WORSHIP OR SUICIDE

THEOPOLITICAL VISIONS

SERIES EDITORS:
Thomas Heilke
D. Stephen Long
and Debra Dean Murphy

Theopolitical Visions seeks to open up new vistas on public life, hosting fresh conversations between theology and political theory. This series assembles writers who wish to revive theopolitical imagination for the sake of our common good.

Theopolitical Visions hopes to re-source modern imaginations with those ancient traditions in which political theorists were often also theologians. Whether it was Jeremiah's prophetic vision of exiles "seeking the peace of the city," Plato's illuminations on piety and the civic virtues in the Republic, St. Paul's call to "a common life worthy of the Gospel," St. Augustine's beatific vision of the City of God, or the gothic heights of medieval political theology, much of Western thought has found it necessary to think theologically about politics, and to think politically about theology. This series is founded in the hope that the renewal of such mutual illumination might make a genuine contribution to the peace of our cities.

FORTHCOMING VOLUMES:

Adam Joyce
No More Pharaohs: Christianity, Racial Capitalism, and Socialism

Maxwell Kennell
Mennonite Metaphysics: Social Critique out of the Sources of the Radical Reformation

Andrew Sutherland
Debt in the Divine Economy: Creation, Salvation, and the Redemption of Our Obligations

WORSHIP OR SUICIDE

On Paradox Between Religion and Society

OLEG DIK

◣ CASCADE *Books* • Eugene, Oregon

WORSHIP OR SUICIDE
On Paradox Between Religion and Society

Theopolitical Visions 29

Copyright © 2025 Oleg Dik. All rights reserved. Except for brief quotations in critical publications or reviews, no part of this book may be reproduced in any manner without prior written permission from the publisher. Write: Permissions, Wipf and Stock Publishers, 199 W. 8th Ave., Suite 3, Eugene, OR 97401.

Cascade Books
An Imprint of Wipf and Stock Publishers
199 W. 8th Ave., Suite 3
Eugene, OR 97401

www.wipfandstock.com

PAPERBACK ISBN: 978-1-6667-4715-7
HARDCOVER ISBN: 978-1-6667-4716-4
EBOOK ISBN: 978-1-6667-4717-1

Cataloguing-in-Publication data:

Names: Dik, Oleg, author.

Title: Worship or suicide : on paradox between religion and society / Oleg Dik.

Description: Eugene, OR: Cascade Books, 2025 | Series: Theopolitical Visions 29 | Includes bibliographical references and index.

Identifiers: ISBN 978-1-6667-4715-7 (paperback) | ISBN 978-1-6667-4716-4 (hardcover) | ISBN 978-1-6667-4717-1 (ebook)

Subjects: LCSH: Worship. | Political theology.

Classification: BV10.3 .D54 2025 (paperback) | BV10.3 (ebook)

VERSION NUMBER 10/02/25

Scripture quotations are from the Holy Bible, New International Version®, NIV®, copyright © 2011 by Biblica, Inc.® Used by permission of Zondervan. All rights reserved worldwide.

To Lisa

For the circle is perfect and infinite in its nature; but it is fixed for ever in its size; it can never be larger or smaller. But the cross, though it has at its heart a collision and a contradiction, can extend its four arms for ever without altering its shape. Because it has a paradox in its centre it can grow without changing. The circle returns upon itself and is bound. The cross opens its arms to the four winds; it is a signpost for free travelers.

—Gilbert Keith Chesterton, *Orthodoxy*

But one must not think ill of the paradox, for the paradox is the passion of thought, and the thinker without the paradox is like the lover without passion: a mediocre fellow.

—Søren Kierkegaard, *Philosophical Fragments*

Contents

Preface ix
Introduction xiii
Abbreviations xxii

Part I: The Birth of Secular Society from the Religious Womb

1 How Myths and Rituals Form Society 3
2 Conceiving the Sacred Person in the Judeo-Christian Womb 25
3 The Birth and Growth of Secular Imagination Within Judeo-Christian Dominion 48
   Critical Interlude 66

Part II: *Incurvatus in Se*: The Triumph and Decay of Secular Society

4 Success, Estrangement from a Devouring Mother, and Exhilarating Hubris 73
5 Crumbling Mythical Horizons and Ritual Alienation 101
6 Exhaustion and Social Decay 120
   Critical Interlude 144

Part III: Götterdämmerung and Emergence of Re-Enchanted Society

7 Disembodied Jesus, Mad Virtues, and Chaos 151
8 Resurfacing Manichaean and Gnostic Interregnum 169
9 The Emergence and Seductions of the Megalomaniac Leviathan 189
   Critical Interlude 210

Part IV: How Idiotic Worship Unintentionally Births a Flourishing Society

10 *Soli Deo Gloria*: Envisioning Paradoxical Patterns 217
11 The Eucharist: Embodying the Living Center 230
12 Peace Through *Ecclesia Militans* 250
    Critical Interlude 271

Conclusion: Paradoxical Worship and a Flourishing Life 277

Acknowledgments 283
Bibliography 287
Index 299

Preface

A YELLOWED SOVIET BLACK-AND-WHITE photo catches the attention of my wife Lisa, who is American. She points out that it looks like it was taken in the 50s. However, the photo dates to the year 1985. In it a five-year-old boy, dressed in a traditional Russian peasant costume, plays a balalaika, while young girls dressed in folk gowns form a circle. Above the dancing children is the portrait of a seemingly benevolent leader: Vladimir Ilyich Ulyanov, a.k.a. Lenin. He towers over the entire scene, his gaze stern yet smiling from the eternal realm.

I am the boy in the photograph, and I can clearly recall chanting with other children in sync, "Lenin always lived, Lenin is alive, and Lenin will live in eternity." If our questions sketch the horizons of our answers,[1] perhaps the origin of the question of the following book could be traced to this Soviet kindergarten. It may be that this experience subconsciously planted in me a persistent doubt that perhaps there is no godless society after all, contrary to what I had been told all through my childhood in communist Soviet Union.

I am tempted to write a book addressing one particular tribe. One of the deepest divides today runs between those who claim to believe in the existence of God and those who don't. I seek to demonstrate that while on the individual level one is able to live as if God does not exist, on the social level this illusion evaporates and the centrality of the divine remains solid. I grew up in a world that seemed devoid of God and came to perceive a world where God is present, albeit often opaque and vague. I have also met some who made the exact opposite journey. Yet, independent of our beliefs, most people agree that we have a lot in common.

---

1. Gadamer, *Hermeneutik im Rückblick*, 162.

Every human being comes out of the womb naked and helpless. Every baby has the same needs in order to survive. According to the Hebrew creation story, every human being is created in the image of God. Today, people with various cultural/religious identities and beliefs share the same space in a common world and societies. At holidays, many families are faced with a diversity of views. Most people decide to simply celebrate and eat together and not view the other family member as alien. Those who believe in God usually acknowledge that the unbelievers are part of the same reality. And thoughtful agnostics give a nod to the persisting religious patterns that still orient our societies. Perhaps the only precondition for my intended audience is the ability to extend charity to the other, to view the other as a member of the same humanity despite deep differences.

I intend to extend charity through my clear writing style.[2] If you are not familiar with the particular academic slang, I hope you will still be able to follow my train of thoughts. I mostly abstain from referencing too many names in my text as it would interrupt the flow and signal to those outside that they are not part of the conversation. The main text represents the result of my dialogue with various cultural and intellectual traditions in the past and present. The details of the process are referenced in the footnotes, for clarity and if the reader wishes to understand how I arrived at the story I tell. I intentionally begin every chapter with an anecdote from my life to signal that I am part of the story I tell. St. Augustine hinted at a strange convergence between the individual's story and the larger whole in his *Confessions*. Academics are embodied human beings and not a brain in the vat, even though they often create the illusion of having "the view from nowhere."[3] Yet we are all like fish in the aquarium, attempting to get outside and have a glimpse from beyond, to reach a larger perspective. While I do intend to sketch larger horizons transcending our particular waters of time and place, I am still returning to my particular aquarium, from where I began.

Just as we must not forcefully divide people according to their beliefs and segregate our societies, so I believe that stories that seek to split asunder religious from secular realms, the church from society,

---

2. For this purpose I employ the male/female pronouns interchangeably. Moreover, I quote from the NIV.

3. Subjective standpoint is irreducible, even though it can be transcended. However, as Nagel writes, the "good, like the true, includes irreducible subjective elements" (*View from Nowhere*, 8).

are neither historically plausible nor ethically desirable. Therefore, I tell a story of how we got here and where we are going through the lens of intertwining paradoxical relations between religion and society. Hereby, I am attempting to be both sympathetic and critical alike of the Judeo-Christian tradition and secular liberalism. Both the church and the current social order are intrinsically intertwined. While the church survived various political constellations, liberalism is contingent on the existence of the Judeo-Christian metastory and the rituals that gave rise to it. I do not intend to defend the current secular liberalism, although I do hope that it will continue to flourish as it is perhaps the best by-product of the Judeo-Christian tradition, despite all its flaws and current suicidal drive. The breadcrumbs that fell from the liturgical table are sufficient to feed an entire civilization.

I am not attempting to write an all-encompassing metanarrative on the genesis and decline of secular liberalism. My practical aim is more modest. I hope to stir a curiosity among those who are "religiously not musical"[4] about the enduring centrality of religion for the social order. Instead of satisfying the scholarly obsession with details, I seek to paint with broad strokes. Scholarly precision is central in generating knowledge. Yet at times one must glimpse the forest once again in order to see the trees. Without the wider horizons the details become meaningless. I also hope to encourage people within religious traditions to view their faith not merely as social capital or as a therapeutic individual tool. Instead, I would like Christians to arrive at a new appreciation of their core stories and rituals as central for society, thus gaining both humility and confidence within secular societies, which are at the threshold of re-enchantment.

In particular, I seek to arrive at the best possible arrangement between church and society, which will produce synergy between them. In the final part, I sketch the contours of a theopolitical vision, with the intent to unite Christians from various traditions and provide a hopeful way forward beyond the current suicidal drive of the Western church and society. Amid the seismic shift within the very center of our societies, we need a shared courage, love, wisdom, and humility in order to prevail and flourish.

---

4. Max Weber referred to himself as "religiös absolut 'unmusikalisch'" (*Briefe 1909–1910*, 65).

Introduction

GREAT CIVILIZATIONS ARE NOT destroyed from without but rather first collapse from within. Only thirty years ago, at the end of the Cold War, it seemed like the idea of liberal democracy had eclipsed all other rivaling myths. It could have been argued that God's kingdom had finally arrived in its secular disguise and the West[1] had reached "the end of history."[2] Instead, we have awoken from this illusion to the sound of crumbling foundations.[3] The ideal of the individual's dignity, upon which all Western institutions rest,[4] has disintegrated to a level of no return, yet we lack an adequate understanding of how we arrived here. Larry Siedentop summarized well the current impasse:

> It is a strange and disturbing moment in Western history. Europeans—out of touch with the roots of their tradition—often seem to lack conviction, while Americans may be succumbing to a dangerously simplistic version of their faith. On neither side

---

1. I am well aware that grand delineations like "the West" or "Judeo-Christian tradition" are not unproblematic due to the allusion to clear demarcation lines and exclusion of other traditions. Every universal or seemingly solid identity marker can be deconstructed under the historical gaze. Yet in order to think clearly and live, we need both fluidity and temporary closure of definitions. I choose to pragmatically employ these larger identity markers to differentiate one set from others without implying their complete independence from other cultural influences.

2. Fukuyama, *End of History*.

3. In his address at Harvard University Solzhenitsyn traced the decay of Western civilization to its hollow spiritual core. He described lucidly the malaise and inner contradictions that he encountered in the US ("Harvard Address"). I intend to put Solzhenitsyn's intuitions into a larger narrative.

4. Perhaps this idea is expressed the clearest in the German Constitution (*Grundgesetz*). The first sentence lays down the most sacred value: Human dignity is inviolable. The next sentence outlines the task of the state to respect and protect the individual dignity. This sacred value forms the center of German society.

of the Atlantic is there an adequate understanding of the relationship between liberal secularism and Christianity.[5]

I agree with Siedentop and build on his historical analysis to tell a story of the birth and growth of secular liberalism from its religious roots.[6] However, I go further by showing how the church also destroys the sociopolitical order it once birthed and nurtured, creating a vacuum, from within which ancient gods are able to emerge and establish a re-enchanted society.

The stories of decay are as old as humanity itself.[7] Humans crave a larger orientation in the world in order to adjust to and survive within very diverse environments. Narrative plots weave together the now to the distant past and provide horizons of a possible future. Myths of the past explain the larger catastrophic events through human relation to gods. Perhaps the latest civilizational collapse, which to this day haunts Europeans, is the fall of the Roman Empire. Already in late antiquity various Greek philosophers and Christian intellectuals debated possible explanations for the decline of Rome,[8] and in particular the role of Christianity. To this day two contrary plots persist. The first views Christianity as primarily responsible for social decay. The second views internal causes within the empire itself as leading to the collapse and portrays the Judeo-Christian tradition as preserving everything that was good, true, and beautiful.[9] I weave both strands toward a paradox: Christianity is both

---

5. Siedentop, *Inventing the Individual*, 363.

6. In political philosophy, liberalism is traced back to the thinkers after the Renaissance to conceptualize a sociopolitical order *etsi deus non daretur* (Grotius and Hobbes). The meaning of this term is culturally and historically embedded. On the historical development of this idea, see Voegelin, "Liberalismus und seine Geschichte." In the following study I employ the term *secular liberalism* as a broad category to signify a sociopolitical order that centers around the notion of the sovereign individual without a necessary recourse to divine authority.

7. E.g., the Gilgamesh epos and the flood story in the Bible are some of the earliest accounts for civilizational catastrophes.

8. Already in the second century Celsus viewed Christianity as a force of decay. Edward Gibbon revived this tradition in the eighteenth century, and Nietzsche made it more popular through his polemical style. St. Augustine defended Christianity against this critique in *City of God*. Perhaps the best summary of various theories on the decay of Rome is Alexander Demandt, *Fall Roms*.

9. This tradition goes back to church fathers like Ambrose and St. Augustine. While French philosophers during the radical Enlightenment sought to establish a break between modernity and Christianity, German Enlightenment philosophers like Kant and Hegel sought to reconcile the Enlightenment with the Christian tradition. The current popular proponent of a positive civilizational force of Christianity is Tom Holland's bestseller *Dominion*.

the source of decay and renewal of the Western civilization. Both death and life are birthed from her womb. I seek to discern the conditions and causes for decay and flourishing.

The plot of the following book is simple: Sacred ideals form the center of every society. These ideals are embodied through rituals. The embodied sacred lends directionality to societies.[10] Despite the differences of Western societies, they are united by the idea of individual dignity within a secular sphere. This is their common core, around which their constitutions and institutions center. This idea was conceived in and embodied through the Judeo-Christian imagination and worship. Thus, the destruction of the core sends shock waves out to the rest of society. The primary agent causing the collapse of the sacred center is the church. Therefore the church plays a paradoxical role in this social upheaval. On the one hand, the church conceived the secular humanistic social order within its womb and nurtured it since antiquity. On the other hand, the church also contributed to the demise of this social order by disembodying itself through inner corruption.[11] I call this failure of the church extended suicide. Through the failure to worship the triune God as the highest ideal, the church commits suicide. Consequently, by ceasing to worship truthfully, the church destroys its unique gift, around which secular liberal societies are centered: the idea of human inherent dignity. As a consequence of this increasing vacuum the old sacred patterns of Manichaeism and Gnosis resurface. These ideals constitute the core of the re-enchanting emergent social order.

Since this social upheaval does not stem from surface pragmatic causes, it cannot be easily reversed. The solution does not lie in the realm of politics. Ultimately, the church is both the cause of the problem and its only long-term remedy. Yet the healing can't occur through direct engagement with the world by fixing social problems. The church must

---

10. Mellor and Shilling distinguish between the secular and religious forms of the sacred, thus integrating Weber's and Durkheim's theories on religion (Mellor and Shilling, *Sociology of the Sacred*, 21–48).

11. The inner-ecclesial critique on the corruption of the church reaches back to various monastic movements within medieval Roman Catholicism. These reform movements viewed the mainline church as corrupted from within. These voices were further institutionalized through the Reformation in the sixteenth century and became the mainline critique coined against the ancien régime during the French Enlightenment. Ivan Illich further elaborated this strand of critique, and Charles Taylor borrowed Illich's insight as a premise for his genealogy of modernity. See Cayley, *Rivers North*; Taylor, *Secular Age*. Yet the origins of this line of reasoning lie in the fiercest critique of Hebrew prophets toward their own tribal idolatry.

embrace its conflicting legacy first in order to shed any attempt to redeem the world through sociopolitical power and coercion. My premise leads to the conclusion that the church must first exclude the world by focusing its gaze on God's glory. By focusing primarily on the worship of the triune God, the church embodies patterns, which in turn model a symbolic social structure.[12] Paradoxically, the church will include the world in its cosmic vision unintentionally, by embodying the central ideal, from which all other social relations will be reordered in an ad hoc manner. Yet, similar to the history of the church, the messiness resulting from the tension between the ideal and reality will persist. In order to endure this fact, sober realism must be paired with hope. My argument rests on three key premises. Let me be transparent about them and put the cards on the table up front.

First, I assume that religious rituals constitute the social order. The ancient civilizations of Sumer, Babylon, Israel, and Greece expressed this belief through their creation myths. The church fathers developed their theology in confrontation with Greco-Roman polytheism, which assumed the centrality of gods. For Muhammad, the founder of Islam, the primary motif for his emerging monotheism was the overthrow of the Meccan idol worship in order to reinstate Allah as the central ideal to organize society. Emile Durkheim as the founding father of modern sociology viewed sacred rituals at the social center, emanating power and thus constituting all other social spheres.[13] Accordingly, social institutions were formed around the totem pole. The vacuum left by the departure of one God must be filled by a new one for a society to persist. A godless society is therefore an impossibility. Building on this insight of the primacy of ritual, I explain the current sociopolitical transition from the age of secular liberalism to the post-individual and post-liberal order through the lens of ritual conversion.

Second, I assume the objectivity, unity, and irreducibility of the world. The external world exists objectively, and theories can be tested against the weight of reality.[14] This is the reason various theorists can

---

12. I follow here the central thesis of Karl Löwith on the relation of Christianity and Western historiography and extend his insight to the general social patterns (Löwith, *Meaning in History*).

13. Durkheim, *Elementary Forms*.

14. Broadly, I follow here the philosophy of science, which is articulated under the umbrella of critical realism. For a good application of Bhaskar's ideas to social sciences, see Sayer, *Realism and Social Science*.

genuinely disagree and readjust their conceptions of the world. Due to the complexity of the world, we are able to employ different disciplinary angles to hopefully arrive at a larger picture of the whole. I do not believe that all of reality is reducible to physical causes without losing in fact that which makes life human. Due to this theological/philosophical conviction, I view various epistemic and ontological perspectives as complementary, at least in an ideal scenario. Physics/biology and theology/philosophy/history are distinct angles of looking at the world and forming patterns, yet they rarely compete, and if so, then only on the surface. I seek to engage diverse fields of knowledge from history, sociology, and theology/philosophy to advance a hypothesis and sketch a framework on how to grasp social change on a larger scale. I seek to arrive at the convergence between these disciplines in my central claim of the centrality and persistence of religious myths and rituals.

Third, I assume that history is progressing concentrically. Although history does rhyme due to recurring patterns, it does not repeat itself ad infinitum, as Nietzsche maintained. I elucidate such a pattern, which I view in the recurrence of gods, as societies can't flourish with a vacuum at the center. History is also not merely advancing forward toward utopia, as secularized eschatology would want us to believe.[15] Humans do not possess a rational core that could be laid bare by washing off the filth of tradition and religion.[16] As the tradition referring to Heraclitus states: "We can't step twice in the same river." Therefore, while the pattern can be recognized, it transforms itself with the progress of time. Yet whether the curve is rising toward the blissful future or dropping toward apocalyptic doomsday—this judgment depends on the overall normative background of the one who judges. An apocalyptic interpretation is just as contingent upon the larger evaluative judgment as the utopian one. And often what is apocalypse for one group is the breaking in of paradise for the other. The "post" in modernity is a mere descriptive prefix for the progression of time, and the advancing era a mere prelude to the return of gods.

Due to the concentric nature of events, we can both rise and fall as humanity, with relatively stable stages in between. Yet we are not able to fix this stable point. Although we are able to transcend our particularities through reflection, we are not able to completely exit this spatiotemporal

---

15. This Enlightenment tradition is alive and well and finds one of its most eloquent proponents in the Harvard psychologist Steven Pinker.

16. Charles Taylor coins this view "subtraction theory" and develops a sophisticated genealogy against this simplistic view in his magnum opus, *A Secular Age*.

realm and achieve "the view from nowhere."[17] The ideal of a stoic indifference and a mystical flight from history can't be made permanent.[18] Equilibrium remains a fleeting moment in between. Therefore, I do not seek to arrive at an ideal solution. Instead, I believe that this type of harmony is often an unintended by-product of the social embodiment of the ideal. Even in my final, explicitly theological part, I do not pretend to escape the agonistic up and down of history. I am only pointing to the best possible way to shape the center in the hope of reordering the chaos around it. The final part is a mere signpost and not a prescriptive attempt to stabilize liberal democracy through theological means. Theories are reductions of social complexity and must refrain from the prideful ignorance to lay down an ultimate path of action.

Contrary to my historic approach, current theorists of post-liberalism employ the pragmatic prism to explain the waning power of liberalism. Accordingly, the demise of liberalism is attributed to the failure to deliver on its socio-material and ethical promises. As a consequence, the disappointed worshippers turn toward a post-liberal order. This thesis is advanced from political,[19] ethical,[20] economic,[21] and technological angles.[22] Although I do not discard these explanations, I view them as mere surface consequences of a deeper history of religions. The limits of the pragmatic explanation lie in its lack of explanatory power due to its historic shallowness and reductive anthropology. I maintain that humans are not merely rational choice agents and join the trajectory of those who employ the genealogical method.[23] The discourse on post-liberalism suggests that we are witnessing a return to the polytheistic future. The immanent framework is but a temporary intermittence as the gods begin to vie for dominion once again.

17. Nagel, *View from Nowhere*.
18. This view goes back to the Stoic tradition as expressed by Cicero. Recently, John Gray as political philosopher argued for stoic indifference and a mystical flight from the politics infested by Judeo-Christian apocalyptic violence (*Black Mass*).
19. Krastev and Holmes, *Light That Failed*.
20. Gray, *Heresies*.
21. Zuboff, *Age of Surveillance Capitalism*.
22. Harari, *Homo Deus*.
23. I follow in the trajectory of Rémi Brague, Marcel Gauchet, Larry Siedentop, Charles Taylor, and Eric Voegelin. These thinkers address contemporary issues through a careful genealogical investigation.

Another popular paradigm is to explain social change as a result of biophysics and geopolitics as primary causes.[24] I do not discard these theories but view external causes, whether ecological, economic, or macro social, as secondary. These theories fail to account for radical differences of societies under similar material conditions. Every society deals with environmental changes, plagues, economic recessions, and wars. Yet some deal with these stresses better than others. What accounts for this difference in resilience? Ultimately every society either masters external challenges or collapses under their weight. Yet whether societies succeed or fail depends on their inner strength, which is ideological in nature.

We are at a historical juncture. Intellectuals from diverse traditions seem to perceive the gentle susurrus that the old is fading while the new is not yet born. Despite the differences in envisioning the future, there seems to be a growing consensus that change is in the air. I join this chorus. The disagreement runs through various camps. Secular intellectuals are as divided as theologians on the interpretation of change and the way forward.

Increasingly, European intellectuals are split between two irreconcilable groups. On the one side stand those who mourn the decay of the liberal secular order while seeking to revive it. By now, even some intellectuals, who in the past could afford to postulate an abysmal difference between religion and Enlightenment, begin to point out the indebtedness of the Enlightenment to the Judeo-Christian tradition.[25] Yet this group lacks a compelling vision beyond a nostalgic repetition ad nauseam of returning to "Enlightenment values."

On the other side are those who welcome the emerging post-liberal order by celebrating the Nietzschean will to power and the vitality of the ancient gods. After dismantling the idea of Enlightenment progress as Christianity in disguise, some predict a form of mysticism,[26] digital Gnosticism,[27] or resurgence of tribalism as a post-liberal scenario.[28]

---

24. Two contemporary proponents of this view are Yuval Harari and Peter Zeihan, and to a lesser degree William Patrick Ophuls. However, Ophuls does admit that moral reasons are primary for a decline of social order (*Immoderate Greatness*).

25. Jürgen Habermas is one of the most prominent philosophers within this growing chorus (*Zeit der Übergänge*).

26. Gray, *Black Mass*.

27. Harari, *Homo Deus*, 372–403.

28. Both Huntington and Schlesinger warned that the end of the Cold War does not lead toward the hegemony of the West but to resurging tribalism (Huntington, *Clash of Civilizations*; Schlesinger, *Disuniting of America*).

In light of interruptive global changes, religious metaphors resurface and nature is deified once again as a desirable telos of social and ecological harmony. A global transformation is presented as a necessity by economic and political elites, replacing the current sociopolitical liberal order, which views the sacred individual at its center. In the new enchanted global society the individual is superseded by the collective harmony, thus extinguishing the egoistic desires.[29]

I seek to present an alternative view. Those who seek to discard the present order grounded in the belief of human dignity open themselves up to be possessed by demons well beyond their abilities to handle.[30] Those who seek to conserve the Enlightenment are like the nostalgic elderly who would like to hold on to time, which runs through their fingers like dry sand. Their wish, although I sympathize with it, is historically naïve, as the Enlightenment was mostly an inner-Christian conversation and can't offer a solid vision without its sacred underpinning.

The church is caught in a political impasse since the advance of modernity. The breakup of Christendom and the loss of sociopolitical power breeds resentment, as Nietzsche rightly diagnosed. Yet reactionary modes of the church toward modernity lead us into a dead end as they get mired in the immanent frame, failing to provide an alternative view beyond the eternal struggle for domination. Consequently, the church often fails to conceive of the centrality of God's glory and embody it communally in a nonantagonistic, gracious way. The way forward lies in being captivated by God's glory and thus abandoning resentment and the will to power. Christians must faithfully restore the good, the true, and the beautiful through reimagining the ecumenical Judeo-Christian tradition and embodying this imagination contextually from within locally rooted communities of faith. Herein lies the main struggle of the church.

Most likely, secular liberal democracies, as we have known them, will not survive the crumbling of their central ideal. However, some of the passing order will find refuge within the Judeo-Christian rituals, just like antiquity was preserved in part in the medieval monasteries, within which the seeds for the renewal could germinate. The idea of a sacred, spacious, free, creative, and reasonable person who is constituted relationally can survive in the Judeo-Christian exile. Ideal relationality of the person is not established in a mere discursive manner,

---

29. E.g., Schwab and Malleret, *COVID-19*.
30. Dostoevsky, *Besi*.

nor through eternal struggle, but through sacramental participation in the Trinitarian love, abandonment, and giving of the self. This will remain the main struggle for the church in the re-enchanted totalitarian order. The church must awaken to the fact that its Trinitarian worship is crucial not merely to its own survival but as well to the flourishing of entire civilizations. Worship is inevitable; suicide is not.

Abbreviations

BKAT   Biblischer Kommentar, Altes Testament
Eth. nic.   *Ethica nicomachea* (*Nicomachean Ethics*)
WUNT   Wissenschaftliche Untersuchungen zum Neuen Testament

Part I

The Birth of Secular Society from the Religious Womb

CHAPTER 1

How Myths and Rituals Form Society

Gotta serve somebody

—Bob Dylan, "Gotta Serve Somebody"

The one essential condition of human existence is that man should always be able to bow down before something infinitely great. If men are deprived of the infinitely great, they will not go on living and will die of despair. The Infinite and the Eternal are as essential for man as the little planet on which he dwells.

—Fyodor Dostoevsky, *The Possessed*

What constitutes society? All major civilizations in history believed that gods create and maintain society. This myth was communally embodied through rituals. This historical observation can be grounded in the human relational nature, which must be mediated in order for life to flourish. Myths and rituals—these are basic ways for humans to establish order amid chaos. Around myths becoming real through rituals all other social institutions are formed.

Part I: The Birth of Secular Society from the Religious Womb

TRUTHFUL INTUITIONS OF SYRIAN CONSTRUCTION WORKERS

From 2007 until 2011, I lived in Beirut, Lebanon. Many of my friends were Syrian construction workers from rural areas who lived in temporary construction containers. They extended their hospitality by welcoming me to drink tea with them and practice my broken Arabic. During these conversations my friends alluded on several occasions to Europe as "Christian." I protested vehemently and secretly attributed their faux pas to their ignorance. Some of them were even completely illiterate. Well, if Europe is not "Christian," they retorted, what is it then? I struggled to convey to them in my limited Arabic the conventional story detailing the roots of our liberal secular democracies, which could be summed up as following:

The origin of our social order lies in antiquity, mainly in Greece and Rome. Greek philosophers like Plato and Aristotle developed critical thinking in opposition to the naïve Greek belief in gods. Cicero, a Roman philosopher, further chiseled the idea of democracy and natural law. These ideas were forgotten with the advance of the dark Middle Ages and lay in decay for around a thousand years. Yet the chains of the church were broken and the filth of tradition washed off with the breaking in of the Renaissance. Suddenly, man liberated himself like Prometheus and discovered his own capacity for reason and creative genius. From the fifteenth century onward, antiquity was revived, which led toward the breaking in of the Enlightenment, which in turn expanded the space of human-accelerated freedom and progress in opposition to religion. With the exception of a few low moments, the overall trajectory was one of positive development. With some generosity one could even admit some positive contribution of the Judeo-Christian religion and Islam in preserving the Aristotelian heritage. However, these monotheistic religions are for the most part a negative backdrop for human emancipation, which consisted of wrestling our spatial and temporal imagination free from God's intrusion.

This is the conventional story in our culture. I also believed aspects of this plot in 2010, trying to convince my uneducated friends that they were fully mistaken to imagine Europe to be religious. I had a déjà vu of this conversation in 2015 encountering refugees from the Middle East in Berlin/Germany. They also assumed they had arrived in a Christian country, and I also attempted to enlighten them. I intended to paint a contrast to their conception: in civilizations permeated by Islam, religion sought to envelop all of society. At least that is the ideal as presented in the recourse to the first four caliphs since the death of Muhammad, the founder of Islam. I insisted that it is vastly different in Europe and presented to them a stark contrast of the relationship between society and religion as experienced in Europe.

On the surface I was right, as empirical data suggests clearly that institutional Christian religion has been in decline across Europe since the modernization process began to erode the social conditions for organized religion. Everyday experience also confirms the primacy of secular experience. We are able to lead our lives and structure our societies without any reference to a religious authority. In fact, we need to make a conscious effort to escape our dis-enchanted lives for a few hours when we go to the movies or to some religious activity—be it yoga or a church service.[1] Usually, we take the cold, rational structure as the bare reality, and the religious experience resembles a theater. Sometimes we even allow this different reality on the stage to touch us existentially. Yet when the curtain closes and the lights are turned on again, we return to objective reality, where recourse to God is not necessary. The religious experience quickly fades and takes on an ephemeral glow within the solid routines of our material experience.

This plot could also be backed by a theological argument that still appeals to me. Growing up in the Soviet Union with a father who taught Marxism/Leninism, I remember vividly a particular caricature in a schoolbook: a bourgeois, a czar, and an Orthodox priest—the holy trinity of obese exploiters—were riding on a skinny factory worker, who was close to collapsing under their weight. My initial observation of the state-church alliance in Germany seemed to confirm this preconception. Due to this biographical experience, on my journey into the Christian faith, I was drawn to Anabaptist theology, which emphasizes a sharp delineation between church and state. The only way I could reconcile being drawn toward Christ was by emphasizing the apolitical Jesus and his church against the corrupted church after Theodosius I. Within this view the division was as clear as night and day: on the one side, the corrupted church, which ushered in Christendom, from which all current evils of the West were born; and on the other side, the pure,

---

1. Berger and Luckmann employ the analogy of theater to clarify the relation between the everyday, solid experience and other, lesser, real realms like religion. Eventually every spectator must return to the concrete everyday reality (*Social Construction of Reality*, 23–26).

powerless church, which remains in its clandestine state in opposition to public evil.[2] This stark dichotomy lent me an Archimedean point to develop a clear view of Western society. I was able to present a pure Jesus and an ideal church to my Muslim friends, while agreeing with them in their rejection of all the evils within Western society, partly resulting from Christendom. While this dichotomy was useful for my youthful, simplistic concept of Western societies, it could not stand up to historical and sociological realities. I had to face the true historical church of flesh and blood and the unintended consequences of its actions. What emerged was a more nuanced image.

Under closer scrutiny, my ideal demarcation line evaporated. It began to dawn on me that the relation between church and society is more entangled and complex, at times tragic and comic and overall paradoxical. After delving into history and sociology, I began to realize that in an odd way my illiterate Syrian friends were right on a deeper level: at the center of every society in the past and present stands a sacred ideal that becomes real through rituals. Therefore, every society, both in Europe and the Middle East, exemplifies a core similarity, even though the sacred ideals are different. I in fact had been the mistaken one with the popular story I had tried to convey to them. I was the ignorant one under the illusion that the West exemplifies at least an exemption, if not progress, from the backward notion that society needs to be grounded in some kind of transcendental ideal. In this first part, I seek to begin with the ancient myths and slowly make my way to the present. All myths paint a large horizon of meaning beyond immediate experience. Both myths and rituals are modes of mediation of human relational nature. Both modes are indispensable for flourishing societies.

Relationality

Once upon a time, in a distant past, the universe was cold and void. Chaos permeated space. Somehow this chaos turned into order, which brought forth human life. This is the most basic myth. Yet at this juncture the plots

---

2. I am indebted to Yoder for having discovered the political power of the apolitical church, the paradox of power through powerlessness (Yoder, *Politics of Jesus*). However, contrary to Yoder, I believe that it is not sufficient to merely consider the biblical sources in order to construct a theological orientation for the church. Just like the Bible is a product of deep engagement of particular historical people of God with their culture, so Christians today must articulate their view of reality through engaging various myths and scientific disciplines.

differ. One story emphasizes the self-organizing properties of the universe or posits a multiverse.[3] This is a relatively recent plot invention. Historically, the most common narrative is to attribute everything to intelligent agency and not toward chance. Thus most mythological plots entail gods. Yet the core statement remains true for both bio-evolutionary and religious myths: there needs to be a certain delineation between chaos and order for life to emerge. The definition of *human life* could be: the form that emerges at the threshold of an ideal physical, biological, and social condition. Humans are relational beings and have the capacity to discover the ideal proportion and negotiate between conflicting forces.

Humans are intimately tied to ecology. In order to survive and multiply, humans invented creative ways to adjust to very diverse geographical environments like the Saharan desert or Siberian tundra. Humans interact with the material surrounding by transforming it into culture. Through material culture, humans create new ways to protect themselves from hostile environments. Humans were able to create and improve tools to hunt more efficiently. From stone to bronze to aluminum—the development of material culture has been staggering. Humans were also able to develop means of communication that led toward their collective agency. Humans are the only species that has been able to act collectively on a grand scale, and this gives them an advantage over all other species. Orcas and apes form small groups, yet they do not form societies. Geography precedes humans and shapes both their imagination and bodies. Our basic metaphors, which provide us with the ability to reason, stem from our bodily orientation in time and space.[4]

Human perceptions are shaped differently in the blazing sun of the equator or the dark and short days close to the North Pole. The physical environment leads toward microevolution of the human physique and skills. However, over the past three thousand years, humans have made huge strides toward insulating themselves from the original ecology by building civilizations that shield them from the pressures of everyday survival. Now the majority of the world does not need to wrestle to obtain food and warmth from the cruel environment. Whereas our ancestors struggled to keep their fires going, modern man is concerned with artificial lights interrupting his sleep. Our biological organism has porous boundaries toward the environment we find ourselves in. The

---

3. Victor J. Stenger argues against the fine-tuning of the universe and divine origin in favor of a multiverse theory (*God and the Multiverse*).

4. Lakoff and Johnson, *Metaphors We Live By*.

relation between the human organism and geography underwent a dramatic shift within the last five hundred years.

Whereas for most of history, nature was a dominant force, humans increasingly came to dominate and subjugate nature through culture. Now we rarely interact directly with brute nature but are increasingly shielded from its breathtaking beauty and deadly viciousness through the safe wall of our civilizational achievements. We emancipated ourselves from the natural cycles of day and night through artificial light. Most people are freed from the pressure of either hunting or growing food through highly technological agriculture, which produces plentiful food for all. People in industrialized societies are not exposed to extreme heat or cold and are used to a pleasant room temperature. Our bodies are mostly not interacting with and are not shaped by the natural environment but rather by the artificial one. Our own tools form us in reverse. The tools, once crafted, begin to shape us in their image. We become what we do. By crafting artificial systems humans become the product of their own inventions.

Interaction with the world around us mostly happens subconsciously: we breathe, eat, drink, move, and have rhythms of waking and sleeping. These interactions influence smaller relations within our body—blood flow and heartbeat—all the way down to the molecular level. For the most part we are not conscious how the civilizational wall and the technological tools we have created shape our brains and bodies. It takes conscious effort to create cognitive distance in order to become aware of this continuously malleable biological boundary.

Physical and biological processes give rise to an even higher and more complex system of relations: human society. A social group precedes the individual and extends beyond the particular human being; it works back on him through soft, unnoticed force, similar to the culture that envelops him. Contrary to most animals, humans are born helpless and unfinished.[5] Perhaps this fact caused the human brain to develop in ways beyond the instinctive ones to survive. Therefore, human babies need the larger community in order to survive. Babies' bodies naturally appear cute and attract empathy from adults. Yet through growing up, the child needs to develop a relationship to the past of its society and to its ways of arranging communal life in order to become a full member and further sustainer of a flourishing civilization. The child becomes

---

5. Arnold Gehlen builds his sociological theory on the fact that human babies lack survival skills (*Mensch, seine Natur*).

aware of the specific ways that society structures space and time in order to live together.

In the last stage of this development, the individual also becomes aware of herself and her role in the larger whole. The relationship to oneself develops not merely through the awareness of being shaped from the outside but through the capability to exercise agency as well. Mirroring the relation to others, the individual develops a relation to the inner self through the process of socialization. The relation to self emerges from prior biological and social relations, which are absorbed unconsciously and imitated through everyday life.

Humans are relational beings. Relationality constitutes life. In the Christian tradition, God as the highest ideal is relational within himself. Within the Christian Scriptures and the first four centuries' theological disputes this nascent diversity within unity was further elaborated into Trinitarian dogma. Thus, in order to mediate the life-giving boundary due to human physical, biological, and social embedding, a relational ideal is necessary. Relationality does not merely describe the "is" but also outlines the highest ideal, the "ought." While humans are relational beings, their relations are not static as they have the capacity to shape these relations in reverse. In fact, they constantly shape their relational nature in the world, sensing that death could occur when the boundaries are too tight or too open. Uncertainty about the ideal state of openness or closure remains a constant companion. Boundaries must be accepted and transcended at the same time. This paradox gives rise to fundamental ways of myth and ritual to mediate human relationality and form societies. Humans are able to imagine the widest horizons and act together in ways unprecedented in the animal kingdom.

Mediating Society

Every human being is born into a culture that existed before her. Already in the womb the fetus is intimately connected to the mother via the umbilical cord. The moment the fragile infant body leaves the mother's womb, the child leaves the enclosed, warm, and safe space and finds herself surrounded by a vast, cold environment. The baby employs the five senses in order to orient herself in this strange world. Humans are at the core relational beings due to their orientation in the world through sense perception. The separation from the mother heightens the employment of the baby's own senses. Her identity emerges from the hearing and interpretation of strange sounds. The baby develops her own sense of taste, which was dormant in the womb. Now the child actively explores new foods through taste. The feeling of disgust is acquired, which helps to avoid possible harm. The child is able to focus her sight on a particular object and feels the surface of objects through touch.

However, the baby also quickly learns the limits of the senses. The peekaboo game is fascinating to the child as he experiences the person emerging from behind an object as a miracle. With time the child learns object permanence, thereby grasping that there exists a reality beyond his immediate perception. He learns to live with the tragic realization that human senses are inadequate to envision a larger whole. The sense of vision is severely limited when blocked by physical objects. Voice fades with distance as well. Human beings are limited due to their embodied being in the world. They can exist only at a particular place at a specific time.[6] Yet they have learned to cross this threshold through imagination.

Humans are able to imagine a reality that transcends their immediate senses. We imagine because we have an intuition that the larger reality influences us. When the storm clouds form on the horizon, we anticipate danger. When our loved ones die suddenly, we seek for answers. From our daily experiences we develop a habitual perception of cause and effect. Yet we also observe that this causation works on a grander scale. Just like an intergenerational story influences the particular relation between the grandfather, father, and son, so perhaps there is a story of the clan, and there must be reasons for human existence that extend into the dawn of history. These cause-and-effect observations were passed on as wisdom before they developed into hypotheses and were scrutinized through scientific methodology. An example of this might be the following. The Bible speaks of intergenerational blessings and curses. Epigenetics is a recent field of study that explores how external causes such as wars or environmental changes influence the operation of genes—thus also affecting the future generations.

Those humans who were able to anticipate larger-scale causation were also the ones who were most likely to survive. Thus the

---

6. Blumenberg views the possible origin of mythos in the "absoluteness of reality," according to which humans do not have the conditions of their own existence under their control. Consequently, humans developed a sense of expectation toward the wider horizons. By naming the unknown forces, humans regained a sense of control and minimized the existential dread in light of the life-threatening forces (*Arbeit am Mythos*, 9–11).

interpretation of large-scale patterns is useful for communal flourishing. Human curiosity awakens at the moment when they sense that something influences them from beyond their immediate perception. Humans burn with curiosity to explore what it is and delve into speculative tasks—this is the birth of mythological thinking. A myth provides the widest horizon of meaning for humans as it paints a world beyond the empiric reality. By this definition the distinction between religious and secular myths collapses. So-called secular myths such as a Marxist philosophy of history also operate with nonempirical projections, which are, from a historical angle, theologies in disguise.[7]

Every child gets introduced to a world beyond his immediate senses. For thousands of years, old sages were telling stories to young children sitting around the fire. As humans, we are embedded in time and space, and this is the basis for narrative as our most basic way of orientation.[8] A narrative plot is able to offer the child the widest possible map of meaning, well beyond the child's immediate experience. A good story explicates how the child is not merely a product of brute forces but of meaningful events in the past. Myth takes on a narrative structure and addresses at its core the temporality of human life. I suggest a working definition of myth: a *myth* exemplifies a narrative structure and outlines the widest possible horizon of meaning as orientation within time and space.

Similar to myth, the exact origin of rituals is clouded in mystery. Some evolutionary biologists view rituals as facilitating and stimulating processes of adaptation.[9] Both nature and biological life exemplify reoccurring patterns that could be a blueprint for ritualistic behavior. It has long been observed that animals also exemplify ritualistic behavior.[10] An exact definition of ritual remains problematic as it is not always easy to distinguish ritual from other social actions.[11] "Ritual" is an abstracted vague term from within a particular civilization. The meaning of the concept of ritual hinges on the cultural and religious background of a particular society. These emic perspectives must be considered in order

---

7. I agree with theorists/historians (e.g., Carl Schmitt, Eric Voegelin, Karl Löwith, Charles Taylor, and Michael Gillespie), who traced various twentieth-century humanistic ideologies to the transformation of their theological roots.

8. Carr, *Time, Narrative, and History*.

9. Snoek, "Defining 'Rituals,'" 13.

10. Baudy, "Ethology."

11. Harth, "Rituals."

Part I: The Birth of Secular Society from the Religious Womb

to arrive at a specific cultural understanding of the broader term.[12] Yet in order to facilitate understanding, I propose a working sociological definition: *rituals* are communal, reoccurring actions that are imbued with the highest significance and thus distinguished from routinized behavior. Rituals emerge through the communal performance of individuals and mediate the relational human nature. Yet the ritual dynamic is more than particulars and works back on individual bodies.[13] This definition does not resolve all the conundrums relating to this concept, yet it allows us to employ it pragmatically within the following argument. How can the relation between myth and ritual be conceptualized?[14]

Some scholars argue that rituals enable myth, as rituals create a shared framework for trust and development of language, which requires the acceptance of the other.[15] Thus, rituals create conditions for a communicative setting. One can also argue for the priority of myth as a script for ritual performance. Instead of arguing for the priority of myth or ritual, I maintain their distinctiveness yet relatedness.

Imagining kneeling and actually bending my knees are both similar and different. They are similar as both actions originate in the brain. Yet they also differ as the actual kneeling requires more bodily energy than imagining doing so. Once I kneel, I engage my senses through my bodily movement. The performed experience is imprinted more strongly on my memory as it cost me more energy. One can say that imagination and bodily experience are at the same time distinct and yet related. They can't be collapsed into each other, thus leading toward a fundamental tension of human existence.[16] Myth expresses itself primarily through

---

12. Stausberg et al., "Ritual."

13. Catherine Bell views the ritual as an "interactive process" wherein "the ritual is created through the body, but the ritual as such is more than individual bodies and shapes the individual bodies in return" ("Embodiment," 539).

14. On the history of this discourse, see Segal, "Myth and Ritual."

15. Rappaport makes an elaborate case for the primacy of the ritual in the creation of meaning (*Ritual and Religion*).

16. This can be traced back to the way human minds and bodies interact. Lambek views the relation between mind/body as incommensurable: "Incommensurables do not exclude each other, but by the same token they cannot readily be mediated since they share no common measure along which an intermediary position could be staked out. Since . . . mind/body dualism is at once everywhere transcended in practice yet everywhere present, in some form or the other, . . . we have to attend to body and mind in body (embodiment), and also to body and mind in mind (imagination)" ("Body and Mind," 105–9).

imagination, and ritual through the movement of the body. Yet they are intrinsically related.

In an ideal case, myth and ritual are intertwined and mutually reinforcing. However, they can also compete for the interpretation of reality and seek to subvert the other. When they are mutually reinforcing, social reality appears solid. However, when myth and ritual contradict each other, the solid reality begins to crumble and is perceived as social crisis.[17] Putting this specialized discussion on the relation between myth and ritual aside, I maintain that both myth and ritual are fundamental in mediating human relationality.

Human experience arises within a particular place and at a specific moment of time. In this moment as I sit at my desk, typing this essay, my senses perceive the immediate environment of my apartment with its windows facing a tree-lined street. Yet in the back of my mind, I am aware of the larger orienting place that is the neighborhood of Wedding in the city of Berlin, the capital of Germany. Already in this brief orientation within the larger space, upon deeper reflection, I become aware of how myth structures space. The idea of an apartment, city, and nation-state emerged within particular metastories on how people should organize themselves. These orientations within space are not as self-evident as they appear to me. Thus a story can be told of how humans organized their spatial orientation from wandering hunter and gatherers to settling farmers and how their campfire stories either reflected this fundamental change in living or even gave rise to it.

Every myth mediates between the particular experiential place and the larger space, employing basic bodily metaphors: up, down, behind, and forward. The imagining of space outlines possibilities and ways of action. For example, if ancestors are venerated and their postmortem dwelling place is designated in certain locations, these places will become taboo for intrusion. Many civilizations have allocated sacred topographies as places where ancestors and gods dwell. The Greeks associated Hades with a place of the underworld. These deeply entrenched mythological evaluations of space influence collective actions. We are more fascinated by the vastness of the universe, which we perceive as above us, than by the depth of the earth underneath our feet. Myths mediate between our immediate and imaginative perceptions of space. Usually, the furthest possible spatial horizons are inhabited by

---

17. I will further unfold this thesis in the chapters below.

superhuman beings and gods. Each myth tells a particular story of how these various spatial segments interact, including some mediators who are able to move between these layers.[18]

While myths structure the imaginative spatial orientation, rituals enable people to access different dimensions and thus experientially weave together this vast order within a specific communal performance. From animistic dances to Christian liturgy—the basic structure is similar. Ritual serves as a way to connect the layered nature of reality to particular bodies. The result of these mythological and ritual mediations of space is the enlarged, meaningful horizon, both within imagination and experience. This enlarged, ordered universe forms a background for communal action. We can act beyond the visually perceived horizon only if we are able to envision a horizon beyond the eyesight. Imagination enables steps into the dark abyss of the unknown.[19]

Similar to space, we are able to perceive time only in the limited now. In order to capture the past, we must rely on our memory; and in order to anticipate the future, we must engage in speculative imagination. Myths weave together these dimensions of time through a meaningful plot about where people came from and where they are going. This time arc allows for identification between various people as they find themselves in the same metastory. By extending the spatial perception and offering an overarching orientation within a large historic plot, both myth and rituals create conditions of shared identity for a society to emerge beyond the immediate drive to survive.

This imaginative cosmology and experiential incorporation of time and space into communal identity creates a culture within which biological boundaries are negotiated. How each body is nurtured and shaped depends on this mostly unseen mythological and ritual background. For example, rites of passage are established in order to enable male youth to enter a different symbolic space and mark an interruption of time.[20] Within this ritual, both symbolic and very concrete physical dimensions become reality through the often-painful initiation experience.

---

18. Lévi-Strauss analyzed structural similarities within various myths. In particular, he described various trickster figures who served as mediators of the everyday experience (*Structural Anthropology*, 206–30).

19. On the relation between mental imagery and action, see Dörnyei, *Vision, Mental Imagery*.

20. Van Gennep, *Rites of Passage*.

Similarly, social hierarchies are cemented through these most basic mediations of time and space. Those associated with power and prestige are elevated to the higher realms, while the lowest castes are literally positioned with the garbage and pigs. To this day the lower classes are assigned jobs that bind them to the earth: from garbage collectors in Egypt to the "untouchables" in India who are assigned to dirty jobs—spatial orientation orders social imagination. Higher classes rule over lower ones and justify this inequality through myths and rituals. These basic orientations provide the pattern for individual reflexivity.

Before the child develops a reflexive understanding of the self, he is subconsciously orienting himself within a world as mediated through myth and ritual. The child listens to the story, inhaling its orienting patterns, learning the language, which carries within it the normative preconditions on how to perceive and structure the material world. Thus, the conscious self emerges as the latest relational mode. The self evolves within a prefabricated world, and while later on the individual is able to offer a critique of even the basic myth and rituals, he can do so only from within them. The individual possesses only the means that were handed down to him previously. Critique and change of myth and ritual necessarily lead toward modified myths and rituals, as the form itself can't be transcended. A clear indication of a mythical and ritual innovation within modernity is the strategy of negation. New religions pretend to achieve a clear unprecedented break with the past, thus obscuring the enduring force of the old. By casting myth and rituals in a pejorative light, one is seeking to promote new myths.

The primary function of myths is to mediate between spatiotemporal, biological, social, and individual-reflexive boundaries, seeking to establish an embodied ideal through ritual performance. A myth requires a communicative setting: the one who narrates an ancient story needs listeners who accept his authority and a special place. Often a group gathers in a circle, symbolizing eternal continuity. Similarly, a ritual requires a shared performance. Through the act of speaking and dancing, a shared identity emerges. Kinship relations form a biological bond, and stories on this level do not suffice when the group outgrows the immediate kinship relationships. Societies that are not bounded by blood must be knit together by the invisible spirit that creates a bond stronger than blood. A myth ties a particular group to the largest spatial and temporal horizons. Creation stories narrate how this particular society emerged from prehistoric times, mostly through some divine intervention.

Moreover, the mythological plot also provides a basic orientation for the current society by describing the relation between spatial hierarchies. Borrowing from the present material and symbolic culture of a particular society, myths place a temporary society in the primordial beginnings and project its continuation toward a desired future. Mythological plot sketches the notions of the true, the good, and the beautiful. The individual listener feels elevated and energized to strive toward a much higher and broader reality, beyond his egoistic desires.

Through rituals, this anchoring in the overarching horizon of time becomes real as performers feel they are participants in the larger tragedy, drama, or comedy, connected to their ancestors. Even though in Judaism the veneration of ancestors was absent, various rituals evoked the continuous story of God with his people. In the psalms, which were performed songs, the writers constantly evoke God's action in the past in light of the current threat. Thus, the very act of singing reinforces collective memory and creates a stable overarching plot despite the particular chaos Israel experiences. Rituals are perceived as unchanging in their form, thus preserving social continuity amid chaos and interruptions.

Yet paradoxically, change is also mediated through rites of passage. Thus rituals are collective ways to secure both the continuity and discontinuity of a particular society. Both continuity and discontinuity can endanger every society and must be performed at the right time with communal consensus. A fossilized society might collapse by failing to adapt to the changing environment. Similarly, a society that is constantly disrupted might break apart due to the power of centrifugal forces. Rituals offer a collective mode of reflexivity to mediate between these moments.[21]

A myth also establishes core hermeneutical principles that become deeply embedded in every society and that guide the normative prism through which the world is perceived. For example, the Hebrew creation story begins with a sovereign God who creates order from primordial chaos through his all-powerful word. Creation is the result of an original harmony and ushers in a universal state of peace. This original shalom rings through various messages of Hebrew prophets as the true origin and final vision. Violence is introduced as a result of humans turning

---

21. Michael Stausberg points out that reflexivity does not only refer to the cognitive framing by the critical observers of rituals, but is employed in order to construct new rituals within reflexive modernity, which deconstructs its solid appearance ("Reflexivity," 643).

away from God by not trusting his loving care. Thus, the created world is framed by peace as the ultimate reality, and therefore violence is described as an aberration. Contrary to this mythological plot, the Babylonian creation story views the origin of the created order in an act of violence.[22] The prism of ontological peace or violence serves as an orienting normative frame for a particular group.

Thus, myth produces a hierarchy that then guides collective perception and individual evaluation. A group is able to act together only if certain values are elevated over others, if there is a collective agreement that one ideal is higher than another. These hierarchies create an orienting map of meaning within time and space. The human sense of vision prioritizes some patterns over others, as our brain is unable to focus on everything at once with the same precision. Thus, in order to focus, we must attribute a particular value to an object. Once our vision has zoomed in upon a particular object, a discriminatory pattern emerges. This complexity of perception can be reduced only through prior discrimination, which is possible through the mythological creation of value hierarchies. Thus myths are foundational for perception and action. Without the discriminatory ability, human brains would "freeze" in indecision.

Yet while mythological creation of an ideal solves the problem of perception, it also creates a new problem. Since the highest ideal is not self-evident, humans are prone to miss the mark. The failure to perceive the highest ideal leads toward a skewed pattern, which provides a false map of meaning, thus leading toward aimless wandering. It matters whether ultimate reality is perceived as peaceful or violent at its core. If the ultimate deity is violent, then societies might as well abandon the illusion of permanent peace and accept the fact that violence is woven into the very social fabric. The question about the highest ideal is of utmost importance for the survival and flourishing of every society. This is the reason most myths narrate a battle between conflicting gods. The main message of the Hebrew prophets was the call toward right worship of Yahweh and the warning of social destruction if Israel surrendered to the worship of lesser gods. Similarly, the relation between the rightful worship of God and social flourishing was intimately at the core of St. Augustine's apologetics as well and central to the message of

---

22. "Marduk's first creative act was the severing of Tiamat's body.... The upper part became the heaven, the lower part the earth" (Lambert, *Babylonian Creation Myths*, 169).

Muhammad as the founder of Islam. Yet how does this ideal become a living reality for people?

This ideal becomes real to people through rituals of sacrifice. Sacrifice functions according to the logic of exchange. Through the persuasion of the myth and socialization, people are willing to give up something dear to them or even endure physical pain, in the belief that through this sacrificial act they are elevating the highest ideal, which structures the best possible society. As people feel loss and pain in their bodies, the ideal is inscribed into their bodies through the memory of this event.[23] Through the conscious decision to enter pain, whether by the sacrificing of time, material means, or bodily comfort, the ideal is elevated above other values. This ideal is often manifested materially in a form of a totem or image, whereby a society acquires its center. The most primal way to express this double effect is to dance ecstatically around a totem pole and experience this collective energy, which then extends to all other social realms. Durkheim noticed this, describing Aboriginal tribal life:

> Life in Australian [Aboriginal] societies alternates between two different phases. In one phase, the population is scattered in small groups that attend to their occupations independently. Each family lives by itself, hunting, fishing—in short, striving by all possible means to get the food it requires. In the other phase, by contrast, the population comes together, concentrating itself at specified places for a period that varies from several days to several months. This concentration takes place when a clan or a portion of the tribe ... conducts a religious ceremony.... These two phases stand in the sharpest possible contrast. The first phase, in which economic activity predominates, is generally of rather low intensity. Gathering seeds or plants necessary for food, hunting, and fishing are not occupations that can stir truly strong passions. The dispersed state in which the society finds itself makes life monotonous, slack, and humdrum. Everything changes when a [ceremony] takes place.... Once the individuals are gathered together a sort of electricity is generated from their closeness and quickly launches them into an extraordinary height of exaltation.... Probably because a collective emotion cannot be expressed collectively without some order that permits harmony and unison of movement, [their] gestures and

---

23. In his essay *Zur Genealogie der Moral* Nietzsche speculated about the origins of morals in the experience of pain. Recently, Mellor and Shilling summarized sociological research on pedagogic techniques of pain (*Sociology of the Sacred*, 72–92).

cries tend to fall into rhythm and regularity, and from there into songs and dances.[24]

The sacred ideal often manifests itself through its central position. Its power is maintained through continuous communal sacrifice. The Islamic core ritual resembles the Durkheimian portrayal. Every Muslim is required to go on hadj at least once in a lifetime. This powerful ritual becomes the central orienting experience for the Islamic worldwide community. Moving in sync with millions of people from all over the world, over a time span of thirteen days, all dressed in white robes, sacrificing comfort and circling the black stone of Kaaba—this central ritual creates a strong cohesion within the Islamic community. Contrary to Christianity, Islamic solidarity is reinforced through the prescriptive requirement of communal fasting over the month of Ramadan and five daily prayers in the basic posture of submission in one language: Arabic. Despite local variance, Islam is more rigid in its form in comparison to Christianity, and thus achieves high uniformity and cohesion among its worshippers.

The sacred ideals create the basic social structure. Through this structure, people are able to recognize a common pattern, thus synchronizing their individual actions. Ideals give directionality to every society. Common actions further create solidarity. The highest ideal of a particular society can be found in examining what the people are prepared to sacrifice themselves and ultimately die for. In premodern societies, people were dying for the glory of their deity and immortality of their tribe. In the nineteenth and twentieth centuries, Europeans were dying for their nation-states. Many Muslims are willing to die for their prophet Muhammad. Many Europeans are not able to comprehend the use of violence as a means of defending the honor of Islam. Yet they accept the abstract ideal of human rights, which is used as the legitimization of European and US war interventions. Secularized citizens can't comprehend violence in the name of a particular God, while they view themselves as justified spilling blood in the name of universal human rights. Every myth provides a justification for violence and outlines possibilities of peace.[25]

So far, I have described myth and ritual as fundamental ways for mediating human relational modes and thus forming society. Yet is

---

24. Durkheim, *Elementary Forms*, 214–16.

25. René Girard analyzed the distinct character of the biblical corpus in relation to the logic of sacrifice. Accordingly, biblical mythos departs from the universal centrality of violence and sacrifice. Divine love in Jesus ends the cycle of violence (*Ende der Gewalt*, 290–95).

there a way to achieve not "a view from nowhere" but at least from a privileged position? By analyzing the basic function of myth and rituals, am I not pretending to have glimpsed the primitive reality from beyond? This in itself is a mythological plot, which requires a sacred position outlined by rituals: Since dawn, humans have desired to break out from within spatiotemporal confines and fly like Icarus to the sun. Rituals outline a place beyond the everyday contingencies, from which to glance upon this world.

The latest attempt for this privileged position is the academic myth and academic rituals. The power of the academic formation of reality stems from the disguise of its mythical and ritual conditions by creating a dichotomy toward its religious roots. While seeking to make visible the myths and rituals of the past, the lone scholar is able to do so only from within untold myth and invisible rituals. However, he resembles more the ancient shaman than he is himself aware of. Academia evokes the illusion of ascending to the higher and unchanging realms, from which academics are able to illuminate the ever-changing reality of fleeting forms. This mode betrays the Platonic enchantment. I take up the cave imagery and spin it a bit further: Climbing from one cave, the scholar stumbles into another one, while mistaking this new surrounding for a higher plane.

The Inescapability of the Cave: Academic Myth and Rituals

The core plot for the academic creation of reality is outlined by Plato. Plato's allegory of the cave has had a lasting impact upon the European conception of education. In particular, it outlines a mythological plot and provides rituals for current academia. The larger intention of Plato in *The Republic* is to envision a just society. Justice can be established in an ordered, stable state, where each person is expected to contribute according to one's abilities and in turn receive from the state according to one's needs.[26] Thus, metaphysical contemplations on the nature of reality are embedded within the practical task of education, and education serves the greater political task of establishing an ordered society. Plato also describes a state of chaos, where rulers are seduced by their own vanity. They do not perceive the higher nature of being, instead succumbing to shadows in their lust for power. Thus, the key task of

---

26. Karl Marx borrowed this ideal from Plato.

education consists of elevating the ruling class into a higher realm. A person who has glimpsed the true nature of being, who is able to distinguish between the everyday changing fleeting moments and the unchanging forms—this person becomes a wise and just philosopher-king. A state that is ruled by these kind of elites flourishes. Thus the Platonic allegory provided a stabilizing plot for the Greek polis.

The allegory unfolds its captivating force upon our imagination due to its metaphoric language. Spatiotemporal everyday existence is cast in the image of a dark cave. People who dwell in it are imprisoned. Yet with time, they come to affirm their imprisoned state as the ultimate reality. A tragic plot is present here as the people live in the illusion that they were forced into and came to embrace with time. A dramatic plot captivates the listeners as Plato describes one prisoner who was dragged outside and came to perceive the true nature of things. This liberated man decides to return and free the other prisoners. However, they feel threatened, and Plato concludes that they would murder him. This myth provides the core plot that to this day guides the academic enterprise.

Academia promises to elevate the individual through knowledge. The academic seeks to lay bare the deeper conditions of the surface reality, envision wider horizons, and thus ascend toward a pinnacle of perception that surpasses the point of view commonly taken up by naïve people entrapped in their everyday lives. Philosophy promises depth, history opens up width, and natural sciences guarantee control over solid nature, breaking the shackles of entrapment to the whims of nature. Once the rituals of passage are successfully completed, the academic priesthood grants the seal of recognition: a piece of paper that bears the mark of authority and initiates the entrance of its bearer to the elite circle. This person is now better qualified to judge the nature of reality than the unenlightened commoner trapped in the menial professions. Similarly to the experience of the one dragged from the cave to the surface, the initial methodological gaze is bound up with pain as the light hurts the eyes unaccustomed to daylight. Yet the experienced pain is justified through the deep satisfaction of finally glimpsing a qualitatively higher world. The heroic mission to liberate the masses trapped in the dark is invigorating. Thus, the torturous, lonely, mechanical repetition of academic rituals serves the higher goal of emancipation. The body must be disciplined through repetitive rituals in order to ascend to the higher order of being.

Academic institutions function according to the Platonic myth and are structured through rituals, which are at the same time negated.

By obscuring the operation of myth and ritual within its own walls, academia is able to reproduce a fiction about its privileged point of view beyond the primitive myths and rituals of the cave dwellers.[27] Yet by removing the veil of disguise, the production of knowledge through academic myths and rituals reemerges with an ironic twist: if you escape one cave, you will inevitably stumble into another. The new cave might be a bit brighter and the prisoners might live in an even-greater illusion about their condition, as they are able to move freely. Yet the core conditions do not change. Humans are not able to permanently leave their bodies and detach themselves from their perception within a particular experience of time and place.

What if, instead of presupposing a cave and an exit toward a higher reality, Plato had posited a world existing of a multitude of caves, some better than others? The only possibility for those cave dwellers would have been to enter other caves, narrate their stories, and seek to build a cave according to the best ideal. What if this ideal is not reached by the elitist ascension toward the abstract and eternal but can be touched and tasted within the very low everyday confines? The Judeo-Christian myth emphasizes the downward movement of a God revealing his will in the cave and then even entering the contingent and illuminating the cave through his presence. The shadows acquire another, thicker, and fuller dimension, and the ephemeral takes on an eternal veil.

Perhaps one could object to my story in this manner: Even if myths and rituals are inescapable, we nevertheless loosened their grip and thus escaped from them toward more pluralistic and fragmented rituals and myths, which we are able to choose at will. It is useful to know how primitive societies evolved through myth and ritual at their center. However, we live now in a secular liberal democracy, which is not centered upon myths and rituals. We do not dance and shout around a totem pole, we do not sacrifice to a tribal deity. At the heart of our civilization lies the idea of human dignity, which we protect through the universal declaration of human rights. If someone trespasses this established taboo, the secular state possesses the legitimacy to punish the one who offended this sacred value. We don't have a religious punishment system, and priests barely play a role in a secular society. Even their last ground of authority in the realm of the soul is contested by secular

---

27. Grimes recognizes this disguise and writes, "In short, the grand and guarded divide separating academic and popular culture is at best a fragile construction and at worst a defensively guarded fiction" (Grimes, "Performance," 394).

psychologists. We have evolved away from these superstitions toward a society governed by consensus based on rational discourse.

This objection sounds plausible on the surface. However, once we dig a bit deeper, we become aware of the same deeper patterns that we witnessed for all of human history: God remains at the social center. We might object that the gods have lost their power, as many people do not believe that they truly exist. Gods have become an object of legends that entertain us through such television series like *Game of Thrones* or *Vikings*. We use gods and demons to be entertained, knowing that their impact upon us has faded away and survives only as a memory in the pages of history. This statement might ring true for some on the individual level. Yet on the collective level, the gods never left. We can't form societies without myths and rituals. They simply evolve and change.

Theological myths are transformed into bio-evolutionary and sociological plots of explaining all of reality. Therefore, to reiterate Ludwig Feuerbach, even if the gods do not exist, man needs to invent them in order to provide a deeper justification beyond communal consensus. Judeo-Christian myth and rituals split apart and created a "nova effect" of diverse myths and rituals.[28] To build upon Feuerbach's assertion, one might also acknowledge that Marxism is just another myth, which splintered off from Judaism and Christianity, forming a syncretistic religion with its own rituals. Thus, Feuerbach is not at all unlike the Hebrew prophet Isaiah, who ridiculed other pathetic gods, contrasting them to the one true God (Isa 44). Yet both Isaiah and Feuerbach were able to do so only by assuming the reality of their own God, who is not made of human hands but who is the source of all reality.

On a surface level, Western secular democracies differ from Hindu or Islamic societies, where religion is more visible on all social levels. The juxtaposition of God versus humanism, religion versus secularism, is popular in our society. Yet from a larger historical distance, nothing has changed. We are more similar to Babylonian civilization and current non-Western societies than some secular academics in their mythological caves dancing around the goddess of reason are willing to admit. The idea of individual dignity, around which all our institutions are centered, is the product of a particular religion. We are still dancing around a totem pole without realizing that we are involved in a ritual. The irony of modern man lies in the fact that while he believes himself to have

---

28. Charles Taylor introduced this metaphor in his book *A Secular Age*.

evolved further than primeval man, he is more naïve, as he believes himself to have outgrown myth and rituals while he narrates the myth and circles the totem pole unconsciously. Furthermore, that of which we are unconscious has us even more strongly in its grip.[29] In the following two chapters, I lift to the surface of consciousness the myth and rituals that to this day form the core of secular, liberal democracies.

---

29. Perkins, in her book on the persistent significance of Christendom in shaping European identity, quotes Toynbee: "If one cannot think without mental patterns—and, in my belief, one cannot—it is better to know what they are; for a pattern of which one is unconscious is a pattern that holds one at its mercy" (Perkins, *Christendom and European Identity*, 346).

CHAPTER 2

Conceiving the Sacred Person in the Judeo-Christian Womb

So God created mankind in his own image, in the image of God he created them.

—GENESIS 1:27

IF IT IS TRUE that religious myths as embodied through rituals constitute the core of every society, where did the idea of a sacred person originate, around which Western societies center? The idea of inherent human dignity is anchored in the Judeo-Christian story and became social reality through worship. The origins of this idea lie in the minor departure points of the Hebrew creation narrative from its surrounding Mesopotamian myths. The original setting of a sacred personhood can be traced to Hebrew theology. This anthropology ripened with the advance of the Christian movement, maturing further for over a thousand years during the medieval period and coming to fruition in the Renaissance.

IMMANUEL KANT IN ARABIC

While living in Beirut, I met a remarkable young man from Syria. During the day he worked in construction, and in the evening he studied for his university entry exam. One evening he invited me to his construction shack for tea and conversation. While sipping sweet tea and chewing dried figs, he pulled out a book on the history of Western philosophy. With delight he declared that this book had been written by a professor of the university in Damascus where he hoped to study. He then carefully handed the book to me and asked me to check as to whether he understood the philosophy of Immanuel Kant, a German philosopher. I protested, explaining to him that my Arabic was not sufficient to understand him speaking about Immanuel Kant. My friend smiled and reassured me by explaining that all I would need to do is to see whether he rightly remembered the passage, which summarized the philosophy of Immanuel Kant. He proceeded to repeat the passage by memory—word for word. I was stunned. First, I was blown away by his ability to memorize a passage that I struggled to read in Arabic. Second, I was confused as to why he had such motivation to invest so much energy in memorizing a secondary text about Kant's philosophy. On the surface, he just wanted to pass the exam. However, was he required to repeat the text written by his professor? The obvious irony was hidden from my friend that he was memorizing an explanation of Kant's imperative *sapere aude*: the courage to think for oneself. This experience triggered further questions about a core difference between Germany and Syria. Why was it so obvious for my friend to repeat the words of an authority, and why was there such an emphasis in my German education to critically examine the claims and come to my own conclusion?

This question is complex and can be answered from various angles. Yet perhaps the deepest layer, the original deviation, is found in the mythological departures. The Quranic and biblical creation stories differ in some seemingly minor details, which grew into major cultural differences. In the Hebrew creation story, God asks humans to name the animals. Within the cultural tradition at this time, to name a thing meant to give it existence. Thus God gave humans a power to create. In the Quran, Allah dictates the names of animals to people, who must repeat them.[1] It would be a tremendous task to trace the history and social impact of these normative plots. Assuming that civilizational differences can be traced back to minor mythological deviations, let us dare to jump over the glaring, unbridgeable gap of history and examine the mythological beginnings of our current anthropological social core.

---

1. Quran 2:31–33.

Deified Kings

In ancient myths humans are only side characters upon the main stage of gods. Humans understood themselves within the grander story, with gods being the main agents. By narrating the actions and traits of gods, humans comprehended themselves indirectly by looking into the mythological mirror. Historically, anthropology derived from theology. Our earliest written accounts suggest that our early ancestors did not look inward but rather up and beyond the perceivable horizons. Designated people who mediated between the widest horizons and highest ideals were crucial to give orientation to society. Consequently, priests as mediators between the divine and human took a high position within the social hierarchy. Yet society had to be structured in practical matters as well. Exceptional humans with special skills and useful wisdom were appointed as leaders. In the earliest societies separate spheres of politics and of religion were not distinguished. Thus the priestly and the kingly roles often merged within one person:

> In the ancient world the king stood between the divine and human realms mediating the power of the deity in his city and beyond. He communed with the gods, was privy to their councils, and justice, for leading in battle, for initiating and accomplishing public building projects from canals to walls of temples, and had ultimate responsibility for the ongoing performance of the cult.[2]

Due to this central social role of the king, many myths described the king as set apart from the people, both in his origin and attributes. The king was elevated toward the gods. In Egyptian and Babylonian mythology, only the king was given the privilege of having been created in the image of god. The pharaoh was described as a living representative of Re.[3] The authority of the king was legitimized through this sacred anchoring. The king's power was further extended through the presence of statues as a symbolic representation of his rule over a territory.

This hierarchical conception of social reality extended to the Greek imagination as well. Plato's ideal society, which is both ordered and just, presupposed a clear hierarchy governed by a philosopher-king, who was able to perceive the unchanging, divine reality. Considering various

---

2. Walton, *Ancient Near Eastern Thought*, 278.
3. Westermann, *Kapitel 1–11*, 210–11.

modes of government, the philosopher-king and monarchy surpassed oligarchy, democracy, and tyranny. Contrary to the mythological justification of the king as divine, Plato also emphasized the human effort of the perfect ruler ascending to the divine knowledge. The king is not above his subjects due to divine origin alone but also due to his rigorous philosophical training. Although social position was determined from birth, Plato also advocated for the value of merit, which further stabilized this hierarchy.

The Romans took up Greek philosophy and applied speculative reasoning to their pragmatic conception of the republic. The essential hierarchical conception was not touched but democratized. To create a balance of power and thus secure stability due to higher representation, democratization was necessary in order to prevent tyranny and chaos.[4] However, this democratic gesture included only a small minority of Roman free male citizens, just like its democratic precursors in Athens. In order to strengthen the weakening solidarity and to unify the large empire, the divine king returned with new force. The emperor cult was established throughout the Roman Empire as a unifying religion amid the cultural, ethnic, and religious pluralism.

The idea of a divinized king did not disappear with the advance of Christianity. The image of a king as having both an earthly and celestial body, representing both heaven and earth, exercised a formative force in shaping both medieval political theology and nation-states.[5] The Byzantine emperor had both worldly and sacred power in his hand (Caesaropapism). Muhammad as the founder of Islam embodied these double roles as late as the seventh century. Although he initially viewed himself as a peaceful prophet, he became a warlord as well after his pilgrimage to Medina. For Muslims, Muhammad became the embodiment of the perfect union of religious and political powers, which the subsequent caliphs sought to emulate and which many Muslims around the world today nostalgically remember as the golden age. In Western Europe, the roles between earthly and heavenly powers were more clearly distinguished, in part due to the influence of St. Augustine's political theology. However, the king also needed the blessing of the pope. The ideal of a Christian king exercised a disciplinary restraint over the power of the king. The power struggle culminated in the investiture controversy (1076–1122).

---

4. Cicero was one of the leading Roman philosophers to translate Greek philosophy into Roman law.

5. Kantorowicz, *King's Two Bodies*.

Yet this tension never disappeared. Instead, the power slowly shifted from the Roman Catholic Church in the medieval age to the advancing nation-states since the Renaissance.

Historically, the most natural way to govern society was to let the most able person represent the divine ideal at the center. The assumption that underlies this form of structuring society is the empirical observation of basic inequality. Whether by nature or nurture, people enter society as adults with differing skills and abilities. Since we constantly must evaluate our perception according to hierarchical categories, we conclude that all of reality is structured hierarchically. Therefore, some people belong at the top as philosopher-kings (Platonic imagination) or as divine kings (Mesopotamian/Egyptian myths), and others must serve at the bottom. Historically, the value placed on a person has varied according to their perceived usefulness. In antiquity, this was evident in the adoration of those at the top rung of society, while those deemed less worthy were relegated to the bottom as slaves, often then viewed as akin to useful objects.[6] For this reason, slavery was viewed as a "natural" state in all major civilizations, since ontological inequality was accepted as a given and cemented through myths and rituals.

For most of history, priests and kings formed the social center, and often these roles merged in the person of a divine king. This idea was so prevalent that in the secularized twentieth century, divinized kings reappeared in the form of dictators like Stalin, Mao, Hitler, Mussolini, and others, who surrounded themselves with a sacred aura and established personality worship akin to the Roman imperial cult. Yet one particular religion, firmly rooted in ancient Near Eastern soil, thus sharing most of its mythical assumptions, nevertheless departed in some minor conceptions of how God relates to humans. When train rails split, the initial minor shift does not seem significant. Yet the initial deviation grows into a wide distance as each rail follows its separate course. This minor separation was sown within the Hebrew tradition and came to germination within one particular Hebrew branch, which became the largest world religion. Let us look more closely at this juncture of departure as a historical anomaly.[7]

---

6. Aristotle, *Eth. nic.*

7. It takes a gut honesty to admit that the current secular, liberal, democratic order is built upon this unnatural religious departure from the more evident assumption of ontological inequality. Nietzsche was one of the rare prophets who clearly unmasked the secular intellectuals promoting democracy as Christianity in disguise.

Deified People

The roots of the Western intuitive understanding of our identity as humans and our held ideals of how we ought to be lie four thousand years back in the mythology of the ancient Near East. In order to understand the unique contribution of the Bible toward modern anthropology, we must begin to understand the different way that Israelites conceptualized their God in relation to the wider religious culture surrounding them. From a sociological perspective, *God* can be defined as the highest common ideal of a particular group of people. By projecting an ideal, humans established a norm and a common definition for their species. Humans turn into what they focus their attention on. The ideal images that we contemplate seep into our very being. The imagined ideals, which we imitate through recurrent rituals, shape our bodies and our behavior. Human societies begin to resemble their God. In this way anthropology follows in the footsteps of theology. While the Bible is firmly rooted in the cultural soil of the ancient Near East and resembles its surrounding culture, it nevertheless exemplifies some distinct differences.

The ultimate link between theology and anthropology lies in the description of God creating man in his image (Gen 1:26–30). This qualification applies to men and women in their corporeality. At the end of creation God proclaims the material creation as good, not making a qualitative distinction between matter and spirit. While the history of interpretation on the meaning of this proclamation is vast, the context of the creation story makes clear that humans are elevated above the rest of creation. All humans are elevated to the position of divine king and are assigned with the responsibility of representing God by ruling over creation and taking care of it, much like a benevolent king. At the outset a democratizing principle is presented in the way Yahweh relates to his people. The hierarchy is flattened as the Israelite king is lowered to the level of a mere human (1 Sam 8). Simultaneously, the common Israelite is lifted up. God makes a covenant with the entire people and not merely with the king. God rules through his covenant, and every Israelite is called to understand and obey the Mosaic law. By singling out God as the only ideal and commitment to him through covenant, which is clarified through law, every Israelite is required to become a responsible citizen. The creation story does not offer us an essential definition of what a human is. Instead, human nature is defined in its relational mode to its divine origin. What makes humans distinct from animals and the rest of nature is the ability to respond to a God who is relational within himself.

God creates. This is the common pattern in various creation myths. Yet the crucial difference lies in the detail: How does God create? Or, to go one step further: What is the origin of God? In various Babylonian and Egyptian myths, gods have a beginning, and among various gods there is an eternal struggle for survival. Gods kill and replace weaker deities. They emerge with the cosmos through the process of separation and procreation. Contrary to this, the Genesis account portrays a God who has no beginning and stands outside the created order.[8] While the existence of tribal deities depends on the success of their people, Yahweh stands outside of the particular history of the Jewish people. Isaiah polemically contrasts the idolater, who must constantly recreate his own god and sustain him, with a God who comforts Israel: "Do not be afraid, I have created you" (Isa 44:2, 21). The fact of external stability serves as a precondition for the inner condition of peace. This cosmological stability is contrasted to the instability of the idol worshipper, who must constantly uphold social order through continuous construction. While Israelites can lean back and rest while God creates, idolaters must uphold reality through their own creation, as their idol does not move.

Amid the chaos of historical upheaval, the fact of God's unchanging nature is reiterated through the psalms and prophets, and the people hang on to the conviction that God will persist regardless of any life-threatening changes. In a similar vein, Jesus' mission is presented as both a sudden interruption in history and yet in continuity with God's unchanging love for his people. When departing from his disciples, Jesus comforts them by reminding them that all authority is given to him. Similar to Yahweh's miraculous manifestation to Israel, Jesus exerts his power over natural chaos. While initially Jesus' sovereignty seems contradicted through his shameful death on the cross, the resurrection event reinstates him as the all-powerful ruler over the cosmos. In the final book of the Bible, Jesus is portrayed as sovereign judge over the Roman Empire. He is revealed as the one before whom every knee will bow.

Ultimately, the stability of the world is guaranteed through Yahweh's nature as independent from his creation. The reason for creating and sustaining the world lies within his own generosity. This understanding stands in contrast to Mesopotamian deities, who must be fed

---

8. Walton, *Ancient Near Eastern Thought*, 91.

and constantly upheld, so that they in return hold up their side of the bargain and stabilize the social order. This basic difference appears throughout many stories in the Bible.

In the ancient world the temple designated not merely a concrete place of worship but a symbolic center of the cosmos. The creation as a whole was represented through the temple complex.[9] Most temples in the ancient Near East encompassed gardens, where food for the deities worshipped in these sacred spaces was grown. The garden of Eden in Genesis is also rooted in the same cultural practices, yet it contains a core difference. The garden of Eden is the place where God dwells and where he seeks to have a relationship with humans. It is also a gift, which God in his generosity provides for humans. He grows this garden in order to give food to people and satisfy their aesthetic desire. God is portrayed as caring for people, and contrary to the Mesopotamian gods he is not in need of the people's service. God as the primary caretaker and creator invites humans to rest. The ability to step back from work is rooted in the assurance that the world around humans will not crumble, as God is the one who maintains all of reality. In John's Gospel, Jesus exemplifies this theme by embodying God's generous love through his first miracle by turning water into wine at the wedding of Cana, thus demonstrating God's abundant provision for his people.

Another story that exemplifies this difference is the post-flood sacrifice.[10] In both the Atra-Hasis mythos and the Gilgamesh epic, gods depend on humans. Thus, exterminating humans through the flood also held consequences for the gods, namely, they starve and thus gather hungry around the smell of sacrifice like flies. Gods and humans are co-dependent. They need each other in order to survive. To the contrary, in the Noah story, God does not need the sacrifice, yet he accepts it thankfully and is touched by the human desire to restore the relationship. The biblical account accentuates the relational-moral nature between God and humans. This is further emphasized in how Yahweh is understood to be in the biblical stories. The names of deities designated their attributes.

> If ancient cultures considered something to exist when it had a name and a function, the name of a deity is more than simply

---

9. Walton, *Ancient Near Eastern Thought*, 124–25.

10. The following is a summary of a comparative study of how the sacrifice after the flood is presented in the Mesopotamian and biblical account (Baumann, "Opfer nach der Sintflut").

a moniker by which he or she can be invoked. It is the god's identity and frames the god's "existence."[11]

The biblical God introduces himself by the name Yahweh. Etymologically, this name could indicate the meaning as "a causative form of the verb 'to be.'"[12] In the understanding of the ancient Near East, to create is to give function and names. Tracing this etymology further, John Walton concludes that the key identity of Yahweh is the ability to create a people and enter into a relationship with them. God is the one who initiates the relationship, yet the human answer also matters. Humans are endowed with full responsibility, and the creation story already introduces the idea that God partners with humans to bring about his plans. He does this initially by asking humans to name the animals, thus bringing into existence a distinct culture, as naming a thing is also taking part in creating.

The relationship between God and his people rests upon a number of mutual obligations, which are summed up through the covenant. Contrary to the Egyptian and Mesopotamian deities, the biblical God does not enter into a contractual relationship merely with the king but with the entire people. Although the idea of minor personal deities existed at that time, we see in the Abrahamic story a clear difference. In various Mesopotamian sources, people are portrayed as complaining about their personal deities, who do not take care of them. To the contrary, the God of Abraham is elevated above all other gods and still maintains his personal, caring nature. The most common mode of relation was a sense of dread in light of the powerful yet unpredictable gods. Consequently, the worshippers sought to appease these whimsical gods. To the contrary, beginning with Abraham and later developed in the exodus story, we perceive a God who limits his independence by entering a committed relationship with his people. Jesus operates within this understanding and renews the covenant with his people through his own sacrifice. The biblical God makes the first step toward his people and keeps pursuing them in love. He assures them of his trustworthiness through covenant by providing the sacrifice. In the story of Abraham's sacrifice, God himself provides a ram, which foreshadows the sacrifice of Jesus.

From the Israelite perspective, these characteristics elevate the God of Abraham over all other gods. While in Mesopotamia the worship of various deities was a matter of human pragmatic management of

---

11. Walton, *Ancient Near Eastern Thought*, 92.
12. Walton, *Ancient Near Eastern Thought*, 93.

well-being, the biblical God is portrayed as requiring the only allegiance. Therefore, the prophets call the Israelites to disassociate themselves from polytheistic practices and cut all ties to local deities. This requires Abraham to cut ties with the most basic unit of life: family, land, and tribal religion. The sovereign God would appear as more abstract than local deities, because he is not represented through a material image and is not tied to a particular ethnicity and land. This God calls Abraham into the unknown future. Freedom from the particular is enabled by a God who guarantees a freedom toward the wider reality. The transcending of boundaries, which guaranteed life, is made possible by a God who is sovereign over all creation and at the same time particular in his affection. This movement of transcending ethnic and cultural boundaries is further radicalized through Jesus. The particular tribal religion was transcended by Abraham and then made into a national religion through Moses. The Hebrew prophets hinted at the universal calling of Israel, whose special election comes with the mission to gather all nations at the table of Yahweh (Isa 25:6–8). This prophetic vision was embodied through Jesus and transformed into a global, boundary-transcending movement through the apostle Paul.

God speaks reality into existence. The universe is not hollow and empty but is shaped into a dynamic and creative order. The psalms also introduce the idea that just as God speaks, so all of creation echoes the overabundance of meaning. Since God is portrayed as the source of all life, truth, and beauty, humans are most human when they are transformed into this original image. This creation story finds its culmination in the story of Jesus, who is presented as the perfect image of God and who invites humans to be restored to their original purpose by becoming like him.

A seemingly minor Israelite deviation from the mythological culture of the ancient Near East has had huge implications as the biblical story unfolds and ushers in the revelation of Jesus, who confirms the original meaning, corrects some Jewish deviations, and embodies God's ideal in a tangible manner. In the person of Jesus, God and man reunite, thus establishing the lost dwelling place of Eden. Let me sketch briefly the anthropology that emerges from this biblical theology.

The relationality of humans is manifested primarily in their relation to God as the highest ideal, to nature as their cocreated environment, and to their fellow human beings. Since humans are created in the image of God, they are set apart in the hierarchy. This privilege comes with the responsibility of stewardship for the creation and accountability to the creator. God also guarantees their equality. In relation to God, both men and women are created equal, and the biblical creation story does not set up hierarchies between people groups. Humans cocreate with God, and in this ability they exemplify the creative potentiality to establish new networks. This engagement is made possible through demystified nature. When the earth or the sun are not viewed as deities, they are not worshipped but become objects of inquiry. Human reasoning is encouraged within such a conceived cosmology and anthropology. The ultimate reality is peaceful. Struggling and evil are subsumed under the unifying reality of the good, as guaranteed by the all-powerful God. Goodness and continuity generate a stable inner attitude amid the dynamics of change. This cosmology gives rise to attention to patterns that persist through change and to the ability to abstract from the particular; similar to the elevation above the local deities of the transcending nature of God.

Human interiority is further developed through abstraction and the moral nature of God. That which one can't see, one must imagine. Imagination is the ability to construct a subjective reality that differs from external nature. The Israelites are invited into a dialogue and love relationship and not mere outward, passive submission. Since God is reliable in his promises, the believer develops an inner conversation within himself and is challenged to interpret history in light of God's revelation. Several psalms reflect on the struggle of the psalmist to make sense of what is and ought to be the case. Thus, the biblical writers develop a rich inner texture through constant dialogue with God, with nature, and with each other. This inner-biblical polyphonic conversation extends to the story of Jesus. Jesus' entry into history triggers a controversy on the nature of God's action with his people. The inner-Jewish dialogue circles around the identity and mission of Jesus, culminating in the birth of the movement that believes that Jesus is the promised Messiah in the line of David, the fulfillment of Yahweh's promises, and the seal of the new covenant.

Christianity further develops the language of interiority. Correcting the slide toward external ritualistic obedience only, Jesus emphasizes the intention of the law given to Moses. Jesus takes the idea of a God desiring an intimate relationship with his people a step further. God's glory no longer dwells only in a certain area of sacred space but becomes real through his bodily presence, thus furthering God's passionate movement toward his people. Those who believe in him become like the sacred temple, whose bodies become the sites of God's indwelling through his Holy Spirit. The language of intimacy and interiority comes to its pinnacle in the Gospel of John. Humans are invited into the mutual harmonious indwelling of the divine persons (John 14–17).

God's freedom is portrayed in contrast to local deities. The Israelite God is not bound by creation, ethnic, or political restrictions. His freedom springs from his desire to glorify himself, and seeking his own glory comes from his love. Since God is the sole sovereign creator, all of creation acquires its realness in relation to him. Biblical stories constantly portray characters who transcend particular boundaries by reaching out to the higher, liberating goals set by Yahweh: "freedom from" is intelligible only in relation to "freedom toward." Freedom as a human imperative is good only within a world that is permeated by a loving God, who guides his people toward union with himself.

Anthropology as a discipline grew out of theology. The distinction of being human lies in our capability for complex relationality. The right proportion of this relationality emerges as people contemplate God as the highest ideal, who orders the entire cosmos. The main message of the Hebrew prophets is the call to the people toward right worship. By the failure to worship God, horizontal relations become skewed and social chaos follows suit. What was once good becomes perverted. The relational human is set apart. Both men and women are endowed with special obligations toward creation and other human beings. Humans are equal before God, they have creative capacities and rich inner lives, they are able to reason and are called toward freedom, which is outlined by the perfect will of God. The drama of the biblical story unfolds as humans turn into a caricature of themselves by turning away from God. Yet God pursues Adam and Eve and subsequently their descendants as well. God continuously calls rebellious people to himself in order to restore them to a true humanity. Yet contrary to the unmediated communication with God in the garden of Eden, human interaction with God is now mediated by rituals. While the fact of humans being created in the image of God is never revoked, the brokenness in the relationality toward God affects all other aspects of human life. Humans become truly human through communion with God. Biblical worship provides the path back to this union. Thus to worship Yahweh rightly is to keep chaos at bay and promote social flourishing. For the Israelites, the key question, from which everything else flows, is: How and whom to worship rightly? Due to this all-encompassing understanding of worship, the secular discourse on ritual does not do justice to the Hebrew emic understanding: "True worship involves reverential human acts of submission and homage before the divine Sovereign in response to his gracious revelation of himself and in accord with his will."[13] As Block succinctly points out, the Hebrew Scriptures emphasize a God who invites people to dwell with him. Thus, worship is always a human response of thankfulness. This response involves the entire person and permeates the entirety of the Israelite social life. The inner attitude must be aligned with external ritual practice. Moreover, the cultic practices in the temple are condemned by the prophets if these do not correspond to everyday life. God requires a holistic worship, a God-pleasing life ushers in the temple rituals, and the rituals overflow into righteous living. This idea extends to the Pauline definition of worship as surrender of the believer's entire life as a sacrifice pleasing to God (Rom 12:1–2). For the Israelites, worship is embodied through elaborate cultic and social prescriptions. At the center stands the covenantal mode of relationship between God and his people. The detailed law is an expression of God's gracious revelation as to how the believer can please his God, contrary to the surrounding deities, who remain vague and leave the worshipper in uncertainty and therefore agony concerning their obligations.

Hebrew worship involved all the senses. The aesthetics of the temple building offered spatial orientation: the temple was seen as the center of the universe due to God's presence. Yet the prophets also relativized this widespread conception in the ancient Near East, emphasizing that the temple couldn't contain God. The hearing of the Torah was a regular practice. The words were meant to become an integral part of the life and action of believers. Various yearly celebrations structured the perception of time and engraved a divine pattern that permeated the entire sociopolitical life of Israel. As smell has the potent ability to trigger memory, the smell of sacrifices and incense imprinted upon the deep collective subconscious the first recorded sacrifice, when God pledged not to exterminate humanity. The tasting of food during communal celebrations reminded the Israelites of the gracious character of God. Touching the sacrificial objects made it tangible for the Israelites that God provides even the sacrifice, as he did for Abraham. The detailed command in Leviticus for the daily life of the Israelites created coherence for the life of an entire people.

---

13. Block, *For the Glory of God*, 23.

While the Christian movement retains this view of God, it also develops further the inherent anthropology in continuity with the First Testament by changing the mediating rituals, which enabled the new movement to transcend the cultural boundaries of Judaism. By accommodating non-Jews in the covenantal relationship, various specific ethnic forms of mediations were proclaimed no longer essential. The rich bodily and cultural means of relation toward Yahweh were concentrated in the core rituals of baptism and Eucharist, leaving room for further elaborate cultural appropriations.

Hebrew theology departed from the surrounding Mesopotamian imagery in some minor yet crucial points. From this theology an anthropology emerged, which was also distinct in relation to the ascending Greco-Roman world. The main difference was a view that every human was made in the image of God and therefore equal before God, thus confronting the prevailing natural ontology of inequality. Moreover, the advancing Christian movement further universalized this anthropology, setting a stage for the revolutionary upheaval of the ancient world.

One man embodied a link between this Hebrew imagery and the Greco-Roman philosophy like no other: Saul of Tarsus, who later became the apostle Paul.[14] Proficient in Greco-Roman culture and deeply steeped in the Pharisaic tradition, Paul had a dramatic encounter with the risen Christ and offered a theology that provided fresh answers to urgent questions of antiquity. One of these answers was a radically new conception of what it means to be truly human.

Intercultural Genius

The crisis of antiquity consisted in the chaos that ensued from the antagonism between local and universal powers. The particular tribal gods, who were seen as ruling over city-states, lost their potency through shifting their authority to the abstract structure of the rule of law through the distant Roman Empire. While the Roman conquerors left local cultural structures and deities in place, they were drained of their efficacy to govern. The prevailing experience of submitting to a remote ruler undermined the established hierarchies and social conventions. This destabilizing effect led toward the proliferation of various

---

14. In the following part, I follow the basic argument as developed by Siedentop, *Inventing the Individual*, 51–79.

religious movements to fill the vacuum of the collapsing hierarchy of the ancient cosmos in its conception of the family and the city-state. Within this state of social confusion, the early Christian movement offered a cosmic vision, a new form of association, and an attractive image of what it meant to be human.

As an answer to the collapsing ancient hierarchies, the gnostic movement offered a hierarchy of ascent through knowledge. Contrary to this gnostic conception, Paul's point of departure was the idea of Jewish election and its ultimate universal mission through the Messiah. In Christ, the specific Jewish-ethnic distinctions and cultic boundaries were relativized as a new community of human beings was envisioned, whereby social status, ethnicity, and power based on gender became secondary (Gal 3:28–29). Through Christ, God extended his invitation to restore humanity, and by receiving this gift through faith, each person was given a new identity. In working out this anthropology, Paul employed the spatial metaphors of depth and inwardness.

While on the surface Roman law and imperial ideology ordered all of reality, and Jewish resistance through Mosaic law established a counterculture, Paul presented an entirely other imagery, in which the ultimate reality is that of an all-powerful God who enters history through Jesus and conquers the power of sin on the cross. The solution to Roman coercion and the Jewish particularistic interpretation of the Mosaic law was to recognize God's universal agency within a particular history through every human agent. Divine revelation did not come through external association with the Roman Empire or ethnic religion. Instead, every human could experience a deep mystical union with God by trusting in Jesus as the Messiah and experiencing this reality through the ritual of baptism. This transformative event came about not through coercion but through human participation in what God did in Jesus. However, contrary to the stoics, even the human will was seen as permeated by God's internal grace and cannot be made into an ultimate means of human self-redemption. Jesus' liberation does not consist in the external overthrowing of powers but in the defeat of invisible evil and the end of imprisonment through its powers. The ultimate problem is invisible and internal. The core event for change and fulfillment consists in renewal of the self.

Neither birthright as a Roman citizen nor rational ascent defined the worth of a person but merely trusting the descended God in Jesus, whose presence was made permanent through the Holy Spirit. Thus this

God, who was seen to stand above all of creation and political powers, moved toward the inner core of the individual. This type of reconceived anthropology appealed not only to the slaves within the Roman Empire but to the Greek nobility as well. The slave was granted a personal will, responsibility, and power for agency. The ancient nobility, whose hierarchical conceptions had begun to crumble, were given another cosmic imaginary, where they were not merely ascending toward unchanging forms but could enter into a personal relationship with the personal and triune God.

This reconception of the self did not remain a purely individualistic and elitist experience as in the case of many gnostic sects. Paul combined this sense of a gifted new self with strong communal obligation. Freedom from sin created an obligation toward freedom to love—to love God through loving the fellow believer and the neighbor. The moral impetus became internalized. A freely received gift created a sense of obligation. Humans received immeasurably more than they were able to give back. The imbalance between eternal gifts and temporary life created a strong push toward loving the fellow human, who is made in the image of God. In this Christian conception, the only way to love God was by loving his creation, which most closely reflects his image. Thus, giving back toward God could be achieved via the concrete human. With the idea of God's presence within, the Jewish imagery of law written on hearts became reality, and the idea of human ability to weigh the nature of the good developed into the category of conscience.

For Paul, this experiential encounter with Christ fulfills the requirement of the law. The social body of this expressed love is the church. The church creates a radically new form of association that upsets the hierarchical social structure of antiquity. The core requirement of membership was an individual experience independent of any external marks. In summary, the achievement of Paul was immense:

> Paul overturns the assumption of natural inequality by creating an inner link between the divine will and human agency. He conceives the idea that the two can, at least potentially, be fused within each person, thereby justifying the assumption of the moral equality of humans. That fusion is what the Christ offers to mankind. It is what Paul means when he speaks of humans becoming "one in Christ." That fusion marks the birth of a "truly" individual will, through the creation of conscience.[15]

---

15. Siedentop, *Inventing the Individual*, 61.

This Pauline anthropology lays down the foundation of how Western civilizations conceive of their social core today. Working from within the Hebrew theological tradition while employing Greek concepts, Paul develops a vision of human equality, freedom, and inwardness. He alters the Greek conception of hierarchical reason by domesticating it through the Christian virtues of humility and love. This anthropology is deeply seated within the Christ event. For Paul, the agency of God can't be separated from his view of human nature. What God did creates an obligation for what humans must do.

This anthropology does not remain within the realm of individual knowledge. Instead, this view of what it means to be human becomes a living reality through the social body of the church and the reoccurring pattern of the Eucharist. The eucharistic experience provides an experiential pinnacle of God's gracious invitation through his self-sacrificing love. The believer is invited to receive this gift and to remember the redemptive God in history. At the same time, by taking the Eucharist, believers proclaim that God is sovereign over history. The individual embodies God within herself, she becomes one with God, symbolically returning to the union with the creator in paradise, and aligns to his will toward a perfect freedom.

Paul was the first Christian theologian who worked out the implication of Jewish theology within the setting of Greco-Roman antiquity and institutionalized the messianic movement, thus lending it durability through a social body. This renewed image of humanity disrupted antiquity and led toward the transformation of society centered upon the idea of sacred personhood. In the following centuries this idea put an end to the ancient ontology of inequality, and through the medieval ages it permeated the sociopolitical dough like a grain of yeast. Although the medieval period was pejoratively framed as a time of ignorance and regression by radical Enlightenment philosophers, one could retort that all seeds germinate in the dark. In fact, the medieval period became the laboratory of ideas and associations that prepared the foundation for modernity.

Germinating Sacred Personhood in Medieval Christendom

Radical ideas do not change societies overnight. It usually takes a messy process for these ideas to become part of a social imaginary, to acquire an aura of the factual and become the ruling norm for social institutions. Christianity both accelerated the decline of antiquity and stepped into the increasing vacuum. One theologian, who similarly to Paul served as a link between decaying antiquity and the ensuing chaos, was Aurelius Augustine. Both his theological vision of the sociopolitical reality and the prayerful lens through which he interpreted the world as he spoke with God laid the foundation for the medieval age. Augustine further elaborated the inwardness of the Hebrew and Pauline anthropology. Accordingly, the cosmic battle rages within each heart, which can find ultimate rest only in God. Being well versed in Manichaean and Platonic philosophy, Augustine turns away from dualistic-hierarchical ontology and explores the inner realm, which becomes the lens through which the world is discovered.

In some regard, Augustine continues from within the Greek anthropological vein. Plato views the human as a rational self who ascends toward the eternal order through perception. This stands in stark contrast to the then-prevailing ethics of glory, "where what is valued is strength, courage, and the ability to conceive and execute great deeds, and where life is aimed at fame and glory, and the immortality one enjoys.... The higher moral condition is where one is filled with a surge of energy, an access of strength and courage." Moreover, Plato distances his highest anthropological ideal from the poetic view wherein the gods imbue the individual with the creative spirit. "Plato's work should probably be seen as an important contribution to a long-developing process whereby an ethic of reason and reflection gains dominance over one of action and glory."[16] While Augustine borrows some Platonic categories to communicate his newly found faith, he nevertheless departs from Greek anthropology in some core assumptions.

Augustine further develops the Pauline conception of the will as prior to reason. Departing from Platonic dualism, Augustine emphasizes the necessity of loving God. The Platonic hierarchy of values breaks down, as every aspect of human nature needs to be redeemed by grace. Instead of ascending dispassionately toward the highest good, every human must be gripped by personal divine love in order to reorient her entire life toward God. This conception introduced a different spatial orientation. Instead of looking upward only, St. Augustine looks for God everywhere and most of all inwardly:

---

16. Taylor, *Sources of the Self*, 117.

> God is not just what we long to see, but what powers the eye which sees. So the light of God is not just "out there" illuminating the order of being, as it is for Plato; it is also the "inner" light. It is the light in the soul.[17]

Contrary to the Platonic conception of the divine, the biblical God is more dynamic. His presence within the individual motivates Augustine to explore the inward by talking about this process. Language creates a reality, and ultimately, it creates a higher form of reflexivity, wherein the individual begins to reflect about his own reflections. Taylor calls this second order of reflexivity "radical reflexivity."[18] Augustine remembers his own remembering; in this way he meticulously descends into inner realms in search of God's working. Augustine often narrates a particular experience in his life where he discerns God's gracious working:

> What agony I suffered, my God! How I cried out in grief, while my heart was in labour! But, unknown to me, you were there, listening. Even when I bore the pain of my search valiantly, in silence, the mute sufferings of my soul were loud voices calling to your mercy. You knew what I endured, but no man knew. How little of it could I find words to tell, even to my closest friends![19]

Augustine's anthropology emerges through prayer as a way of continuing communication. Prayer establishes a relationality toward God, and from this renewed sense of self, all other spheres are reordered. Augustine is aware that he is not able to rationally lay bare all of his motives. Therefore, he constantly appeals to God to search him and relay to him the true condition of his inner realm and the nature of reality. The relationality is both established from the inside out and also caused externally by God communicating through the Scriptures, external events, and nature. Throughout Augustine's continuous dialogue, the world emerges as dynamic and overflowing with meaning.

This particular experience of prayerful discernment serves him as a lens to interpret his society and discern larger meaningful patterns in history. The person is not trapped within a predetermined fate, damned to counter it with stoic will. Instead, Augustine paints a dynamic reality where each person is able to respond and change. Each person renews the

---

17. Taylor, *Sources of the Self*, 129.
18. Taylor, *Sources of the Self*, 130.
19. Augustine, *Confessions*, 143.

relationship toward self, others, and the world as she converses with God and narrates a larger story through confession.

The place of God's revelation becomes the center of the universe. From here, patterns are perceived and evaluated. For ancient Near Eastern culture, the temple formed the divine center. Yet within the Israelite myth, the temple is an imperfect mediatory site, which reminds Israelites of the original unity in the garden of Eden and creates an expectation for a more intimate communion. Jesus fulfills this expectation by reconciling humans with God through himself as the true dwelling place. Through Jesus, God indwells the body of each believer through the Holy Spirit, and the body of each believer becomes the site of God's presence. In a paradoxical sense, each individual is rendered the center of the universe through her connection to the divine center. Yet this individual centrality remains conditional on the connectivity to the absolute center. Augustine further elaborates this Judeo-Christian spatial restructuring of the world by describing a mode in which the world and history could be grasped through the divinized personhood.

This mode of conceiving of reality through inward conversation with God becomes the primary mode for the Christian mystics of the following centuries. By cultivating and articulating the presence of God within, this practice challenged the political powers by subverting the established hierarchies of birth lineage, gender, and knowledge. Where and how God reveals himself lays down the foundation for how authority is perceived and exercised. Within the Islamic myth, Allah primarily reveals his will through a book, in the form of prescriptive law. Thus authority remains external, and those who interpret the religious law become the primary authority in all social matters. To the contrary, Christians view the final revelation of God made manifest in Jesus and, through him, within every human person who embraces him. This understanding of revelation prepares the way for individual conscience. Thus, in principle, every individual is endowed with authority from within.

While the temporal order is hierarchical, the equality of every person before God poses an alternative potential that could at any time break into the temporal order. Various monastic movements, individual mystics,[20] and apocalyptic groups claimed this inner revelation to

---

20. One impressive example of a female mystic who challenged the male ecclesial structure of the eleventh century is Hildegard von Bingen. Although Hildegard von Bingen came from lower nobility, she challenged the male hierarchy of the church through her visions. Her theology falls in a genre similar to the Revelation of John. She

confront the status quo. The appeal to the divine voice within and the equality of people as the accepted social imaginary provide a powerful mechanism to raise a social movement against abuses of power by kings and the established church. The social imaginary of equality and inner authority due to divine presence becomes a continuous social ferment within medieval societies. The fuel for the engine of social reforms comes from the idea of divine authority within every ordinary believer. The external hierarchies are relativized as being temporal.

The early church embodied equality by welcoming people from different social classes. Although neither the Pauline Letters nor the early church called for a violent abolishing of all inequality in society, they sought to embody an alternative, eternal, and all-encompassing reality, which ultimately began to permeate the established social relations. Due to its subversive, slow nature, the imagery of principal equality took even deeper roots as it could be embraced voluntarily over time. The church became a place where people from all social and cultural backgrounds encountered each other and were made equal by the same need of God's grace expressed in the rituals of confession and Eucharist. The church sought to keep the balance between loyalty to earthly powers and following the radical call of Christ. This tension led toward changes over a long temporal span. For example, the church did not confront slavery directly and did not call for the immediate overthrowing of this practice, which was regarded as natural in all civilizations. However, the Christian sense of equality at times stirred some Christians to critique slavery against all odds. For example, in the fourth century, Gregory of Nyssa condemned slavery in one of his sermons head on.[21]

---

claimed to write down what she sees. This allowed her to create vivid images, which reframed the perception of the reader and yet refrained from confronting the ecclesial power structure directly as she did not claim to have authoritative teaching. Yet her images offered a wide range of interpretations, thus cracking open the status quo. See Hildegard von Bingen, *Weg der Welt*.

21. In one of his sermons Gregory preached, "For what price, tell me? What did you find in existence worth as much as this human nature? What price did you put on rationality? . . . God said let us make man in our image, after our likeness. If he is in the likeness of God, and . . . has been granted authority over everything on earth from God, who is his buyer, tell me? Who is his seller? To God alone belongs this power; or rather, not even to God himself. For his gracious gifts . . . are irrevocable. God himself would not reduce the human race to slavery, since he himself, when we had been enslaved to sin, recalled us to freedom. . . . Is there any difference in these things between the slave and his owner? Do they not draw in the same air as they breathe? Do they not see the sun in the same way? . . . If you are equal in all these ways, therefore, in what respect have you something extra, tell me, that you who are human think yourself the master of a human being" (quoted in Siedentop, *Inventing the Individual*, 119).

As the Roman Empire began to break apart and solidarity within the hierarchical vision of society weakened, even open critics of Christianity like the emperor Julian acknowledged that the social attractiveness of Christians came from their charity toward strangers and the moral appeal of their communities.[22] However, as Christianity became the officially privileged religion of the Roman Empire during the reign of Theodosius I, Greco-Roman elitism once again raised its head; this time in an ecclesial disguise. The temptation was very real to reestablish the hierarchical understanding of power, in particular for bishops, who suddenly found themselves at the pinnacle of power. As a response to this temptation, some Christians consciously sought to preserve the revolutionary notion of Christianity.

From the third century onward, the Christian egalitarian impulse was embodied through monks, who distanced themselves from the seduction of power in order to live out the new form of association. Within monastic communities the radical conception of the individual could evolve in contrast to the virtues of antiquity:

> The first striking thing about that new identity was that its basis lay in voluntary association, in individual acts of will. This was a radical departure from the beliefs and practices of the ancient world. Family cult, civic status and servitude had been assigned by birth or imposed by force. . . . The transition from solitary hermits to communal monasticism confirmed a new form of sociability, a sociability founded on the role of individual conscience, on accepting the claims of a universal moral law.[23]

This reality of individual will led toward a freedom from social expectations. Women could also establish their own monastic associations. At first, mostly upper-class women led this emancipatory movement. Within monasteries, manual labor acquired a new dignity. Democratizing principles were embodied in how leadership was conceived and monasteries organized. For example, St. Benedict "sought to eliminate social distinctions within the monastery. . . . By taking individual responsibility so seriously, the ideas of moral equality and limited government became closely associated. Outward conformity of behavior was all that was expected in the ancient family and polis. But monasticism consecrated a vision of social order founded on

---

22. Siedentop, *Inventing the Individual*, 89.
23. Siedentop, *Inventing the Individual*, 94–95.

conscience.... However difficult to achieve, there was in theory 'no distinction' between persons on the grounds of social status, whether of higher or lower class, slave or free-born."[24]

The mystics, monks, and nuns led the way in preserving the radical anthropology and embodying it through their visions and communities. The individual increasingly became aware of her own genius as God was perceived as working from within each person to renew her soul.[25] In the eleventh century, scholastic canon lawyers democratized the Greco-Roman idea of natural law by grounding it in Judeo-Christian equality. This creative reinterpretation was a birthplace of the idea of individual rights.

The history of the church and its impact upon social and political realities is not straightforward. Desired consequences often do not follow pure intentions. Perversions creep in—good and bad are mingled together. Monks sought to be faithful to God and unintentionally cultivated the seed of modernity by watering the idea of the equal individual. How much Platonism and Manichaeism did Augustine smuggle in through theological disguise? This is still being hotly debated. Just like Augustine functioned as a link between antiquity and the medieval age, so Martin Luther, as an Augustinian monk, embodied the ferment of the medieval age and transitioned it toward modernity. The irony of Martin Luther lies in the fact that by reforming the church he unintentionally secularized it.

This leads us to the question in the next chapter. If the idea of the sacred personhood was conceived in the Judeo-Christian womb, how did it disconnect from these sacred roots and develop the imaginary of a god-free space, which ultimately led toward a disconnected, atomized individual? Liberal democracies center upon the idea of human dignity, from which concrete human rights are deduced. Yet this anthropological core is surrounded by the secular atmosphere that permeates all social segments. Western society is comprised of institutions centered upon the sacred individual. These institutions are imagined to exist within the broader secular space. Where did the idea of the secular originate, and how did it evolve in the Western world?

---

24. Siedentop, *Inventing the Individual*, 97–98.

25. Benoît Godin traced the idea of innovation. He located a positive view of innovation as understood in early Christian theology regarding the divine renewal of the individual soul (*Innovation Contested*, 42–45).

CHAPTER 3

The Birth and Growth of Secular Imagination Within Judeo-Christian Dominion

La religion de la sortie de la religion

—Marcel Gauchet, *Le désenchantement du monde*

The idea of sacred personhood was conceived in the Judeo-Christian womb. Yet how did this idea become the core belief around which a secular social order was formed in the wake of the Renaissance? The very idea of a place free of divine coercion is already inherent in Judeo-Christian theology. This "god-free" space grew rapidly within medieval theology and accelerated after the Renaissance through translation. Hereby, Christendom as homogeneous space was inverted and turned into a secular space. The result of this development was the secular liberal order, which is held together through a paradox: at the heart of secular liberalism stands a religious idea. Yet the secular acquires an aura sui generis through obfuscation of its sacred center.

How Dare You? Beirut vs. Berlin

Charbel came every summer from Paris to visit his elderly mother in Beirut. She rented the first floor of her house to us and extended warm hospitality and generosity. When Charbel came to visit, she invited us to meet him over refreshments. Over the course of conversation, I learned that Charbel viewed himself as atheist. However, he would often accompany his mother, who attended the Maronite Mass regularly. Moreover, he traveled with her to visit the sacred site dedicated to a local saint. When I asked him how he could engage in these events, considering his atheism, he answered that this is a cultural way of his people and that religion is an intrinsic part of Lebanese culture. He closed his explanation with: "What else would there be, if not this Maronite church?" Atheism for him seemed a matter of individual, cognitive preference, which did not require the rejection of his culture, which was obviously saturated with Christian imagery and practices.

In Berlin, my wife and I planted a Christian center in a storefront space. Sometimes neighbors drop in for events and activities that we hold in the same space. On one occasion, a German neighbor expressed to me her opinion how utterly absurd it appears when modern people today listen to a pastor and accept religious authority. In response, I asked her about her university classroom and why she accepts the authority of a professor by listening to her for hours. In Berlin, the relation between individual cognition and culture seemed to be reversed: religion resided within individual decision and needed justification vis à vis secular culture. In other words, many people hold the premise that personal faith cannot possibly exist in a society bereft of God's presence. Charbel migrated between these two worlds when he flew between Paris and Beirut. Europe conceived and embodied the imagination of a time and space devoid of God. This myth became social reality through particular rituals. Where did the idea of the secular originate, and how was this imagination extended like a blanket over an entire society?

The Judeo-Christian Origin of Secular Imagination

The origin of the secular imagination lies in the dissatisfaction with randomness and chaos and, in particular, the chaos that was associated with cunning gods vying for power. Subsequently, a desire for a unifying principle and archaic origin arose. This unifying principle does not necessarily need to be a naturalistic cause. Initially, polytheistic chaos was ordered through a transcendent, all-powerful God who creates a stable hierarchy. However, since nature was also deified in the earliest myths, our clear distinction between immanent and transcendent spheres does not apply to these archaic creation myths. Gods emerged out of primeval waters, and water was also viewed as a deity due to its life force.

In the pre-Socratic tradition, philosophers searched for a simple causation for everything that exists. The speculative reasoning of Democritus even hinted at a theory of reality consisting of atoms. Pre-Socratic philosophers sought to glance beyond appearances and trace all of reality toward a unifying substance.[1] Even earlier than Greek speculation, Mesopotamian myths narrated the emergence of the gods from primeval waters.[2] The experience of conflicting forces and the unpredictability of nature led toward a desire for a unifying harmony. The experience of plurality and unity is fundamental for humans. Myths and rituals seek to balance the experience of plurality and unity in a perfect tension.

Egyptian gods, similar to the Greek gods, were more powerful and wiser than humans. Yet they also exemplified many of the same weaknesses as humans: being vain, whimsical, and often unpredictable. Socrates came to critique these gods, who seemed all too human, and Hebrew prophets kept reminding the Israelites about the complete otherness of Yahweh, contrary to the Mesopotamian and Egyptian deities who surrounded them. Plato developed a philosophical speculation about the highest ideal, which he came to envision as transcending human arbitrariness. Thus, instead of corrupting people with tales about immoral gods, Plato sought to create an abstracted ideal, toward which people could strive and thus elevate the sociopolitical order. Similarly, the Hebrews emphasized a God transcending creation and ethnic particularities. Instead of merging with nature and being tied to a particular tribal fate, the Hebrew God stood outside of all creation and claimed to guide all of humanity and history. Yet while the Platonic divine remained abstract and vague, the Hebrews envisioned a dynamic God who enters into relationship.

Within polytheistic experience, social spheres are undifferentiated and are permeated with sacred power. Religion is present everywhere as all of life is enchanted. Paradoxically, by elevating one all-powerful and omnipresent God over nature, an idea emerges of a space and time

---

1. Osborne, *Presocratic Philosophy*, 61–80.

2. Walton, *Ancient Near Eastern Thought*, 88. Blumenberg rejects the hypothesis that logos emerges from mythos by ironically juxtaposing water as a source of life in ancient mythology and modern evolutionary biology, whereas the latter "logos" is paler in its explanatory scope (*Arbeit am Mythos*, 34).

distinct from this God, where people are enabled to make independent choices.³ The Hebrew creation story presents this desacralization of nature and introduces a difference between God, who stands beyond his creation, and all of creation, which is devoid of divine attributes. While biblical cosmology still contains traces of polytheism and admits the existence of all kinds of intermediary beings like angels and demons, it nevertheless continuously emphasizes the final authority and power of one God, who rules over all of reality through his sovereign will.

The Hebrew creation story tells a tragic plot: God's immediate presence with his people was broken through people's rejection of him, and the consequent distance became a permanent reality. Secularity as experience of God's distance became a reality, and the Bible tells a story of how God seeks to bridge this space. However, due to his loving nature God will not violate people's will. Therefore, he continuously seeks to win his people back but does not overwhelm them. Instead, the god-free space remains the genuine space of freedom, leading toward a delicate balance between presence and absence. Since God seeks a love relationship with humans, he is compared to a lover who waits for the answer of the beloved. In order to enable human response, God hides his glory, which is manifested indirectly via immanent means. A secular space emerges as a result of the idea of God's voluntary retreat in order to enable humans to make a deliberate choice to love him or reject him. Secularity is a gift bought at the price of divine agony.

God's gift of a secular space is further reinforced by abstracting him from a particular image within a cultural and ethnic setting. On the one side, abstraction allows for a universal conception of God. On the other side, abstraction requires a continuous mediation of an invisible, atemporal God within the here and now. This translation puts the emphasis on the human interpretation of history and marks the beginning of theological reasoning. God chooses to be vulnerable due to continuous human mediation. From this abstraction and the need for mediation, a constant danger arises of false representation. The Hebrew prophets critiqued idolatry as perverted worship, wherein humans mistake their own illusions for the highest ideal. Feuerbach later extended this critique to all of religion as a form of false consciousness, while excluding himself from his critique. By retreating, the Hebrew God allows for a god-free space to exist, even if temporarily. Augustine takes up this notion and refers to

---

3. Gauchet describes the paradox between divine greatness and human liberty in the development of monotheism (*Désenchantement du monde*, 64–73).

saeculum as the time in between Jesus' departure and his return; there is a time for decision, where people are able to exercise their freedom.

In Christianity, this distance is not mediated merely through prophets and law but by God himself entering history in the person of Jesus. Yet, this event also requires further mediation due to God's particular spatiotemporal revelation. Within Christianity, this is solved through the presence of the Holy Spirit as the one person of the Trinity who dwells within the body of believers. By entering his creation God assures people that he continues to uphold and care for the world he created. This reality is regularly mediated via the ritual of the Eucharist.

Secularity as spatial and temporal absence of God carried a positive nuance within the Judeo-Christian story. Secularity as absence allowed for the possibility of making a genuine choice to reenter into the lost relationship. The early church refused to worship various local deities by claiming allegiance to the invisible, universal God. Consequently, some Romans accused Christians of being "atheists." What was meant as a pejorative label became an unintended prophecy. Every myth contains potentials that lie dormant until they are awakened. The oxymoron of this theological secularity bled into historic reality when the early church took over responsibility for the collapsing empire and was challenged to draw a sharper distinction between the heavenly and the earthly realms.

Accidental Secularity

The tragedy of history consists in the fact that the results of one's actions often stand in opposition to original intentions. Secularity can be viewed as an unintended result of the church having taken up social responsibility at a time when chaos ensued and social institutions crumbled. Through the increasing worldly success of the church, it inhaled some cultural Greco-Roman air, which it had once resisted. Some Christians viewed this development as compromise and sought inner reforms. Once again, these reforms, both theological and practical, grew and became a successful blueprint for the rest of society.[4] Yet by scaling the ecclesial reform, the once-holistic spiritual practices were cut loose from their sacred roots.

---

4. Taylor views both strands, "intellectual deviation" and "reform master narrative," as complementary in understanding the rise of the secular age as normative experiential background (*Secular Age*, 773–76).

As the Western Roman Empire weakened due to internal reasons and external pressures, the church increasingly became the most solid functioning institution. Within only four centuries the church had risen from a Jewish sect into the central Roman institution, willing to take responsibility for society amid the collapsing order. Bishops rose to new prominence in the fifth century. This development led toward a new social constellation of authority:

> The first of the innovations was an unintended consequence of the new urban role of the bishops and clergy. As the bishops were so often the de facto rulers of the cities, they assumed—and had to assume—a primary role in dealing with the Germanic invaders of the empire. At stake was not only the safety of the cities and their Romanized populations, but also the very future of the church. It was a pope, Leo the Great, who succeeded in "dissuading" Attila and his Huns from sacking Rome itself in 452, with the help, perhaps, of a quantity of gold. This new role of the clergy in defending the cities and dealing with the "barbarian" invaders confirmed their ascendancy over the traditional magistrates of the city. The clergy became diplomats and administrators.[5]

The shift in responsibility from divine matters to concrete administrative responsibilities changed the core of ecclesial leadership. Formerly, the main tasks of the clergy were divine matters, how to lead and nourish believers by connecting them to the triune God through liturgy and counseling. The clergy had to look upward and horizontally within their parish. Now, their validation shifted to sociopolitical success. The pastoral/visionary tasks stood in tension with the administrative everyday business. These had been separated in the early church in order to free the apostles to pursue their primary calling (Acts 6:1–7). Once the clergy defined itself as administrators, the lifeline of the church to the divine weakened, further pushing spontaneous-relational communities outside. Secularity, as humanly ordered space, grew with the spiritual justification that the Christian service must be conducted with dignity and order (1 Cor 14:26–40). With time, the logic of efficiency took over. By trying to save the collapsing Greco-Roman world, the church inhaled a dose of its air, yet it also exhaled a Judeo-Christian breath into the collapsing antiquity. One could say that by making the world Christian, the church also made itself worldly.

5. Siedentop, *Inventing the Individual*, 126–27.

By the sixth century, the chronicler Gregory of Tours recorded that the Frankish kings complained about the power of the bishops: "'There is no one with any power left except the bishops,' King Chilperic lamented."[6] Bishops increasingly mimicked the class that had traditionally provided the curia of the ancient city. Wealth, power, and reputation introduced moral compromise within the church and reintroduced the ancient hierarchical structure. The position of the bishop was more likely to be filled by an aristocratic contender, who knew how to manage the affairs of the church and convince the masses in order to create compliance. The self-understanding of the church as the persecuted body of Christ shifted toward being a central institution and heir of the Roman Empire. This shift in sociopolitical status led the church elites to focus their attention increasingly on immanent affairs, thus creating a spiritual vacuum, which was increasingly filled by monastic communities, various apocalyptic movements, and local saints, who offered an alternative vision to the current church, which had compromised its countercultural appeal.

These reformist movements halted the manifestation of the secular sphere only momentarily. In the long run, the reforms laid the foundation for even steelier secular dominion by succumbing to the same illusion of power as the compromising church against which the reforms were developed. Monasteries created an appealing alternative. Within a monastic community the idea of equal individuals was embodied through the election of superiors by all members, and the representative form of government took roots, wherein the one in authority was accountable to govern as Christ did. The vision of a hero was replaced by the Christian idea of humble leadership, as St. Benedict sought to promote and model for the medieval monastery movement. The paradoxical effect consists in the fact that as "Christianity became more 'other-worldly'—as it sought a clearer idea of another world—it was forging a powerful instrument for social reform."[7] By drawing a strong separation from the secular world, the monasteries created a perceptible and tangible alternative.

This hard separation also arose from the pragmatic necessity to maintain authority over the brute force of Germanic invaders. One of the most visible examples of this strategy in the fifth century was a clear emphasis of bishops to distinguish between spiritual and temporal powers vis à vis Germanic invaders. The clergy insisted that the authority of

---

6. Siedentop, *Inventing the Individual*, 137.
7. Siedentop, *Inventing the Individual*, 161.

the church stems from the invisible realm. While the Germanic barbarians possessed brute force, the church appealed to the "sword of spiritual power."[8] By insisting on a sphere independent of physical coercion, the idea of individual conscience arose: "Distinguishing spiritual from temporal power rests on the premise of the individual conscience. For that premise can be construed as meaning that there must be a sphere within which everyone ought to govern his or her own actions, an area of choice, governed by conscience."[9]

Monasteries embodied an alternative to coercive power, which lent them credibility among people. The decisive secularizing impulse occurred when the church used this moral and symbolic capital to once again extend its reach into medieval society after the tenth century. As Siedentop states: "Altogether, the Cluniac reform movement raised the sights of the church, inciting it to defend moral authority in a world apparently given over to mere power."[10] While the church grew in power by offering an alternative to brute force and injustice within tribal feudal Europe, it succumbed once again to the temptation to translate its spiritual capital into political power. The monk Hildebrand of Sovana, who became Pope Gregory VII, set a pattern for translating spiritual power into concrete political influence. Spiritual revivals and inner-ecclesial reforms contributed to him consolidating power. The pope began to extend the dominion of the church over all of sociopolitical reality, creating a prolonged confrontation between popes and kings (investiture controversy). Yet by seeking to transform the world, the church was transformed in the process as well, as Taylor noticed: "The irony is that it somehow turned into something quite different; in another, rather different sense, the 'world' won after all. Perhaps the contradiction lay in the very idea of a disciplined imposition of the Kingdom of God. The temptation of power was after all, too strong, as Dostoevsky saw in the Legend of the Grand Inquisitor. Here lay the corruption."[11]

Secularity as unintended by-product of ecclesial corruption emerged from noble motives,[12] which were then deeply transformed as the church attempted to impose the inner-ecclesial order over all of society. From a

8. Siedentop, *Inventing the Individual*, 133.
9. Siedentop, *Inventing the Individual*, 134.
10. Siedentop, *Inventing the Individual*, 186.
11. Taylor, *Secular Age*, 158.
12. Taylor borrows this interpretative lens from Ivan Illich (Taylor, *Secular Age*, 158).

historical distance, scholars recognize that spiritual capital is not simply scalable without the perversion of original intentions. What was attractive on a small scale within monastic walls turned into a caricature when imposed on the whole of society.

Martin Luther unintentionally repeated this monastic secularization of the world. By returning to biblical roots, he embraced a biblical liberating authority against the ecclesial corruption of his age. However, what had been a powerful, life-giving message, when embodied in Luther's ascetic piety and the communal movement of the Reformation, turned out to be the seed of secular modernity when the initial ecclesial reform was transformed into a sociopolitical reality. By seeking to correct the excesses of the Roman Catholic Church, the correction itself turned into an excess, failing to embody the richness of the Judeo-Christian tradition. As the sociocultural background of the Reformation receded, the overcorrection accidently provided the building blocks for the coming secular age. Luther elevated individual Christian freedom against the stifling authority of tradition and ecclesial hierarchy.[13] Yet he meant it as correction and never as antithesis against the church community. However, without the concrete sociocultural background, Luther's correction paved the way for the secular individual free from any constraints. While Luther still anchored his individual authority in Scripture and tradition, this impulse increasingly turned into solipsistic individualism. Luther emphasized justification alone through grace. The thick background of this discovery was a lifestyle of sacrifice as thanksgiving for the costly love of Jesus. As Bonhoeffer rightly recognized, once this background receded, grace was reduced to a cheap justification of the individual—which eventually turned into positive psychology.[14] Even worse, once the Augustinian elaboration of inwardness grows to the point that God as active sovereign agent is all but ignored, the possibility of a genuine relationship with a God who answers is eclipsed. The complete transformation of theology into anthropology was achieved via liberal Protestantism. The sovereign God shrank to the degree that human inwardness extended. Ultimately, God was transformed into human subjectivity via psychology.[15]

---

13. Luther, *Von der Freiheit*.

14. Bonhoeffer, *Nachfolge*.

15. I follow here Barth's basic critique of Schleiermacher's mutilation of God's otherness (Barth, *Theologie Schleiermachers*).

The Protestant critique of thick religious culture and art as mediation between the people and God was transformed into disembodied religion, which became an easy target of Enlightenment philosophy. The corrective emphasis on the authoritative role of the Scripture changed from "the word became flesh" to "the word became a lecture." This development paved the way for the excarnation of religion from its deeper cultural and bodily function and its migration into the discursive realm of the educated elites. Religion, which has been reduced to a cognitive discourse, can be more easily subjugated by and reshaped by the religious elites. Luther sought to minimize the power of the pope and give the Bible back to the people on the streets. However, he unintentionally created a multitude of Protestant popes in the emerging theological faculties, who did not submit to any authority except to the rules of Enlightenment rationalism. Spiritual discipline, once cut off from the roots of Christian practice, became the driving force behind the disciplinary secular society. Once the accountability before God vanished, the ideal of being true to oneself remained. Yet with the dissolution of the self, the virtue of authenticity is decaying as well.

Luther sought to overcome the two-tier medieval society and extend the divine calling over the profane as well. The distinction between "calling" (German: *Berufung*) and everyday "profession" (German: *Beruf*), was to be minimized. However, without the theological underpinnings, calling collapsed into profession, by sacralizing the latter and elevating it to the central identity marker. Centuries before Luther, all aspects of his theological insight and the subsequent birth of modernity were already germinating within ecclesial reforms and theological articulations. In a sense, Luther only cracked open the ripe fruit.

William of Ockham emphasized God's free will. He contrasted God's dynamic action to the immovable, fixed, rational, and hierarchical understanding of reality in antiquity. This voluntarist theology with emphasis upon the moral equality of all people corresponded to the Franciscan revolution and the call toward poverty: "Human freedom and God's freedom were becoming mutually reinforcing characteristics. That is why contingency and choice, rather than eternal ideas and a priori knowledge, loomed so large in his thinking."[16]

This theological innovation stemmed from biblical and Augustinian tradition, inner-ecclesial reform, and the sociopolitical upheavals of

---

16. Siedentop, *Inventing the Individual*, 309.

the thirteenth and fourteenth centuries. Ockham could not have conceived an idea of human freedom and equality separated from God. His emphasis on the economy of explanation and avoidance of unnecessary multiplication of entities was a continuation of the Judeo-Christian disenchantment of polytheism, wherein God was seen as the primary agent, thus reducing the causal powers of all other entities. This nominalist revolution has divided theologians ever since.[17] I believe that these differing conceptions can be reconciled in the idea of glory performed in worship (see chs. 10–11). However, without the larger mediating myth and ritual, nominalism migrated from theology into anthropology and pinnacled in epistemology, which reduces reality to mere human choice, ushering in complete indeterminacy and randomness.

Secularity is inherently present within the Judeo-Christian myth. It accidently became a social reality due to the engagement of the church with the world. Yet one can also posit a secularization device at the very heart of Judeo-Christian theology. Judeo-Christian myths are transformed into secular ones via a process of translation.

Translating Religious into Secular Myths

Translation becomes necessary when difference precludes understanding. Difference manifests itself through distance. Distance can be felt as geographical remoteness or qualitatively as a difference of culture and language. Often that which is physically removed from us is also relationally distant, as we are not able to enter into a deeper mode of understanding. Since the Israelite creation story introduces a God who stands above all of creation, he constantly introduces mediatory ways for how people can enter into relationship with him. As being complete other and yet loving his people, God continuously translates his nature in order to be understood and loved.

Translation occurs through symbols, anthropomorphisms, and metaphors, by employing a particular language and material culture. The Israelites insisted that God is beyond all spatiotemporal reality and therefore incomprehensible. Yet they continued speaking to God and of God. This

---

17. For example, while Siedentop hails Ockham's achievement as in line with biblical and Augustinian tradition and views it as "the birth of secular liberalism" (*Inventing the Individual*, 316), John Milbank interprets nominalism as a distortion, calling the church back to the Platonic-participatory view of reality. See Milbank, *Theology and Social Theory*.

creates a tension, as translation reveals as much as it hides. Any analogy contains both similarity and difference. This fact creates a peculiar culture of continuous meaning making through the deciphering of God's self-revelation and seeking to translate the received message to other people, as the Hebrew God is universal in nature, sending his people out to be the light of the world, to shine in darkness. God's universal nature relativizes human culture and creates a challenge to the Israelites to seek to transcend ethnic boundaries and enter into a process of understanding foreign gods. Although these encounters were often polemical in nature, as recorded in prophetic literature, they nevertheless created a constant tension between the highest ideals across different religions.

This translation process is visible throughout the Bible. God did not just dictate his will once and for all, requiring his people simply to repeat the words and obey his laws. Yahweh enters history, is continuously present in history with his people, and speaks continuously through different people at different times. Even the Ten Commandments are continuously interpreted and can be narrowed down to the double command to love God and the neighbor or elaborated upon into a full-bodied legal text as is presented in the book of Leviticus or later by the rabbis in the mishnaic and talmudic traditions.

Jesus translates God's intention in the most tangible way. Reverberations of God's physical communion with people in the garden of Eden ring through his presence with all people who are on the fringes of society. Jesus restores this original unity and seeks to demonstrate God's original intention for his people, initiating a spark that flies beyond ethnic-cultural particularity. The apostle Paul extends this vision and translates this embodied culture into Greco-Roman culture. Furthering the translating logic of its Jewish roots, Lamin Sanneh attributes Christianity's success across cultures to its translating impetus.[18] Yet translatability also introduces an unstable relation at the core of the Christian experience, a tension that can't be avoided:

> I see translation as a fundamental concession to the vernacular, and an inevitable weakening of the forces of uniformity and centralization. Furthermore, I see translation as introducing a dynamic and pluralist factor into question of the essence of the religion. Thus if we ask the question about the essence of Christianity, whatever the final answer, we would be forced to reckon with what the fresh medium reveals to us in feedback.

---

18. Sanneh, *Translating the Message*, 51.

> It may thus happen that our own earlier understanding of the message will be challenged and even overturned by the force of the new experience. Translation would consequently help to bring us to new ways of viewing the world, commencing a process of revitalization that reaches into both the personal and the cultural sphere. This locates the message in the specific and particular encounter with cultural self-understanding, although it is important to stress that the encounter still leaves culture subject to God's law.[19]

Dynamism and creativity, which was generated through translating the message, relies on an encounter with the other. These dynamics were at their strongest at times and places when Christian movements were in a minority position, without official political backing. Theological creativity was at its peak during the first stage of its understanding, vis à vis Judaism and the subsequent centuries as the church fathers sought to articulate their new faith within Greco-Roman antiquity. Once Christianity became the religion of the state, the translating dynamism weakened. If one can suppress heretics via an order, one does not need to meet them on their turf and to enter their mode of arguments. It is no accident that by the fourth century, as bishops became administrators and maintainers of the sociopolitical order, their theology was increasingly rooted in judicial metaphors.

Translatability as the essence of Christianity reveals a double effect: it can either sustain its dynamism through permanent struggle about the original intention of the message or lead to a dead end. Translatability leads into a trap if Christianity merges with a powerful sociopolitical order and sheds its focus toward God and the stranger. When Christianity arrives at a stable position, it begins to fossilize. This occurred as Christianity translated the dynamic vision of a Jewish street Messiah to Greco-Roman civilization, transforming it in the process. Yet Christianity's own success also led toward stability, which lessened the tension of being a minority "in between." The creative translation did not suddenly stop in the fourth century but continued throughout the medieval period well into the Renaissance, thus laying the foundation for a secular society with powerful political, legal, economic, scientific, moral, and artistic institutions.

The Roman Catholic popes shaped the idea of sovereignty as a sphere where the church governed itself independently from earthly

---

19. Sanneh, *Translating the Message*, 53.

powers, with full authority over individual Christians. This understanding of sovereign rule was anchored theologically in the mandate given by Christ himself to care for the souls. During the tenth and eleventh centuries, this monastic reform gained ground and began to establish itself over all spheres of social life by means of canon law:

> The union of papal supremacy with canon law helped to introduce order not only into the affairs of the church but into secular life as well. Canon lawyers continued to invade the sphere of civil lawyers. It could hardly have been otherwise, for the church was interested in all the principal moments of life, from birth to burial.[20]

Centuries before the modern nation-state would be crafted from theological ideas, the church modeled a sociopolitical reality that became the prototype for all subsequent modern secular states. Secular ordering of the sociopolitical reality can be understood as a circle with three layers. The outer layer consists of the cosmic legitimization of the sovereign ruler. "In the *Dictatus Papae*, Gregory VII puts forward a dramatically unitary vision of authority within the Church, which begins and ends with the papacy, due to its God-given ... responsibility for the care of souls."[21]

Thus, the cosmic legitimacy lays the ground for moral authority through the beneficial contribution of the church to ordering society. The pacifying role of the church in fostering the realm of the "peace of God" within the medieval world driven by brute force and tribalism lent the church an identity as establishing the widest possible identity of "Christendom." This identity was further solidified against those outside the borders of the Christian order, as visible in the Crusade mobilization. Finally, the moral vision was made concrete through the development of canon law, which permeated every sphere and established the equality of all citizens in relation to the law, giving the final blow to the inequality of antiquity and whatever was left of it in the feudalism of the early medieval age.

By the time the political theorists of the Renaissance had begun to envision a political sphere outside of the church, they could copy and paste ecclesial practice into a different framework: "The example of the church as a unified legal system founded on the equal subjection

---

20. Siedentop, *Inventing the Individual*, 229.
21. Siedentop, *Inventing the Individual*, 203.

of individuals thus gave birth to the idea of the modern state."[22] In his groundbreaking vision of the earthly sovereign Hobbes does not invent new ideas. Instead, as a political theologian, he translates the ecclesial into secular categories. Over six hundred years after Gregory VII, between 1618 and 1648, Europe was torn apart by tribal wars again. However, this time it was not the church that acquired credibility by establishing the peace of God but the state, which mimicked the fading church in establishing a permanent secular peace. The church gave over its all-encompassing corporeality to the state, which was then viewed as the primary agent of care and protector from harm and death. Thus, authority shifted to the state, and the church lost its supremacy.

Hobbes engaged in some theological hermeneutics in the second part of his work, in order to reconfigure the relation between sacred and secular realms. In this undertaking he mirrored the argumentation of Pope Gregory VII in establishing his sovereignty. Simply put, power shifted from church to state due to the fact that the state was envisioned as the entity with the largest extension, means of care, and authority over the bodies of citizens.

This secularization of the sociopolitical order rests on the deeper presupposition that grew out of the Judeo-Christian tradition, namely, that divine authority and creative agency are internalized within the individual. In the beginning of this process God is maintained as a necessary presupposition in order to prevent a slide toward solipsism. The seventeenth to eighteenth century was a time of imagining scientific, artistic, and moral orders without explicit recourse to God. Yet the Judeo-Christian myth nevertheless was present as invisible background. God served as a safeguard against the slide into complete human autonomy.

Descartes kept the reverence to divine trustworthiness as a bulwark against the possibility of a malicious demon deceiving the human mind. Descartes resurrected the age-old Jewish insistence on the trustworthiness of God against the polytheistic confusion due to the indeterminacy of the world. Similarly to Descartes, Immanuel Kant insisted in his moral philosophy on the practical necessity of God in order to allow for human freedom and responsibility in ethics.

Moral and scientific authority was grounded in the individual's ability to observe the world as it is and draw logical conclusions. This turn toward the empirical began as a theological movement of nominalism.

---

22. Siedentop, *Inventing the Individual*, 207.

Ockham's razor presupposes the theological reality that God as a simple, unifying causation is better than a multiplication of causes due to various gods vying for power. The origins of empiricism lie in the desacralization of nature, which allows for humans to approach nature as an objective reality. Ockham's insistence on contingency and choice further undermined the Greek idea of eternal immovable reality, which can be discerned only through a priori rational insight. By distinguishing between deductive and inductive reasoning, Ockham emphasized the need for verification by the senses, thus laying the groundwork for the development of rigorous methodologies in the sciences. By emphasizing God's freedom and voluntary faith as the primary way toward God, Ockham also prefigured the Kantian critique of natural theology, further splitting the unity of knowledge and separating the human realm of an empiric world from the transcendent realm. On a generous note, both Ockham's and Kant's protection of theology from natural theology could be traced back to the prophetic warning of making God in the image of man, thus preserving the sovereignty and otherness of God. This apologetic concern, however, would lead to the increasing distancing of God as the immanent and the transcendent spheres moved apart. The empiric world as worthy of human exploration acquires its importance through God's evaluation of creation as very good. The Israelite creation story lacks the Platonic and gnostic gradation system between the material and spiritual worlds. Moreover, by entering his own creation through Christ, God once again emphasizes the ontological goodness of this world. Salvation happens not through expulsion into a spiritual realm but through a very concrete historical man. Jesus' life consists of everyday acts, which are imbued with eternal meaning.

The Gospels tell a story of how the mundane events at the periphery of the Roman Empire point to divine action. Everyday life is pregnant with meaning and is worthy of symbolic exploration. The natural world points beyond itself to the creator himself. The motivational force of the Scientific Revolution consisted in reading creation as general revelation via the book of nature in a manner similar to reading the special revelation of the Bible—both were ways to glorify God. Similar to truth, the beauty of the world was seen as symbolizing divine order. The human being is not merely the crown of God's creation but is endowed with creative powers. In the wake of the nominalist shift within theology, the human being is increasingly viewed not merely as imitating the stable order but as actively cocreating with God. Within the agonistic world of

Ockham, which is marked by hunger, plagues, and isolation through the experience of religious banning, it is hardly surprising that the notions of freedom and will come into prominence—first within God himself and subsequently within anthropology as well. This development peaks with Nicolaus Cusanus's proclamation of the human as *hominem esse secundum deum*—the human being a second God. Cusanus borrows this quote from *Corpus Hermeticum*, and the ambiguity can be resolved in different directions.[23] Emphasizing the "second" one could maintain the Judeo-Christian understanding of the creative potential in humans' continuous dependency on the primary God. However, in the wake of modernity, this ambiguity was resolved by a gnostic understanding of self-divinization through a creative act.

During the Enlightenment, the exceptional theology turned into ordinary anthropology.[24] Due to their divine nature, humans increasingly viewed themselves as capable of ordering their sociopolitical reality through mutual discourse and of governing themselves through reasonable laws. Moreover, God guaranteed the nature of reality and the human mind in such a way that humans were able to deduce stable laws and thus control nature. However, humans were not merely discovering the given cosmos but were also able to create—even if not ex nihilo, at least through rearrangement of the given, thus arriving at new combinations.

The authoritative realm of the church receded with the expansion of human autonomy in politics, science, arts, and economy. The last bulwark against the increasing human emancipation was the realm of moral authority. The nurtured and developed idea of inwardness led toward a logical conclusion that to listen to yourself is to some degree equivalent to listening to God as God reveals himself within. Through Christian mystics and the period of Romanticism, the idea of an individual consciousness became a self-evident space for leading an autonomous, authentic life.[25]

The emergence of European secularity from the translation process of theological ideas begs the question as to why this secularity became a

---

23. *Corpus Hermeticum* refers to a collection of dialogues that were collected between 100 and 300 CE and translated into Latin during the fifteenth century.

24. Paraphrasing Leidhold: "Aus dem exzeptionellen Theologicum wird ein ordinaeres Anthropologicum" ("Kreative Projekt," 61).

25. Brague views the relation between the idea of revelation and individual conscience as causal ("Are Non-Theocratic Regimes Possible?").

sealed-off, solid, "immanent frame," as Charles Taylor coined it.[26] Returning to Charbel, whom I mentioned at the beginning of the chapter, we could imagine various modes of secularity, including the one where the secular remains within the individual cognition amid the overall religious culture. If the secular imagination was conceived in the religious womb and emerged through translation of theological ideas and practices, how did secularity acquire the aura of the factual to the degree that it is taken for granted? How did the secular move from within the religious sphere into its opposition? How did it succeed, and can it survive without its roots? These are questions for the second part of this book. However, first, I will seek to address three possible objections to my core assumptions.

---

26. Taylor, *Secular Age*, 542–57.

Critical Interlude

There is a saying in Russian, "That is neither fish nor meat," meaning that the thing one is referring to is not solid or real but somehow in between and bland. This saying could be leveled at my story so far: to postulate the origin of society from myth and ritual is to deny a deeper, more solid causal category, which gave rise to myth and ritual in the first place. Two possible primary causes could be suggested. The first primary cause could be a bio-evolutionary-conceived life force, which guides the organizing logic of humans in building societies, functionally employing myths and rituals. This story would acquire the following plot:

For most of history, humans survived within small tribes—similar to other intelligent animals, like orcas, apes, or wolves, who organize their survival in small packs. This lent them a relative advantage in raising their young and in hunting. However, the cooperation involved in such tribes also required higher communication skills, which hinged on developed language. The higher level of adaptation caused the development of the brain, and conversely, the development of the brain further enabled the refining of communication skills, which further improved survival. A certain circular reasoning is not problematic for a story, as causes can't be projected into infinity. This development happened to people as they were guided by their instincts for survival. The bio-evolutionary scientist inserts a teleological structure in retrospect, contrary to the view held by the people living through this history, who for the most part attributed this teleology to gods. A good story requires a plausible goal and plot. The bio-evolutionary narrative suggests that survival as the highest goal produced rational skills, which enabled humans to organize themselves in larger groups, thus outperforming all other living species by adapting to all possible environments on earth.

The ability to innovate is what distinguishes humans from animals—to form large networks based on trust and communication.

Like all good stories, this one can't be deconstructed easily. Once the core assumption is accepted, the rest naturally follows. Once survival as the highest goal is taken for granted, everything else is interpreted functionally as serving this highest goal. Once one embraces the highest ideal, all other patterns are structured accordingly. The contemporary scholar inhabits a strange position: the scholar is a part within the larger historical process of evolution and is in fact a product of genes and forces unconscious to himself. The irony is that while the bio-evolutionary scientist insists on the blindness of the evolutionary process and denying teleology, she is telling a good story, pretending to see.[1] This is then not unlike the religious believer who insists on having figured out his God. Yet this would be ultimate hubris, and this God would cease to be a God per definition. Nagel rightly recognizes that the bio-evolutionary account in its reductionist brand can't provide any meaning to human existence:

> As it is usually understood, evolutionary naturalism is radically antiteleological. This implies that it is not suited to supply any kinds of sense to our existence, if it is taken on as the larger perspective from which life is lived. Instead, the evolutionary perspective probably makes human life, like all life, meaningless, since it makes life a more or less accidental consequence of physics.

Nagel concludes that a "genealogy of this kind gives us nothing to live by."[2] Without prior assumption of the meaningfulness of the universe, bio-evolutionary reasoning as scientific practice is also impossible. The contradiction is obvious when a reductionist bio-evolutionary scientist claims to be a conscious agent, transcending these blind forces. In short, by telling a plausible story, the scientist assumes an elevated status above the primordial chaos, thus glancing at it from a distance. And it is this distance that provides a reflexive pause, which allows humans to act back upon the environment and not merely be acted upon.

---

1. One example of this apologetic redrawing of a line between true science and religion is the work of Paul F. Lurquin and Linda Stone, *Evolution and Religious Creation Myths*. While infringement from both religious and scientific angles can be real, the apologetics of religion against science, or as in this case of science against religion, is simply mistaken, as Conor Cunningham argued convincingly in his book *Darwin's Pious Idea*.

2. Nagel, *Secular Philosophy*, 15–16.

By telling a good story humans also escape the environment's gravitational force, as every plot introduces various possibilities for action. The bio-evolutionary scientist can't escape the priestly role. One could then assert that a boundary exists, albeit a fuzzy one, where science collapses back into the myth from which it came. Bio-evolutionary science collapses back into mythology when it seeks to replace the historically preceding myth that gave rise to it.

If a myth splinters into diverse substories, these can create mutual illumination without competition. However, once the substories seek to replace the foundational myth, they by definition narrow the widest horizons. The historic origin of science from religious myth is unquestionable. However, once science becomes a myth, it oversteps its radius of operation, as it can't paint the widest horizons. Scientific perspectives seek to satisfy the how questions. However, once they seek to address the why questions as well, they stumble into the mythical realm and, in so doing, abandon their explanatory power and morph into a caricature of true myth. Once bio-evolutionary science dissolves into a myth, it reduces the complexity of the primary myth. The scientist-turned-priest senses the obvious contradiction between what is being proclaimed and what is being lived. No human seeks merely to survive in a manner to preserve his genetic pool but is confronted with the grand questions of meaning at some point in life. The core question is not how to survive but how to thrive.[3]

Of course the mythological bio-evolutionist could object that the guiding principle of biological survival tricks us into imagining a realm of meaning. Yet this objection could be seen as exemplifying a phenomenon present in religious ritual: the priest perceives a reality that is hidden from the vision of the naïve believer. To reduce myth and ritual to a mere evolutionary survival mechanism is to miss the genuine question of meaning, which is not separate from biology but nevertheless not reducible to it. At the threshold where bio-evolutionary science crosses over into myth, it begins to resemble the Mesopotamian and pre-Socratic creation plots, wherein the origins are postulated to arise from a life force, which permeates all of reality akin to a deity. This pattern is legitimate. However, from a historic angle, one must honestly argue for one myth against another and not pretend to elevate reasonable science against gullible superstition.

---

3. The chasm between mere biological survival and life worth living became obvious during the COVID-19 period.

Once the historic genesis of the bio-evolutionary story is laid bare, deeper presuppositions can be discerned. Without projected teleology this plot would simply collapse. Every good story needs a larger goal, which allows us to assess the practical rationality of actions. As humans, we are embedded in time and space, and the story ontologically structures our experience and thought.[4] Historically, the bio-evolutionary story evolved from a deeper background. Within the political struggles for authority at a later stage of modernity, the primary myth was pitted against its progeny. This religion vs. science war was then fought by both the ignorant Christians and historically and philosophically unversed agnostic scientists alike.

Demarcation lines between science and myth, although in constant flux, matter. For the prideful scientist, in his historical and philosophical ignorance, could turn science into scientism. As a result, rigorous science is threatened to dissolve into a reduced myth, thus creating a caricature of both. Durkheim put it lucidly: Although science is a child of religion, religion must reckon with science as established authority. However, science must also acknowledge that there always will remain a speculative moment, as life encompasses more than our mind is able to elucidate.[5] Yet humans must live and act without fully comprehending. Myth as the widest possible horizon of meaning remains not merely as filling the gap of temporary ignorance but as keeping alive the prescientific background. Empiric methodology requires nonempirical assumptions. Thus just like religion and politics can meddle with rigorous scientific methodology, so science can destroy itself from within due to its overreach.

Another cause for myth and ritual could be located in the social force itself. Durkheim speculated about this collective force, which permeates all of social reality. Yet, upon closer examination of this primal cause, one could assert that it begins to resemble the traditional notion of God, or at least a gnostic demiurge.[6] Durkheim refers to society as social being, which permeates all social segments in its totality. It hovers above, not unlike the creative spirit in the book of Genesis. Durkheim attributes agency to society and divine attributes, such as hiddenness. Perhaps the attempt to move from empiric description and understanding to explanation inevitably introduces a narrative structure and incidentally stumbles into the myth one sought to break off from. Myth and rituals are

---

4. Carr, *Time, Narrative, and History*.
5. Durkheim, *Elementary Forms*, 433.
6. The following summary is from Durkheim, *Elementary Forms*, 441–47.

inevitable at a certain depth. Perhaps it is better to acknowledge this fact, as it creates a leveling field for all to join.

One could still object that by writing about myth and ritual, I myself have taken up a higher ground from which I assess myth and ritual. I do not claim to have such an ideal view from nowhere. Instead, as will become clear in the final part of the book, I am writing from within the Judeo-Christian myth and ritual, which I believe to be a "true myth."[7]

Finally, a historical argument could be leveled against my narrative. Against my plot of continuation, one could also posit a plot of interruption. Accordingly, modernity emerged through a sudden human awakening, in which individuals liberated themselves from the oppressive forces of tradition and religion. The Enlightenment appears like a secular miracle, a Promethean liberation from the oppressive gods. The medieval ages are seen as dark times in between, and the Renaissance came primarily through the rediscovery of antiquity. Historically, this plot was shaped by a few philosophers of the radical Enlightenment and gained popularity during a polemical struggle for authority between the state and church. Due to the habitual nature of human actions and the complexity of societies, continuity is the norm, and new social associations usually emerge from deep practical and ideological transformations. Those secular scholars, who postulate sudden interruption, ironically emulate a theological device they seek to overcome. Sudden interruption is reserved to God only, as he stands above and beyond time and space. Theologians call this event "miracle." And by definition, miracles occur as exceptions to the rule. Historical beings must be understood within the continuum of time.

Contrary to the stories that locate the origin of secular liberalism in the post-Renaissance period, I locate the beginnings in the minor deviations of the Israelite creation story, which grows and matures into a full-blown conception of the individual through antiquity and the medieval period. The deep roots of the tree are nurtured by the rich mythological soil. The idea of the sacred personhood, which creates a society from within one's own reason, freedom, and creative energy, stood at the beginning of modernity and was the result of a long historical process. After the Renaissance, we have witnessed both the triumph and demise of a secular social order centered around sacred individual dignity. The seed of destruction is already sown within the hubris of success.

---

7. The term "true myth" was introduced and elaborated by C. S. Lewis.

Part II

Incurvatus in Se: The Triumph and
Decay of Secular Society

CHAPTER 4

Success, Estrangement from a Devouring Mother, and Exhilarating Hubris

> *That the Christian saeculum has become secular shows modern history in a paradoxical light: it is Christian by derivation and anti-Christian by consequence. Both aspects derive from the worldly success of Christianity and, at the same time, from its failure to make the world Christian.*
>
> —KARL LÖWITH, *MEANING IN HISTORY*

> *The power of prayer, moreover, had recognized limits; it would have been impious to ask too much. But the power of science has no known limits. We were told that faith could remove mountains, but no one believed it; we are now told that the atomic bomb can remove mountains, and everyone believes it. . . . Some of our activities will do good, some harm, but all alike will show our power. And so, in this godless universe, we shall become gods.*
>
> —BERTRAND RUSSELL, *THE IMPACT OF SCIENCE ON SOCIETY*

Part II: Incurvatus in Se: *The Triumph and Decay of Secular Society*

SECULAR LIBERALISM HAS BEEN the most successful sociopolitical order since the Enlightenment. The collapse of the Soviet Empire seemed to confirm Western hegemony. Due to scientific and technological progress, political stability, economic prowess, and cultural hegemony, secular liberalism came to dominate the world order as the best model, which others came to imitate *nolens volens*. Success is objective to the degree it can be measured empirically. People in secular liberal societies are wealthier and live longer in stable socioeconomic and political environments. I argue that this success is rooted in the fertile Judeo-Christian soil. Yet slowly, the roots are being torn from their soil due to the church behaving like a devouring stepmother. The primary cause of subsequent decay has been the accelerating hubris that has been growing in the heart of the West, exhilarated by its own success.

EVERY REFUGEE'S WAKE-UP

I remember, upon first arriving in Germany as a ten-year-old, experiencing life as a continuous fairy tale, despite the harsh reality of the refugee center. We celebrated as a family the first sum of money handed to us by the German state, and we headed together collectively to a shopping mall. Upon entering the mall, our heads spun as we tried to decipher the content of all the packages and cans. As we carried all the goodies home, we felt like we were returning from a treasure hunt. As refugees, we had as much and even more exquisite foods than a Communist Party leader in the Soviet Union. In our tiny room, my mom tried to persuade me, in vain, not to eat everything at once. The dream of paradise-like abundance ended for me abruptly with a rumbling in my stomach shortly after midnight. I was unable to react quickly enough, and the hastily devoured food splashed down from the bunk bed upon my poor sister sleeping below. The feast ended up in misery. The miracle turned into a nightmare.

This memory encapsulates a very common reality experienced by many refugees. The initial infatuation disappears like a fata morgana, and the hidden costs previously unknown stare squarely in one's face. At this stage, many refugees experience an upending of their view of their host country. In their homeland, they often idealized Germany and viewed their country only through a negative lens. Afterward, Germany becomes the dump with a thin glittery layer around it, while the country of origin is viewed through rose-colored glasses. Some get stuck in this simple dichotomy and never manage to progress toward a more nuanced view. The idealistic view of home on one hand and antagonistic view of the host country on the other precludes any attempt to accept reality. The cost of this naïve view is the inability to develop a realistic perception and arrive at acceptance of German society. Growing resentment fuels ascending fatalism and keeps the refugee in a state of paralysis, unable to embrace the opportunities present.

Every change brings with it wins and losses. Life is a trade-off. Sometimes the losses are not immediate and therefore not as evident. In the parable of the lost son, the younger son demands to receive his inheritance immediately. As a result, his status and popularity increase disproportionately. On the outside, he appears to be a success, even though on the inside, he is guilty of dishonoring his father, thus breaking God's commandment. Therefore, his external success is won at a great cost. Moral reality is objective to the degree that it always reasserts itself against anyone cracking one's head against its solid nature. The son's success came to an abrupt end as it was not sustainable. He rapidly descended the social ladder and found himself with the pigs, at the lowest social stratum (Luke 15:11–32).

A memory from my childhood also confirms the moral of this biblical story. Our grandfather allowed us to help in the slaughtering of chickens. After chopping off their heads, we would release their bodies, which would run frantically, often even for a long time. Yet their collapse was just a matter of time. We would even cruelly bet on whose chicken would outrun the others. How one evaluates secular liberalism depends on the normative criteria one assumes and the time span one applies. The chicken could run faster without its head. One could view it as short-term success. Yet the short sprint always ended in a collapse.

Success

Many Western intellectuals exemplify a stunning hypocrisy by profiting immensely from their civilization's success while simultaneously denying anything good in their own culture. It has become fashionable and a distinction of intellectual merit not merely to critique but to flagellate the West.[1] Ironically, the masochistic flagellation of their own civilizational heritage is unique to the West and is rooted in a specific, though

---

1. Stark, *How the West Won*, 1–2.

perverted, Judeo-Christian tradition, namely confession. Contrary to the Judeo-Christian tradition, secular society lacks rituals of confession and the divine authority to forgive. Instead, historic guilt is endlessly recycled and weaponized. The unfortunate result is the inability to both attain a nuanced view of their own heritage and experience a truthful encounter with the stranger, as Pascal Bruckner lucidly summarizes:

> It is a mistake to think that self-devaluation is going to open us up, as if by a miracle, to distant peoples, put us on the track of goodness and dialogue. In Western self-hatred, the Other has no place. It is a narcissistic relationship in which the African, the Indian, and the Arab are brought in as extras in an endless drama about settling scores: and that is why we are witnessing the conjunction of remorse with racism, of affliction with the stalest egoism. . . . Let us beware of anyone who values the foreigner only out of disdain for himself: his self-aversion will end up infecting his sympathies.[2]

Confirming Bruckner's analysis of permanent guilt as inner Western perversion, Bassam Tibi describes the new class of intellectuals who master the language of perpetual self-accusation, equating it with an elevated moral ground and thereby negating the stranger through patronization. Tibi relates his own experience with German secular academics forbidding him to deviate from their opinion on Islam and immigration and seeking to explain to him his own culture and religion (Islam).[3] In a strange way, by keeping historical guilt as a permanent burden, those with power manage to use it as a weapon against those less sophisticated within their own civilization and as a moral badge signaling virtue to outsiders. As long as I condemn my entire civilization, I am perceived as a moral authority. As long as I proclaim my virtues to the world, I will not be asked to do penance and sacrifice my money or status. Instead, the continuous self-flagellation increases the social capital of the chattering class.

Let me return to my refugee experience to untangle the bewildering surprise of many refugees who have encountered a similar mood in Germany, and perhaps as well in the larger West. As I mentioned in the story at the beginning, the affluence we encountered at the lowest social strata in German society was preserved only for the elites in the Soviet Union. The degree of freedom and comfort, the miracle of

---

2. Bruckner, *Tyranny of Guilt*, 101.
3. Tibi, *Europa ohne Identität?*, 338.

functioning state institutions, and just everyday impressions that I as a human am respected and my dignity preserved made clear to me at the time why Germany was a haven in comparison to the crumbling Soviet Empire. Yet, my bourgeois German peers from school, whose parents were medical doctors, lawyers, and teachers, did not share my sheer amazement. Instead, they preferred to wear Che Guevara T-shirts and bear images of Stalin's and Lenin's profiles with hammer and sickle. This expression extended to the university, where students were more familiar with Marx and Adorno than with Solzhenitsyn. After a period of time living in both the US and the Middle East, as well as encountering people from many countries of the world, I realized that nowhere have I experienced the same level of denigration of one's own heritage than in Berlin, Germany. Debt that is not settled and perpetual guilt lead to the decay of cooperation and trust in society and in this way to death. The apostle Paul distinguishes between guilt, which leads toward repentance and changed behavior, and guilt unto death, which perpetuates broken relationships (2 Cor 7:10). Both Bruckner's and Tibi's analyses would fall in line with this premise of Paul.

A discussion as to whether the European story has been a success or an utter failure can't be settled discursively as it depends on the normative ideal of what makes up a success.[4] The disingenuous posturing of many intellectuals, decrying the West as the worst civilization while enjoying its success, is an attempt to wipe away historic complexity with a moralistic argument that does not withstand the scrutiny of scholarship and the historical reality, which depicts the convergence of both good and bad.[5] It is a truism to state that every civilization has both evil and good in it. Without a solid anchoring in the complex myth, we tend to stumble from one simple extreme into another, from idealization and triumphalism into complete self-loathing and abasement. In order to analyze perversion, one must first perceive the good. Without an ideal, no deviation can be discerned.

---

4. Moreover, even if one admits that it has been a success, it can be undermined by the argument that it was chiefly won through the exploitation of the rest of the world.

5. Even one of the worst aspects of European civilization, like colonialism, is, as Nigel Biggar argues, a mix of good and bad motives and consequences (*Colonialism*). Living in Beirut for four years, I repeatedly encountered Lebanese who had a nuanced view of French colonial influence, including thanking the French for having built universities and hospitals. In the parable of the weeds, Jesus is portrayed as viewing reality intermingled with good and bad, which can't be clearly separated until the end-time (Matt 13:24–43).

The European West developed a successful civilization, if compared with existing historical sociopolitical orders and not utopian dreams. Perhaps the weightiest argument for the success of the West is a pragmatic one: the West exerts an attraction on people from all over the world, who want to migrate to either Europe, North America, Australia, or New Zealand. The gravitational force of the West is undeniable, and the level of education, political stability, wealth, equality, and freedoms can be measured empirically. Countless immigrants in Germany have explained to me that they came to Germany seeking peace, economic opportunities, personal freedoms, rule of law, and educational opportunities for their children. These accounts contradict the prevalent narrative in academic ghettos that the West is the worst exploitative and racist civilization. It is true that in its thirst to dominate and enslave, Europe resembles the grand civilizations of the Babylonian, Persian, Greek, Roman, Islamic, Mongolian, and many other empires preceding it. Yet there are unique positive features that made the West stand out and contributed to its overall success. I would suggest that this success emerged from the fruitful Judeo-Christian soil that had been tilled for many centuries by countless Christian communities.

Both the Jewish and Christian Scriptures emphasize the virtue of humility. The special status of Israel as God's people is not due to its size or achievements but lies entirely in God's own character. This idea of bestowing special status entirely as a gift is then continued in the Christian Scriptures and is introduced as the idea of "grace"—an unmerited gift. Both the Jewish and early Christian communities were minor and insignificant, surrounded by powerful empires. The danger to one's identity of being a minority is either complete dissolution or self-assertion by destroying the enemy. Christian communities of the first centuries exemplified a strong identity in Jesus and simultaneous humility and openness to the culture surrounding them.

Rémi Brague views the key identity of Europe in its "eccentric" nature.[6] Europe has nothing solid at its core that it did not borrow and meld into a new network.[7] Its core religious myth has been adapted from the Middle East. Of course the danger of borrowing lies is devouring the other and not preserving the other's distinct identity. While medieval

---

6. Brague, *Voie romaine*, 142–71.

7. Brague even uses a more opaque metaphor for the contribution of Christianity to the formation of Europe. Accordingly, Christianity illuminated the already given; it provided a new way of seeing ("Was hat Europa," 29–30).

Christianity has been guilty of incorporation and annihilation of the other, the distinctiveness of antiquity has nevertheless been preserved. To admit your own insignificance and borrow from others requires humility. Humility opens up potentiality for improvement.

To the contrary, pride goes before the fall, as is stated in Hebrew wisdom literature (Prov 16:18). Pride is rooted in the view that fundamental differences exist between people, and due to certain innate qualities, one human being or group is superior to the other. To the contrary, the Judeo-Christian tradition claims that all people share a fundamental equality before God, in spite of relative differences between humans. In the beginning of the medieval ages Europe was far behind in technological innovations. For example, by 1018, China already had a successful iron industry and the most superior navy, setting the stage for industrialization and expansion. However, a hierarchical society and the suppression of entrepreneurship by the Mandarins, as well as a sense of self-sufficiency and cultural superiority, stifled its development.[8] The first miracle of innovation, in both ideas and technology, occurred in Greece due to the relative egalitarian conception of society and the value given to humility to learn from others.[9] However, Greek democratic ideas allowed for only a few male citizens to be considered as equal. Greek city-states remained slave societies, not able to transcend the ontology of inequality and antagonism, thus exhausting themselves in wars between various Greek city-states.

Science and technology are not unique to Europe. In fact, other civilizations were much farther ahead in technological advances. However, what was unique to the West was the deep and overarching social embedding of innovation. Innovation and knowledge were not reserved for a specific caste but had to be extended to every individual. Since this idea was fundamentally rooted in the Judeo-Christian myth, the elites could not prevent the spread of innovation throughout the entire society. For example, within the caste system of India technological innovation was reserved to higher castes only.[10] In both China and India, and to a lesser degree Rome and Greece, one might add, the ontology of inequality sealed any innovations within a very narrow social stratum.

In Europe, the historically predominant hierarchical structure became porous. Scientific, medical, technological, and economic

8. Stark, *How the West Won*, 12.
9. D'Angour, *Greeks and the New*, 27–32.
10. Mangalwadi, *Wahrheit und Wandlung*, 59–73.

innovations had begun in the elitist circles of monasteries. However, the vision of monks was to serve the common good. Even more so with the advance of the Reformation, the two-tier model of society being divided between the religious elites and the common believers was completely abolished by Martin Luther in his challenge to every Christian to live a life of sanctity. If every citizen is equal in the eyes of God, then every citizen is worthy of a life lived in dignity. This idea enabled various social reforms to improve the life of the poor, to develop medical care for all citizens, to eradicate child labor and forbid slavery. European Christendom was the first civilization known in history to eradicate slavery. First the English abolished slavery within their own borders and then fought against their own interests to eradicate slavery globally.

This moral impulse of equality is counterintuitive and contradicts both the empiric and historical experience. The main argument against the abolition of slavery that Wilberforce faced was the breakdown of the economy. However, the egalitarian impulse unleashed productivity, as free people have higher motivation to work and increase their own wealth. Personal freedom, paired with property rights and political stability, guarantees high ingenuity and a greater motivation of citizens to innovate. After the liberation of slaves, women were also increasingly granted the same rights as men. The earliest feminist movements were also fueled by Christian concerns for equal participation of women.[11] In the building of a modern nation, women contributed greatly to social reforms, and since the Second World War, women have entered all social institutions and the market successfully. Today women even outperform males in some economic and educational sectors. A society that views all its members as equal in principle will have a much larger pool of highly motivated individuals than societies that privilege a tiny minority only. Equality before God and subsequently equality of opportunity proved to be a powerful resource to mobilize energies that had lain dormant.

Equality of all men and women before God and the emphasis of the Protestant Reformers upon *sola scriptura* as the crucial guiding path toward God led to an explosion of production and circulation of knowledge. Literacy was increasingly considered not as the privilege of idle nobility but as the right of every citizen. Without Luther's emphasis upon the priesthood of all believers and the validation of ordinary Christian life, the Gutenberg press would most likely have remained a

---

11. Sohn-Kronthaler and Albrecht, *Faith and Feminism*.

toy of the elites, or perhaps even would have been forbidden, as in the case of the Ottoman Empire. The Information Age would not have happened. The Judeo-Christian impetus to know the will of God, which had been written down in a book, even superseded the first literacy development of the Greeks, who had restricted learning to boys only.[12] A society that is able to utilize more brainpower will have a more vibrant culture and better solutions to complex problems.

The egalitarian impulse also required an objective standard that would allow people to contribute to the common good based not on their heritage but on their skill. A meritocratic system cemented the idea of equality and was a final blow to the ontology of inequality. Meritocracy as an objective standard was first practiced in monasteries and then extended to the free city-states in the medieval period, first in Italy and then in Northern Europe.[13] With the advance of the Industrial Revolution, the new world allowed for the masses of previously disadvantaged classes to rise in the social hierarchy through skill, knowledge, and effort.[14] The seal of distinction, which formerly had been passed down through heritage in the European nobility, could now be earned by every citizen, through either education or skill. The new bourgeois class replaced the old nobility in its social significance. Many self-made entrepreneurs surpassed by far the old aristocracy in wealth and influence.

Of course meritocracy as ideal is weakened through inequality, and the rise to the top through the social capital of the rich. That said, Europeans and North Americans can't imagine the agony of intelligent youth who grow up in countries where society is governed publicly by hereditary, religious, or ideological class belonging. In the Soviet Union, Jews and other minorities were often excluded from rising in social institutions.[15] While in the West, social connections as advancement are hidden, in the Middle East, the concept of *wastah* is publicly acknowledged. I met countless bright young Palestinians in Lebanon who were not allowed to study at universities. Not the brightest advance but those who are born into a certain family of privilege. As an ideal, a meritocratic

12. Stark, *How the West Won*, 21.

13. The religious spirit of capitalism by far preceded Protestant ethics. Max Weber advanced his thesis amid anti-Catholic sentiments of the culture wars in Germany at the beginning of the twentieth century.

14. On recent advocacy for the meritocratic principle, see Wooldridge, *Aristocracy of Talent*.

15. E.g., Edward Frenkel on his experience in Soviet Union academia as a Jewish minority ("Reality Is a Paradox").

system selects the best minds without partiality from the largest pool and thus creates a pull toward higher social mobility and innovation, which benefits the majority in the long term. Meritocracy as a social concept is not merely founded upon the idea of equality of worth but also upon the basic assumption that truth and goodness also exist outside one's own tribe. Openness toward the other requires a conception of reality beyond one's own tribal boundaries.

Paradoxically, admitting that one is inadequate and in need of the other also requires an ontological sense of security. The admission of weakness comes from a stance of strength. Both of these preconditions are met in the universal nature of God and his trustworthiness due to his commitment and the stable covenantal promise he provides. These theological Judeo-Christian ideas provide a structure of reality that is trustworthy and reliable, while admitting that humans are able to err. This conception of the relationship between the larger cosmos and the human allows for the assumption of truth as objective reality outside of the human mind and calls for a search to find these laws of nature. Within this mythological soil, modern science could emerge: "Science arose only in Christian Europe because only medieval Europeans believed that science was *possible* and *desirable*. And the basis of their belief was their image of God and his creation."[16]

Belief in the external reliability and stability of the world produces an obligation to pursue truth. This Hebrew foundational view about creation is further complemented by the Christian notion that it is only truth that sets us free from illusions. Humans are able to grasp truth, although only partially, and be realigned with an objective reality. This teleological drive, which underlines all scientific enterprise, is crucial and can't be deducted from the scientific method itself. Every scientist must commit to follow the truth no matter where it leads and be willing to become a martyr for truth's sake, no matter the personal consequence. In fact, scientific progress occurs through both the incremental accumulation of knowledge through reliable methodology and sudden paradigmatic shifts.[17] In the case of the second, the individual scientist

16. Stark, *How the West Won*, 315; emphasis in original. Stark goes on quoting Alfred North Whitehead, who concluded in his 1925 Lowell Lectures at Harvard "that science developed in Europe because of the widespread 'faith in the possibility of science . . . derivative from medieval theology.'"

17. Karl Popper emphasized incremental progress. Thomas Kuhn and Paul Feyerabend viewed progress in scientific discourse as the revolutionary succession of paradigms.

must be able to question established paradigms and have the courage to stand against the pressure of the majority. However, faithfulness to both continuity on one hand and sudden disruption on the other requires a higher norm, to recognize when to follow and when to deviate. The Judeo-Christian story provides this ideal, which allows for both continuity and disruption of the status quo.

The Greeks also discovered the unity and reasonableness of the world. Yet they lacked a decisive component in order to develop scientific methodology. By overemphasizing the rational ability to discern reality through mere contemplation, they too often equated the musings of philosophers with reality. Platonic shadows hovered over the world, suggesting that the highest goal was to transcend the mundane reality through abstractions. Although Aristotle dabbled more in observations, empiricist methodology in its true sense evolved during the medieval scholastic period, due to the Christian realization that human reasoning is also flawed and requires an intersubjective rigorous method.

Another reason for the emergence of empiricism has been the appreciation of empirical reality as the site of God's revelation, thus viewing the material not as a mere shadow of eternal forms but as good creation and worthy of exploration. The scientists of the Renaissance viewed both the Bible and nature as "God's two books," seeking to glorify him through their scientific enterprise.[18] Scientific progress and technological innovation are not causal. In fact, pragmatic innovations often preceded scientific reasoning. However, the scholastic speculations on the nature of knowledge and how the rational a priori relates to empirical sensory data laid the foundation for testing, and thus increasing certainty. Theoretical contemplation in combination with continuous empirical testing allowed for the progress of knowledge and an increasing ability to control nature. The result was the explosion of technological and social innovation, which leads toward wealthier and safer societies:

> The leadership of the West, both in technology and in science, is far older than the so-called Scientific Revolution of the 17th century or the so-called Industrial Revolution of the 18th century. These terms are in fact outmoded and obscure the true nature of what they try to describe—significant stages in two long and separate developments. By A.D. 1000 at the latest— and perhaps, feebly, as much as 200 years earlier—the West began to apply water power to industrial processes other than

---

18. Howell, *God's Two Books*.

milling grain. This was followed in the late 12th century by the harnessing of wind power. From simple beginnings, but with remarkable consistency of style, the West rapidly expanded its skills in the development of power machinery, labor-saving devices, and automation. Those who doubt should contemplate that most monumental achievement in the history of automation: the weight-driven mechanical clock, which appeared in two forms in the early 14th century. Not in craftsmanship but in basic technological capacity, the Latin West of the later Middle Ages far outstripped its elaborate, sophisticated, and esthetically magnificent sister cultures, Byzantium and Islam. In 1444 a great Greek ecclesiastic, Bessarion, who had gone to Italy, wrote a letter to a prince in Greece. He is amazed by the superiority of Western ships, arms, textiles, glass. But above all he is astonished by the spectacle of waterwheels sawing timbers and pumping the bellows of blast furnaces. Clearly, he had seen nothing of the sort in the Near East.[19]

The slow tide of social and technological innovation before the Renaissance burst into skyrocketing productivity since the Industrial Revolution due to highly motivated individuals in Western liberal democracies constantly improving technology, which produced ever-cleaner, reliable, cheaper, and abundant energy. Energy equals life. In the past, people invested a lot of time and muscular energy to collect wood to prepare food and warm themselves. Within only a century, machines had replaced muscle labor in the fields, in the factories, and at home. This newly won time was harnessed to reinvest into research and further improvement. We have moved from burning wood at home to burning coal and gas and finally to wind, water, solar energy, and nuclear power. The combination of high tech and constant, cheap energy led toward a super abundance someone living two centuries ago could not have dreamt of. The average person in Europe or the USA today lives like the nobility did in the past centuries. The pessimistic outlook on scarcity and the alarmist predictions in the 70s about the effects of overpopulation[20] were proven wrong.[21] In the twentieth century, the average citizen in the Western hemisphere has achieved a better standard of life than almost anyone else in history. People live much longer, healthier, in stable political entities,

19. White, "Historical Roots," 1204.
20. E.g., the study by Meadows et al., *Limits to Growth*.
21. Pooley and Tupy make an economic case against the scarcity assumption (*Superabundance*).

and with drastically reduced violence.[22] Of course, as humans we still have a negative bias, as this is the way we survived. Therefore, we still select news that tells a negative story of decay. Moreover, negative emotions are more useful in creating attention and selling products or peddling news. Therefore, the system has an inherent selection bias. Yet, if we compare ourselves within real human history and not some imagined utopia, we must concede that Western societies of the second half of the twentieth century have achieved a level of flourishing incomparable to any other in the whole of history. For most of human history, starvation was just one natural catastrophe away. Thus, being overweight was a marker of a higher social status, just like it is still today in some developing countries. This problem has been reversed in the West. Now the marker of poverty is being overweight. Around 1415, one of the bestsellers was the book entitled *Ars Moriendi*—the art of dying, since death from the plague or early childhood deaths was ever present. We live at a time when someone dying in his sixties is deemed "dying young."

Yet equality and scientific transformation of society alone would not be sufficient to explain the magical transformation of society observed through history. Equality presupposes trust, in order to enable cooperation. Science requires a philosophy of time that allows for the idea of progress to develop. In order to build stable, reforming institutions over a longer period of time, a conception of time and trust is required. If a group of people believe that a better future is in its grasp, they will strive toward it. Moreover, if they are able to trust each other, their institutions will be stable and require less investment of energy. Trust frees up resources, which can be invested into further innovation.

The Judeo-Christian conception of time is complex. One could deduce a circular movement. Similar patterns occur not only in nature but also in history.[23] Through careful observation these patterns could be deduced, and humans could gain wisdom by adapting their lives to the inevitable. We also see notions of apocalyptic decline. History is spiraling down toward an inevitable catastrophe, a sudden interruption. Yet in the biblical view, the apocalypse is never final but is rather followed by God's restoration and redemption. Therefore, the overall image of history, despite the circular and the descending apocalyptic patterns, is the view that time progresses linearly toward final bliss, as God's reign will be

---

22. Steven Pinker makes a case for progress based on statistical evidence about the reduction of violence (*Better Angels*).

23. A striking example of this circular repetition is the cycles in the book of Judges.

fully manifested over the entire universe. This Judeo-Christian imagination was secularized and turned into a truism of progressivism. Yet, "even those who attack the idea of progress as a bourgeois illusion hold that they are more progressive than their opponents."[24] The inevitability of progress has been a powerful motivational force since the Renaissance. Tomorrow will be better than today, and we are able to become active agents in this divine grand plan. Granted, this originally religious idea was secularized, yet it maintained nevertheless its motivational plot. Up to the First World War in 1914, the spirit of the age was an exciting expectation about the rise of humanity.

A group might be as motivated as they want to be. However, they will not progress far if they do not possess mutual trust. The core precondition for building cooperation on a larger scale, and thus achieving a highly specialized and innovative society, is indeed trust. Individual persons are limited beings within an infinitely complex world. The complexity surpasses human perception. One of the main functions of the brain is to reduce complexity and provide us with patterns of perception. Once these patterns prove to be useful, humans can fall into habitual actions and turn on the cruise button, thus preserving energy. We think in order to stop thinking, one could say. Another mechanism to reduce this complexity is to delegate part of our responsibility to other members of society whom we deem to be better equipped to handle some aspects.[25] This always entails a risk. Once tribes delegated the protection of their borders to the king, they were able to invest the time and effort needed for military activities into developing trades, thus growing wealth. However, the risk remained that they might become vulnerable in some other aspects. Trust is beneficial in developing a highly specialized society of professionals who are able to improve in their fields and thus lift the overall level of well-being. As Luhmann concluded, it is impossible to constitute a complex society without trust.[26]

To the contrary, the lack of trust eats up resources and lowers the quality of life for all. My US-American wife was surprised that in Germany you could order goods on Amazon and pay later, after receiving the item. My Nigerian friend told me that life insurance would not work in Nigeria as doctors would be easily bribed to give a certificate of death.

---

24. Löwith, *Meaning in History*, 111–12.

25. Luhmann defines trust as a mechanism for reduction of social complexity (*Vertrauen*, 27–38).

26. Luhmann, *Vertrauen*, 126.

Where trust weakens, bureaucracy grows and lawyers multiply. Precious resources are wasted in order to enforce and surveil cooperation. Investors stay away from countries with high corruption, as the lack of trust must be paid in cash. Both economic and political interactions require trust. However, where does this foundational resource come from?

In tribal societies, trust is established through blood, territory, and tribal allegiance to a common history and deity. This has been a fact for the overwhelming majority of human history. In many nation-states today, these tribal ties are the main hindrance to establishing stable political order. Europe was not different and perhaps even more tribal than the current Afghanistan. Despite the Pashto and Dari speakers worshipping the same God, they are nevertheless deeply divided. The Germanic tribes were as divided among each other as they were hostile toward Romans. What was the miracle that brought together the conquering marauding Germanic barbarians and the civilized Romans to establish a sense of shared identity and cooperation in the deeply fragmented Europe? In a nutshell, it took centuries for the warring tribes to establish trust. By feasting on a common God who transcends ethnic boundaries, they became part of the same reality. The God whom they incorporated is a God who entered into a trustworthy covenant and sacrificed himself to uphold his side of the bargain. Thus, backing up the promise through action became the highest ideal and a precondition of trust in political and economic interactions. If God commits and can be held accountable, this then also applies to a king, who does not stand above God or above the law.

It is therefore not by accident that in 1215 the Magna Carta was authored by the archbishop of Canterbury, which served as a tangible document the subordinate rebel barons could use to hold King John of England accountable. This idea, wherein the more powerful side of the treaty submits to a higher authority, was already present in the First Testament and worked its way through antiquity and medieval monasticism into the very political fabric of nation-states. The idea of commoners holding accountable those in power over them created the basis of a deep notion of public trust. Moreover, the personal sense of individual agency is elevated, which encourages personal investment in the upholding of the political order.

Trust is the precondition for smooth cooperation and the development of a highly specialized society. Trust allows for political stability, which provides the background for long-term strategic agency of accumulation of wealth and reinvestments. It is therefore not surprising that the first proto-capitalist communities, who acquired immense wealth through production and investment, were medieval monasteries, where the social capital of trust was immense due to the voluntary commitment of each member.[27] In a society where basic solidarity exists, the surplus is reinvested and the fruits are redistributed. While inequality is not completely eliminated, the entire society overall is elevated through charity as the sacred virtue.

While trust creates the social glue and enables cooperation and growth of knowledge and wealth, it likewise, however, has the potential to lead to abuse. Unlimited trust is naïve in light of psychopaths, who might take advantage of it and manipulate the system toward their gain. Therefore, a successful society must have a simultaneous existence of trust and distrust. Distrust creates checks and balances, which hinder a few who would use the system toward unjust gain. The Judeo-Christian myth views humans as broken, as fallen from unity with God. While the human is open toward perfection, it is nevertheless also open toward the deepest pits of hell. These extremes permeate human nature. Therefore, a system based on this theological anthropology must be designed in such a way as to reinforce the good side and minimize the evil. This complex anthropology laid the basis for the division of power and institutional checks and balances in order to prevent abuse. Mistrust does not need to be personified by any particular superior, as it is built in into the system. It is therefore activated only negatively, allowing for trust to be at the fore.

The paradoxical feature of the West has been overall stability with constant simultaneous dynamism. Mere stability could lead toward fossilization. Yet constant change without stability would also lead toward dissolution. The ingenuity of Western success lies in the preservation of a solid structure with internal flexibility. The agreement on the ontology of peace allows for continuous political pluralism and discourse with the possibility of a peaceful change of power. Ideally, power transitions occur through best arguments and not hardest fists. Similarly, the affirmation of pluralism as the core feature of reality allows for playful competition in the marketplace of ideas and the growth and development of the best ideas. Yet pluralism presupposes the humility of each actor to admit that he does not grasp the entire reality. Moreover, the exchange of ideas requires the existence of a relatively free public space. Innovative cultures, whether Greece in the third century BC or England in the eighteenth

---

27. Stark, *How the West Won*, 131–34.

century, exemplify the similar preconditions of cultural openness with a healthy dose of confidence and a playful love of freedom.

The dynamism of Western civilization is also fueled through holy unrest, which arises from the simultaneous affirmation of the "is" and the "ought," without collapsing this embrace into dry realism or lofty idealism. The Hebrew prophets held this tension. Their social critique would satisfy Marxist empiricism. Yet they do not reduce reality to political power and economic inequality. They always paint a larger picture of God's action in history and evoke hope through projecting how God will bring his purposes toward a harmonious end. This tension allows for real change, as the material reality is taken seriously and is transformed through incremental steps by people who envision a divine ideal. Innovation, if defined pragmatically as ideas that work,[28] dissolves into a cynical tool of manipulation. Innovation always entails a normative idea that both the vision and its realization must elevate life toward a better state. Collective visions are necessary for a coordinated agency. Humans can act only toward that which they can envision.

The earliest visionaries were prophets, who presented to people images received from divine revelation. In secular liberal societies, prophets were mainly replaced by produced images on the screen. Hollywood's core identity consists in the production of dreams that satisfy human desires for a larger image amid the fragmented modernity. Individual dreams are fed by collective myths. These myths outline the perception of reality. American movies seeped globally into every culture. In the 80s, I remember sneaking into illegal video places in the Siberian city of Omsk to watch Rocky and Rambo, the man who with a bow fought on the side of the Afghan Mujahideen and struck down a Soviet helicopter with an arrow. We did not care about being perceived as traitors for cheering for our enemy, since we were hungry for eternal archetypes, which were offered to us through these movies. The hegemony of a civilization is measured primarily by its ability to produce dreams that captivate people. The Hebrew metastory grew immensely in its Christian form and enchanted the European pagans. Through Europe, the Judeo-Christian myth was transplanted into almost every cultural setting globally. Even in its secularized form of Hollywood blockbusters, the Judeo-Christian myth continues to captivate hearts and minds. Eternal themes of love and hate, death and life, beauty and ugliness are explored through captivating plots. Of course,

---

28. Mulgan, *Social Innovation*, 8.

one could debate whether Hollywood presents a syncretistic mythology. However, one can still recognize the biblical tropes.

Ideas become real when embodied through people. The power of ideas over time is exerted through social institutions, which form a larger society. The central institution where the core ideas of the West were initially embodied and transmitted was the monastery. The success of the West came from the monasteries as think tanks and experimental laboratories, where those who thought the ideas also put them into practice. The Judeo-Christian conception of society became real within the monastic community. The origins of political liberalism, scientific reasoning and technological invention, economic practices as proto-capitalism, and the origins of modern universities—all of these building blocks of Western success were first rehearsed in the monasteries before they were scaled to success in the larger society from the Renaissance onward.

To point to the success of the West does not imply denigration of others, which have merits of their own. Yet to sideline the success story of the West is to be disingenuous both to the European tradition and to others, who would like to learn and flourish as well. Just like the West came to its success through humble learning and copying from others, so it must generously offer its best lessons to others as a gesture of gratitude. If the European success was nurtured by its religious roots and the first prototypes were tested in monasteries, why has this story been forgotten? Instead, a different plot became popular. Within the popular consciousness, we believe that Western success was won against theology and the church. Moreover, it has become fashionable to attribute Western success primarily and solely to exploitation of the other. Why did this dichotomy between the seeming secular reason and religious irrationality become so popular, between the scholastic backwardness and the light of the Renaissance? I locate the reason for this split in the church itself, which pushed its secular child into the wilderness. Once outside its maternal realm, the secular sphere became intoxicated with its own success and stumbled into hubris, which led toward an illusion of complete independence from its religious origins.

Devouring Mother and Exhilarating Hubris

The worst abuser is the one closest to the child, as this breaking of trust leads toward the shattering of ontological trust and subsequent deep trauma. The church as ideal mother, modeled after the image of Mary, the mother of Jesus, became complicit in the abuse of her children. This traumatic abuse has also been stored in the German collective memory as seen in the fairy tale of Hansel and Gretel. When the children's mother dies, their father marries a woman who hates them. She drives them out into the woods, leaving them to die. Eventually, they stumble upon a witch's house, which is made of sweets. They are enticed and are almost devoured by the evil witch. One could also equate the stepmother with the evil witch. Whereas their true mother would extend loving care and release them into a space of freedom, where they could mature within a safe frame, the stepmother kicks them into the wild. The world becomes a dangerous place because the children did not first experience the roots of security through motherly love. Without ontological security, the children became easy prey; the evil mother entices them in order to control them and destroy all sense of agency and dignity. The fairy tale ends with the struggle between the siblings and the witch. The siblings manage to push the witch into the oven, where she meets her demise in the flames. Hansel and Gretel liberate themselves from her spell as they run free.

This is, in a nutshell, the popular story of the secular emancipation from the religious stepmother. In the face of abuse, if the victim is not completely broken and there exists a spark of resistance, the victim will struggle for freedom in order to escape the devouring stepmother. Yet the transition from the view of the church as a caring mother with Jesus as her Lord, for whom Christians were willing to give their lives in the Roman Colosseum, to that of a devouring stepmother from which only the strongest sought to break, was a gradual one. The beginnings of this transition can be located in the fourth century, as the church was elevated from a persecuted beggar to the queen of the empire. Within this elevation to power came the birth of hubris, which transformed the holy, loving mother into a devouring witch.

Paradoxically, the moment of ecclesial victory has turned out to be its defeat. The last book of the Bible portrays the church as struggling against evil, which could be viewed as manifesting itself in the seemingly all-encompassing power of the Roman Empire. The minority of faithful martyrs stood the ground against the cunning and cruel attacks of the ancient evil, as embodied in concrete sociopolitical structures, against those who upheld their faithfulness to Christ as the final victor. However, this apocalyptic imaginary lost its historic significance the moment the church became the most powerful institution in the Roman Empire.

Eusebius of Caesarea, as one of the first theologians of the empire, could not relate to the images of the struggling church and even advocated the removal of Revelation from the Christian canon. Instead of viewing the history of the church in opposition to the earthly empire, he merged these and interpreted Constantine's life as a tool of God's redemptive purpose in history. This view created a conundrum, which St. Augustine sought to disentangle in his masterpiece *Civitates Dei*. If God used the Roman Empire to realize his plan with the church, did the collapse of the Roman Empire undermine God's sovereignty and goodness? Augustine distinguished clearly between the earthly and heavenly kingdoms, and if these touch, as in the case of the Christian Caesar, then even this overlap can never bring about the heavenly kingdom. Eusebius collapsed this critical distance and fueled Christian confidence in embracing the view of God's kingdom within the particular sociopolitical space. Yet it takes only a few steps to cross the line between confidence and hubris.

The justified triumph of the church as the institution that could permeate the decaying Roman Empire with the good, the true, and the beautiful lent it moral authority. For three centuries, the church proved to be a flourishing counterpart to the decaying Roman Empire. However, once in power, the church elites began to justify the use of political coercion for supposedly spiritual ends. The early church practiced excommunication on a personal level and through the moral authority of church leaders. However, as the church merged completely with the sociopolitical order, the unity of Christendom as a religious-political order also required the citizen to be Christian. Thus, behind every bishop's spiritual authority stood a king with a sword. The church conquered the Roman Empire through free persuasion and moral example. Yet in subsequent centuries its status was backed by political power, which made dissent almost impossible. The church began to employ its spiritual authority in matters of political power. This development began first in the East and later followed in the West as well. Examples abound.

Catherine Nixey describes vividly the excesses of the Christians in the East between the third and sixth centuries. In Alexandria, Athens, and Damascus as centers of classical philosophy, Christian mobs persecuted philosophers and pillaged Greek temples and ancient libraries. This development peaked in 529 with the Justinian law prohibiting religious practices other than Christian ones and enforcing Christianity as a way of life:

Everyone now had to become Christian.... Those who refused would be stripped of all their property, movable and immovable, lose their civil rights, be left in penury and, "in addition"—as if what had gone before was not punishment by mere preamble—they would be "subject to the proper punishment." If any man did not immediately hurry to the "holy churches" with his family and force them also to be baptized, then he would suffer all of the above—and then he would be exiled. The "insane error" of paganism was to be wiped from the face of the earth.[29]

Only two hundred years later, this Justinian law was mimicked by Charlemagne in the West as he forced Christianity upon the Saxons. The wandering monk Lebuin-Liafwin set the stage for the Frankish military conquest. He preached a fiery sermon to the Saxons, offering them to either convert and keep their freedom or be conquered by Charlemagne and become his subjects. The proud, freedom-loving Saxons rebelled against the Christendom coercion. The subsequent political conquest in the name of the Christ the Victor was dragged out for thirty-three bloody years and ended with the massacre of 4,500 Saxons in the year 782, who were beheaded as a public display of Charlemagne's sovereign power.[30] These two examples, in both the East and the West, were not exceptional events. Instead, they represented a pattern of collaboration between ecclesial authorities and political powers.

Hubris as attitude was born at the moment the church envisioned itself as the victor over the Roman Empire. Once the church was either pulled into governance or freely stepped into the vacuum, it faced the challenge to create clarity and precision, both conceptually and on the organizational level. Yet precision also required hermeneutical stripping. One can't rule through poetry. The plurality of biblical genres was overlooked and the reading of the Bible reduced to philosophical-propositional theology, leaving the poetic-visionary mode to the mystics on the fringes of the established church. The medieval Roman Catholic Church stood under constant tension. The dogmatic-practical side was always suspicious of the mystical-individual spirituality. The split between the administratively minded clergy and the monks, which occurred in the fourth century, widened and continued to produce various reform movements on the fringes of the established church. Some of these movements were successfully incorporated into the church, and others

29. Nixey, *Darkening Age*, 248.
30. Padberg, *Christianisierung Europas im Mittelalter*, 95.

were brutally suppressed. Yet these visionaries and prophets, who often critiqued the abuse of power and moral compromise of the clergy, did not just disappear. Toward the end of the medieval ages, the apocalyptic movements intensified.[31] By being branded and rejected as completely other, they often doubled down in their self-righteousness. The hubris of the established church gave birth to the hubris of the prophetic revolutionary. Both claimed to be on the right side of history, lacking the humility of recognizing evil within. The hubris of the church to establish God's kingdom on earth gave rise to various critical religious groups that sought to uncover the glaring hypocrisy of the church and the wide gap between their claim and reality. In becoming outcasts, these groups often wanted to prove their superiority, only to be entrapped by the seduction of hubris. Hence, the late medieval age witnessed an amalgam of reform movements, both within and outside the church. Some of these movements spiraled down toward self-destruction. Perhaps the worst case was the Anabaptist excesses in Muenster. These and other cases prevented Luther and other Reformers from going further in their separation from the political powers and made them weary of decentralized, spontaneous expressions that evoked the Holy Spirit.

Did the medieval church prepare the soil for the emergence of the Renaissance and the success of the West, or did it lay perverse patterns of violence and hubris, which were then taken up by the secular nation-states? History rarely fits within one category. The church laid down the best and worst patterns for the advancing secular age. Just like a mother who became drunk on power and drove out all children who dared to call her out, so secularity mimicked this abusive totalitarian certainty. Just like there had been no free space to exist outside of the all-encompassing Christendom, so now there seems to exist no space outside of the encompassing secular age. It has become unthinkable, a ubiquitous taboo, to imagine a space to live and thrive outside of the secular liberal consensus. It often takes the view of an outsider to notice this religious core of secular liberalism, which Talal Asad brings to the surface:

> The "nature" of early liberalism, the "humanity" of our own day, may be talked about as if they already exist but the point of talking about them is that they are still to be created. The essence of the myth of liberalism—its imaginary construction—is to assert human rights precisely because they are *not* built into the structure of the universe. The frightening truth concealed by the

---

31. Cohn, *Pursuit of the Millennium*.

liberal myth is, therefore, that liberal principles go against the grain of human and social nature. Liberalism is not a matter of clearing away a few accidental obstacles and allowing humanity to unfold its natural essence. It is more like making a garden in a jungle that is continually encroaching.... But it is precisely the element of truth in the gloomy picture of society and politics drawn by critics of liberalism that makes the project of realizing liberal principle all the more urgent. The world is a dark place, which needs redemption by the light of a myth.[32]

Asad recognizes that secular liberalism can't shed its mythological roots, which imply a redemptive purpose and must be imposed upon the other. The tragedy is that the child repeats the violence of its abusive mother and raises the level of violence due to the absence of the redeemer:

In secular redemptive politics there is no place for the idea of a redeemer saving sinners through his submission to suffering. ... Instead there is a readiness to cause pain to those who are to be saved by being humanized. It is not merely that the object of violence to connect an optimistic project of universal empowerment with a pessimistic account of human motivation in which inertia and incorrigibility figure prominently. If the world is a dark place that needs redemption, the human redeemer, as an inhabitant of this world, must first redeem himself.[33]

The redemptive vision remains, while the modus shifts completely. The gnostic motif of self-redemption is introduced, and violence becomes a justifiable means toward the immanent goal. Utilitarian logic creeps in. If the highest good is achievable for the masses, why not sacrifice a few along the way? At the heart of secular liberalism lies the hubris of human salvation of self, if necessary, through coercion and extermination of all those who reject the immanent paradise.

The rebellious, often-prideful spirit did not disappear with the expulsion from the church. The political fragmentation of the late medieval ages allowed for various intellectual rebels to find their niches. As the church was losing its authority by being mired in worldly affairs, it increasingly came to be seen as the negative foil for any forward-looking free inquiry. The reaction was fiercest where the ecclesial hegemony was strongest. The Enlightenment in France was wrought mainly against the church. To the contrary, the Protestant Reformation in Germany and the

---

32. Asad, *Formations of the Secular*, 59; quoting Margaret Canovan.
33. Asad, *Formations of the Secular*, 61–62.

religious diversification of the landscape prepared the way for a more irenic Enlightenment, often framed as theological reform. Kant, Schelling, Fichte, and Hegel were positively open toward religion and even sought to secure its meaning and place in light of the fundamental shifts they saw. Of course, one could debate whether fierce opposition toward the church or taming through patronizing is in the long term worse for its robustness. Within the more amicable relations between secularity as a god-free space and the church, political and intellectual elites granted the church a space to influence the public space to the degree it was willing to transform itself into a civil religion, thus losing its distinct shape. Rousseau and later even Comte realized that humans need religion on a social level. Thus, the niche was created for the usefulness of theology and the church to dilute itself into the broader, abstract, and general form of religious bond between diverse citizens. The Christian church changed its role from a prescribing authority on the nature of reality to a tolerated useful institution that could operate "within the bounds of reason"[34] as long as it fed the poor, cured the sick, and provided a sacred legitimation for the crown, thus securing social balance and stabilizing the monarchy and later the nation-states.

Yet the church lost not only its cosmic vision; it also lost its prophetic edge by driving out its visionaries and prophets, who came to live outside the church walls. In the ideal image of the church, all gifts are channeled toward the common goal of love. Love must be tested and lived out in the practical community. Visionary prophets must integrate their skill within the day-to-day concerns of pastors. The razor-sharp critique of the prophets must function like a scalpel to heal and not to kill. Once the visionary prophets and intellectual teachers are driven outside the relational community, they develop a skewed perception, with totalizing visions and systems of thought claiming to encapsulate all of reality. They become like Nietzsche's caricature of the intellectual, a big ear on a tiny stick of a body, a man who has too much of one thing, lacking everything else.[35] Yet the individual hubris to perceive the whole without the need of community creates a simplistic perception of reality and a totality that forcefully either drives out or subjugates the other. This is the beginning of modern hubris, with intellectuals posing

---

34. Kant, *Religion innerhalb der Grenzen*.
35. Nietzsche, *Also sprach Zarathustra*, 136.

questions to themselves and then proceeding to solve them in a solipsistic mode without glimpsing wider horizons.

Examples abound. The history of modernity could be written as the myth of Icarus in his prideful flight to the sun and subsequent fall when ultimately reality reasserted itself against his ignorance of reality. The Marxist rebellion against Hegel's all-encompassing spirit led only toward another totalitarian ideology, which required the sacrifice of hundreds of millions to achieve its secular utopia.

One could tell of modernity as the story of prideful certainty. Descartes locked himself up in a room and sought to arrive at certainty via introspection. He stared at a flickering candle and forgot to consider the thick relational background of his reflexivity. Before he began to think, he was raised by loving parents and a community of people. Before he became aware of himself, he was already formed through tradition and language. Amnesia of history is a dangerous side effect of hubris that has plagued modernity since its branding of the medieval age as darkness. People without roots are not able to evaluate the present. Since they are not anchored in the present, they are open to demagogues, who promise them paradise on earth in exchange for their total sacrifice. Existential uprootedness transforms persons into a malleable mass.[36] Once oral history was superseded by professional historians in service to the state, people lost access to collective memory and became more vulnerable to state propaganda. Historical amnesia turns citizens into a malleable mass, since they are not able to properly evaluate the present, as they lack proper patterns of evaluation. Yet remembering requires humility to stop and look back, to expect to learn from lessons of the past.

One could describe modernity as the story of human independence and prideful confidence to order their relations on a micro and macro scale without any reference to God. Beginning with Hobbes and subsequent political theorists, isolated aspects from the religious myth became the sole foundations. Yet pride is blind. It is not able to see further than its own narrow assessment of reality, as it can't endure images that contradict its wishful illusions.[37] Reduction is therefore necessary, and megalomaniac theories that enshrine the prideful view of the world are the result. As Hobbes viewed humans as evil in their original natural condition, the

---

36. Both Simone Weil and Hannah Arendt saw the anthropological fundamental need for roots in community, history, and culture (Weil, *Need for Roots*).

37. Ironically, this sentence also sounds prideful. Perhaps the discursive mode only reproduces pride. Humor would be more fitting in exposing pride.

need for the state as redeemer arose. To the contrary, Rousseau imagined and romanticized the innocent wild man and viewed the advance of civilization as the source of all evil. Voltaire completely severed the relation between sacred and secular time, between the theological interpretation of history and the purely secular philosophy of history. He did so due to embarrassment at particular roots of the Christian theology in the Hebrew people and the desire to paint a universal history of progress.[38]

Man was imagined to be either rational or completely irrational. Hubris runs into contradictions, as it wants to control the myth. By breaking single pieces from the mythological plot it is able to hold on to the piece while losing the entire treasure. Dissatisfaction with theoretical limitations does not drive it back to the original myth. This would require humility. Instead, the prideful intellect attempts to bury its crimes by further elaboration of the theoretical tower of Babel. Thus, theoretical production functions like a perpetuum mobile, despite the disastrous consequences. It must continue to reassemble the pieces that were broken off from the original fuller image. Yet those who reassemble the shiny pieces either forgot the location of the gold mine or are too proud to admit the origin of their little treasures.[39]

One could tell of modernity as the tragic illusion of humans who mistook the divine spark within themselves for a God. The initial nominalist appraisal of divine freedom and will ended in the proclamation of man as God, who freely creates the world from his own creative genius. Modern man is akin to Goethe's Prometheus, who creates after his own image. Heinrich Heine called for a heroic rebellion of man, not to endure the tension between heavenly ideal and earthly reality. Instead, he insisted on creating heaven on earth now, through human will. Nietzsche's insistence on the creation of new myth and values from the heroic human will of the Übermensch is the pinnacle of this implosion. Marx sought to translate this hubris into a socioeconomic reality. Ultimately, Soviet gulags grew from this soil, justified as a necessary means to achieve this worldly Marxist utopia. Divinization of the self leads toward a punctual obsession and loss of humility to endure the complexity and tensions within a tragic world. Relative innovation turns into a curse of total and perpetual renewal by breaking every continuity and stability.

---

38. Löwith, *Meaning in History*, 105–14.

39. Habermas is one of the notable exceptions. In his conversation with Ratzinger, he pointed to religious background as the reservoir of meaning for modern philosophy (Habermas, *Zeit der Übergänge*).

Yet the worst hubris of all is Christian pride, because it cloaks itself in a guise of humility. It sounds humble when reason takes up the task to outline its own limits and secure a space for faith, as Immanuel Kant sought to accomplish. Yet if someone claims to outline one's own boundaries, one must be able to glimpse beyond them. If one would like to safeguard a space for religion, one must at least intuitively inhabit a larger space and somehow have knowledge of a greater myth. Kant even notices the contradictions of reason, yet he does not return to the myth but creates a transcendental nirvana, where these contradictions might be overcome.

Hubris eventually leads to collapse due to the erasing of larger horizons of orientation as a result of its punctual obsession with self and particular theoretical aspects that are cut loose from the larger web of meaning. Moreover, hubris creates historical amnesia, cutting off the present community from resources of experience in the past. Although not immediate, collapse is inevitable. The initial effect of pride is exhilaration, as one feels unrestrained, in the illusion of a limitless reality with oneself as the arbiter, around whom the universe circles. This myth was elaborated by Nietzsche and seeped into Schumpeter's view of how the economy grows. Schumpeter describes the entrepreneur as a godlike creator who invents the needs of people and envisions means to satisfy them, while also possessing the will to bring about his visions. He is restless and never satisfied, he is a Nietzschean Übermensch, who is independent of his social and natural environment, who imprints his own image upon this world.[40] Schumpeter's view of the entrepreneur became the normative view for Silicon Valley and the current fashionable slang of innovation. There is no end to the growth of economy due to the fact that there are endless combinations, which the genius can bring forth to satisfy prefabricated needs. The exploitation of the eternal longings within the human heart is the precondition for the heroic calling of the superhuman entrepreneur, who creates a culture of acceleration due to the dogma of effectiveness and creativity.[41] Yet without the anchoring of the creative person in the ritual of rest and without relation to God as the ultimate creator, the gift turned into a curse.

Hubris permeated the heart of Western civilization and led toward a curse of constant transformation, which through its glittery success

---

40. Schumpeter, *Theorie der wirtschaftlichen Entwicklung*, 127.

41. Hartmut Rosa critiques modernity by analyzing various accelerating modes (*Weltbeziehungen im Zeitalter*).

blinds us to the darker secret. Humans were gifted with a divine nature. They were gifted with creative powers. Once they cut themselves loose from God, the gift turned into a curse. Creativity was once viewed as a thankful response. However, when the individual is doomed to create himself, unless he evaporates, it turns into a curse, akin to Sisyphus and the subsequent exhaustion.[42] As Godin rightly concludes in his exploration of the idea of innovation, innovation turned into a magical formula, an empty slogan to manipulate the masses.[43] Innovation without history and normative telos is transformed into a forced feeding of the masses by the few godlike entrepreneurs who profit from creating the cravings in people. People who can't rest, who are always kept in flux, turn into a malleable mass, which is a precondition for advancing totalitarianism.[44] At the heart of the primal hubris exists a lie that the individual human stands above God. Lies negate reality and must ultimately shatter against it.

The myth concerning sacred personhood is able to unfold its power even without its ritual embodiment—at least for a while. The once-liberating space of secularity as God's invitation for humanity turned into a suffocating cage at the moment men fell into the absurdity of a gift without the giver. Let's return to the headless chicken and the lost son. The chicken can accelerate without its head, albeit without direction. The lost son was the most popular guy in town. Yet it was just a matter of time until he would end up with the pigs. The removal of roots, which gave nourishment to the blooming tree, does not lead toward a sudden death. The plant can even continue to keep the appearance of life. On a social level, exhilaration leads toward acceleration and the appearance of success. Thus, the binary as to whether secularization leads toward success or failure is misleading—at least in a short span of time. Like most important questions, the answers can be given only in retrospect. In the short term of a few centuries the cleavage between the mythological-ritual soil and the outward success can go unnoticed, despite the growing symptoms of advancing decay.

---

42. Andreas Reckwitz traces the development of creativity from the elitist classes during European Romanticism to the current general imperative for everyone. However, as Reckwitz concludes, once voluntary creativity turns into a coercive imperative, it becomes oppressive (*Erfindung der Kreativität*).

43. Godin, *Innovation Contested*, 286–87.

44. Arendt, *Elemente und Ursprünge*, 679.

CHAPTER 5

Crumbling Mythical Horizons and Ritual Alienation

"Whither is God?" he cried; "I will tell you. We have killed him—you and I. All of us are his murderers. But how did we do this? How could we drink up the sea? Who gave us the sponge to wipe away the entire horizon? What were we doing when we unchained this earth from its sun? Whither is it moving now? Whither are we moving? Away from all suns? Are we not plunging continually? Backward, sideward, forward, in all directions? Is there still any up or down? Are we not straying, as through an infinite nothing? Do we not feel the breath of empty space? Has it not become colder? Is not night continually closing in on us?"

—Friedrich Nietzsche, The Gay Science

The sleep of reason produces monsters

—Francisco Goya, title of an etching plate in Los Caprichos

Part II: Incurvatus in Se: *The Triumph and Decay of Secular Society*

PRIDE LEADS TOWARD A posture of being bent into oneself, hindering the individual from imagining wider horizons. The gnawing sense of loss accompanied the secular story of success from the beginnings of its alienation from sacred roots. First the mad prophets sought to awaken the masses to the fact of the crumbling world, which is not held together by God. Then academics caught on and began to glimpse the contours of the encroaching paradoxical condition: as the sacred mythical horizons were being wiped away while the secular boundaries were being pushed further, the world began to contract. Through the process of the detachment and fragmentation of rituals, alienation as an existential condition crept in.

CRUMBLING MYTHICAL HORIZONS

The collapse of the Judeo-Christian myth has led to a sense of exhilaration due to the illusion of a world without limits. It was believed that once the rigid religious authority as the limiting force of human potential was overcome, the flight toward the sun would be in reach. This optimistic mood prevailed in the eighteenth and nineteenth centuries and led toward rapid acceleration and the success of European societies. My main assumption is that myths and rituals organize society on a fundamental level. Due to the human relational nature, societies can't enter a post-mythological state. The only option afforded society is the transformation and/or partial or entire replacement of the original given myth. Modernity evolved through the fragmentation and recomposition of the Judeo-Christian myth. Historically, we can't merely posit a theological mythological unity that splintered into various fragments—Charles Taylor lent us a fitting image of a "nova effect."[1] Upon a closer look into the Judeo-Christian Scriptures, one can discern a complex polyphony, which is held together through God's agency and through shared rituals. These basic central features of the Judeo-Christian myth emerged as unifying for the medieval ages. However, there were always fierce debates and struggles over the interpretation of God's nature and the mediatory ritual practices. Today, these religious disputes appear to us like eccentric hobbies reserved for ivory-tower clergy. Yet they touched the very core of society and the nature of reality: the question of how we perceive God as the highest ideal also determines what we take reality to be.

---

1. Taylor, *Secular Age*, 299–423.

When the unifying agency of God throughout the biblical corpus is removed, along with the shared rituals, the paradoxical features that are held together and thrive in the communal performance of the ritual and reading of the text, a complex text like the Bible deteriorates into simple contradictions. The mythological paradoxes are held together through the covenant as the foundation of trust and the shared response. Christians keep this performative structure in place and enhance it. The new covenant in Jesus must be celebrated by all members regularly. The image of diversity and unity as organism is embodied through the ritual of the Eucharist (see ch. 11). Every Christian member is attuned to a particular aspect of the myth. Teachers transmit the continuity and propositional aspects, prophets are intuitive to the overarching whole as they perceive God's action underneath the surface, deacons apply the myth to the everyday needs. Yet they all act in symphony with the larger resonating melody of love. How does the visual relate to the sense of hearing, the propositional discourse to the image? One could seek to reconcile these paradoxical features discursively, which would require a lot of time and energy. Discursive frames without a communal ritual create exclusive theories, which squeeze out paradoxical tensions in order to achieve a higher degree of clarity. The proper response to God's action in history and his communication is communal response in loving God and neighbor. The paradoxical tension must not be resolved but activated in the communal performance of teaching, singing, reciting, eating, celebrating, and acting in everyday life.

The cracks within the paradoxical Judeo-Christian myth appeared at the moment the church shifted its focus from the table of Jesus to the table of Caesar. The performative unity suffered its first crack with the increasing secularization of the clergy due to the church's administrative responsibilities in the fourth century. The apostles delegated the practical tasks to deacons and kept their main tasks of teaching and prayer (Acts 6). At this early stage these differentiations were still held together, even though the Pauline Letters indicate the first fractures and divisions.[2] However, with increasing power and the invitation to build the new world on the ruins of antiquity, the focus shifted, causing distance to form between administrators, teachers, and prophets. Due to the lack of a shared ecclesial body, each claimed to represent the most authentic form of Christianity. Governance required clarity, and dwelling in the desert

---

2. E.g., various cases Paul addresses in his Epistles to the Corinthians.

allowed for unifying vision and simplicity. Of course, some exceptional saints managed to hold this tension together and release new energy, bursting forth, leading toward reforms. The spiritual reform of Cluny, which led toward social and political innovations, is but one example. However, the weakening of performative unity widened the gap between paradoxical parts within the Judeo-Christian myth.

The nominalist controversy that simmered through the late medieval ages prefigures the subsequent modern splits. Although initially a purely theological controversy, it spilled into the wider society, shaping anthropology and affecting how we perceive reality today. At the core of this debate stood the question concerning the perception of ultimate reality as stable or dynamic. Dominicans sided with Aquinas, incorporating Aristotelian philosophy and supporting a hierarchical, stable view of God and the social order. Franciscans sided with St. Augustine and were more critical of the Greek philosophical heritage. They took a more dynamic view of reality, which is not merely given but comes into being through the will of God. Both could have been held in fruitful tension, as both are reflected in the biblical narratives. However, once the church elites chose to emphasize stability, they expelled the proponents of dynamic reality and made them into external critics over time. The end result of nominalism is a solipsistic individual, whose only recourse to the real consists in his will.

Power requires clarity. Clarity leads toward conceptual splitting and reduction of larger metaphors. What once existed in the larger frame is now made to fall outside of it and thus begins to create a life of its own, disconnected from and often in opposition to the arrogant mother who gave birth to it. Yet what emerges from this existential hurt is not something completely other. The overall framework is still in place, while the picture in detail seems to oppose the original one. The paradox between nature and grace is held together in the ritual of the Eucharist. Nature and grace become one in the piece of bread that is the body of Christ. However, this sacrament was split asunder politically once the administrative church sided with nature, while the monks left the city and in so doing came to represent grace as outside this material world. This distinction was then fatefully cemented through Luther's juxtaposition between a theology of glory and a theology of the cross. On April 26, 1518, Luther presented his thesis in Heidelberg contrasting these two theologies. Luther associated "glory" with the Roman Catholic aberration from grace and the human tendency to redeem oneself through good works.

Moreover, "glory" encompassed the Roman Catholic moral compromise and desire for recognition and power. Instead, Luther emphasized the cross as the only path to being justified by God. God's justice is met only in the destruction of one's pride, insofar as the sinner acknowledges that nothing can be done for one's own salvation except by receiving God's grace in Jesus. Luther's bifurcation between glory and the cross makes sense within his historical context, as he sought to reform the church by clarifying who God is and what he has done for humans in Christ, contrasting it to the church, which had succumbed to immanent false glories. Yet in the subsequent history, Luther drove a wedge further between nature and grace, thus prefiguring the secular divisions between reason and faith, pushing apart the immanent and transcendent spheres. Discursive theology, once disembodied, runs wild and causes the splintering of original unity. Within the widening cleavage between the spirit and the flesh, gnostic speculations thrive.

The original theological unity is not conceptual in nature but teleological, imaginary, and performative. The gathered church seeks to glorify God as it views itself as the body of Christ and experiences this reality through a communal ritual. The various mythological parts complement each other simultaneously in a network through interactions and not through analytical, linear reflection by an intellectual. Once this performative unity is lost and the gnostic master becomes the sole center responsible for holding these various narrative strands together, the various paradoxical modes drift apart and turn into mere contradictions. It takes a community to keep the paradox alive and vibrant. The desire for knowledge and control kills the living organism. Antagonistic plots emerge in its wake, which resemble the dualistic Manichaean narrative. The main task of the modern intellectual endeavor consists in creating a unifying myth that restores the relation to nature, to others, and to self without a necessary recourse to God as a unifying whole. Underneath modern philosophy and literature lies the search to find a formula that will somehow restore the holistic meaning and experience of the cosmos.

Modern man seeks to reinvent the experience of stability and dynamism. Movement results from a difference of motion. I can say that an object moves only in relation to the background, which doesn't move. If God is not the ultimate point of reference, what is? If everything is in flux, then the world is experienced as either highly unstable or completely still. Initially, natural laws were conceived of as stable variables that undergird change. That which persists through change can be trusted. Durkheim was right at the beginning of the twentieth century in claiming that we merely traded our faith in God for faith in science.[3] It is therefore only consequential that science turned from mere methodology, which was temporary and in constant need of falsification, to an object of faith. Totalitarian political regimes of the twentieth century, both in Russia and Germany, justified themselves with recourse to scientism, which defied any modesty and purported to speak with total certainty. Polanyi's path to philosophy of science occurred through his encounter with the Soviet ideological perversion of scientific methodology and freedom of thought: "I was struck by the fact that this denial of the very existence of independent scientific thought came from a socialist theory which derived its tremendous persuasive power from its claim to scientific certainty. The scientific outlook appeared to have produced a mechanical conception of man and history in which there was no place for science itself."[4]

Initially, the modern myth split between the impersonal, objective order and the expressive, meaning-making human. Taylor rightfully noticed the inherent tensions within these types of anthropologies. On the one side, a person is conceived as detached mind, and on the other hand the Romantic rebels invoke an expressive genius, who infuses the cold universe with meaning.[5]

This initial split caused extensive crumbling. The hegemony of naïve positivism was deeply shaken by the deep current of epistemic suspicion, which has been deconstructing any certainty ever since Kant. Already Descartes recognized the possibility of the acid effect of skepticism and sought to mute it by postulating God as the last harbinger of the trustworthiness of the external world in relation to the human mind. Any theoretical knowledge hinges on the little human brain, which is fallible. Thus, any form of knowledge is temporary and merely a projection. Since Kant, any reference to simple, given, objective reality must be elaborately propped up and justified.[6] The loss of an overarching horizon of faith leads toward a frantic search for absolute certainty. This can take up different ideological frames, like for example Hegel's idealism, in which the philosopher turns into a gnostic magician. Within positivism, the scientist turns out to have the last authority over the nature of reality.

3. Durkheim, *Elementary Forms*, 432.
4. M. Polanyi, *Tacit Dimension*, 3.
5. Taylor, *Sources of the Self*, 368–93.
6. Perhaps this is the reason Heidegger's language verges on the esoteric. The nebulous language obscures the world, which is not available.

Yet any hard system increases in fragility at the same time as it fossilizes. As the system fractures, various strands battle against each other, seeking to encapsulate a larger part of reality.

The Romantic rebels rightly noticed the loss of meaning when nature is reduced to a mute, useful, material order. They sought to restore the organic, living, mysterious, larger whole by emphasizing the experience of nature, folk traditions, and simple, collective memory. The restoration was envisioned through the artistic genius, who demonstrates aesthetic experience and thus creates a pattern for emulation. However, due to the lack of unifying rituals, this lone prophet was also viewed in opposition to society, thus promulgating the bifurcation of the theological myth, thereby fueling the antagonism. Romanticism rightfully critiqued a reductive rationalism, yet it failed to provide a unifying myth and rituals. Even worse, Romantic geniuses further accelerated the divinization of the human ego by proclaiming its absoluteness.[7]

Moreover, the theological deification of every human person as created in the image of God was ripped apart by monstrosity on both sides. The Romantics elevated the human being into the realm of God without the concrete relation to Jesus Christ and the mediation of sacraments. To the contrary, various materialistic ideologies emptied the human of any reference to the divine, robbing the person of any divinity. The Marxist critique viewed the individual as nothing more than a product of class interest. Freud considered the individual a product of much deeper psychological forces in which the individual's consciousness only reproduces deeper unconscious traumas. Nietzsche emphasized the plot that humans are driven by biological forces. Modern sociological constructivism and naturalism portrayed the individual as a penetrable sponge, who is driven at will by larger systemic forces, permeating him without any resistance. At the end of this fierce deconstruction of the idea of an individual stands the proclamation of the "death of the subject."[8]

Against this annihilation of self and fragmentation into random details, a philosopher envisions the whole building and the eternal organizing logic that transcends the empirical realm. He is able to point to the way the single bricks must be put together in order to achieve a larger synthesis upward. Due to the lack of unifying rituals, modernity must have gnostic, speculative priests, who like Hegel are able to hold

---

7. E.g., Fichte, *Grundlage der gesammten Wissenschaftslehre*.
8. Heartfield, *"Death of the Subject."*

the random pieces together in a unifying vision. Contrary to the vision of St. Paul in the Letter to the Corinthians, our secular age has proven the temporality of love and the self-proclamation of knowledge to be eternal. Love as a soft component must be covered with the steely logic of knowledge. When the paradox is not alive in the loving participation of different people within the Eucharist, there arises a need for Hegelian philosophers to become master dialecticians who incorporate all the disparate pieces and present a unifying ideology, incorporating everything into a total system.

However, one could counter that the mythological fragmentation does not need to be integrated. The disparate pieces can be appreciated on their own without the need for a grander story. In fact, smaller stories could be more exciting and liberating, and we as a society could develop a shared suspicion of any narratives that lay a normative claim to a bigger representation of reality.[9] The same scientist can study nature as a dead object and then marvel at it as something personal and beautiful. The same scientist can declare that the human emotion of love is nothing other than a biochemical process in the brain and then declare passionately his love to his beloved on a romantic date. In principle, this could be possible.

Yet to lead a life individually and to act coherently, humans are making strong value judgments. Moreover, due to the finitude of human life, humans orient their actions according to a larger telos, thus seeking coherency.[10] This applies even more strongly on a collective level. When disparate pieces are perceived as unconnected, life is experienced as fragmented and meaningless. Directionality arises from the evaluation of some aspects as deeper than others, and adventure comes from seeking to integrate the pieces into an ideal order. With the increasing drainage of value from our perception, life becomes boring. The result of dis-enchantment and the loss of a larger plot is ennui, which produces phlegmatic, passive societies. In order to act, one must perceive something worth striving for. Sameness produces aimlessness. Without an orientation, both individuals and societies stumble in the dark.

One could object that the loss of an overarching telos brings into focus the particular, the formerly overlooked aspects. This is true as long as the larger myth remains as a background. However, the initial thrill of

---

9. Lyotard declared as early as 1979 the end of grand narratives (*Condition postmoderne*).

10. Charles Taylor elaborates this claim in his essay "Leading a Life."

the idiosyncratic, when completely detached from the larger background, loses its significance as humans make sense of the particular in light of the larger conceptual framework. When a small child does a paint by number, her face lights up the moment she notices a larger pattern from previously disconnected points. Once the larger myth has been cut in pieces that can't be connected, once the plot has been deconstructed and parodied, what remains is a deep sense of boredom. Instead of compelling new stories that have the power to engender dreaming, old stories are recomposed, ridiculed, and ultimately buried. While the Hollywood budget skyrocketed, the cinema rows emptied. Perhaps this is a symptom of a deeper malaise of the mythological imagination.

Following Charles Taylor, the German sociologist Hartmut Rosa describes the result of the modern fracturing of meaning as a loss of resonance.[11] A universe that reflects the communicating God speaks. Without God nature becomes mute and man is imprisoned within self-talk to fill the void. Ultimately, deeper meaning is not discerned in nature, nor in the archetypical stories, nor in the individual's inwardness or the other. Instead, meaning is reduced to brute power. The other human being ceases to be viewed as a reflection of the face of God and turns instead into an object to exploit. There is no answering, as one does not perceive a calling. First, a dialogue is transformed into a monologue. Yet ultimately even the self-talks exhausts itself due to the collapse of resonating relations.

Moreover, this fragmentation of the Judeo-Christian myth is enshrined institutionally. A scientist is free to do yoga but must do so by crossing the clear demarcations between the various segments. Through this process, the person is trained to inhabit various fragments while lacking the possibility of somehow integrating them. The proliferation of esoteric religions reflects the hunger to transcend the bureaucratic rationality of everyday life. However, since these esoteric religions function according to the logic of the individualist consumer market, they fail to provide a communal ritualistic integration.[12] Without the higher ritual anchoring of the fragmented myth, people stumble like a drunkard from one extreme to the other. Conditioned citizens unconsciously embody the fragments and reproduce them through their life. The more sensitive

---

11. Rosa, *Resonanz*.

12. Mellor and Shilling argue that once religion functions according to bio-economic logic, it undermines its own corporeality and ultimately weakens social solidarity (*Sociology of the Sacred*, 24–28).

ones seek to somehow individually integrate the cold and narrow rationalism with the highly individual, anti-institutional spirituality in order to endure a reductionist, mute universe.[13]

The once-unifying Judeo-Christian myth gave rise to various fragmented outlooks on reality that break pieces from their mother and reshape them. Politics, science, and economics keep this secret by obscuring their mythologies and hiding their rituals in plain sight. In prideful moments, they forget their religious origin, and at times their idolatrous nature resurfaces. This is when people break out into open worship of the nation, when science turns into scientism, and economics displays its superstitious nature.[14] These mythologies exemplify a similar structure, but they obfuscate any reference to the transcendent while seeking the same powers and functions in the immanent. In short, they deny being religions while functioning as such. Every myth becomes a reality through the embodiment of it via rituals. Conversely, the Judeo-Christian myth fragments due to alienation from its ritual.

Ritual Alienation

Since rituals are the most basic modes of mediation of human relationality, they can't be destroyed but only replaced by another religious ritual. In the case of our secular order, the central Christian ritual of the Eucharist has been splintered into various elusive rituals, which disguise themselves as non-rituals and seek to satisfy the former unifying experience. The Eucharist is the symbol of human relational nature to God, to nature, to other humans, and to oneself. The Eucharist provides a unifying experience and meaning within the concrete sociopolitical world (see ch. 11). The secular rituals emerge from the recomposition of this unifying ritual and splinter into various reductive sub-rituals. Before rituals are replaced or transformed into something else, they first weaken from within. The crack came, as with the mythological nova effect, from within Christianity itself.

Rituals are most stable when in coherence with myth and everyday behavior. Just as the triangle is the most stable structure in nature, when rituals, myths, and everyday behavior refer to and reflect each other,

---

13. Sam Harris is a prominent example, who publicly pronounces his atheism while also promoting meditation practices in the Western form as Buddhism lite.

14. McCarraher argues that dis-enchanting social forces progressively acquire a divine-like function (*Enchantments of Mammon*).

they create a social stable order. Conversely, when one of these three components is undermined, the entire social structure weakens. Usually, prophets point out basic contradictions with the intent to renew relations and restore a flourishing social order. Throughout history three ideal-type constellations are possible to clarify the relation between myth, ritual, and ethics (everyday behavior).

The prophets in the Bible critiqued the blatant contradictions between public religious statement, cultic practice, and everyday behavior. At times the external performance was in place, yet the prophets accused people of a lack of inner attitude, of failing to grasp the meaning of the ritual or contradicting the ritual behavior through their ethics. Jesus continued in this prophetic vein by pointing out the gap between what the Pharisees professed, their rituals, and obvious hypocrisy in their everyday behavior. Jesus sought to point to the true intention of the Jewish myth and its rituals in order to renew the life of people. He even went beyond this prophetic task and claimed to embody the myth and ritual. One can say that in Jesus, myth and rituals merge within a particular person and become tangibly experienced in the everyday life of people.

The central ritual for all Christians, which symbolizes the continuation of this real divine presence in Jesus, is the Eucharist. Within this ritual, various narrative strands unite (see ch. 11) and culminate in a powerful peak. The social vision of the church flows from the Eucharist. The everyday behavior of Christians also affects how the Eucharist is perceived by those observing from outside. A blatant contradiction weakens the ritual. For example, when the medieval church invited Christians to partake in the experience of a loving, self-giving God and then condoned violence against heretics, this undermined the very core of its logic.

Biblical prophets did not question the need for ritual mediation per se. They only pointed to the fact that contradictions destroy the reality of the ritual by emptying it of its meaning. The Protestant Reformers continued in this vein. Luther's pamphlet on the sacraments continues the vein of discussions at the end of the medieval age on how God relates to humans.[15] The question of what really happens when Christians eat the bread and drink the wine, whether this is a symbolic event or whether transubstantiation really occurs, seems like an exotic but irrelevant argument to modern people. However, the question on the nature of the relation of humans to the world has been central to modern philosophy.

---

15. Luther, *Von der babylonischen Gefangenschaft*.

Since the rejection of sacraments, the mediatory task has shifted to the mind. Epistemology has replaced sacramental theology and practice. Since then, humans have been grasping for certainty through inner introspection, concealing the theological question and attempting to provide answers without reference to theology.[16]

Protestant Reformers sought to restore and correct the mediatory rituals by answering the why question. In their perspective, rituals were warped into a form of magic through which people sought to attain the favor of God. Protestant Reformers sought to explain the significance of sacraments in the biblical story and draw out the consequences for the everyday life of believers. However, by correcting the sacramental abuse of the late medieval church, they also overcorrected by focusing on the spoken word at the expense of the material-bodily aspect of ritual mediation. From a rightful critique that rituals could be abused to exploit people and prevent them from entering into a relationship with God, the path was slippery into suspecting rituals to be unnecessary, meaningless, anachronistic forms. On the heel of rightful critique came a general suspicion of rituals being empty of meaning and a means to exploit and coerce the poor into submission.

Thus ironically, the Protestant critique of ritualistic abuse served as a transition for the general secular suspicion of rituals. The Protestant renewal was disconnected from its context and turned into a secular anti-ritualism perpetuated by Kantian, liberal-economic, and Marxist assaults. Kant dismissed concrete ritual practices as unnecessary in light of a pure ethical religion.[17] The liberal-economic dismissal of ritual arose from the hubris of human autonomy. God does not need rituals; he creates everything ex nihilo. This theological belief was reversed. Accordingly, humans, who are creating the world according to their image, don't need archaic, useless rituals. Rituals are akin to breaks in the well-oiled machine of economic growth. Rituals appear as irrational from a mythological perspective, which views the human as a Promethean God, who attributes value only to that which is useful for him. From this perspective, rituals are useless leftovers from the archaic past. Maximizing of profit required the erasure of rituals. Medieval societies were structured according to many sacred markers of time and spatially oriented around sacred ritual sites. This ritual structure had to be erased in order to create

---

16. Gillespie, *Theological Origins of Modernity*, 255–89.
17. Kant, *Religion innerhalb der Grenzen*.

a malleable and constantly available factory worker, who could guarantee a predictable production process. The sacred becomes real through rituals, which organize space and time in a particular manner and create a perception of reality. By eliminating sacred rituals, the Promethean myth became reality. When God lost the authority to decree a Sabbath rest, machines stepped in by instituting breaks.

The Marxist critique took up the question of the biblical/Protestant critique of empty ritual and essentialized it by declaring ritual a mechanism of concealment. Accordingly, rituals are empty manipulative tools, which obfuscate the true nature of reality and prevent people from emancipating agency toward social justice.[18] In retaining the Judeo-Christian mythological plot while secularizing it at the same time, Marxism performs the same rituals once it takes up political power. Both the liberal-humanist project and the Marxist shaping of sociopolitical reality require rituals that fulfill the same function as the previous religious rituals, yet without being recognized as such.

Due to the inevitability of ritualistic mediation (see ch. 1), the once-unifying ritual of the Eucharist splinters into many pieces. Sociologists of religion and theologians alike glimpse various scattered ritualistic pieces throughout secular society. The difference from the medieval experience is that the ritual is not presented as a given but must be consciously created within the different social segments. Some rituals that are viewed as necessary by the secular powers are implemented in order to secure some minimum mediation of the secular subject. The state needs its civic religion, as Rousseau rightly observed, and some basic rituals in order to safeguard a semblance of solidarity.

Capitalism weaves its enchanting grip around the world not merely by providing goods to the people but by creating the illusion of its own power being divine. As McCarraher remarked, within the capitalist system "money occupies the ontological throne from which God has been evicted."[19] He further elaborated on why Europe was never dis-enchanted. Instead, the former divine was dispersed into the immanent divinities: "The world can *never* be dis-enchanted, not because our emotional or political or cultural needs compel us to find enchantments—though they do—but because the world itself is . . . charged

---

18. Bloch argues that rituals are empty events that solve the problem of deference ("Deference"). Thus, in line with Marxist logic, rituals are replaced with reductive materialist ontology.

19. McCarraher, *Enchantments of Mammon*, 11; emphasis in original.

with the grandeur of God.... The earth is a sacramental place, mediating the presence and power of God, revelatory of the superabundant love of divinity. In Christian theology, another way to say that the world is 'enchanted' is to say that it is *sacramental*."[20]

In order to satisfy the human desire for a larger whole, both spatial and temporal, mythological and ritual mediation are necessary. Once the Eucharist loses its mediatory power, secular liturgies begin to satisfy this innate thirst.[21] Consumer products turn into a fetish, which does not satisfy permanently. Instead, they keep alive the eternal longing and commitment to a global market, which is turned into a deity through divine attributes. Smith lucidly exposes the shopping experience as liturgical mediation of our desires and habits.[22] While capitalism promises to still the thirst for abundance, nationalism created its own myths and rituals to still the desire for security. Popular culture in entertainment and sports keeps alive the myth of universal resonance. In Durkheimian fashion, the crowd experiences its own dynamics as eliciting a grander energy flowing from the center, creating an illusion of a transcendent deity. The parallels between the choreography of a soccer stadium and a Pentecostal-charismatic revival are striking. Sociologists describe this diffusion of the former religious phenomena into a secular mode, which is still mediated and crafted through rituals.[23] Yet these secular rituals acquire their power on the ruins of public religious rituals. Anti-ritualism brought together unlikely allies.

Anti-ritualism has formed a powerful barrier in alliance with secular humanism, Kantian moralism, Marxism, and liberal Protestantism. Moreover, evangelical revivalism insists on the "informal" non-traditional and non-ritualistic mode of worship. This powerful alliance created a blind spot in academia in the study of religion. Asad pointed out that Western scholars projected this Protestant bias onto their study of religion and were unable to see the material-ritual side of other religions, like Islam.[24] Yet ironically, since rituals are inescapable, the non-ritualism must be ritualized in order to remain stable over time. The unifying divinity did not merely migrate but was cut apart into many gods, each one

20. McCarraher, *Enchantments of Mammon*, 11.

21. James K. A. Smith makes a strong case for the inescapable function of ritual ("Secular Liturgies").

22. Smith, *You Are What You Love*, 27–57.

23. Mellor and Shilling, *Sociology of the Sacred*, 21–48.

24. Asad, *Genealogies of Religion*, 40–54.

vying for power and the attention of its worshippers. On the surface, this new polytheism appears harmonious due to the illusion of voluntarism, yet underneath the question of allegiance surfaces.

As the ritualistic structure of secular liberalism becomes visible and the secular myth is exposed through encounter with the ritualistic modes of Hindu, Buddhist, and Islamic civilizations, a romantic desire for ritual awakes. A contrary development is set in motion in scholarly attention to the ritual. The myth is ignored and the ritual is imbued with almost magical power, in the hope of returning to Rousseau's primitive stage. The 60s saw a powerful return of various Eastern rituals. Now it is not uncommon for CEOs to meditate in Buddhist temples and sweat with shamans in the Amazonas. Office clerks dutifully perform their breathing exercises after work. Influencers captivate teenagers about their daily morning rituals on TikTok. Rituals celebrate a powerful comeback and are hailed to reconnect the estranged Western individual to the larger world. We are stumbling back into the primitive stage of ritual for ritual's sake, seeking redemption and connection to the divine through meticulous obedience to ritualistic prescriptions without the larger narrative arc.

Western societies have come full circle. While the biblical prophets sought a vision of integration of ritual, myth, and everyday behavior, these were torn apart throughout modernity. Without the larger orienting myth, secular society stumbles like a drunken man from one partial truth to another. The evaporation of the larger orienting myth and voluntary everyday ethics requires the imposition of rituals, which increasingly function as the steely frame that must hold societies together. In light of the threat to Jewish communities from the Roman Empire, the Pharisees doubled down on strict obedience to rules. Rituals serve as the last bastion of solidarity to prevent the breaking apart of societies. Crumbling empires, before imploding due to the mythological vacuum and increasing resistance to their rules by the citizens, resort to imposing obedience through ritualistic prescriptions. The Roman Empire imposed the cultic worship of the emperor; the Roman Catholic Church forced heretics into a prescribed liturgy; the French Revolutionaries erected the temple to reason; and Auguste Comte, the founder of positivism, realized that rituals in the worship of humanity are necessary. Every totalitarian regime forces its citizens to perform public displays of ritualistic loyalty in order to create the appearance of unity.[25] However,

---

25. Václav Havel, in his essay on the power of the powerless, famously told a story of a grocer who had to put up a sign in the window of his store in praise of the Communist

the rigid imposition of rituals to somehow hide the absence of myth and everyday ethics is doomed to crumble. Rituals for ritual's sake, to uphold the status quo, do not work in the absence of a larger narrative and grounding in everyday actions. When meaning is lacking, it is inevitable that some people will refuse to comply and create a visible sign of difference, breaking the illusion of ritualistic unity.

When both the myth and rituals splinter into many pieces and do not cohere, neither to each other nor to the everyday experience of people, alienation occurs. A secular society still provides pockets of existence where the individual can create a mythological bricolage and particular rituals through which relationality can be experienced. This fragmentation presents an opportunity for entrepreneurs of meaning to exploit this desperate attempt to preserve a small pocket where relationality is not cold and mute but somehow resonating. Offers abound. Whether survivalist nature adventure for bored office clerks, cuddling parties for hedonistic urban dwellers, or instant yoga for busy individualists—all these are attempts within a fragmented society to cling to a moment and practice that could secure a deeper connection beyond the instrumental logic of everyday life. While these attempts could be compared to a floating device in a raging sea, they do not overcome the deeper conditions of alienation, which stem from fragmentations of the original myth.

Within the Judeo-Christian view, *alienation* refers to the separation of man from God and subsequent evil and decay that permeate all relational aspects. Similarly, in the Second Testament humans are described as "alienated from the life of God" (Eph 4:18). Incoherence occurs when an idea is broken from its original semantic context while seeking to preserve its particular meaning.

The Marxist employment of this term as a tool of social critique was initially unquestioned. However, as the idea of alienation gained an ever-widening radius in neo-Marxist social critique, questions of the deeper presuppositions resurfaced. Alienation implies an ideal from which one deviates. Marx did not develop well his normative assumptions on the ideal state of humans in archaic society. He seems to have remained a Romantic follower of Rousseau, assuming an ideal state of

---

regime. Even though everyone knew that this ritual lacked meaning and real reference, it still acquired social force to create the illusion of unity ("Power of the Powerless"). In a similar vein, many enforced rituals during the COVID-19 period were useless from a medical perspective. Instead, they served as powerful rituals of solidarity to create cohesion and solidify the power of the ruling class.

innocence, a paradise-like community where people lived in a classless society in perfect harmony. However, if the ideal is neither God nor an essentialist human nature, does the idea of alienation even make sense? It would appear that Marxism bit off too large of a chunk, which it can't spit back out nor swallow. Various attempts have been made to validate the concept of alienation without recourse to God, in order to keep its ubiquitous usefulness within Marxist theory.

Rahel Jaeggi sought to reinterpret alienation primarily as alienation of the individual within oneself, thus turning attention to personal autonomy. From this focal point, the individual seeks to extend this idea to other types of relations, demonstrating that various modes of relations to the world are already implicit in the self.[26] Hartmut Rosa critiques this definition as too narrow. Accordingly, people often feel alienated, at least in moments when they lose control over their lives. When people fall in love, they are enraptured by a transcendent experience, be it religious or aesthetic.[27] Rosa borrows from Jaeggi the interpretation of alienation as "relation of absence of relation." The various relations that form the network of every person do not resonate with meaning, they do not speak. Instead, they stand across as "mute and/or threatening." Resonance is the opposite of alienation.[28] While I agree with Rosa on his definition of alienation, I ground the evaporating of resonance and thus the rise of alienation primarily in the fragmentation of the unifying mediations of most basic relations. Accordingly, the conditions of modernity are necessary and not sufficient causes for the destruction of a resonating world. Contrary to Rosa, I locate the primary causes in the deeper genealogy of modernity.

Modernity emerges from the recomposition of Judeo-Christian myth and rituals. The once-unifying framework is fragmented, and the once-encompassing order splinters into various patterns. Gillespie lucidly concludes:

> What actually occurs in the course of modernity is thus not simply the erasure or disappearance of God but the transference of his attributes, essential powers, and capacities to other entities or realms of being. The so-called process of disenchantment is thus also a process of reenchantment in and through which both man and nature are infused with a number of attributes

26. Jaeggi, *Entfremdung*, 14.
27. Rosa, *Resonanz*, 302.
28. Rosa, *Resonanz*, 305–6.

or powers previously ascribed to God. To put the matter more starkly, in the face of the long drawn out death of God, science can provide a coherent account of the whole only by making man or nature or both in some sense divine.[29]

One can say that the previous harmonious picture was cut into pieces, and the modern project consists in putting these pieces, which were repainted, into a new coherent order. At its core, our secular age is antagonistic, as glaring contradictions are now not mediated via the Eucharist in the ecclesial space but rather via individual thinkers, who must imagine to be a god, seeing the larger whole. Those who are able to paint the largest horizons of meaning become the guiding figures for the followers. In the past these were shamans and priests. In secular modernity, trust shifts toward experts within the realm of their knowledge.[30] While the priest painted the unifying framework, which encompassed all of reality, the experts are able to represent only their particular area of knowledge. Therefore, a modern man, who accesses reality via the mediation of various experts, always experiences it in part and remains well aware that in the same area there are other experts who might hold a completely different view on the same issue. As Giddens describes, traditional societies provide the mediation of the whole via locally rooted authorities. Modernity abstracts these relations in order to scale the powers and control of the nation-state. This leads to the experience of disembedding: "But the impact of the three great dynamic forces of modernity—the separation of time and space, disembedding mechanisms, and institutional reflexivity—disengages some basic forms of trust relation from the attributes of local contexts."[31]

The unifying sacrament was cut into pieces and spread over a volatile landscape of conflicting ideologies. There is no divine presence via the Eucharist, which invites every person to be lifted up and participate in the divine reality of love. Instead, everyone must reassemble the disparate parts through her own efforts and trust experts, who float like brains in the vat, disconnected from their social relations and particular belongings. Zarathustra's perception of humanity as shattered limbs on the battlefield expresses well the consequence of the prior shattering of

---

29. Gillespie, *Theological Origins of Modernity*, 274.

30. Giddens, *Consequences of Modernity*, 28. Helmut Schelsky analyzed the migration of authority from religious elites to secular professionals (*Arbeit tun die Anderen*).

31. Giddens, *Consequences of Modernity*, 108.

the divine metanarrative.[32] Francisco Goya glimpsed the monsters who arise from the splitting of reason and imagination long before Nietzsche did. What distinguishes the biblical prophets and modern artists is the inability of the latter to point toward redemption and hope.

The story I have told so far could also be told through the genesis of modern art.[33] Picasso's monstrous images; Kurt Schwitters's nonsensical dada stammering; and Fontana's slitting of canvas with a razor blade, naming this destruction of all foundation *The End of God*—all these expressions could be read as convulsions of the last man in light of the shattering of prior myth and rituals. Cubists conveyed monstrosity, the Dada group pointed to meaninglessness and anger. Surrealists perceived irrationality and created a sense of dread and decay. Losing any sense of hierarchy, trash was turned into art, and everyday objects like soup cans or urinals were displayed in museums.

While modern art can be read as a commentary upon the true condition of a world estranged from God, as art itself is also cut off from the larger horizons, it can't point to anything higher. In the absence of any sense of meaning, even the raison d'être of art itself becomes questionable. Even destruction in emancipatory disguise requires an agreed-upon myth. In a truly absurd world, no value judgment is possible. Therefore, an artist can't point out otherness. Everything blurs together into a swampy grey. Within the decaying world filled with the same images, the idea of art as presenting a deeper and higher perception becomes obsolete. The expansion and fracturing of the once-encompassing myth and rituals leads toward confusion, which is a precondition for various social pathologies.

---

32. Nietzsche, *Also sprach Zarathustra*, 136.

33. Hans R. Rookmaaker makes this point in his classic *Modern Art and Death*, 131–225.

CHAPTER 6

Exhaustion and Social Decay

> *Sir, I'm in desperate straits!*
> *The spirits I summoned—*
> *I can't get rid of them.*
>
> —Johann Wolfgang von Goethe,
>   "The Sorcerer's Apprentice"

> *This is the way the world ends*
> *Not with a bang but a whimper.*
>
> —T. S. Eliot, "The Hollow Men"

An alienated society finds itself amid increasing cross-pressures and sinks into dread, madness, and finally exhaustion. The shrunk horizons lead toward a boring myth and create a world collapsing into itself. The splintered rituals evaporate the experience of the whole. The overarching ritual is not given but must now be continuously recreated by the individual. The constant companion to this Sisyphean work is dread of the void. In desperation of this loss of meaning, society descends into madness. The last attempt to craft the self only increases the exhaustion.

Within the atmosphere of fatigue, the very idea of sacred, personal dignity seems like a distant dream, like a fata morgana receding in the fog of amnesia. Our cultural obsession with zombies in dystopian cities is symbolic of the progression toward decay.

Vodka or Opium and Meth?

Visiting my grandparents in the Siberian village of Ivanovka, it was not uncommon to see drunk men lying in the ditches of the dirt road. During holidays, the village descended into a drunken stupor, with women and children bracing themselves amid an increase in violence. My mother's friends were surprised by the fact that her father never beat up her mother. In winter, drinking could be deadly if those who stumbled home took a break in the snow, only to fall asleep, which resulted in freezing to death quickly or, in less worst-case scenarios, just loss of some limbs. A running joke emphasized the need of Russian men for strong women, who could rescue them from freezing to death by carrying them home on their backs. The contrast could not have been more extreme: the exhilarated men, shouting and dancing just moments earlier, would drop into complete exhaustion and passivity. The following day, they would appear like overcooked vegetables. One could compare the stage of late modernity with the image of a drunken Russian: initial intoxication and the burst of high energy eventually lead to complete exhaustion.

However, I believe this living metaphor does not do justice to the simultaneous and contradictory working of forces. Exhilaration did not stop, and yet it dawns on us that without a break from incessant creation of the self, exhaustion is inevitable. As a society, we keep pushing the gas pedal while pulling the hand brake at the same time. Perhaps another example from life in Berlin might bring it into focus.

One day, at 2 a.m., a friend of mine came to my apartment, ringing the doorbell in complete desperation. Upon first glance, I noticed weird symptoms. His limbs were jerking uncontrollably. His eyes were widened, and he seemed in agony. He stuttered something incomprehensible. I understood only: "I am exhausted and must sleep." Yet he could not stand still and was constantly making uncontrollable movements. I accompanied him home. Later on he confided to me that he had taken drugs with accelerating and sedating effects at the same time and that this combination had put him in a spiral of forces, battling inside himself. He felt as if he could drop and die, and yet he felt at the same time as if something was churning inside him, keeping him awake. This experience is akin to torture, as contradictory forces must be endured simultaneously within one body.

Late modernity can't be compared to the effects of vodka. One could also say that it would have been better if late modernity could be compared to someone partying with speed and then smoking a joint in the afterglow. Yet the current condition can't be compared to a rational agent, who acts in a linear fashion. Late modernity is simultaneously on both opium and meth.

Secular liberalism has been like a zombie that can't die. So many funeral speeches have been given. Romantic critics since Rousseau pointed out that the increasing alienation of humans from nature and from each other would lead toward destruction from within. Marx, a Romantic in disguise, added a moral critique by asserting that capitalist societies create social inequality, which tears them apart from within. The neo-Marxists from the Frankfurt School pointed toward the deep inner contradictions of modernity. The instrumental reason prepares the grounds for the reemergence of mythological barbarity. The Enlightenment is pregnant with evil.[1] The more conservative/communitarian thinkers, both from the left and the right, pointed out that excessive liberalism destroys the very precondition of functioning societies: loving, primary communities.[2] Here both the traditional left and conservative thinkers converge in their analyses. These critiques of liberalism are symptomatic descriptions of deeper historical causes, which are ultimately the fracturing of myth and rituals. Exhaustion and subsequent social decay radiate from within this deep center.

Before proceeding, I must consider a powerful rejoinder to my perception of decay, which has been addressed by existentialist thinkers as the condition of the absurd. Some felt the collapsing myth and absent rituals and sought to provide a way forward in light of the collapse of meaning. Albert Camus's reinterpretation of an ancient myth is worth noting, as Camus sought to touch on the deepest cause of the current decay, facing the suicidal consequence head on.

---

1. Adorno and Horkheimer, *Dialektik der Aufklärung*, 1–9.

2. Robert Nisbet is an example of a conservative critique of liberalism (*Quest for Community*). Honneth represents the neo-Marxist Frankfurt School (*Kommunitarismus*).

A Heroic Stance?

Camus sought to establish a way to live in light of nihilism without referring to belief in God. He accepted the Nietzschean proclamation about God's death and in his essay "The Myth of Sisyphus" claimed that "even if one does not believe in God, suicide is not legitimate."[3] First, Camus outlines the reality of the absurd, which arises from the breakdown of any meaningful relationality and a deep insight into contradictory nature of all reality:

> A world that can be explained even with bad reasons is a familiar world. But, on the other hand, in a universe suddenly divested of illusions and lights, man feels an alien, a stranger. His exile is without remedy since he is deprived of the memory of a lost home or the hope of a promised land. This divorce between man and this life, the actor and his setting, is properly the feeling of absurdity. All healthy men having thought of their own suicide, it can be seen, without further explanation, that there is a direct connection between this feeling and the longing for death.[4]

Camus acknowledges the drive for death as a powerful motivational factor in modernity.[5] Camus goes on to resist the Kierkegaardian leap of faith in the light of life's absurdity. Even if the absurd man faces the consequence of the absurd in the form of utter despair, he must not succumb to the temptation of a cowardly escape. Instead, he must face fearlessly the truth without squinting. Camus reconstructs the Judeo-Christian myth. He reinterprets the reality of sin and constructs a road of redemption without any reference to God: "For sin is what alienates from God. The absurd, which is the metaphysical state of the conscious man, does not lead to God. Perhaps this notion will become clearer if I risk this shocking statement: the absurd is sin without God."[6]

Since man must face reality without being able to fall back on any divine support, what remains for Camus is the lone hero: "Thus I draw from the absurd three consequences, which are my revolt, my freedom, and my passion. By the mere activity of consciousness I transform into a

---

3. Camus, *Myth of Sisyphus*, preface (unnumbered page).

4. Camus, *Myth of Sisyphus*, 6.

5. Freud acknowledged this drive for death on the individual level. Igor Schafarewitsch views the death drive as the core motivational, collective force for socialism (*Todestrieb in der Geschichte*).

6. Camus, *Myth of Sisyphus*, 27–28.

Part II: Incurvatus in Se: *The Triumph and Decay of Secular Society*

rule of life what was an invitation to death—and I refuse suicide."⁷ Suicide is a real consequence of life's absurdity. Yet Camus paints a compelling vision of a hero whose mission is to revolt against it through his free choice and exert his passion upon this world. A paradigmatic example of this heroic overcoming of absurdity is the character of Sisyphus, who is viewed by Camus as a tragic hero, who faces the absurdity of his task. Moreover, Camus pictures Sisyphus finding happiness as he descends from the mountain to repeat his task into eternity:

> But Sisyphus teaches the higher fidelity that negates the gods and raises rocks. He too concludes that all is well. This universe henceforth without a master seems to him neither sterile nor futile. Each atom of that stone, each mineral flake of that night-filled mountain, in itself forms a world. The struggle itself toward the heights is enough to fill a man's heart. One must imagine Sisyphus happy.⁸

Today, we encounter this cynical hero in Hollywood films. He is completely disillusioned and after once again saving the world, he sits alone with his whiskey bottle; the last scene suggests a fleeting smile upon his face. While this mythological plot to face the absurd and yet find meaning without recurrence to God seems plausible and even desirable at first glance, I believe it does not hold up under closer inspection. Camus claims tough honesty by facing the world without God, yet he smuggles God in through his unarticulated background.

I agree with Camus that one might find happiness in punishment. Simone Weil rightly viewed punishment as a deep human need to restore meaning and dignity.⁹ Yet punishment presupposes a hierarchy, which must be maintained, and force, which secures the continuation of this task. Sisyphus does not live in an absurd world. He lives in a world maintained by the highest ideal, and within this structure even his repetition acquires meaning due to orientation. Sisyphus knows why he is being punished. His punishment still upholds the larger structured universe, whereas in a truly absurd world, punishment dissolves. What distinguishes the modern man from Sisyphus is the absence of punishment and thus any sort of negativity.¹⁰ The absence of punishment heightens

---

7. Camus, *Myth of Sisyphus*, 42.
8. Camus, *Myth of Sisyphus*, 78.
9. Weil, "Needs of the Soul," 123.
10. Byung-Chul Han describes the excess of positivity as the source of autoimmune

agony. The analogy between Sisyphus and the thoroughly secular man breaks down at this point. If Camus would truly deconstruct his Judeo-Christian background, he would tell a different myth of Sisyphus:

Sisyphus wanders aimlessly, as he is not able to perceive any horizons. He senses exhaustion, yet he is not able to refer to himself, as there is no "I" nor hierarchies that could orient him in space. Sisyphus yells and begs for the privilege to push the stone up, to have the privilege to sense his own agency in a world with delineations of up and down, forward and back. Instead he is left to perceive forces piercing him as he sinks into nothingness and madness. The modern version of Sisyphus resembles Ted in Harlan Ellison's novel, whose final thought encapsulates the finality of nihilism: "I have no mouth and I must scream."[11] One could extend this agony to: "I have no hands and I must scratch. I have no body and I must move. I have no sense of direction and I want to arrive."

Camus unwittingly exposes his own blindness by claiming that it "is always easy to be logical. It is almost impossible to be logical to the bitter end."[12] The nature of the absurd is such that it undermines the very condition of revolt, any energy or will. Camus still views the logical possibility of suicide but revolts against it. It is a revolt that springs from the willful decision of an agent. However, suicide, at least on a collective level, can also occur as the slow draining of the will to live, as gradual exhaustion. Camus lived in a different world, where he could still take for granted the Judeo-Christian thick background in constructing his absurd hero. Nietzsche was far more insightful in portraying the last man as an exhausted, porous being who does not resist. Suicide can't be avoided through the individual act of protest if the person does not inhabit a larger myth and is not upheld through rituals. Once the person is sedated, suicide is perceived as a redemptive falling asleep. Suicide does not present itself as an individual option but rather descends upon individuals as an atmosphere of social exhaustion.

Exhaustion

Exhaustion is the diagnosis of our age. Psychologists and economists alike point to the self-exploitation of people within the neoliberal order

---

sickness, which manifests itself as exhaustion (*Müdigkeitsgesellschaft*, 57).
11. Ellison, *I Have No Mouth*.
12. Camus, *Myth of Sisyphus*, 8.

as they internalized the dictum of self-authenticity.[13] Sociologists point to the systemic acceleration and external pressures upon the individual to function within a society that is constantly in flux.[14] Philosophers like Byung-Chul Han describe the spirit of our age as exhaustion due to the disappearance of boundaries. Alain Ehrenberg put it succinctly: "Depression is the guardrail of the person with no roadmap."[15] Within such a total positivity, the individual turns against oneself, resulting in neuronal exhaustion. The resulting symptoms of this exhaustion are the prevalence of depression and burnouts. The absence of moral boundaries led not toward more sex but toward an increasingly asexual society, wherein young people retreat into their safe zones, both physical and mental cocoons.[16] Humans have created a world of safety and convenience, which works back on humans and undermines their fertility.[17]

This diagnosis of Western contemporary societies lacks a deeper understanding of historical causes. Therefore, the surface analysis suggests a quick cure. Thus books on how to solve exhaustion only deepen the condition. It is like attempting to extinguish fire by tossing gasoline on it. Why do people exploit themselves and are not able to resist the accelerating forces? Why are people not able to erect boundaries and protect themselves from the excess of the possible? Byung-Chul Han points to the deeper causes without further espousing them. According to him, the loss of religious faith leads toward the "lack of being."[18] Han points to the deeper ontological conditions of the current exhaustion, which ultimately result from the deeper causes of crumbling mediating myths and rituals.

Within my assessment plot so far, I have sketched how the breakup of the Judeo-Christian myth and the disappearance of rituals leads toward alienation. Alienation as a sense of dried-out relation to the larger whole leads toward a sense of loss and the shrinking of the individual. The universe is perceived as vast, empty, and cold. Giddens points out that as individuals and societies, we rely on the givenness of the world as the pre-reflexive background. Yet this meaningful web of relations is

---

13. Zuboff, *Age of Surveillance Capitalism*.
14. Rosa, *Weltbeziehungen im Zeitalter*.
15. Ehrenberg, *Weariness of the Self*, 233.
16. Lukianoff and Haidt, *Coddling of American Mind*.
17. Colino and Swan, *Count Down*.
18. German: "Mangel an Sein" (Han, *Müdigkeitsgesellschaft*, 35).

undermined through alienation. Giddens refers to this glue of our social world as *ontological security*:

> The phrase refers to the confidence that most humans beings have in the continuity of their self-identity and in the constancy of the surrounding social and material environments of action. A sense of the reliability of persons and things, so central to the notion of trust, is basic to feelings of ontological security; hence the two are psychologically closely related.[19]

We take for granted other persons, objects, and our experience of time as a continuous world, which guarantees stability. This givenness is necessary for life as routinized cooperation and provides us with the condition to project patterns upon the external world. In a world that would constantly change radically, everything would become unstable and unreliable, threatening our very biological organism, which needs time in order to adapt to new environments.

Giddens traces the emergence of this foundational security, which undergirds all healthy interactions on the micro level, to early childhood. The routinized loving care of the parent instills into a child a pattern of trust, which is then transferred to all other relations. However, on the larger social scale, Giddens points out that religious cosmologies and rituals have a stabilizing effect, which creates a perception of meaningful continuity:

> The meanings of routine activities lie in the general respect or even reverence intrinsic to tradition and in the connection of tradition with ritual. Ritual often has a compulsive aspect to it, but it is also deeply comforting, for it infuses a given set of practices with a sacramental quality. Tradition, in sum, contributes in basic fashion to ontological security in so far as it sustains trust in the continuity of the past, present, and future, and connects such trust to routinized social practices.[20]

Giddens describes the change from premodernity to the modern world through destabilization. Premodern trust was established through kinship relations, the local community, religious cosmologies, and tradition. For the sake of rapid social change and economic profit, these stable relations were disembedded from their locality. Modern trust relies on personal relations, which must be continuously upheld

19. Giddens, *Consequences of Modernity*, 92.
20. Giddens, *Consequences of Modernity*, 105.

by individual choices. Moreover, abstract systems of experts must be trusted, and religious myths are replaced with future-oriented utopias. One of the benefits has been an immense rise of wealth. The cost has been a deep crack in the prevalent modes of ontological security. In the modern world, nothing is given—neither family nor local community, neither religion nor tradition. Everything is malleable and held in constant flux for the sake of possible networks, which are deemed as innovation. Nothing remains in its proper place but can always be recreated by the divine entrepreneur. Ultimately, the disappearance of ontological security creates a precondition for deep insecurity about the world and self: "If basic trust is not developed or its inherent ambivalence not contained, the outcome is persistent existential anxiety. In its most profound sense, the antithesis of trust is thus a state of mind which could be best summed up as existential *angst* or *dread*."[21]

The initial excitement might persist as long as one sees the creative potential that emerges from the destruction of the given. However, the Nietzschean madman is filled with dread at the moment when the consequences of destruction of the highest ideal begin to dawn on him. Dread overtakes the individual who realizes that he is not able to contain the forces that have escaped from Pandora's box. Why is the sense of persistent dread both the precondition and result of madness? In order to elucidate the relation between dread and madness, it is crucial to differentiate dread from fear.

Individual fear arises as a signal of concrete danger. The human body responds instinctively. Fear causes humans to switch into flight, fight, or freeze modus. Yet these instinctive responses are subject to evaluation in any given social context. If I react instinctively and everyone around me remains calm, I will most likely register my initial reaction of fear as a false alarm. In other words, the feeling of fear is mediated. We also learn when and how to fear. In stoic, heroic societies, fear is viewed as something to overcome. To the contrary, as Frank Furedi laments, within the last decades a culture of fear has been superimposed upon Western societies, which arises from "worship of safety."[22] Furedi rejects the culture of fear as it creates a fatalistic mood, wherein people are viewed as not in control of their actions and the entire society descends into a sense of powerlessness.[23]

21. Giddens, *Consequences of Modernity*, 100; emphasis in original.
22. Furedi, *Culture of Fear*, 8.
23. Furedi, *Culture of Fear*, 170.

While Furedi views this systemic construction of anxiety as an aberration from the true spirit of Western liberalism, Bell points out that the diffusion of fear into every crack of the social fabric is inherently useful for the system to remain stable. The birth of liberalism was accompanied by Hobbes's analysis on the usefulness of fear to instill loyalty into subjects. When a sense of threat is constantly maintained by the state, citizens automatically rely on the authority of the state to protect them. Thus continuous fear is necessary to awake the trust of citizens and legitimize the subsequent authority of the state. However, fear is not merely diffused top down by the sovereign ruler. Instead, it is constantly inscribed through and by the citizens themselves. Bell concludes:

> The politics and culture of fear that envelop us is not the intrusion of an extra-political force kept at bay by the liberal political order. To the contrary, liberalism needs fear and so it produces it, and it does so not simply by the imposition of the heavy, disciplinary hand of the state and its apparatuses, but by the velvet touch (one that we even desire!) of the vast array of technologies of the self that constitute the complex space of civil society.[24]

While liberalism as political form promises to liberate its citizens from fear, it needs fear in order to legitimize both its political and economic power. Systemic anxiety is good for business—at least in the short term. People who freeze due to the constant systemic pounding of fear turn into docile subjects who can be "cured" by the crowds of secular professionals.

Flight as the second reaction to fear leads toward all types of addictions, whether drugs, gambling, or workaholism. Perversely, it also boosts economic growth, which is gained at the cost of the parasitical destruction of those caught in the rat race. Drugs create new markets. Gambling creates new incentives for work. Work can serve as a temporary diversion from deeper naggings of fear. In comparison to the reactions of freeze or flight, the most powerful engine of modernity is the fight modus. Fear is converted into anger, and anger is known to be the motivational force leading toward frenetic hyperactivity.

One feels in control of fear as long as one is able to act. Fear turns into dread the moment one senses a loss of agency. Loss of agency is experienced when the sense of fear is decoupled from a particular object and a particular moment. A sense of constant danger everywhere,

---

24. D. Bell, *Divinations*, 12.

an overwhelming, haunting feeling from inside and out—this is dread. Furedi hints at the deeper roots of the culture of fear, which he views in the loss of the wider historical consciousness. Once systemic fear acquires the aura of the actual due to loss of the larger myth and rituals that safeguard ontological security, dread sets in as Damocles's inevitable sword, hanging over each one by the single hair of a horse's tail. Without a mythological orientation, fear can't be grasped; and without a ritual, there is no way to escape it. Cicero rightly concluded that dread spoils any sense of enjoyment, as it kills any possibility of rest. Any organism, whether biological or social, needs a time of recuperation. Rest is the protective barrier against madness, as Chesterton lucidly observed: "It is the happy man who does the useless things; the sick man is not strong enough to be idle. It is exactly such careless and causeless actions that the madman could never understand; for the madman (like the determinist) generally sees too much cause in everything. . . . If the madman could for an instant become careless, he would become sane."[25]

Letting go of the incessant compulsion to establish causal links between everything requires ontological security and trust. This compulsion arises when the givenness of the world breaks apart. Disorientation paired with constant pressure to gather the broken pieces without knowing the why and how, without the larger orientation pattern, creates a deep contradiction, which presents itself as absurd. The absurd eliminates any sense of meaning as all hierarchies are flattened and one does not know where to focus. Yet one must somehow make sense in order to ease the pervasive dread. The simultaneous focus everywhere overheats our selective mechanism, which always reduces complexity. Without the ability of this prior trust to accept complexity before selecting and framing parts of it, the mental capacity is overloaded. As Chesterton put it:

> Poetry is sane because it floats easily in an infinite sea; reason seeks to cross the infinite sea, and so make it finite. The result is mental exhaustion. . . . To accept everything is an exercise, to understand everything a strain. The poet only desires exaltation and expansion, a world to stretch himself in. The poet only asks to get his head into the heavens. It is the logician who seeks to get the heavens into his head. And it is his head that splits.[26]

---

25. Chesterton, *Orthodoxy*, 7.
26. Chesterton, *Orthodoxy*, 6.

The compulsion to squeeze all of reality into analytical thinking without the intuitive sense of the whole leads toward strikingly similar patterns between schizophrenia and modernity. The person suffering from schizophrenia becomes a mirror of the shattered mythological pieces. It dawns on both the philosopher and the madman that the modern world is split open in a myriad of chasms that can't be reconciled. Yet the madman is more honest about it. Immanuel Kant pretends to transcend the antinomies of reason by delegating them to different uses of reason and by positing the realm of consciousness, where pure and practical reason, naturalistic causation and freedom, are conjoined. Gillespie demonstrated painstakingly that the medieval discussion on the nature of God migrated to the discussion of anthropology and later to nature as well.[27] At the core stands the question of necessity and freedom. While early Reformers like Erasmus and Luther could disagree on this question, they still had a larger shared framework. However, the subsequent discussion between Descartes and Hobbes shows the widening gap, wherein man is increasingly viewed as part of deterministic nature. Immanuel Kant's solution is not satisfactory. A basic contradiction remains at the heart of modernity, while the mediatory modes of faith and sacraments fade away. The individual can be viewed as either a godlike subject or dirt-like object at the same time. A schizophrenic person embodies this modern anthropology and swings between megalomania and wormhood. Zarathustra's nightmare of spread limbs is at the heart of this modern dread. Madness and modernism mirror and reinforce each other.[28] The prideful shattering of unifying myth and rituals by philosophers lays the tracks for systemic insanity, upon which individuals slide into schizophrenia. The parts can't be gathered into a whole, and philosophies in the wake of Hegel, which attempt to do just that, create a structure for totalitarianism, an even worse nightmare.

This problem was recognized by the Romantics. The paradox can't be gathered together in the analytical mode of philosophy. They rightly sought to recover the intuition and the foundational role of myth, the arts, and poetry to point to the absolute. However, the Romantics were

---

27. Subsequent summary is based on Gillespie, *Theological Origins of Modernity*, 255–89.

28. This insight is based on Louis Sass's analysis of modernity's structure. Sass discerns at the core of secular modernity contradictory and clashing modes of experience, which form the patterns for various psychological pathologies (*Madness and Modernism*, 270).

not able to offer an alternative to the shattered Judeo-Christian myth nor to establish unifying rituals. Instead, they elevated the individual genius and will to the divine throne. And through this fateful move, they influenced the Hegelian image of a philosopher, who knows by overlooking the entirety of human history.

Wouter Kusters seeks to reappraise the modern madman by viewing him as akin to the ancient prophet. The madman points to the deeper reality by engaging in modes of performance that upset normal perception. The person suffering from schizophrenia is personifying the fractured modern reality, in which a sense of the given reality is shattered. What is perceived as mental illness in fact mirrors a hidden reality. Kusters makes references to prophetic literature, as the prophet was often in his thought patterns outside of the majority consensus.[29] While I agree with Kusters's intention to rehabilitate the madman from his captivity, without the deeper background and community, madness will not contribute to any new insight.[30] The prophets operated in a world of depth. Their visions could be discarded as false, but generally, they were not dismissed as illusions. Moreover, prophets operated within communities who could at least test their visions. To the contrary, the modern madman is simply dismissed and drugged into a comatose condition in order to "function" on the empirical surface of reality. Without the social body of the church, where myth and ritual offer a place for someone who envisions strange images of depth, the prophet ends up either homeless on the street or locked up in the psychiatric ward.

The church I currently attend in Berlin welcomes people with "mental illness." While they are viewed in the secularized society as problems to be fixed, we as a community have observed them employing their perceptive sensibility in order to point to the deeper layers of reality at times. As leaders we have sought to take their cues seriously. A secular psychiatrist who lives in the same block as our street church confided to me that her years of experience have highlighted the centrality of communities where mentally ill people can experience a connection to other people. These relations create intersubjective webs of differences, which are continuously tested. Without these networks, the one dealing with

---

29. Kusters, *Philosophy of Madness*, 626–34.

30. MacIntyre rightly observed, critiquing the absolute doubt of Descartes, that the epistemological ideal of doubting all beliefs, independent of reference to the historical and autobiographical context "is not meaningless; but it is an invitation not to philosophy, but to mental breakdown" ("Epistemological Crises," 12).

Exhaustion and Social Decay 133

mental illness drowns in utter isolation. The idealized notion of the mad prophet can be uttered only by the sane.[31]

As Chesterton rightly pointed out, one can't reason against insanity, because insanity is in itself reasonable, like a very narrow circle. Therefore, "insanity is proved not by any error in their argument, but by the manifest mistake of their whole lives."[32] Exhaustion as a living condition, both individual and collective, both mental and physical, is a tangible proof of madness. In utter exhaustion, even words sound hollow and one is too tired to think. This condition is the strongest final living argument against the secular hubris of perpetual motion and negation of the given sacred patterns.

Late modernity can be compared to opposing drugs. The drive to accelerate is constant due to the absence of constraints as any larger patterns and given rituals are shattered. There are no givens; everything is in flux. It seems that the remedy is so simple: if one is exhausted, one should rest. Rest presupposes ontological trust that the world will not crumble and that the gods do not need to be fed (see ch. 2). In short, resting implies a myth where each person is invited to rest by an all-powerful God. However, if the individual is made to be god, upon whom everything depends, then rest is not an option. All totalitarian ideologies of the twentieth centuries sought to eliminate the holy ritual of rest. One could also add the neoliberal elimination of Sabbath. Within the myth where rest is commanded, a shared ritual of rest leads toward rejuvenation of entire community. Rest allows for contemplation and a higher plane from which to evaluate everyday life. The Babylonian myths return in a new disguise. This time the worshipper is not under constant pressure to feed the gods. Instead, the individual has become god and therefore carries the divine burden of universal responsibility.[33] Perpetual motion remains as the only viable plot. Communal rest is unthinkable if the survival of both nature and the human species depends on the perpetual self-exploitation of humans. Consequently, as Byung-Chul Han remarked, today everyone is exhausted in his own

---

31. Chesterton, *Orthodoxy*, 5.
32. Chesterton, *Orthodoxy*, 13.
33. Perhaps like no other philosophical ethics, Hans Jonas articulated in his book *Das Prinzip Verantwortung* the universal, holistic responsibility of humans in light of various global threats. Due to the absence of God, it becomes the sole responsibility of humans to preserve the earth from environmental collapse and nuclear threat. Although well meaning, Jonas prepared a mythological ground for collective exhaustion.

lonely way, without a shared space and time.³⁴ This type of exhaustion isolates, whereby people lose the ability to face the other and communicate. Everyone sinks into his own mental and physical exhaustion within his own cell, amid the broken pieces of the former myth and ritual.

Social Decay

Exhaustion can be described as a state of energy depletion. The symptoms of this state are various modern pathologies like depression and burnout. The final stage of exhaustion is the lack of will to live, which can be observed through physical passivity. The baby boomers, who won the sexual revolution, who tore down the seemingly outdated religious boundaries and pushed society toward a liberating utopia, are surprised that society without restraints produced a burst of energy for only a brief moment. The long-term result has been exhaustion and individual retreat. Within the pervasive social exhaustion, individuals retreat into their own cocoon, cuddle into the fetus position, and fall asleep. This is not a willful, heroic suicide but a cowardly retreat into the slow extinguishing of life.

Both Plato and the apostle Paul employed the body as a metaphor for society. I believe it is a better social imaginary than a machine, as it lends an organic quality. Surface descriptions of social decay abound on popular and academic levels. Mourning and nostalgia set in, similar to Treebeard's words in *The Lord of the Rings*: "For the world is changing: I feel it in the water, I feel it in the earth, and I smell it in the air. I do not think we shall meet again."³⁵ While the explanations of the causes of this decay and prescriptions differ, the symptoms can be perceived unanimously. Similar to the body, the causes for the external symptoms lie deeper, under the skin and tissues. These causes can't be perceived through a quick empirical survey. I might perceive chest pain, yet only deeper analysis might reveal that I have had a heart attack.

I trace the surface decomposition to the central core. Crumbling myths and ritual alienation produce exhaustion and finally lead toward annihilation. The individual can't experience self-agency. Once each person was lifted up and made unique through the Judeo-Christian myth and rituals. Once these crumble, so does the idea of the sacred individual. The death of the subject is a result of both civilizational exhaustion and

---

34. Han, *Müdigkeitsgesellschaft*, 57.
35. Tolkien, *Lord of the Rings*, 3:281.

the impossibility of imagination. According to Nietzsche, the self dissolves amid life forces. Marxists negated the self by declaring individuality an illusion and subsumed it under class consciousness. Freud lucidly exposed the rational self as driven by deeper biological drives. Without divine anchoring, humans are just beasts, slaves of larger evolutionary forces. Once the manifesting relationality to the divine breaks, the idea of the sacred individual can be easily deconstructed. Once the individual can't be experienced or imagined, the ideal of individual dignity collapses. Like a sinking ship, the suction pulls everything around to the ground. Social decay is a mere symptom of this deeper collapse.

Western societies have been centered around the idea of sacred dignity. Once the core collapses, we begin to sense the shock waves on the surface. Society begins to decay from the inside out, which explains why the effects are delayed. One could also compare this decay to a dying tree. Even though the roots of the tree begin to disconnect from its nourishing ground and the dryness moves upward, the external foliage might still appear as in full blossom. By the time one begins to notice leaves losing their color and strength, the decomposition is further along than one might suspect. I will now attempt to show how the decay extends from the inside out.

Individual dignity is an embodied idea. It exists as an ideal only insofar as it can be experienced within one's own society, and even extended to the enemy, as seen in the Geneva Convention. Therefore, the Western outrage concerning crimes of humanity, as in the Rwandan genocide, or more recently the Russian-Ukrainian war, or the torture carried out by US servicepeople in the Abu Ghraib prison, still points to the presence of consciousness that all human beings have a spark of divinity in them. Both the left and the right sides of the political spectrum like to point out the prevailing harm done by the other to human dignity. However, human dignity is increasingly torn into ever-smaller political fractions and hereby loses its universality.

The Left likes to point to human dignity and the subsequent human rights of refugees and cultural minorities, while the Right seeks to protect the dignity of the unborn. This disagreement is not per se on the underlying normative assumption but how to balance it in complex situations. As long as these discussions occur, the underlying normative assumption is upheld. However, increasingly political fractions accuse the other of using the argument of human dignity in order to gain power. A deep suspicion arises that a reference to the most holy is nothing other than a mere power game. In order to win the war, both parties are ready to use the holy as a means for short-term gains. Through this desacralization the holy loses its status as set apart, as untouchable, and is reduced to a mere tool. The irony of culture wars is that while each group accuses the other of using human dignity merely as pretense, both bemoan the increasing instrumental treatment of humans.

While the Right and the Left have different explanations and selective interpretations of whose dignity is under attack, they would agree that increasingly humans are treated instrumentally. Both traditional left-leaning intellectuals and some conservatives[36] point out that the goal of maximizing profit by any means, with ravaging market forces, uproots people and produces malleable robots who are robbed of their human dignity. The prize of the economic success of the twentieth century has been bought with the very core that defines us as human. We have sold our souls for our material well-being. The ideal of human dignity erodes as humans lose the very central relations that define what it means to be human. Society is transformed into a cold machine upheld by spinning wheels. Robert Putnam summarized the collapse of community under the fitting title of his book: *Bowling Alone*.

The once-revolutionary practices of proto-capitalism, invented in monasteries and scaled to success as regional economy, got severed from their local roots. With the disappearance of ritual as a bulwark, the economy was uprooted and elevated into an apersonal apparatus, thus devaluing local relations and perverting meaningful exchanges.[37] Marxist insight on the acid effects of capitalism on genuine human relations has been demonstrated by various scholars. The erosion of social capital and deeper trust stems from malleable individuals, detached from any meaningful embedding, who serve the capricious whims of the unpredictable divinity called "the market."[38] Increasingly, abstract corporations, not accountable to anyone, exploit the masses of people. A sense of mutual obligation, which existed through the shared ritual of the Eucharist, has long been replaced with the cold logic of exploitation. Thus the same

36. E.g., Nisbet, *Quest for Community*.

37. Karl Polanyi described in his masterpiece *The Great Transformation* the uprooting of local economies through intentional market economy and the modern nation-state.

38. Richard Sennett extends the analysis of Karl Polanyi by describing how the new capitalism of the twenty-first century created a global iron cage, which forms the individual in a particular manner, uprooting him further and demanding a constant availability (*Culture of New Capitalism*).

proto-capitalist practices, once detached from ritual soil and mutual obligations, turn into tools of subjugation. Slowly, the deeper imaginary of the sacred person at the center, uniting the diversity around it, is transformed into a friend-foe binary.

The more progressive Left in the tradition of the Frankfurt School view the human dignity of various minorities, whether cultural, religious, or sexual, under threat from the majority. Conversely, the Right and conservatives view the human dignity of the majority under attack. The good news amid the raging cultural war is the fact that both sides still operate with the presupposition that humans have inherent value, which must be defended. However, decay sets in when this dignity can't be extended as universally given but begins to be granted under specific conditions.

At this point, the paradoxical *unum et pluribus* tilts toward either tribalism or suffocating totalitarian order. A pluralistic society is a living organism that requires continuous equilibrium between unity and diversity. However, diversity can't exist without a minimum consensus of shared identity. The foundation must grant that all members of society share the same human nature. Based on this common nature, differences can be distinguished and appreciated.

Neither totalitarian order nor anarchistic tribalism is desirable. The paradoxical simultaneous existence of unity and diversity can be rooted in the idea of human dignity, as it provides a framework that is inclusive enough to create a broad sense of oneness while allowing for particular differences. Once the idea of human dignity weakens, various groups begin to perceive the same social phenomenon from diametrically opposing views.[39] The progressive Left seeks to promote diversity of various sexual, cultural, and religious identities. Conservatives point out that what really matters is diversity of opinion, independent of particular racial or sexual identities. Decay occurs at the moment when both sides are not able to extend generosity to the other due to inherent human dignity. It is then a slippery slide from the other losing humanness to being considered the enemy.

---

39. Schlesinger warned already in 1991 that a pluralistic society, the equilibrium of *e pluribus unum*, could be torn apart from the extreme Left and the extreme Right. The danger of the Left lies in the fracturing of majority consensus through identity politics, and the danger of the Right lies in excluding diversity by creating a homogenous totality (*Disuniting of America*). However, my main critique of Schlesinger consists in his blind spot concerning liberalism. I maintain that the main problem lies not with the fringe extremes but with the weakness of liberalism itself due to its inner unresolved contradictions (Dik, "Dilemmata und die Zukunftsfähigkeit").

A society that loses a sense of shared broad and strong identity is unable to welcome a stranger. When the centripetal forces weaken, centrifugal forces accelerate. What makes us different is enriching only as long as we are all aware that we have something uniting us. In the absence of a uniting bond, difference turns out to be threatening. In decaying pluralistic societies, diversity is increasingly viewed as something dangerous, and people begin to think in terms of a zero-sum game. These dynamics are most likely to accelerate with the decline of economic growth.

In a tribal society, intergroup cooperation decreases. The idea of human dignity can't be extended toward all citizens if increasingly large groups feel that state institutions are selective and not impartial. In an exhausted society, every individual and group turns inward and is primarily concerned with its own survival. Trust in state institutions as stabilizing factors of the public good decreases across all Western countries. This lack of trust in institutions to fairly distribute goods and services only further exacerbates the tendency to seek gains for one's own group. Paired with the popular academic myth in social sciences, which leaked into the streets, that at the core, society is manifested through relations of power, the general direction of every individual and group turns to: How can I play the system for my own advantage? Once the system allows for too many free riders, who do not pay into it but rather only take out, the system will inevitably break down.

Meritocracy, which once was a powerful tool to enable the working class to improve their lives through education and hard work, turns into a cynical empty ritual to favor the already privileged. Whether meritocracy leads toward social flourishing or the widening of inequality does not depend on this mechanism alone but on the level of solidarity within society.[40] Meritocracy is empowering in a society where every person is believed to be the bearer of God's image and solidarity between people from various socioeconomic classes is high. The medieval church managed to hold powerful elites accountable. Once this common reference to the higher authority disappears, the chasm between elites and commoners grows. The moment arrogant elites openly despise people, resentment begins to fester from the bottom up. With the return of the pre-Christian ontology of inequality, meritocracy turns into a shibboleth of the ruling

---

40. Thus I claim that both Sandel's critique and Wooldridge's defense of meritocracy are justified. Whether meritocracy enhances or reduces the common good depends on the larger background of social solidarity. This social capital is in itself not economic or political but grows out from religious practices, as I demonstrated in ch. 4.

elites to preserve their power.⁴¹ At this point the system breaks down in providing porosity for the lower classes to ascend the social latter.

Once a large swath of people begin to suspect that the current economic or political system is rigged and is in some fundamental way against them, they lose trust in complex pluralism and open themselves up to simple solutions offered by demagogues. Already Plato pointed out that the weakness of democracy lies in the susceptibility of people to charlatans. In a decaying society people are too tired to think and hope. Instead, they fall for the sweet promises of immediate relief. With every lie and condescending, patronizing gesture of the elites, the exhaustion of the masses increases and the resentment toward "the rich man north of Richmond" grows.⁴² Neither Hitler nor Stalin could have abused their societies to that degree without prior exhaustion and their complete resignation.

Distrust and a "hunkering down" mentality,⁴³ starting from immediate neighborhoods and extending to national politics, weaken the sinews of a pluralistic society, which depend on trust and cooperation. However, a charitable gesture to extend human dignity and good will to the other requires risk, as one does not know whether this trust will be reciprocated. Risk involves a higher energy level. For this reason exhaustion causes one to remain within the known boundaries of one's own tribe. For an exhausted individual and society, elaborate arguments that purport that freedom of speech and a diversity of opinions are in the long term a better strategy to solve complex problems are not convincing.⁴⁴ One must have a spark of energy to take the other seriously before one can begin to think about successful strategies. An exhausted society can't trust, as trust requires taking the risk to be vulnerable and delegate control to the other. Without such trust, critical discourse can't emerge, and complex problems, which require as many brains and perspectives as possible, can't be solved. Society descends into ideological currents, which further isolate groups from one another.

41. This has been the critique of Sandel (*What Money Can't Buy*).

42. The song "Rich Men North of Richmond" by Oliver Anthony became a viral hit overnight and hit the nerve of many people, who felt unjustly treated by the political and media elites.

43. Putnam has found that rapid diversification of neighborhoods initially leads to a "hunkering down" mentality and erosion of trust ("*E Pluribus Unum*").

44. Mill's classical arguments for freedom of speech presuppose a thick culture of shared values and the psychological state of people who are committed to pursuing truth (*On Liberty*, 49–51).

To the contrary, pluralistic discourse in politics, science, and economics, the continuous wrestling for the best solutions to complex problems, is the life elixir of all successful Western democracies. Pluralism rests on the firm belief in human dignity. Cracks in the foundation lead toward growing tribalism and the inability to find the best solutions. The failing of pluralistic discourse always leads toward disastrous social consequences and immense human suffering. Human perception is always limited. Even if one solution was appropriate at one particular moment, it must be adjusted according to the changing nature of the problem. Ideological closure of science and politics results in simplistic perception and the implementation of approaches that either do not solve the problem or make it even worse. Increasing ad hominem attacks and destruction of the other in politics and science point to the deterioration of pluralistic discourse and the corresponding fossilization of the social body.

The loss of inner elasticity leads toward the inability either to affirm a unique identity or to welcome a stranger. Both European and North American societies are torn by the issue of immigration. The right-wing parties favor walls, while the left-wing parties imagine John Lennon's song coming true. The inability to come to a consensus betrays a deeper failure to agree on the higher ideal, which might make the way for a solution. Both for the Right and the Left, the immigrant becomes a fetish to promulgate the preoccupation with their own identity. For the political right, the stranger serves as a means toward actualization of self through othering the other. If what was once considered solid has evaporated, the stranger accentuates the threat of the void inside. A host who is unstable in his own identity is therefore unable to invite the stranger in. Perhaps the closing of borders across Europe and increasing soaring support for right-wing parties is just an admission of the inner weakness of Europe. The leftist theorists in the wake of the Frankfurt School theorize immigration as continuation of the eternal struggle between oppressed and oppressors. Ultimately, the issue is not about concrete people seeking a better life, about the immigrant's culture or religious identity, but about realizing a social utopia through the masses of the new proletariat. The perverse game of using the poor for fueling social strife does not stop.[45]

The decaying society loses its ability to be open toward and welcome the stranger and new ideas. Instead, it turns inward and descends into pathological unresolved conflicts. Tribalism and an increasing social

---

45. One of the most recent examples of this approach is Naika Foroutan, *Postmigrantische Gesellschaft*.

and moral decay are the results. Countless immigrants who arrived in Germany with great hopes and aspirations turned to me disillusioned and disgusted by the decay they perceived in Germany, asking for explanations. A decaying society either turns to stone due to fear or pretends to be completely open due to naïveté, which grew out of security and wealth. The right proportion of closure and openness, which creates life, can come only from the ability to refer to an ideal. The absence of an ideal leads toward frantic, irrational extremes and the tearing apart of anything sane in the middle.

The loss of the ideal leads toward the loss of the real. If individuals and groups do not have a myth and ritual to discern a hierarchy of values, then they become simply overwhelmed by myriad possibilities of focus and information overload. However, the complexity and conflict soon take over, and another criteria for hierarchy must be negotiated. If the throne of God, the embodiment of truth, beauty, and goodness, is void, another deity ascends to the throne. For the last decades, the ancient myth of brute force experienced a resurrection in literary theory and French philosophical departments, leaking out into the rest of society. When truth, beauty, and goodness disappear, the cold logic of power grips the world and everything is reduced to brutish physical force.

In a society governed by the cold logic of power, scientific enterprise, which relies on a commitment to pursue truth for the sake of the common good, can then be perverted into its caricature. Once mythological soil for scientific practices erodes, it becomes a mere tool to buttress claims of power. Science as the fragile search for truth turns into a strong, positive, and democratically legitimate support of those in power, losing its impartiality and turning into a whore, providing results to the higher bidder. Politics turn into coercive manipulation when belief in the unifying peaceful logos vanishes. Without the idea of a mutual enriching exchange, economics descend into brutal exploitation and slavery. Without the divine spark in each person, education becomes a mere tool of the powerful elite to indoctrinate their subjects into machines.

Our sense of reality is mediated through myth and rituals. The breakdown of the larger myth and rituals is felt as a loss of reality, leading to exhaustion. With the breakdown of the larger religious reality humans must compensate for this loss. The prior coherence between the objective larger reality and the subjective inner dimension is no longer a given. As Thomas Nagel puts it, the religious question remains, while the answer is discarded. Nagel goes on to examine various responses to the religious question without God.[46] In this chapter, I went further than Nagel and sought to show that these basic relations to the larger whole, to nature, to others, and to the self are not possible to reconstruct without the larger Judeo-Christian myth and given ritual. Surely we can fall back on other myths and rituals, yet they would also entail a different social order, as I will show in the subsequent chapters.

The creature that most strikingly symbolizes this prevalent exhaustion, this sense of living without life, is the zombie. "[The] zombie is the icon of the zeitgeist."[47] John Vervaeke traces the prevalence of the zombie in the twenty-first century to the perversion of the Judeo-Christian metanarrative: "[The] zombie has evolved to become a representation of the loss of the sacred canopy traditionally provided by Christianity, and . . . its features have evolved along the fault lines of this loss, representing a world that no longer explains itself, nor provides us instruction for how to live within it."[48]

The human person created in the image of God participates in God's goodness, beauty, and truth through worship. Conversely, the zombie is empty of any meaning, desiring to fill this emptiness by devouring others, yet unable to ever be satisfied. The zombie is completely cut off from the environment around him and is not able to enter any meaningful relationships. Instead, the zombie merely drifts with others, neither dead nor alive, always hungry to devour the other's brain. The zombie has lost its uniqueness and creative ability to create any order. Roger Scruton pointed to the intrinsic relation between beauty and community, demonstrating this point through the painting *The Annunciation* of the Dutch master Joos van Cleve and the architecture of Venice.[49] When the divine beauty reveals itself, its light touches the entirety of our lives, including the arrangement of everyday objects and urban architecture. Subsequently, the absence of this divine illuminating glory leads toward the confusion of any rightful measure. The result is monstrosity due to lack of proportions. Furthermore, zombies dwell in dystopian cities—mirroring the outward decay and ugliness through their own deformity. As long as we are able to write about zombies, there is hope. Zombies do not notice any hierarchies, nor do they care. The moment zombies become invisible to us marks the point of our own transformation.

46. Nagel, *Secular Philosophy*, 3–19.
47. Vervaeke et al., *Zombies in Western Culture*, 24.
48. Vervaeke et al., *Zombies in Western Culture*, 5.
49. Scruton, "Beauty of Belonging."

The zombie is the inversion of the relational human whom we encounter in the creation story (see ch. 2). Christians embody both death and life within themselves as they enter into unity with Christ, who died and rose again. So Christians are alive, destined for eternity, while they are still in their earthly, decaying bodies. Zombies pervert this paradox. They are neither dead nor alive. Instead, they are the walking dead. There is no pattern in their existence, no punishment, nor any sense of heroism. They are more honest representatives of an absurd world than Camus's Sisyphus.

Critical Interlude

OBJECTIONS TO MY ARGUMENT could be raised from sociological and theological perspectives. Even theorists who view the classical secularization theory critically nevertheless admit that the empirically verifiable fact of religious resurgence does not have any bearing upon the structural secularity in Western societies. As Casanova has pointed out, even if the decline and privatization of religion had not occurred, religion still had lost its orienting function within a differentiated society.[1] Increasingly, secularity has become an object of academic inquiry, and with this awareness it ceases to be the ubiquitous normative background. However, secularity still remains like the air around us, which we breathe daily and struggle to articulate.

I agree with Casanova and believe that secular myth and rituals will remain in place and operate, just like the Judeo-Christian ones were not replaced overnight but remain operative, even within and through the secular ones. The moderate claim that I raise is that the secular myths and rituals exhaust themselves even faster than the preceding Judeo-Christian background, due to their internal fissures and inability to unite paradoxical features through a common ritual.

This fracturing could also be explained through the neuroscientific work of Ian McGilchrist, who interprets the decay of civilizations with the increasing dominance of the left-brain hemisphere.[2] Thus, the ever-tighter control through analytical skill weakens the wider relational horizons. Consequently, societies become rigid and their institutions fossilize before collapsing. The mind is formed through bio-evolutionary and civilizational processes, and conversely the mind creates an

1. Casanova, *Public Religions*.
2. McGilchrist, *Matter with Things*.

ever-contracting, suffocating society. This feedback loop continues until its radius becomes too narrow to perceive anything of significance. While this process is observable, it is hard to predict at what stage of decay the fundamental secular assumptions, which govern our societies at a structural level, will also be swept away by another myth.

Some theologians view the genesis of a secular explanation of reality as Christian heresy. Thus the relation between a secular outlook on the world and theological perception must be interpreted as antithetical, with the latter struggling against and seeking to "out-narrate" the first.[3] While I am sympathetic to this view and in particular to the unearthing of theological presuppositions underneath the seeming secular reason, I want to assert a different narrative. From a structural perspective, John Milbank is right in describing the antithetical character between religious thought and secular reason in the nineteenth-century development of sociology. Yet this is just one mode, prevalent since the radical Enlightenment, and does not do justice to the various shades in between. As Taylor points out, the extreme poles present reference points for discourse, and the antithetical view of the theological and the secular is helpful in order to break free from the suffocating embrace of the secular myth.[4] In this regard, Milbank's account could be used as an initial detox.

Yet, as any addict knows, after weeks of extreme detox in the hospital, one must face real life with all its complexities. Within the multifaceted biblical account and the life of the believer, God's seeming absence and presence can't be fit into a clear-cut dichotomy. God's distance could be viewed as a space of invitation, so that the human is not overwhelmed by God's otherness. At the same time, when humans willfully shut God out or attempt to tame him by assigning him a space for his existence, the secular acquires hubris, which Milbank rightly exposes as antithetical to Christian orthodoxy. In the thick of Christian life, in both the biblical story and ecclesial life, believers always struggle with God's simultaneous closeness and distance. Even his presence is mediated via word and sacrament.

Theological narratives, when reacting against one extreme, must be careful not to construct another seeming certainty, which tempts us toward hubris. There is a space to critique how the Augustinian saeculum as time in between was transformed into the aura of the factual.

---

3. Recently, the main proponent of this view has been John Milbank, in his masterpiece *Theology and Social Theory*.

4. Taylor, *Secular Age*, 594–618.

Yet this critique must abstain from the similar temptation to establish sacred time as the realm of the factual. In reality, every Christian and every church is struggling with the honest question of the psalmist: "Where is my god? Why does he not intervene?"[5]

Instead of pitting the theological and the secular against each other, it is more accurate to paint a complex relation of how the secular matured in answering theological questions and ultimately managed to disguise its theological roots, pretending to be an all-encompassing, solid social fact. Both from historical and theological perspectives, secularity appears as a multifaceted phenomenon in its dynamic relationality to religion.

Yet there is another view of secularity as the next stage in the inevitable maturing of modern man. Liberal Protestants interpreted Bonhoeffer's fragments in his letters as a call to accept the immanent framework and translation of Christianity into "worldly" categories.[6] This view is rooted in a simplistic view of history as evolutionary ascent. As I have demonstrated in the first two parts, neither is the relation between Christianity and the secular order simply antithetical, nor is the secular world somehow a pinnacle of Europe's religious history. Secularity is a gift of Christianity as God limits himself in order to invite people to love him. However, secularity is also Christianity's estranged child, which is unable to procreate.

The historical objection could consist in viewing modernity as a sui generis response to the vacuum left by Christianity.[7] Consequently, the pathologies of secular liberalism are inherent to such liberalism and are mostly pragmatic in nature (see introduction). Yet according to my presupposition in chapter 1, these immediate causes are secondary in nature. The deeper primary causes for social change are mythologies and rituals, as they manifest the center of every social order. Social

---

5. E.g., Ps 88 ends with the perception of utter darkness enveloping the psalmist.

6. Somewhat vaguely Bonhoeffer writes in his prison letters about "worldly interpretation of biblical categories" (*Widerstand und Ergebung*, 174).

7. Löwith and Blumenberg disagreed on the nature of secular modernity. Whereas Löwith viewed modernity as arising from Christian concerns via secular means, Blumenberg saw in modernity not merely a Christian project but something different altogether. In particular, the vacuum left by Christianity came to be dominated by the human self. I seek to combine both perspectives into a synthesis. Accordingly, while it is true that Christians translated their concerns via secular means, Blumenberg is also right in pointing out the emergence of an anti-Christian human self-determination. Both processes were parallel. However, Nietzsche was right, that there came a point of complete rupture, where God was murdered as man first put himself on the divine throne and then descended into madness.

change is undergirded not by sudden coming into being but by the recomposition of previous myths and rituals. This is true for both Judaism (see ch. 2) and Christianity. Innovations are usually minor deviations from the previous religious background.

Of course these immediate causes are more appealing to the modern man, as they suggest that we can quickly fix what is wrong with our society without the need to reach into deeper layers of history. This keeps us in the illusion of control and blinds us to the reemergence of ancient patterns in front of our eyes. Secular liberalism, just like any other myth and ritual, creates the aura of the factual, which conceals the alternatives. Yet history and social reality are never static. Various myths vie for power by subverting the old ones and imposing themselves as all-encompassing explanatory worldviews.

When the center collapses, the surrounding social order does not simply evaporate overnight. Institutions still persist habitually, albeit without an inner sense of validity. Yet emptiness extends to the outer realms as well and is perceived as a crisis. The old sacred center collapses. The effects are felt as symptoms of decay. Yet the new order is not yet born. In the third part, I will describe these morbid symptoms and the contours of the ancient myths, which resurface and shape the re-enchanted social order.

In the third part, I will tread into more speculative ground, attempting to discern the contours of the new and yet-familiar sacred order. The discussion as to whether history exemplifies some patterns or is completely random is cumbersome. It seems obvious that to be human is to be able to discern patterns of meaning, without which we would not be able to orient ourselves in this world (see ch. 1). Due to this fact, we are able to read Shakespeare and be moved by his writing, even though we have the glaring historic gap of centuries between us. In order to discern change, some constancy is required. For societies, I view this constant variable in the persistence of myths and rituals, which form the center. Assuming this continuity, I seek to sketch the sacred structures arising from the mist of history. Civilizational decline is never abrupt, unless it is just buried by volcanic ashes, as in Pompeii. Usually, life drains slowly from the body, leading to agonistic pathologies and descending into random zombie-like twitching of limbs. Exhaustion and decay are never final but invite new life growing from within the decaying corpse.

Reappropriating Camus's conclusion, I formulate the initial consequence of the absurd as follows: The absurd undermines individual consciousness, wherein the sense of agency is transformed into passivity. Individual freedom turns into a complete passive attitude toward powers that sedate and devour any notion of personhood. Passions are externalized into complete abandonment of self. The final revolt does not consist in the individual rebellion. Instead, an exhausted society merges with the advancing total powers, which guarantee peace at the cost of extinguishing the self. The invitation to death is experienced as life—a life of complete stillness, like a frozen lake in the depth of hell in Dante Alighieri's *Divine Comedy*. All longings and strife will finally come to an end. The figure emerging from the perversion of the Christian myth is not a heroic smiling Sisyphus, as Camus hoped for, but a brainless, grinning zombie who is always hungry for the minds of other people but overall indifferent amid the ruins. Like the zombie, the new myth feeds off the passing order. The ascending gods recompose the dying body, sucking out parasitically the last juices. The new civilization forms around these gods. In the third part, I will describe this agonistic fading away and the ascent of the re-enchanted society, centering around ancient gods in a new disguise.

Part III

Götterdämmerung and Emergence
of Re-Enchanted Society

CHAPTER 7

Disembodied Jesus, Mad Virtues, and Chaos

Corruptio optimi quae est pessima.

—Ivan Illich, in *The Rivers North of the Future*, by David Cayley

Turning and turning in the widening gyre
The falcon cannot hear the falconer;
Things fall apart; the centre cannot hold;
Mere anarchy is loosed upon the world,
The blood-dimmed tide is loosed, and everywhere
The ceremony of innocence is drowned;
The best lack all conviction, while the worst
Are full of passionate intensity.

—William Butler Yeats, "The Second Coming"

The church is called the body of Christ. This metaphor captures the social significance of the church in embodying the highest ideal. By disembodying from within itself, the church ceases to uphold the central ideal, leaving a glaring void. In this void the remnants of its formerly sacramentally gathered virtues are let loose and wreak great havoc upon the world. The dying church disfigures this world, leading toward agony and evoking hunger for new gods amid growing chaos.

Evangelical Zeal Without Grace

The street church that I colead in Berlin also functions like a neighborhood center, offering a location for music and for neighbors to celebrate birthdays and special events. Over the course of about two years students studying film presented their final projects at our venue. Their friends attended, and the place would quickly fill to capacity. In this context I met a young woman who was at first intrigued by the "cool" atmosphere of the location, as she put it. She inquired about the center, and I shared with her the Christian vision that had led us to open up this space. However, as I talked I noticed that her initial excitement began to disappear from her face until all that was left was a stony, grim expression. She interrupted me with the protest remark that Christians even dare to speak publicly about a religion that in her opinion had propagated so much evil in the world. She went on a litany recounting witch hunts and Crusades. Instead of replying to her indictment of Christianity immediately, I asked about her occupation. Her face brightened as she began to share with me that she is a lobbyist and political activist for vegan policies and lifestyle. Her ecstatic vision of a world of perfect harmony between humanity and nature informed all of her life. The meaning of her entire life seemed focused on overcoming the original sin in which humans elevate themselves over other forms of life, unleashing a cycle of violence. She went as far as insisting that those who resist this vision must be forced to comply, as this would serve the planetary good. Ironically she did not notice a strange mirroring of the evil Christendom she had just condemned in her desire to coerce and subjugate those who resisted her paradise-like dream of the future.

Tragically, in her ignorance of the deeper mechanisms at work in the political religions of the twentieth century, my friend was tilling the soil for another Manichaean religion. Anyone with a rudimentary knowledge of the history of religions will recognize in current social movements and antagonistic forces a strange bricolage from former Judeo-Christian parts.

Yet these parts are glued in a strange way, creating deformed patterns. My vegan friend kept the Judeo-Christian patterns of progress and redemption, yet removed Jesus and the Holy Spirit as divine agents, thus reducing tension between the imperfect present and the eschatological ideal, thereby elevating herself and her fellow activists to the status of the only virtuous group battling external evil. Evangelical zeal to convert without the grace and humility of Jesus leads toward a bitter Manichaean division of the world into friend and foe. The vegan militant missionary is a tragic bastard child of the church without knowing it. Desiring an ideal while giving birth to evil—this tragic pattern between intention and action is typical not only of many social activists today. This pattern has been modeled by the church during the last two millennia.

Disembodied Jesus

The old social order does not die suddenly akin to heart failure. Historical processes rarely end abruptly. The old order usually flickers for a while before going out. Perhaps a quick death would be favorable as the German saying goes: "Better an end with horror than a horror without end."[1] Yet decaying societies are slowly tortured to death by former virtues gone mad. The former limbs are cut loose from the body and create a great havoc on their own. Since the secular order creates a historical amnesia, secular priests can't provide the deeper historical explanation for the ensuing chaos.[2] Instead, they seek to reconfigure the body according to pragmatic considerations without recurring to the higher ideal.

Life-giving social order emerges from the right proportion of the parts in relation to each other and to the highest good. The parts do not constitute the highest good in themselves. Therefore, Aristotle rightly noticed that virtues are good only when they exemplify the right proportion within themselves and in relation to other virtues. Therefore, virtues can also be perverted into extremes and ultimately turn to vices.[3] The Second Testament writers follow the same logic in describing the church. The church is held together by the highest ideal as embodied in the person of Jesus. As long as the church directs its primary attention to this highest

---

1. German: "Besser ein Ende mit Schrecken als ein Schrecken ohne Ende."
2. Helmut Schelsky explained the increasing social impact of secular professionals with the decreasing role of clergy (*Arbeit tun die Anderen*).
3. Aristotle, *Eth. nic.*

ideal, it is able to hold together the differences and the plural goods, which serve to complement one another. The apostle Paul uses the organic metaphor of the body to describe how the freely chosen worship of God by individuals creates a larger community. Divine agency permeates the church through the Holy Spirit, creating a dynamic reality. The worshipping church is pictured as a social body, where the right proportions of the various gifts are maintained through each person worshipping the same loving Lord, who is at the same time the highest ideal and the lowest servant of all (Phil 2:1–11). Chaos ensues the moment that Christians lose sight of Jesus, who holds the entire social body together. The apostle Paul addresses the infighting and confusion in the church in Corinth and seeks to restore the dynamic unity by emphasizing the lordship of Jesus (1 Cor 12:3). The virtues are not good in themselves but only in relation to a vertical ideal and the horizontal balancing with other virtues embodied through worshipping people. Once these relations are strained, the former virtues are loosened from worship and radiate into the wider society, where they produce the contrary to the former function within the worshipping church. First, I will point out the vertical disembodiment of the church, before describing the horizontal consequences.

The disembodiment of the church occurred either as a violent removal from without or as gradual self-mutilation from within. There are various examples of the first case, of which I will briefly name just two. For example, the Bolshevik Revolution in 1917 led toward a violent removal of the church, creating a vacuum at the center, which the Communist Party filled with its political religion. Hitler also sought to either completely control the church or eliminate any independence of it from the state. His attempt at eradication was not as successful as the Soviet replacement of religion, yet the resemblance between these totalitarian orders in relation to the church is striking. Force produces counterforce and so historically the side effect of pressure placed upon Christianity has in fact been mostly its growth in strength, not unlike a muscle which needs resistance in order to grow.

Therefore, an inner subversion of the religious core is in fact more efficient for the weakening of the church in the long run. I have heard an anecdote that Trotsky, perhaps the most intelligent Bolshevik, advised Lenin to import German theologians and let them do the inner perversion rather than slaughter and ban Orthodox priests. Perhaps this is an unfair assessment of German theologians, as most of them sought to defend Christianity and make Christianity palatable to its cultural despisers.[4] The tragedy is when Jesus is slowly supplanted by the noble vision of creating paradise without God and in this way replacing the very best with a lesser good. However, in order to make Christianity acceptable to everyone, it had to be diluted. That which was formerly an accidental by-product turns into a defining feature. Early Christians were passionate about Jesus and accidently transformed the world for the better. Their successors became passionate about improving the world and lost Jesus in the process. I see tragic loss beginning at the third century and continuing into today. Let me employ Zarathustra's vision of spread limbs over a battlefield to paint an ideal-type image of the ecclesial disembodiment that has been reoccurring since the fourth century.

The last book of the Bible offers the tiny Christian communities in Asia Minor through a vision seen by John an image of a future cosmic battle between Jesus and the dragon. Instead of appearing as an insignificant Jewish sect, they are portrayed as key actors in this universal drama. They are encouraged to stay faithful to Jesus as conquerors amid the all-pervasive emperor cult. They proclaim Jesus as Lord over all powers and authorities—this is a proclamation that brought on persecution and even martyrdom. In the book of Revelation the boundaries are clearly defined. The evil empire stands on one side, while the suffering church resisting the onslaught stands on the other. These perspicuous lines become blurred once the empire becomes Christian. The clear allegiance to Jesus as Lord is clouded by the allegiance now to earthly powers. An ideal becomes mired in pragmatist politics, weighing various alternatives. If the emperor is Christian, the allegiance of the church must be negotiated and is not as clear cut as in times of opposition to the pagan empire. The headship of Jesus is not felt as directly. Now the conviction emerges that Jesus also works through the Christian king. Consequently, various relational modalities arise, which are often marked by a power struggle between ecclesial and earthly authorities. From the Renaissance on, the secular powers copied the church as a unifying institution and established a powerful authority that surpassed the authority of the church. However, by that time the church had lost its apocalyptic ability to envision an alternate reality and prophetically resist the hubris of earthly powers. Lacking a spine, the church elites often compromised and became subservient to the secular powers, in this way dismembering the church from within. How it was

---

4. Schleiermacher's classic *Über die Religion* is paradigmatic for this type of apologetic theology.

carried out differed according to time and place. Here I will offer an ideal-type diagnosis of how this dismembering has occurred.

If the head represents the ideal then it is clear that *Jesus as the head was severed and replaced* with another secular ideal. Resources and the loyalty of faithful believers were turned away from the worship of Jesus and from the love of neighbors, and instead turned toward a personal thirst for power by ecclesial and political elites. Too often the church was mired in the power game of the nation-states, lacking prophetic distance and alternative agency. The struggle between loyalty to Jesus or to earthly power remained the constant tension during the medieval ages for all Christian leaders. By compromising the lordship of Jesus, the church turned into a status-quo institution, a mere tool of the powerful. The church, once the harbinger of love and justice within the cruel Roman Empire, turned into a redundant institution of oppression by using its social capital of the past to coerce and subjugate. By trading allegiance toward the highest ideal with immanent lesser ideals, the church lost its potency by abandoning its Archimedean point to speak and act from. The church mired itself into all-too-human power games and lost its moral authority over the secular sphere. The final self-debasement of the church in the present is its identification with recent political parties, regardless of whether left, right, or libertarian. This development points to the loss of the all-encompassing imaginary and identity as being the body of the one through whom and for whom the entire universe was created and who rules over all powers (Col 1:15–23).

By forgetting its cosmic identity as sketched in the book of Revelation and the Letter to the Colossians, the church has become increasingly subservient to the state since the Enlightenment. Immanuel Kant prefigured this dependency while outlining the role of theology within the modern university.[5] Theology was portrayed as a naïve child on the chain of reason. Theology stood with its back to the wall and had to give account to the Kantian notion of universal reason. It is still in this position to this day, even though there was an attempt by Karl Barth and the post-secular theology of the Yale school to liberate theology from its foundational chains to secure its own epistemic ground. Theologians have begun to resemble Munchausen, who claimed to have pulled himself out from the swamp by grabbing his own hair. The Platonic spirit, which detests the particular body and everyday language, came to invade

---

5. Kant, *Streit der Fakultäten*.

theology and the church after all. By extension, once the second-order philosophical language was accepted as the primary mode, it shaped thought as well. Distance came to predominate theology. Once distance is enshrined as the highest mode of relation, love diminishes. Since the eighteenth century, theology turned into a parroting discipline of current secular fads, failing to provide fresh metaphors to shape cultural discourse. Kierkegaard and Dostoevsky were exceptions who dared to speak with a fresh voice. Yet these prophets had to place themselves completely outside the state churches in order to gain a larger perspective. Moreover, they had to develop a different way of speaking in order to break free from the static ontology. Most of the church elites were thoroughly integrated into the secular system.

The tongue was ripped out of the Christian body and transplanted into the Leviathan's head. To this day, the ecclesial elites in Germany are educated at theological faculties of the state university. Their primary reference point is not God, the church, and the street but the questions and praise of other secular academics. Since the human mind is embodied in time and space,[6] how and what we speak and think depends on the context and where we direct our attention. By training future pastors in secular academia, the church was turned into a mimicry of these reductionist servants of the secular state. Theologians became mouthpieces for the secular matrix, unable to perceive or receive fresh revelations.

Within the first three centuries the church had transformed from an obscure Jewish sect to the most potent religious institution in the Roman Empire and had moved from the fringes to the center of power. As the decay of the Roman Empire spread and various barbaric tribes began to invade, the church became the core institution to establish social order. In order to organize the political and economic life of the cities, the bishops became administrators concerned with the efficiency of these worldly affairs. Christian spirituality, which had made the Christian movement so potent in the first place, was relegated to mystics, who moved out from the cities into deserts and remote places. Within the early church, spiritual practice and everyday life were intertwined. In his letters, St. Paul addresses practical, everyday questions on how to live as a Christian community amid the Greco-Roman culture. However, once the surrounding culture had taken on the Christian identity on the surface, the former pressure fell away and confusion set in as to what it meant to be a Christian in

---

6. Lakoff and Johnson, *Philosophy in the Flesh.*

Christendom. Monks preserved the former struggle by relocating into the wilderness. Yet this spatial and organizational separation between everyday life and holistic life in the presence of Jesus served only to manifest the split between the transcendent and immanent spheres. The unity of the Christian incarnation as "God with us," which can't be experienced in everyday life, became a problem to solve through theological acrobatics. Secularity, as God's gift for humans to make a free choice to love him, increasingly turned into a void due to complete drifting apart between the immanent and transcendent spheres.

Saint Paul stressed the importance of prophets in the early church. Prophets were visionaries who discerned the deeper reality and were crucial in directing the church amid complex historical events. These prophets were complemented by teachers, who examined the received images and integrated them into the overall accepted revelation. Prophetic visionary skills were in high demand in the dynamic reality of the early church, in order to pave the way forward amid uncertainties. However, once the church became a stable institution, administrators and teachers became the central pillars of the church. Prophets and mystics were then often treated as annoying troublemakers and at times even burned at the stake. *The eyes were gouged out.* The blind church stumbled forward into disastrous situations, which seemed profitable for the administrators in the short term but came to be judged as horrible mistakes in hindsight. With the accelerating secular space since the Enlightenment these prophets became artists, philosophers, and authors who positioned themselves against the institutional church.

The heart of the church is its continuous remaining in Christ by cultivating spiritual disciplines (John 15:1–7). *The heart was ripped from the worshipping body and transplanted into an efficient institution.* At times the heart was reunited with the body. This is when the church experienced reforms, in which deep spiritual practice was reincorporated into the church and its energy served as innovative force.[7] Yet the tension between institutional efficiency and mystical spirituality remained throughout the remaining church history, and only exceptional saints were able to bridge this abyss.

A church with a transplanted head and tongue, without a heart and with gouged-out eyes, turns into a zombie without consciousness. Its soul is dead. The Holy Spirit as divine agent has been replaced with

---

7. Cluniac reforms in the tenth century being one notable example.

bureaucratic calculation. Zombies are able neither to enter into a loving relationship nor procreate. The lack of procreation points to the sterilized body. No pain of birth is felt. Instead, sanitized halls resemble the sepulchers where the memories of the past are repeated ad nauseam. A number of immigrants expressed their surprise to find, upon entering German cathedrals, only a few elderly individuals in such a huge space, sitting apart in silence, without any notion of fellowship. *The church as sterilized body is not able to procreate.* The statistics in sociology of religion paint a grim picture of a dramatic decline of membership with the loss of the younger generation across Europe.[8]

Infertility is a symptom of aimlessness. Aimlessness arises from the lack of a goal. Without intentionality, any desire evaporates. If the social body is not gripped by an external ideal, no direction through a unifying goal can be discerned. Members fall into apathy, and the only goal becomes mere survival. The loss of orientation creates a sense of meaninglessness and disgust within an institution turned inward. A social organism that turns inward begins to devour itself as it can't draw any external energy. When the feet to proclaim the good news are not used, atrophy sets in. When the blood no longer circulates, the extremity will die and be amputated. The image of the mainline state church in Europe as overweight through historic power and wealth, yet unable to walk, is pathetic and sad. The once-glorious body has made itself unrecognizable to its origin in its parroting of the zeitgeist and attempt to appear relevant to the wider society.

The last attempt to somehow create meaning lies in utilitarian self-justification. A church without identity descends into self-hatred and allows the secular masters to *amputate its hands*. The last twitching lies in a random attempt to appear as good and to do good without discernment of a larger goal and without any internal energy. The actions of the church for the common good were once rooted in the larger vision of God's kingdom. Once the fullness of love and a higher vision evaporate, the pulpit turns into a moralistic-political tool to beat people into activism motivated instead by guilt and fear. Ivan Illich lucidly described the perversion of the good Samaritan story. Under the guise of efficiency, the spontaneous, true expression of love of one's neighbor morphs into his annihilation in the name of love.[9] As Luhmann's historical analysis

---

8. Grossbölting offers an incisive analysis of the decline of German church since 1945 (*Verlorene Himmel*).

9. Cayley, *Rivers North*, 157–69.

shows, the goal of the secular social service is not to empower a real person but merely to maintain a systemic equilibrium in order to cement the continuous power of the state.[10]

The antithesis of love is perhaps not hate but pride. The triumph in its own potency in the world fueled the self-sufficiency of the church. Pride directed the gaze of the church away from the highest ideal and toward its own capacities to bring about "real" change in the world. The exchange of the ideal happened gradually, in the name of the good. There can be no blame shifting between the various traditions of Christianity. They all fell in the past, and they are all constantly in danger of being subverted from within. Worldly power and fame penetrated Orthodox, Roman Catholic, and Protestant churches alike.

Disembodiment occurred through the perversion of worship. The Roman Catholic and Orthodox remained strong in their larger metanarrative and ritual while neglecting the everyday aspect of worship in ethics and discipleship. Protestants, on the other hand, reduced the metanarrative through acidic rationalism, and their anti-ritualism stripped their spirituality, leaving it as naked Kantian imperative. The phenomenal rise of Pentecostal-charismatic Christianity in the twentieth century against all odds makes them vulnerable to repeat the downfall of their predecessors, if they don't learn humbly from the church's mistakes in the past.[11]

Mad Virtues and Chaos

A disfigured church seeking to make the world Christian can't establish the right proportions; neither in itself nor in the wider society. The disembodied church turns into a monster. Monsters, although bearing some resemblance to the original, are a product of the perversion of the original order into chaos. They produce chaos through their destructive agency. The tragedy of a monstrous church breeding chaos lies in its blindness. Without reference to Jesus as the highest ideal, the church is not able to perceive its true condition. It honestly seeks to redeem the world by making it "Christian." Yet the church is not aware of its own monstrosity due to the perverted proportionality. Similarly, the church seeks to infuse the world with its virtues, without realizing that these virtues are good only in relation to other virtues within a social body and in continuous

---

10. Luhmann, "Formen des Helfens."
11. Robbins, "Globalization of Charismatic Christianity."

orientation toward Jesus as the highest good. G. K. Chesterton reiterates Aristotle's insight by describing the destructive Christian virtues disconnected from the church as a social body:

> The modern world is not evil; in some ways the modern world is far too good. It is full of wild and wasted virtues. When a religious scheme is shattered . . . , it is not merely the vices that are let loose. The vices are, indeed, let loose, and they wander and do damage. But the virtues are let loose also; and the virtues wander more wildly, and the virtues do more terrible damage. The modern world is full of the old Christian virtues gone mad. The virtues have gone mad because they have been isolated from each other and are wandering alone.[12]

Chesterton goes on to give a few examples of the monstrosity of Christian virtues. By now, various agnostic intellectuals employ this insight as a heuristic device to understand the current social chaos.[13] In the following analysis of the current chaos, I employ Chesterton's insight.[14] The chaos resulting from Christian virtues gone mad is stronger in the USA due to the more activist church, which is thrashing and affecting the world with its deformity. In Europe, the church is on life support and not moving. Even though the idea of Christendom still shapes European identity,[15] the church does not exert significant social influence anymore.

What makes the church unique is its paradoxical nature of *unum e pluribus*. Simultaneous unity and diversity are guaranteed through Jesus, who is the embodiment of love and the one who governs the church. The modern nation-state, seeking to mimic this paradox, lacks both the divine agent and the ritual soil in which the paradox can live. *Ecclesial vision without Jesus and the Holy Spirit easily fossilizes into a totalitarian cage.* This was theoretically accomplished by Hegel and then materialized through the totalitarian ideologies of the twentieth century. Hegel was fascinated by the mystical speculations of Jakob Böhme and Nicolaus Cusanus. Yet instead of viewing these visions within the concrete-complementary social body of the church, he fossilized the spirit into a philosophical system. Instead of encouraging the worship of Jesus

---

12. Chesterton, *Orthodoxy*, 15.
13. E.g., McWhorter, *Woke Racism*.
14. However, I disagree with Chesterton that this shattering and deformation happened as a result of the Reformation. Instead, I trace this perversion to the fourth century as Christianity became the official religion of the Roman Empire.
15. Perkins, *Christendom and European Identity*.

within the church, the Holy Spirit was reduced to a dialectical tool in Hegel's gnostic vision. The loving, dynamic reality of Jesus' body was turned into total obedience to the steely cage of the Prussian state. A system that does not leave any air to breathe provokes another extreme of complete disorder, creating a pattern of destruction.

God elects his people in order to take the message of redemption to the world. Their privilege requires them to sacrifice themselves for the good of the other. Although chosen, God makes clear that ancient Israel had nothing special inherently; rather God chose them due to his own glory, in order for them to proclaim his name to the surrounding nations. Similarly, God elects people from all nations to form his body in order to praise him. Yet, *election without the higher mission of praise and self-sacrifice turns into prideful nationalism.* This spirit of prideful superiority has continued through the centuries. A plethora of books have been written on the Christian reinforcement of prideful nationalism through the secularization of theological doctrines. However, due to globalization after the Second World War, a global elite emerged with no particular ties to a particular nation-state. They borrowed the secularized notion of being elect and anointed.[16] The emergence of global elites occurred due to the digital revolution and the new economy.[17] Contrary to the feudal lords, they are not accountable to the church; and contrary to the national elites, they are not accountable to the populus. Once a year, they fly in their private jets to Davos, where they consult on how to save the world by imposing ascetic rules on others while themselves indulging in luxury. People perceive this type of moralizing from the top down as humiliation. Consequently, they stop trusting that the political, educational, and media elites represent their interests. Institutions lose credibility in the wider population. The higher order crumbles into smaller and more pluralistic pieces. This is not chaos per se. However, in order to organize some sense of larger unity, trust in higher structures and their representatives is required in the long run. A complete distrust of elites invites chaos, as complexity can't acquire a representative order.

Yet, there is an even more sinister way of destruction when the sense of election is cut off from God. The psalms are full of gratitude for God's provision and guidance of his people. *Election without gratitude invites*

---

16. Thomas Sowell takes up this theological origin in *Vision of the Anointed.*

17. Richard Sennett sketched the transition from earlier industrial, national capitalism to a new, global, and more diffuse form of capitalism, altering substantially human relationships (*Culture of New Capitalism*).

guilt and sacrifice of the other to absolve oneself of this unbearable burden.[18] European nations sought to redeem the other by forcing them into the Enlightenment. Understandably, this effort was mostly not met with gratitude by the natives. Today, secularized elites are aware of their elect status due to their wealth and privilege yet are unable to thank God for it. Their rising guilt calls for new redemption fantasies. Christians were called to be one with Jesus and take their cross upon themselves. The new global elites feel guilty about their privilege, but they abhor the cross. The solution is to present themselves as saviors of the world without any concrete sacrifice, to congratulate themselves in Davos as the elect group saving humanity, all the while eating caviar and drinking champagne. The framing of the problems and the solutions by those who do not have "skin in the game" are at best superfluous and at worst dangerous for people whose lives are affected concretely by the decisions of the most powerful elites.[19] History provides numerous examples of how the attempt by prideful elites to adjust reality to their own ideology has caused catastrophes such as famines and wars.[20]

Guilt is not only driving the actions of the elites but has Western societies in its grip. Mainstream media and academia employ collective historic guilt as motivation for activism. Within the Judeo-Christian tradition, feelings of guilt served as a symptom resulting from sin. Sin as the separation of humanity from God leads toward various splits—of man from nature, from others, and even within the self. In both the First and Second Testaments, God is portrayed as providing rituals of confession and forgiveness of sins. Thus guilt was just a temporary negative burden, which eventually led toward emancipation from the destructive force of sin and toward a progression of holiness—a transformation into the likeness of Christ. Even if this sanctification did not occur, at least no person was condemned to be permanently weighed down by the burden of guilt. Without the prospect of God's forgiveness, the apostle Paul spoke about the guilt that he says leads toward death (2 Cor 7:10). *Guilt without God's*

---

18. As a psychotherapist, Carlo Strenger described this sense of burden, which he encountered in his cosmopolitan, wealthy patients (*Diese verdammten liberalen Eliten*).

19. Taleb explored how having one's "skin in the game" affects both cognition and behavior (*Skin in the Game*).

20. One famous example from Soviet history of how ideological science caused unimaginable human suffering is the story of the Soviet agronomist Trofim Lysenko.

forgiveness suffocates. A person, and even entire societies, ridden by guilt can be extorted and manipulated for evil ends.[21]

If there is no recourse to forgiveness and inner change, the only means of self-absolving becomes the mantra of being compassionate, to just accept everyone as they are. However, Jesus embodied grace and truth (John 1:14). Unconditional love of the sinner and harsh judgment of sin—these extremes were always united in prophetic literature. Prophets were brutally honest in naming evil in its various expressions and simultaneously giving people hope by pointing to a compassionate God who still loved them and did not give them up. *Compassion without God turns into sugary sentimentality at best, and at worst it opens the door for various social evils.* Without any higher ideal, compassion turns into the reinforcement of the narcissistic ego. Without the deeper anchoring of identity in God, every individual becomes fragile and in constant need of recognition.[22] Every word of truth that hurts is equated with the potential destruction of the other's identity. Compassion is weaponized and turns into a coercive command. As no one dares to name a lie, people are left in their deadly illusions. So-called compassion is like a blanket that slowly suffocates the other. Initially welcomed as protection from the hurting cold of the outside world, the blanket also shelters one from perceiving reality. Lies take on the disguise of compassion and construct an illusory reality, resulting in confusion as individuals become more and more fearful of being perceived as lacking compassion. As Solzhenitsyn rightfully pointed out, social evil is able to thrive and take on a systemic hold upon entire nations only when individuals lie to themselves and to each other all the time.[23]

The prescribed expression of "compassion" is brutally enforced by the threat of sanction by exclusion. No one dares to speak one's truthful intuitions, except for a few licensed professional authorities. Pluralistic discourse transforms itself into an echo chamber. These secular priests are elevated as the only viable sources of authority. In the name of science, numbers and proclamations are constantly pushed upon people

---

21. E.g., Ayaan Hirsi Ali encountered difficulties in accessing statistics in her research of migrant assaults on women in Europe, due to fear of being portrayed as racist (Ali, *Prey*).

22. In his essay "The Politics of Recognition" Charles Taylor recognized already in 1994 that the weakening of the divine affirmation leads toward an increase of and demand for human recognition.

23. Solzhenitsyn, *Archipel Gulag*, 771–85.

as naked truth, reinforcing one particular narrative. Without orienting metanarratives, statistics can't be interpreted, thus opening the door for propaganda. Without deep anchoring in divine and ontological security, the numbers trigger individual hysteria. *Reductionist truth without grace kills.* Scientific truth without a deeper embedding in the myth that gave birth to it turns into a utilitarian tool of the powerful. Consequently, people lose trust in scientific discourse. Chaos sets in when a society can't agree on avenues of how to establish consensus to solve problems and face a future.

Perpetual social strife is stoked through the myth that views all of reality through the power difference between victims and perpetrators. In the Judeo-Christian tradition, prophets continuously decry injustice and call believers to lift up the powerless in society. The Bible acknowledges social evil and exploitation, while maintaining the possibility for both good and evil within not only the perpetrators but the victims as well. This view allows for reconciliation between them. The one with the highest social status lowers himself and sacrifices his privilege as he seeks to imitate Christ, so the powerless is elevated, as they both partake in the same God in the ritual of the Eucharist. To the contrary, within the secularized Manichaean myth, hierarchy is cemented and becomes the battle cry for an eternal fight. Those on top remain perpetual villains, while the victim is justified in employing violence to topple them. In this myth, the complex ontology of evil does not envelop all but is divided unequivocally—perpetrators are purely evil and victims purely good at all times.

Victimhood as cemented position emerges through perversion of the biblical notion of evil. Reconciliation becomes impossible. Resentment begins to permeate all of society, preparing the soil for open hatred and strife. The perversion is complete when the former victim justifies evil as a means to counteract historical injustice. Racism, hate, and violence are allowed, as long as they are directed at a group that represents the externalized evil. This simplistic projection of evil upon the other leads toward the recreation of evil. Simone Weil rightly exposed the destructive reproduction of the cycle of evil, when it is not countered through love.[24]

While Christians understand their responsibility to care for creation, they are also equally aware that God is ultimately the one who

---

24. Weil wrote, "When harm is done to a man, real evil enters into him; not merely pain and suffering, but the actual horror of evil. Just as men have the power of transmitting good to one another, so they have the power to transmit evil" ("Human Personality," 94).

maintains and keeps creation together. This allows for deep rest as the final responsibility is delegated to God. *Without God, responsibility turns into a crushing burden and glaring hypocrisy.* Universal responsibility implies universal power. Through this assumption, humans are ripped apart by a sense of pride on one side and complete despair on the other. In our pride, we overestimate our abilities, and at times, by intervening into functioning systems, we cause catastrophic consequences. In our despair, we retreat into fatalistic resignation. In order to hide our inability to bear the responsibility, we seek to hide our own failure and shame by projecting that failure upon the other. This reaction leads to the sacrifice of others and the descent of the system into perpetual disorder, as the inability to bring wrong analysis and skewed solutions into the light cements their failure in the long run. The secular totalitarian systems of Soviet socialism and German National Socialism collapsed due to their own inabilities to self-correct. Failures were always projected upon external powers, upon traitors and saboteurs.

In the Judeo-Christian tradition, a relief was implemented for people who transgressed the set ideal. In his grace, God provided Israelites with clear and elaborate systems of sacrifice to restore their original harmony with God. Similarly, through the sacrifice of Christ, Christians are able to confess and receive forgiveness. On the other side of the painful process of self-critique, which is central to confession, stands the assurance of divine love. Confession nurtures the practice of self-examination and introspection. It allows every person to understand the motivations of one's action and ultimately change one's behavior: empowerment through confession. *Once the hope of divine love is replaced with the cold logic of power, confession is turned from a surgeon's scalpel into a murderous knife.* As Bruno Latour has noted, without the deeper notion of love, the practice of critique turns into "critical barbarity."[25] Latour calls for a critique that would lead toward construction and appraisal of common reality. Yet he does not provide us with the deeper myth for such a practice. If people are afraid to confess due to the fear of being exposed and nailed to the digital pillory for everyone around the world for all time to see, there will be no room to expose evil. Evil will simmer and thrive in the hidden corners of the social body. Agonizing repetition of the collective behaviors that created chaos in the first place will become permanent.

The fear to address lies cements its grip on society. One of the biggest perversions has been the severance of Judeo-Christian freedom

---

25. Latour, "Why Has Critique."

from a positive goal and communal responsibility. God called Abraham to emancipate himself from his family tribe and land in order to follow a higher calling and establish a community. Freedom is good insofar as it is embedded in the divine ideal and is directed toward a constructive intention of building society. Once freedom is cut off from a larger ideal, from community, and ultimately from an objective reality of human relationality, it turns into self-divinization of the human. Historically, Protestantism has been guilty of this perversion. The rightful correction to appraise the individual against the oppressive tradition of ecclesial authority, once set in motion, went too far. *Without healthy relationality toward God and the world, the individual emancipates himself into madness and complete exhaustion.* The one who claims godlike proclamation of "I am who I am" negates his constitutive relationality toward tradition, norms, society, and biology. The moment a person claims to be God and pridefully negates his relational embedding, he self-destructs his own core. A society composed of individuals who negate their own relational nature fragments into pieces and breaks down due to the impossibility of any meaningful relationships. Atomization leads toward breakdown of families and institutions. Fruitful cooperation becomes impossible as all energy is wasted upon establishing a framework of shared reality, which is impossible to achieve as every individual in principle is imprisoned within his own divine-like perception.

It would require a more in-depth study to trace the social process of how the original virtues got disconnected, and by being unhinged from original myth and ritual, cause great havoc. I have touched upon the role of the church. Perhaps a mixture of good intentions to make the world Christian and naïveté about social complexity has led the church toward activism, which unhinges the virtues once gathered through communal worship. One could also tell a story of the secular borrowing from the Judeo-Christian myth at will. Marxism is a prime example of this breaking apart of the original holistic vision. In order to supplant a powerful social reality, one must borrow from its myth and rituals in order to establish a minimal consensus through recognition. Yet one must also put the familiar into another narrative plot and rituals. The willingness of the church to break off its virtues from itself aided in the creation of this secular bricolage.

Once mythological and ritual unity shatters and the church employs coercion against those viewed to be heretics, it robs itself of any trust to function as the largest possible space to gather visionaries and prophets. The rebellious sects of the late medieval ages transformed themselves into full-blown secular ideologies by the twentieth century. The religious wars that tore Europe apart between 1618 and 1648 were precursors for wars fought in the name of various divinities, be they a nation or a vague notion of immanent utopia as a classless or Aryan society. Since humans orient themselves in the world primarily through myths and rituals, perversion and fragmentation lead toward social chaos. Perhaps the ideological bloodbaths are mere precursors of what we are going to witness in the twenty-first-century West. By killing the Judeo-Christian God, the West also buries the idea of human dignity, which has been the bedrock of its civilization. The Holocaust vividly demonstrated what perpetrators are able to do to victims who are stripped of human dignity. Without human dignity, unimaginable horrors are possible and most probably become a grim reality as the West descends into the worst darkness. Hobbes's *homo homini lupus est* will be envied by many, as the wolf's bloodthirst is regulated by its biological intuition. Humans are able to override biology and descend much deeper. The West emancipated itself into the most painful condition of a world without resonance, a world that can't be felt, tasted, heard, or perceived. Inflicting unimaginable pain and suffering upon self and others will be welcomed as the only escape from this nightmare.

Social decay and the agony of virtues gone mad betray a vacuum at the social center. In the physical world a vacuum invites infilling. Similarly, as Jesus pointed out, the spiritual realm also does not know a permanent vacuum (Matt 12:43–45). Demons thirst for fresh bodies. A true vacuum can exist only temporarily and invites new gods, who require worship and subsequently materialize into a social order. The ideological wars between socialism, fascism, and liberalism in the twentieth century and the culture wars shaking the West in the twenty-first century could still be viewed through the lens of the decomposition of Christendom and the shattering into competing secular sects, which seek to establish the sociopolitical world according to their myths and rituals. Now even agnostic observers begin to notice the eerie religious spirit of the post–Judeo-Christian social order. They can't name this new spirit, but they begin to sense its religious nature. However, chaos can never be permanent, as people in a destabilized world desire stability. Chaos calls for old gods in new disguise to establish order.

CHAPTER 8

Resurfacing Manichaean and Gnostic Interregnum

> *In der Geschichtslosigkeit liegt die Chance aller Remythisierungen: In den leeren Raum lassen sich mythische Wendemarken am leichtesten projizieren.*
>
> —Hans Blumenberg, *Arbeit am Mythos*

> *A man cannot fall back on himself in an absolute sense, because, if he tried, he would find very soon that he has fallen into the abyss of his despair and nothingness; he will have to fall back on a less differentiated culture of spiritual experience. . . . Such alternative experiences were at hand in the Gnosis that has accompanied Christianity from its very beginnings.*
>
> —Eric Voegelin, *Modernity Without Restraint*

MANICHAEISM AND GNOSIS RESURFACE as the Christendom shell falls off and historical amnesia sets in. There never was a "pure" religion. After the expulsion from God's presence, humans were caught between conflicting loyalties, as the Bible tells stories of the struggle to maintain allegiance to the triune God. In the felt departure of one God, another idol steps in. From a theological perspective, Manichaeism and gnosis refer to idolatry patterns that reoccur at different times in diverse cultural expressions. Gnosis has accelerated since the Renaissance. The advance of technology produces a new idol from gnostic ancient limbs. Sauron begins to reassemble his body.[1]

Prostitutes for Breakfast

I chatted with my neighbor in Berlin as we stood sipping coffee on our adjacent balconies. Somehow, we ventured into the theme of relationships. Being that marriage is largely viewed as an archaic, unnecessary formality in Berlin, he inquired curiously as to why I married my wife. I shared with him as best as I could the Christian idea of marriage, adding that sexuality requires a covenant due to its sacred nature. Human emotional and bodily unity with the other person is a vulnerable act, and the covenant provides a framework for vulnerability and the giving of self.

My neighbor seemed unconvinced. "Our sexual desires are just like our appetite," he replied. He went on to tell me that he saw no need for a covenant in his relationship to his girlfriend. He insisted that he could love her and do with his body as he pleases. In fact, if she truly loved him, he declared, she would want the best for him, and if he is merely satisfying his physical desires, it would not affect their true love.

I thought for a few seconds and then suggested an experiment: "Next time you go out to the bakery in the morning, you could first stop by the brothel around the corner. After returning to your girlfriend, you could tell her about the pleasurable experience and see how she responds." My friend smiled awkwardly. I interpreted it as an answer that his girlfriend would not be amused.

My neighbor had repeated an ancient gnostic belief in its secular disguise—namely a dualism between the divine inner being and the carnal body. Whatever we do with our body does not have any bearing upon our spirit.

Myths and rituals governing our society must not necessarily be in the open and understood. Instead, their effects are just as powerful, or even

---

1. For the story of Sauron, see Tolkien, *Lord of the Rings*.

more so, when operating as an invisible background. In this chapter, I will seek to show how these myths still operate and hereby expose them.

Ancient Patterns

Within the Judeo-Christian dominion, people are able to pretend to live as if God does not exist. This is possible only as long as Judeo-Christian myth, with its emphasis on human freedom in relation to God, is embodied as a social frame. Once this frame begins to crack, even thoughtful agnostics recognize that the void left by Christianity must be filled with another religion that fulfills the same functions. Feuerbach was right that in the absence of God, man must invent a god. Therefore, it was only logical that Comte, as the founder of scientific positivism, advocated for a humanist religion that was modeled after the church but drained of any specific reference to a particular God and replaced with an abstract supreme great being. The abolishment of the Roman Catholic Church during the French Revolution required a temple built to the goddess Reason. All regimes inspired by Marxist ideologies mimicked Christian rituals, only replacing the Christian God with the particular Communist leader. Contrary to these political religions, which were artificially created overnight due to violent, disruptive suppression of Christianity, contemporary Europe finds itself in the slow but steady decline of the Christian myth and rituals. Therefore, the transition is evolutionary. Christianity is not forcefully removed, as during the French or Bolshevik Revolutions, but gently replaced by another religion. Some intellectuals begin to speculate as to whether Islam or resurgent paganism will supplant Christianity as Europe's core identity. It is of course not impossible. However, I view Islam as the by-product of a stronger competitor to the Judeo-Christian tradition.

Islam spread through its opposition to the Christian empires. Yet there is a deeper religious tradition that posed a subtler and therefore a more dangerous threat. From its birth, Christianity faced a strong opponent that sought to undermine and replace the nascent church. Its strength came not from a complete opposition but from bearing some striking resemblances. Thus, this religious movement could blend in and subvert the church from within. For this reason, the apostle Paul and the church fathers viewed these various religious movements under the label of Gnosticism as the main threat for the church.

The origins of Gnosticism are shrouded in darkness. Gnosticism is a label that refers to a family resemblance between highly syncretistic religious movements, encompassing Zoroastrian, Indian, Jewish, Greek, and Christian elements.[2] Gnostic mythology is highly eclectic and speculative, producing a myriad of splintered schools of thought. In this way gnosis reflects its time and culture of origin. Late antiquity was marked by both a ferment of cultures and ideas and a sense of crisis, as local structures were challenged by great empires and hyper-pluralism:

> The collapse of the ancient empires in the East, the loss of independence for Israel and the Hellenic and Phoenician city-states, the population shifts, the deportations and enslavements, and the interpenetration of cultures reduce men who exercise no control over the proceedings of history to an extreme state of forlornness in the turmoil of the world, of intellectual disorientation, of material and spiritual insecurity. The loss of meaning that results from the breakdown of institutions, civilizations, and ethnic cohesion evokes attempts to regain an understanding of the meaning of human existence in the given conditions of the world.[3]

Similarly to Christianity, gnosis gives an answer, albeit a different one, to this condition. The historic research on gnosis surpasses the scope of my study.[4] I seek merely to outline basic patterns that are useful to recognize reoccurring social and historical phenomena. Despite the plethora of gnostic expressions, it is still possible to recognize the "family resemblance" of various movements and assemble them under the umbrella of Gnosticism. Kurt Rudolph defines *Gnosticism* as a dualistic religion that denigrates the material world and proclaims liberation of man from his imprisonment through knowledge.[5] Upon first glance, this definition could also be applied to Christianity. Yet just like the Jewish creation myth's minor deviation resulted in significant consequences (see ch. 2), so the gnostic departure from the emergent Christian consensus resulted in distinct social and political consequences.

2. Rudolph, *Gnosis*, 59–68.
3. Voegelin, *Modernity Without Restraint*, 254.
4. In the nineteenth and the first half of the twentieth centuries the research on Gnosticism was mostly undertaken by theologians. The main sources were the apologetic writings of church fathers, as for example Irenaeus's *Adversus haereses*. However, the findings of gnostic manuscripts at Nag Hammadi in 1947 invigorated the study of Gnosticism by both religious studies scholars and historians alike.
5. Rudolph, *Gnosis*, 7.

Perhaps the most prominent feature of gnostic myths is their pervading dualism. Gnostic myths negate the Hebrew creator God. Contrary to the Hebrew creation story, the original creation was not spoken into existence by an all-powerful, good God. Creation is the result of a lower deity, and the material world is therefore itself evil. In fact, the seducer who appears as the snake and promises people knowledge and godlike status is often portrayed as the true messenger. His calling appeals to the divine substance in every man. This divine spark is portrayed in abstract terms. Redemption does not occur through a relational God, who continuously reveals himself to people and who enters history and becomes fully human in Jesus Christ. Instead, redemption is initiated through a call from the unknown external realm. Hereby, humans are portrayed as completely lost and estranged in a hostile environment. The world is irredeemable, and ultimately the highest God does not care. The only relevance of human redemption lies in the returning of their divine light particles to the original light, thus restoring the primordial divine harmony. However, this process is a highly abstract, impersonal one. The way to salvation is not through trust in God's unconditional love, which extends to all humans.[6] Instead, gnostic myths appeal to the human desire to be distinguished from and superior above all others. Gnostics view themselves as an enlightened elite, whose salvation is certain due to knowledge of the path to salvation.

The gnostic believer feels superior to the common people, whom he views as trapped in the lower realm. The true God remains distant and unknowable. Positive revelation is negated. All that can be said about the highest God is through negation. The experiential realm of the human lies within the evil material world. Since the highest God is removed and does not act directly upon this world, the gnostic worldview is permeated by a constant dualistic struggle between deities and forces. In its Manichaean version, the world is conceived as existing in constant struggle between competing deities.

Since the true spiritual kernel of the human is static, concrete relations do not bear any significance upon the individual's body. The consequence of this conception is both highly ascetic and libertine ethics, which form two sides of the same coin. Since all the material world is evil, the ascetic gnostic battles against the world by refusing to engage

6. There were also exceptions to this overall trend. Gnostics who were closer to the orthodox Christian teachings, as for example Marcion, did emphasize grace as the means of salvation (Tröger, *Gnosis*, 107–9).

in it through procreation or any enjoyment of it. However, some gnostic schools using the same teaching come to the opposite conclusion for lived experience. Since the ultimate goal of Gnosticism is to escape this evil realm, indulging in sexual or other pleasures does not have any bearing upon the true divine core. The negation of the creator God and the material world leads to two differing consequences—one of indifference and thus transcending the immanent imprisonment or one of active destruction of the material world, which will be burned anyway, as only the divine spiritual substance will ascend and be united with the eternal divine light. The mystical indifference toward the material world in the end is the mirror image of its destruction.

Gnosticism was a highly malleable religious movement. By spreading through different civilizations, it was able to take on various religious ideas and subvert myths and rituals from within. From the inception of Christianity, Gnosticism both took on a Christian disguise and sought to capture the powerful movement. At times, the confusion about what is gnostic and what is Christian was at its peak, as these seemed indistinguishable. Through the first centuries, the differentiation between Christianity and gnosis became more pronounced as prominent church fathers like Irenaeus and Tertullian wrote substantial treaties against various gnostic sects. However, gnosis never left the Christian body. Instead, it lurked in the shadows, ready to subvert it from within when the occasion seemed favorable.

Gnostic Christendom

Scholars debate about the extent of the gnostic imaginary in the writings of the Second Testament.[7] However, it seems clear that both in the Pauline and Johannine Epistles and in the Gospel of John the authors engage gnostic ideas. Paul's anthropology and John's cosmic dualism between light and darkness evoke gnostic imaginaries. However, as Walter Schmithals demonstrated convincingly, Paul and John seemed to engage the prevalent gnostic ideas in order to better express the emerging Christian theology. Yet they put the gnostic ideas in the larger frame of the Jesus event, thus subverting them and even employing this

---

7. For a concise summary of this subject, see Schmithals, *Neues Testament und Gnosis*.

new twist against their original meaning.⁸ In this earliest engagement of gnostic ideas to formulate the identity of the nascent church, gnosis was clearly distinguished as an opposing false teaching. If their concepts were employed at all, then it was mostly from strategic considerations, subsumed within the overall Hebrew messianic narrative. However, as the church became more and more hellenized and grew in sociopolitical power, so it became more open toward increased gnostic influence due to strategic considerations.

Adolf von Harnack goes as far as suggesting that the first Christian theologians were gnostics. Elements of Gnosticism became necessary through translation of the Hebrew religion into a Greek culture and philosophy. The door to speculative gnostic imaginary was opened through the need to make sense of the First Testament stories to the Greek mind. Spiritualizing of concrete historical events through allegorical interpretation leads toward abstraction and arrival at higher orders of meaning. Harnack concludes that, through the allegorical reinterpretation of the First Testament, an intellectual and philosophical element entered the early church.⁹ With the growth of the church and its increasing social status in Greco-Roman culture, Christian leaders were further challenged to present Christianity as a universal, absolute religion. Power requires clarity and systemic width. Thus with the increasing sociopolitical status and in competition with the surrounding polytheism, the early theologians transformed the mostly poetic-narrative Hebrew Bible, the Gospels, and ad hoc letters of the apostles into a coherent system of knowledge (Greek: *gnosis*). One could concede that as long as these theologians used gnostic concepts to articulate Christian faith and remained firmly rooted in the church, they maintained their ties to the Hebrew origins and could still be considered true to the Christian faith. Karl Barth rightly expressed the intuition that Christian theology becomes gnostic when it leaves the body of the church. Barth explicitly places speculative knowledge below the biblical description of faith arising from preaching, in order to prevent gnostic elitism. This has been one of his reasons for entitling his magnum opus *Church Dogmatics*, implying that the proper social context of theologians' reflection is the church. Thus, dogmatics can't reign and judge over proclamation of the gospel but merely serve as an advisor.¹⁰

---

8. Schmithals, *Neues Testament und Gnosis*, 20.
9. Harnack, "Versuche der Gnostiker," 143.
10. Barth, *Kirchliche Dogmatik*, 1.1:89.

Within the church as a complex, dynamic, social body, the polyphonic and paradoxical biblical story can be performed and tensions left without the compulsion of reduction. Jewish and Greek believers with their differing focal points were able to emphasize various aspects of the faith simultaneously. By upholding and embodying the multipolar and transcultural aspects of the biblical meaning, a tension was created that became attractive for people from diverse cultural and socioeconomic backgrounds. Yet with increasing social respectability and the influx of Greco-Roman nobility and intellectuals into the church, both the simplicity and ambiguity of the Bible were placed in jeopardy by the pressure to systematize in service of a more hierarchical conception and clarity. The key question for the church fathers became discerning where this process slipped into Gnosticism. In other terms: At what point did a Christian theologian turn into a gnostic? Since the boundaries were fluid, the answer was not easy. One of the earliest examples of this boundary negotiation was Marcion.

From a Protestant perspective, Marcion could almost be viewed as the first liberal Protestant theologian. His theology was strikingly rational. He rejected both gnostic creation speculations and ecclesial allegorical interpretation. Instead, he favored literal interpretation and conceptual clarity in his system of the Bible. In his lost volume entitled *Antithesis* he juxtaposed law and gospel, establishing a dichotomy between the First and Second Testaments. Contrary to the gnostics, he did not view the human as divine at the core. Instead, he would affirm the Reformation *sola gratia*, according to which every human can be saved only through grace, without any works on his part. Marcion could be ranked among the many liberal Enlightenment theologians who sought to establish a canon according to their own rational principle within the canon. Accordingly, Marcion accepted as authentic only the Gospel of Luke and almost all of the Pauline Letters. He rejected everything that suggested a personal God and the Jewish cultural embedding of the Gospels. While Marcion differed in his orthodox Christian convictions from gnostics, due to his intellectual pride he necessarily slipped into the reduction of both the tensions and paradoxes in the Christian Scriptures. Hans Jonas judges Marcion's reduction of tensions toward logical clarity as being of a "lesser spirit" than his great example, the apostle Paul.[11] However, perhaps what seduced him toward a skewed simplification was

---

11. Jonas, *Gnosis*, 176.

not his intellect but rather the lack of love for God in his complexity as revealed in the Bible and the social complexity of the church. A theologian who is separated from the messiness of life and church is more prone to project his intellectual clichés upon the world. Marcion juxtaposed the evil demiurge of the First Testament against the unknown good God of the Second Testament. Accordingly, he prescribed his followers an ascetic life, even rejecting marital covenant and sexuality as a way to battle the materiality of this world. In retrospect, the service of the Christian gnostics was to provide the nascent church with a challenge to formulate their theological principles. Marcion challenged the church to form the canon of accepted Scriptures and to embrace the First Testament as an integral part of God's revelation. While the church managed to discern the gnostic threat from within and without, it inadvertently created the very gnostic preconditions within the ecclesial body. By splitting itself from within, the church created institutional dualism, which proved to be fertile ground for gnostic dualism to thrive in.

While the early church established criteria for the prevention of a gnostic takeover, it inadvertently created conditions for gnostic patterns to creep into medieval Christendom. The teachings might have been orthodox, yet the church had awoken a desire for certitude through furthering its sociopolitical power. Thus paradoxically, as the church grew in power, it unknowingly prepared the ground for a gnostic takeover. Voegelin points out how the openness and thus uncertainty of Christianity led toward a gnostic desire for closure and certainty with increasing power:

> Uncertainty is the very essence of Christianity. The feeling of security in a "world full of gods" is lost with the gods themselves; when the world is de-divinized, communication with the world-transcendent God is reduced to the tenuous bond of faith, in the sense of Heb. 11:1, as the substance of things hoped for and the proof of things unseen. Ontologically, the substance of things hoped for is nowhere to be found but in faith itself; and, epistemologically, there is no proof for things unseen but again this very faith. The bond is tenuous, indeed, and it may snap easily. The life of the soul in openness towards God, the waiting, the periods of aridity and dullness, guilt and despondency, contrition and repentance, forsakenness and hope against hope, the silent stirrings of love and grace, trembling on the verge of a certainty that if gained is loss—the very lightness of this fabric may prove too heavy a burden for men who lust for massively possessive experience. The danger of a breakdown of faith to

a socially relevant degree, now, will increase in the measure in which Christianity is a worldly success, that is, it will grow when Christianity penetrates a civilizational area thoroughly, supported by institutional pressure, and when, at the same time, it undergoes an internal process of spiritualization, of a more complete realization of its essence. The more people are drawn or pressured into the Christian orbit, the greater will be the number among them who do not have the spiritual stamina for the heroic adventure of the soul that is Christianity, and the likeliness of a fall from faith will increase.[12]

Voegelin goes on to explain as to why the most likely background upon which these Christians unwilling to take up the challenge of the Christian experience would fall would be Gnosticism. The alternative of the Greco-Roman polytheism had disappeared, and Gnosticism appeared like a light version of Christianity with the hard heroic elements extracted from it. The fall was buffered with Gnosticism, which disguised itself as Christianity, promising certainty and realized hope in this world.

The power-thirsty church destroyed the prior unity of the social body, thus inviting gnostic dualism into its center. Already in the third century, the church had split itself into an administrative-sociopolitical body on one side and a spiritual monastic core on the other (see ch. 3). This clear delineation within the church invited gnostic opposition between the material world and the pure spirit. The lax, libertine established church produced its gnostic ascetic counterpart. This split cemented the antagonism that permeated the church throughout the medieval period. While the various splintered sects from Christendom presented a viable theological critique, they were inadvertently drifting into a gnostic pride of pure spirituality, unable to embody matter and spirit.

Toward the end of the medieval ages the gnostic expression accelerated through various sects. Norman Cohn showed convincingly the continuity between these apocalyptic sects and their secularized ideological successors since the Renaissance.[13] This bifurcation within the church was cemented through the Reformation, repeating the tragedy of the split in the third century. The church can't be healed and established through intellectual elites. The paradox that Luther embodied through his person and the dynamic of the church was suffocated through Lutheran orthodoxy after his death. Yet as Bonhoeffer rightly

12. Voegelin, *Modernity Without Restraint*, 187–88.
13. Cohn, *Pursuit of the Millennium*.

recognized, any theological idea, when disconnected from its origin of life and the social context of the church, turns into its opposite.[14] After the Reformation, the gnostic movement was further fueled through the fracturing body of Christ. The established church served as a negative foil for various counter movements, which were tempted to snap and verge into gnostic pride. The established Anglican Church gave birth to Puritanism, verging on the edge of gnostic pride, while the established Protestant Church bore Pietism with its purist and highly speculative tendencies. These movements were reforming the church but also at times venturing into a reactionary gnostic negation.

While German academic theologians rightly view the gnostic movement on the fringes of the established church,[15] they overlook the larger historical dynamics creating gnostic patterns. Once the Roman Catholic Church abused the sacraments as means for gain, it drove believers toward desire for direct encounter with the divine. The pietistic extreme of an unmediated individual experience could be explained as a reaction to the intellectualist hubris of Lutheran orthodoxy. Yet both are lacking the mediatory humility of faith and sacraments. The driving force behind the gnostic reappearance is perverted worship. The established church, initially Roman Catholic and later Protestant, split everyday ethics from the sacraments of the church, producing an illusion that God is not concerned with everyday life. The strong intertwining between sacraments and life increasingly drifted apart. The antinomian rebellion against these hierarchies led only toward new hierarchies, mostly masquerading as direct revelations of knowledge, as in the case of the Munster Anabaptist revolt.

The inability to hold together matter and spirit, word and experience, within one body, divided it into two opposing bodies, which unintentionally reproduced gnostic dualism, setting the stage for secular gnosis as the engine for modernity. Rationalist theologians seeking conceptual clarity without the hermeneutical community of the church stripped Jesus of his Jewish humanity and divinity alike, effectively removing him from the narrative embedding. The German Jesus resembled more the gnostic unknowable abstract deity than the historic Jewish Messiah. Marcion's hatred of anything Jewish was replicated in the capture of Protestant theology through pagan myths to create the political religion of National

14. Bonhoeffer, *Nachfolge*.
15. Tröger, *Gnosis*, 109–66.

180 *Part III: Götterdämmerung & Re-Enchanted Society*

Socialism. Once Jesus has been emptied of his cultural particularity, he may be projected upon by any ideology. Since grace is not connected to the life of the believer, it is perverted into a cheap proclamation and thus sanctification of immanent ideology, as Bonhoeffer rightly noticed. Yet this type of gnostic academic theology awakens another gnostic counterpart: a desire for immediacy without any reference to the word. It is therefore not a surprise that Lutheran orthodoxy and Kantian rationalism produced a theologian seeking to ground the Christian faith in subjective immediacy. While Schleiermacher on the outside seemed to counter the gnostic rationalism, he nevertheless presented another side of the same coin.[16] Similar to Marcion, Schleiermacher's primary motivation was apologia toward cultural despisers of religion. Starting from this premise, it is only logical that he seeks to demonstrate the validity of Christianity by reducing it to the assumptions of the Romantic elite of his time. These gnostic theologies are embodied by churches that fall into the one or the other reduction, thus fueling the gnostic dualism. Institutional antinomianism and the libertine ethics of the mainline churches trigger an ascetic, self-righteous religious populism. Yet what is common to both of them is abandonment of the tension between the good yet broken world and the awaited ideal. Both seek certainty in the now and must therefore reduce the complexity of both theology and the world. Both movements mirror and reinforce each other, heightening the gnostic antagonism and discrediting the Christian faith, as the church is perceived as a torn entity, producing extreme caricatures. Once the church itself begins to reproduce gnostic antagonism through its form, it ceases to be a viable alternative and irenic center for the perceived strife. It is at this state that Gnosticism sheds its Christian disguise and enters into its philosophical-secular stage. One German Lutheran philosopher like no other translated Christian Gnosticism into a philosophical system, which served as inspiration for the warring ideologies of the twentieth century.

Gnostic Modernity[17]

The popular belief that, since the Renaissance, Europe has ascended from religious superstition and uncertainty toward an age of reason and

---

16. Baur rightfully discusses Schleiermacher's theology as gnostic philosophy of religion (Baur, *Christliche Gnosis*, 626–68).

17. Here I follow broadly Voegelin's analysis of Gnosticism as the structuring pattern of modernity (Voegelin, *Modernity Without Restraint*, 175–96).

scientific certainty stems itself from Christian gnostic speculations on the philosophy of history. The biblical account provides a rudimentary structure for the philosophy of history. The early church viewed the incarnation of Christ as the central event in human history and eagerly expected his return. With the perceived delay of Christ's return speculations set in. Already in the second century the Montanist movement divided human history into three parts: the ages of the Father, the Son, and the Holy Spirit, viewing itself as advancing the third age of the Spirit. In the late medieval ages, Joachim of Fiore revived this speculative view of history, which became the blueprint for subsequent secular ideologies. Liberalism, socialism, and National Socialism understood themselves as advancing a third new age. Contrary to Christian speculations of harmonious development, secular ideologies emphasized disruptive violence as an in-between stage. Interpreting crisis as the in-breaking of the new allowed the intellectual elite to discredit tradition and cut off a larger orientation in time.

The late medieval ages generated various crises, which originated in various successful innovations. Technological innovations enabled a population boom. Intellectual freedoms paired with new technologies of communication led toward a rapid rise of literacy and the circulation of new ideas. The old order fell apart into many pieces. The splintering of myths and rituals was followed by the destabilizing of the former equilibrium between clerical and earthly rule as various forms of authority arose, prefiguring the advance of nation-states. Similar to the fading of both socio-material and ideological certainties in late antiquity, the Renaissance enlarged the world due to new discoveries. On top of these ideological and sociopolitical upheavals, the outbreak of the Black Death in the fourteenth century further reinforced the sense of being a stranger in this world, at the mercy of outward forces. Hieronymus Bosch's pictures portraying passive people tortured by active demons capture the essence of the prevailing mood. New religious movements, and Gnosticism in particular, thrive in times like these, offering an all-encompassing plot for those who feel lost, powerless, and estranged from old institutions. The new movements promised an escape from and strategy to overcome this world. With the increasing disembodiment of European Christianity, the new myths borrowed pieces at will from the dominant worldview and constructed a powerful structure that continues to shape modernity since the Renaissance. Yet similar to Marcion, the lines between Christian and gnostic mythologies and rituals were blurry and unfolded their transformation gradually through history.

The allegorical interpretation of Scriptures as further developed by the church fathers is very useful to recognize patterns in the Bible and apply them to make sense of progressing history. Humans seek to perceive some patterns amid chaos in order to orient themselves. The historical speculations of the Christian monk Joachim of Fiore provided such a larger structure of how history plays out according to the divine plan. Christian mystics like Nicolaus Cusanus and Jakob Böhme envisioned a holistic order, which provided stability amid the fragmentation. What makes these speculations so attractive is their immediate accessibility due to metaphorical language and their stabilizing effect upon a world splintering into many pieces. The one who sees remains to some degree outside of immanent forces. Yet these Christian prophets were supplanted by secular intellectuals in providing a mythological explanation on the nature of reality without any reference to a particular God. Only upon a closer reading of both liberal and Marxist philosophers does the notion of a distant gnostic god become evident.

Hegel stood at the threshold of this development. Realizing the fracturing and fragmenting of the modern world and inspired by the Christian mystics of the Renaissance, he sought to provide a gnostic vision par excellence, preparing the ground for secular gnosis.[18] Christian visionaries maintained the distinction between the revelation and their speculations. In principle every believer could read the Bible and, by observing empirical reality, arrive at his judgment about Fiore's theological interpretation of history. A gnostic seer does not merely replace or pervert the perception of reality. Hegel created a simulacrum, a philosophical system, that does not refer to any reality but claims to represent ultimate reality by gathering and shaping the real, be it history, art, science, or politics, into a meta-system.[19] Hegel merely used the real world in order to construct his hyperreality as he ultimately demonstrated in a truly gnostic manner how the absolute spirit comes to himself through historical processes. Hence, in his *Phänomenologie des Geistes* Hegel outlined his intention as seeking to transform "love of knowledge" (philosophy)

---

18. I follow here Magee as interpreting Hegel's philosophy as a gnostic project at its core (Magee, *Hegel and Hermetic Tradition*).

19. I employ here Baudrillard's idea of simulacrum as the ultimate hyperreality replacing the real (Baudrillard, *Simulacra and Simulation*, 2–4).

into "true knowledge" (gnosis).[20] One may add that, by doing so, Hegel successfully transformed Lutheran theology into gnostic myth. While he retained Christian terms, he nevertheless changed their meaning fundamentally. Hegel does not view himself as a mere philosopher, who arrives at his conclusion through wonder and reasoning. Instead, he resembles a seer, who immediately understands the ultimate nature of reality. Since Hegel assumed to have figured out God and offered up a final myth, it would seem that he had turned into a divine-like seer hovering over the rest of creation like God's spirit in the Hebrew creation story. Christian prophets were accountable to the rest of the Christian body, which required any personal revelations to be tested before being accepted. To the contrary, Hegel viewed his philosophy as the final system, subsuming all claims of knowledge under its steely logic.

Voegelin discerned some central gnostic patterns in various modern ideologies and movements. Accordingly, he viewed modernity as gnostic at its heart: "The more we come to know about the Gnosis of antiquity, the more it becomes certain that modern movements of thought, such as progressivism, positivism, Hegelianism, and Marxism, are variants of Gnosticism."[21]

One might judge Voegelin's proclamation as an exaggeration and a sweeping generalization of historic particularities under an overblown, anachronistic category.[22] However, even without employing the artificial concept of gnosis we could easily describe modernity as "immanentization of transcendental truth,"[23] which produces a dynamic recognizable in various modern movements. This immanentization carries within

---

20. Hegel, *Phänomenologie des Geistes*, 12.

21. Voegelin, *Modernity Without Restraint*, 247.

22. On critique of Voegelin's employment of gnosis, see Eugene Webb, "Voegelin's Gnosticism Reconsidered." While I agree with Webb's critique of Voegelin's employment of Gnosticism as too general and imprecise, I still attribute value to Voegelin's insight. A picture might be blurry, but nevertheless express the overall contours. Webb is right that slamming complex phenomena under too broad of a category might lead toward a "lazy polemicism" precluding further understanding. Yet there is also another danger of a death of meaning through a thousand clarifications. Ultimately, I still perceive Voegelin's endeavor as useful in offering a broad pattern that then still can be clarified, as Webb does. Some scholars, like Voegelin, paint with broad strokes, and others then fill in the details. Yet the groundwork is prior and stands on its own. It takes visionary courage to paint the wider horizons that provide the ground for scholars to chisel the footnotes.

23. Voegelin, *From Enlightenment to Revolution*, 265.

itself various destructive potentialities by splitting and reducing the life-giving horizons of the Judeo-Christian tradition.

The gnostic speculation tears apart the spiritual-bodily unity of the human being as portrayed in the Hebrew creation story. Once the material aspect of being human is pitted against the spiritual, agonistic dynamics are set in motion. Marx rejected Hegelian idealism and claimed scientific materialism as the sole basis of his ideology. However, the spiritual was not completely purged from Marxist thought. In Hegel's world, the Judeo-Christian God was turned into a gnostic deity—governing the lower world through dialectical law, whose power is accessible only to the truly initiated and committed Hegelians and their Marxist successors. Accordingly, the material can be manipulated at will in order to achieve spiritual utopia, transcending dialectics into a state of ultimate freedom and equality. In a gnostic manner, even the destruction of the lower material world was permitted for the sake of the pure spiritual renewal. The sacrifice of millions for the highest good was justified from the perspective of the "virtuous" seer.

In secular liberalism, this dichotomy is not as thorough and is mostly postulated between man and nature. In the Hebrew creation story, humans are part of the ecology and are responsible for the best care for it. Once this tie is severed, nature turns into dead matter. Of course one could argue that the first step in the ruthless exploitation of nature had already been performed through the desacralization of nature through the Hebrew conception of Yahweh as the only sovereign God.[24] By declaring nature as a mere creation of the highest God, nature was stripped of its divine power. Man was placed to rule over it. Yet in the Hebrew cosmos, humanity was intimately tied to nature and endowed with the command to represent God's care. With the loss of accountability to God, humanity also lost any responsibility toward nature. Consequently, exploitation and ecological destruction are the consequences of humanity attempting to decapitate God, who commands the maintenance of living ties within his creation. Ecological decay also impacts humans negatively. Instead of restoring the Hebrew myth and returning to nature as their younger sister, humans are tempted to reestablish nature as their mother by divinizing her once again, thus reintroducing her terror over them. Reducing the world to dead matter

---

24. Lynn White traces the roots of our ecological crisis to the dis-enchantment of nature through Hebrew monotheism ("Historical Roots").

triggers the counter perversion to evoke once again the reign of pervasive spirits who must always be pacified through sacrifices.

The Judeo-Christian tension between God's revelation and yet the delay of full presence was reduced to immanent certainty through knowledge. Science, understood as a partial method for discovery, was perverted into a tool that claimed redemptive powers by assuming to represent the exhaustive reality. The multifaceted complex ontology was replaced with narrow empiricism, with scientists acquiring the role of priests, mediating the only access to ultimate reality. Voegelin sarcastically pointed out this parallel: "In the gnostic speculation of scientism this particular variant reached its extreme when the positivist perfecter of science replaced the era of Christ with the era of Comte. Scientism has remained to this day one of the gnostic movements in Western society; and the immanentist pride in science is so strong that even the special sciences have each left a distinguishable sediment in the variants of salvation through physics, economics, sociology, biology, and psychology."[25]

Once all of reality is subsumed under a system claiming finality, openness and inquiry become superfluous. From a gnostic perspective, empiric reality must be manipulated toward the perceived spiritual reality. The finality of the image perceived ultimately structures society. The ephemeral material world must be adjusted, if necessary by force, to the vague yet ultimate goal. The gnostic rejects the real in front of his senses for the sake of the hyperreal received through abstract knowledge. At the core of liberalism, socialism, and National Socialism lies the belief that the concrete must be sacrificed in order to achieve a higher status of being. This sacrificial logic is less visible in secular liberalism, yet as Asad has pointed out, the liberal myth also contains sacrificial logic in the name of vague progress.[26]

This ultimate sacrifice requires the shutting off of the mind and blind obedience, as ultimate certainty demands total agreement. Voegelin exposes the same suicidal structures in shutting down human inquiry in positivistic, Marxist, and fascist ideologies.[27] He ultimately locates this destruction of wonder and openness of the soul in the rebellion against God. The nonrecognition of reality creates a dream world, which is superimposed upon the real world. Yet reality reasserts itself painfully. The gnostic approach can't adjust its perception, and the negation of real

25. Voegelin, *Modernity Without Restraint*, 191–92.
26. See ch. 3.
27. Voegelin, *Modernity Without Restraint*, 264.

consequences requires ever-higher sacrifices. Instead of halting irrational actions, gnostic politics revert to projections and propaganda:

> The gap between intended and real effect will be imputed not to the gnostic immorality of ignoring the structure of reality but to the immorality of some other person or society that does not behave as it should behave according to the dream conception of cause and effect.... The intellectual and moral corruption that expresses itself in the aggregate of such magic operations may pervade a society with the weird, ghostly atmosphere of a lunatic asylum, as we experience it in our time in the Western crisis.[28]

The gnostic reversal of symbols does not lead toward emancipation from the limitations of the world but toward emancipation from reality. Voegelin's interpretation of ideological clashes post–Second World War through gnostic patterns remains useful in the twenty-first century as well. Gnosticism remains a powerful myth in the twenty-first century. In fact, it seems like it has become the only hyperreality, not only providing the interpretative lens but also manifesting itself as sociopolitical reality and, in so doing, turns into a self-referential mirror image. The social conditions for Gnosticism are growing through estrangement from the Judeo-Christian myth and accelerating alienation (see chs. 5–6). The amnesia about the sacred nature of embodied human beings prepares the way for gnostic obsession in transhumanist disguise. While the socialist and National Socialist ideologies sought to create the new human being through forceful removal of what they deemed ephemeral qualities, the advancing transhumanism is able to employ a painless destruction of human embodied nature in the name of its perfection. One might dismiss Yuval Harari's dystopian vision as imagined fiction in which humanity's search to be godlike leads to the creation of an artificial being who supplants them.[29] Yet one can't dismiss the growing dread of the consequences of human hubris to transcend and therefore abolish human relational nature. The Hebrew creation story describes human relationality as the very core of what it means to be human. Once humans modify through technology the very way they relate to God, to each other, and to nature, one can't evade the realization that a fundamental shift has occurred in the way we exist as humans and society. Paradoxically, knowledge and technology served as a way to shield humans from

---

28. Voegelin, *Modernity Without Restraint*, 226–27.
29. Harari, *Homo Deus*.

mythological forces, as Taylor coined it, to create a "buffered self."[30] Yet while modern man would appear to have gotten rid of demons, he is increasingly gripped by forces beyond his own ability.[31] Perhaps Tolkien was right, and the Hegelian spirit reveals himself as Sauron building his own body through technological limbs.[32]

Gnosticism has a paradoxical function within modernity. On the one side it accelerates the engine of progress. By emphasizing salvation of self, it evokes a deep desire for humans to create a paradise on earth. A collective hubris to build a tower for the glory of the nation is a powerful force forward. Yet, on the other side, within this success lies the sinister seed of destruction:

> The death of the spirit is the price of progress. . . . The more fervently all human energies are thrown into the great enterprise of salvation through world-immanent action, the farther the human beings who engage in this enterprise move away from the life of the spirit. And since the life of the spirit is the source of order in man and society, the very success of a gnostic civilization is the cause of its decline. A civilization can, indeed, advance and decline at the same time—but not forever. There is a limit toward which this ambiguous process moves; the limit is reached when an activist sect that represents the gnostic truth organizes the civilization into an empire under its rule. Totalitarianism, defined as the existential rule of gnostic activists, is the end of progressive civilization.[33]

Voegelin's lament on the death of the spirit could also be described as the severance of relationality. Tragically, by severing humans' ties to a creator, nature, and other humans, gnostics did indeed achieve liberation. However, this newfound liberty is indistinguishable from cruel torture. If a person is constituted at the core through relationality, the destruction of these relations does not merely trap a person but injures the inner self. From this anguish, a person will welcome a totalitarian order as relief,

---

30. Taylor, "Buffered and Porous Selves."

31. Perhaps it is not by accident that economists and sociologists revert to religious metaphors to describe the larger structural forces gripping people. Habermas recognized that secular translation of older and deeper Christian symbols can't exhaust their reservoir of meaning (*Zeit der Übergänge*, 190). Zygmunt Bauman compares fear with demons (*Liquid Times*, 26). Shoshana Zuboff attributes agency to surveillance capitalism (*Age of Surveillance Capitalism*, 15).

32. For the story of Sauron, see Tolkien, *Lord of the Rings*.

33. Voegelin, *Modernity Without Restraint*, 195.

since any type of relationality, even a painful one, is better than none. Hence gnostic emancipation from all earthly relations is the worst type of violence since it constitutes the destruction of the human core. "Liberation" is nothing but a euphemistic label for ripping out the heart from the social body. Once human societies are hollowed out from within, people turn into a mass of NPC zombies, who can be molded into any shape and weaponized for any purpose. While various gnostic movements flourished in response to the chaos that ensued from the decomposed Christendom, they only intensified experiential agony through their dualism. In this way gnostic patterns provide both the historical sociopolitical soil and the myth for the emergence of the megalomaniac Leviathan.

CHAPTER 9

The Emergence and Seductions of the Megalomaniac Leviathan

Itaque ex hac maxima libertate tyrannus gignitur et illa in iustissima et durissima servitus.

—CICERO, DE RE PUBLICA

The ... Leviathan is the correlate of order to the disorder of gnostic activists who indulge their superbia to the extreme of civil war.... The victorious Gnostics can neither transfigure the nature of man nor establish a terrestrial paradise; what they actually do establish is an omnipotent state.... Hence, the Leviathan is the symbol of the fate that actually will befall the gnostic activists when in their dream they believe they realize the realm of freedom.

—ERIC VOEGELIN, MODERNITY WITHOUT RESTRAINT

GNOSTIC CHAOS SETS THE stage for a totalitarian society, which emerges on the ruins of exhausted liberalism amid the anguish of decomposed Christendom. Gnostic mythological-ritual core has been growing with the advance of modernity. The re-enchanted dominion is welcomed as redemption from libertine exhaustion. Soft totalitarianism advances through disguise and disruption. As the memory of the old order recedes, both theologians and secular intellectuals alike are seduced to respond in conventional ways, which are inadequate to embody a flourishing society.

Desiring Pain

As a child I witnessed agonizing cycles of abuse. It was not uncommon in Russian families for the man to get drunk and beat up his wife and children. Two of my aunts were regularly abused, but every time after fleeing, they returned to their husbands. At the time I wondered why any sane person would willingly return to a violent abuser. I have since witnessed this same phenomenon, both in other individuals I have encountered and within society. Why does a prostitute submit herself "voluntarily" to her pimp? Why does a teenager "voluntarily" cut himself? Why do entire civilizations willingly accept tyrannical rule? It seems so irrational, and yet it is not.

A teenager who cuts herself once told me that it is better to feel pain and know that one is alive than to sink into complete numbness. This sounded in fact rational. One chooses a lesser pain. The agency, even if it is in itself destructive, feels empowering. The experience of pain would appear to keep the stillness of frozen hell at bay. Similarly, exhausted societies invite abuse by totalitarian powers. The masses assume that it is better to lose all freedoms and feel pain than remain in nihilistic exhaustion.

Dis-Enchantment, Mis-Enchantment, and Re-Enchantment

Re-enchantment suggests the possibility of a dis-enchanted world. Dis-enchantment worked only insofar as a particular myth and ritual allowed for and enabled it (see ch. 3). One could tell a different story. Empirically, dis-enchantment was reserved for only a tiny minority of intellectuals. And even these were dabbling into esoteric and spiritualist experiments as they were espousing their theories of dis-enchantment.[1] While on the surface, pockets were carved out where life could be conceived as structured by immanent forces of bureaucracy and technology, on the

---

1. Josephson-Storm, *Myth of Disenchantment*.

deeper level, the once-unifying medieval myth and corresponding rituals splintered into a myriad of competing myths and rituals (see ch. 5). From the Christian perspective, a secular age is not dis-enchanted but mis-enchanted. As Cavanaugh has convincingly demonstrated in his work, the notion of the holy migrates.[2] The former lesser goods, like material goods, nation, and nature, are imbued with the glory formerly given to the triune God and are therefore elevated to the status of gods. The Judeo-Christian story describes this as idolatry. A fragmented, atomized society is able to function without a unifying myth and rituals on the surface during relative times of calm and peace, wherein every social segment functions according to its own internal logic.[3] Mis-enchantment could be this phase in between as various gods stay within their realms of power, creating an illusion of a peaceful polytheism.

However, any external challenge requires deeper solidarity and triggers a quest for myths and rituals, which are able to provide a stronger foundation of unity. United people are more capable of facing external threats. The Roman Empire allowed for a high degree of cultural and religious diversity at the height of its power. However, during times of crisis, the emperors sought to secure the allegiance of all citizens by introducing the emperor cult. Allegiance to the all-encompassing deity is desired from both top down to consolidate power and also down up to achieve security. The biblical story of the tower of Babel tells a story of people aiming at eliminating prior diversity in order to achieve a name for themselves. Pluralistic liberal democracies tend to be slow in dealing with imminent dangers. Some Western politicians envied China's totalitarian efficiency and speed during the outbreak of COVID-19. Pluralism and freedoms are the goods that are sacrificed first when a threat to biological or social life emerges.

The experience of how liberal democracies can turn into totalitarian regimes almost overnight is not new. Political religions of the twentieth century, both in their National Socialist and socialist guises, are vivid examples of this transformation. Mythological and ritual fracturing remains a temporary phenomenon on the surface. Myths do not simply disappear. They continue to exercise a cohesive force even after their core is removed. The idea of Christendom as developed by Charlemagne in the eighth century worked well into the twentieth century and continues

2. Cavanaugh, *Migrations of the Holy*.

3. Luhmann like no other modern sociologist theorized the structural-communicative order of modern societies (*Soziale Systeme*).

to provide a reference for European identity even now.[4] Similar to Christendom, the myth of the secular age remains intact on the surface while being changed from within. The new deities do not clothe themselves in the religious garbs of the past. Instead, they employ acceptable clothes that disguise their religious nature. As Helmut Schelsky already lucidly noticed in 1975, the new priesthood clothes itself in secular robes while being granted the power of the religious priests and exercising the same authority over their subjects.[5]

However, rusted myths break into pieces, which are then put together into a bricolage. I sought to show that the myth gaining in strength now is the ancient myth of Gnosticism. A myth is very enduring in its narrative core while allowing for a high degree of variations at the fringes.[6] The fragmentation of the Judeo-Christian myth and rituals invites the gnostic threads to be woven further into the very core. Re-enchantment does not merely occur in the pockets of the overall secular society to satisfy some consumer thirst for the beyond.[7] Instead, I argue that re-enchantment occurs at the mythical center. From a larger historical angle, dis-enchantment can be interpreted as an anomaly that occurs at short time intervals within particular mythological traditions. Normalcy reinstates itself. We are witnessing a plunge forward into the ancient past. In a sense, nothing has changed, as every society is structured through the enchanted core.

Modernity is an unfinished project with an open end. Similar to the ancient people, moderns have their own priests who tame the chaos by naming it. By uncovering the mythological past, they seek to establish the final mythos. As Blumenberg remarked, these modern myths do not give adequate answers to deep questions, yet they pretend as though there is nothing left to ask.[8] Since believing in gods would be viewed as regression and allegorical imagination is on the retreat, the vacuum of old names is filled with new names. Since these new mythologies pretend to be the final ones, they seek an all-encompassing totality, which will establish an abstract perfection. Blumenberg mentions only a few of such final myths, hinting at the notion of historic necessity by Hegel, the

4. Perkins, *Christendom and European Identity*.
5. Schelsky, *Arbeit tun die Anderen*, 77–167.
6. Blumenberg, *Arbeit am Mythos*, 40.
7. The phenomena of religions acquiring economic logic in order to market to consumer needs has been well researched in the sociology of religion.
8. Blumenberg, *Arbeit am Mythos*, 319.

notion of being by Heidegger, the unconscious within psychoanalysis, or the idea of the eternal return of the same in Nietzsche's thought.[9] I would add to these the myth of a classless society in socialist societies of the twentieth century and the ideal of an Aryan social body in German National Socialism. These were the gnostic precursors of the abstract deities of the twenty-first century.

These final mythological ideals function as deities because they possess explanatory power, can't themselves be fully comprehended, require sacrifice and obedience, and are imbued with the notion of the sacred. These highest ideals structure social order and give cohesive meaning to societies.[10] There is rarely a simple return to the old gods or a complete break. More often, new mythologies resurrect the old ones in a different guise while also taking up patterns of the established religion. This is how European Christendom established its dominion on the ruins of various tribal religions. And this is how the gnostic trinity emerges on the decaying Christendom, expressing itself in a secular disguise.

The personal, loving godfather is negated. Instead, a distant deity is introduced. This deity does not enter into a covenant relationship with every individual by prescribing rituals designed for everyone. Instead, this deity reveals itself only to a few enlightened priests. The ancient hierarchy is reestablished as only intellectual elites are capable of performing mediations between the deity and the people. Within the secular society, this deity must be communicated within the immanent frame while still maintaining a transcendent appeal. "Nature" or "cosmos" appear as ideal names for this new type of deity. It can be conceived as an immanent deity and at the same time imbued with transcendent properties. C. S. Lewis warned that when nature is elevated from being our sister to the status of a mother, it turns into an evil stepmother.[11] However, it is exactly this dark side that fascinates the modern human, who desires to be punished. Punishment is better than the void (see ch. 6). As Nietzsche foresaw prophetically, after the killing of the Christian God, the last blasphemy would be to use the name of nature in vain.[12] The power of a deity may be measured by the degree of punishment that is bestowed upon those who dare to question the authority of the deity.

---

9. Blumenberg, *Arbeit am Mythos*, 319.
10. They fulfill fully the mythological and ritual functions I have outlined in ch. 1.
11. Lewis, "Living in Atomic Age," 136.
12. Nietzsche, *Also sprach Zarathustra*, 9.

Jesus Christ, the mediator between God the Father and humanity, is replaced with power as blind force. Contrary to the Father God, Mother Nature does not reveal itself through loving commitment by taking on the particularity of human flesh. Instead, Mother Nature is beyond human grasp and can be felt only as a life force or power that permeates everything. The obsession with power and the lack of imagining relations rooted in love in the recent disciplines of philosophy and sociology demonstrates the substitution of the most basic mode of love by the cold logic of power. Granted, Foucault sought at the end of his life to discover constructive notions of power and turned to the Christian pastoral power for inspiration. Yet the overall irony has been the obsession with exposing power in order to empower the disadvantaged group toward higher representation in society. As Foucault rightly recognized, the Christian pastor must lay down his power in order to elevate the powerless: "Pastoral power is not merely a form of power which commands; it must also be prepared to sacrifice itself for the life and salvation of the flock. Therefore, it is different from royal power, which demands a sacrifice from its subjects to save the throne."[13] Hereby, those in power are not destroyed in the process but humbled under the rule of Jesus, the loving master of all, both the powerful and the powerless. Moreover, the power inequality is leveled through the eucharistic encounter in which both priest and layperson recognize their equal need for a savior. To the contrary, the secular priests use the disadvantaged in order to acquire moral authority, as their higher status justifies this ontological inequality. They seek to elevate the disempowered and violently bring down the powerful while viewing themselves in a realm outside of these immanent relations. The enlightened, gnostic mediators, who are able to perceive the discourse of power and redistribute power justly, are authorized to do so because they have special knowledge due to their intelligence. Gnostic knowledge, as the primary distinction for being human, creates a stark hierarchy between the enlightened and the unenlightened classes.

The human being is stripped of the special status of being created in the image of God. The human body is not the temple where God himself resides through the Holy Spirit. The individual is thereby reduced to naked flesh. Abstract immanent deities do not exemplify caring love. Instead, the relation between the person as mere biological organism and the abstract deity is mediated through brute force. The abstract deity,

---

13. Foucault, "Subject and Power."

power, and bare bodies reduced to flesh—this is the new trinity, which constitutes the new social center. This new trinity acquires its plausibility as it is able to function within the secular order while keeping the Christian Trinitarian structure in place and at the same time filling it with ancient gnostic meaning. The new priesthood, which mediates the powers between the abstract deity and the helpless, desacralized individual, is constituted through intellectual elites, who stand above commoners and who are not accountable to a shared covenant. Their authority stems from representing gnostic knowledge, which was bestowed upon them in temples dedicated to the production of knowledge within elaborate rites of passage and sacrificial routines. What type of society emerges around this perverted trinity?

Evolutionary and Revolutionary Transformations

Inequality as the natural historical order returns. Abstract divinity can be mediated only by a few enlightened priests, who guard its power. Every social sphere will be permeated by this new logic and shaped according to the new ontological inequality. Secret knowledge will create a sharp demarcation line. Once the universality of human dignity recedes, the worth of every human being will depend once more on one's enlightened status and utility for the group.

Voegelin viewed Hobbes as reintroducing pagan ontological inequality through his theological reinterpretation of Hebrew history. Accordingly, Hobbes employed the symbol of Leviathan as absolute monarchy under immediate rule of God: "Taking the Jewish theocratic concept as the pattern, the symbol of the Leviathan gains characteristics related to those of Akhenaten's imperial religion. Once more the ruler becomes the mediator of God; God reveals himself only to the ruler; he alone conveys the will of God to the people."[14]

The next step in divinizing the state consists in the removal of God from the sociopolitical world. "Now the link to God in the perfectly inner-worldly symbolism is severed and replaced by the community itself as the source of legitimation of the collective person."[15] The divine manifests itself through the consensus of people, as in liberal democracies, or must be mediated through an elect group, the party, as in

14. Voegelin, *Modernity Without Restraint*, 56.
15. Voegelin, *Modernity Without Restraint*, 64.

socialism or through an exceptional Führer as in National Socialism. The abstract deity will not enter covenant nor provide for his creation. The deity will not reveal his name. Instead, the deity will remain in obscurity, demanding sacrifice and continuous care from the worshippers. Instead of being reassured of one's inherent worth, every person must now prove their worth in relation to the abstract ideal.

The new gnostic trinitarian core acquires its social body through evolutionary and revolutionary modes. Evolutionary transformation occurs through slow change of both myth and rituals alike. Like yeast works its way slowly through the dough, so the new myth changes both the social consciousness and the material world. The meaning of words referring to the old liberal order get increasingly emptied, and the words get refilled with new meaning. Orwell's *1984* dystopia exemplifies this draining of the old substance while keeping the appearance.

The slow transformation of liberalism into totalitarianism begins in its civilizational heart. Sheldon Wolin lucidly begins his formulation of American "inverted totalitarianism" by describing Leni Riefenstahl's propaganda tribute in 1934, comparing it to the American hubris, which clothes itself in a myth.[16] Hubris embedded in a myth is ultimately the deepest force driving civilizations. Wolin shows the secularized Christian myth at work in the American thirst for dominance abroad and increasingly the domestic total control of its citizens as well. Wolin does not pursue his intuition on a deeper historical level. However, he convincingly shows the unconscious transformation of American democracy into soft totalitarianism from both parties, whether the Right or the Left. The monster of big government was built up against the other monster of the big business. Yet, ultimately both have merged and rule ubiquitously by shaping the reality of citizens through new technology. Since continuous motion is at the heart of the American myth, citizens are not able to pause, develop higher perception, and reflect upon this encroaching reality. Pluralistic institutions like politics, business, academia, and media merge into an invisible blanket over a sedated citizen who has lost a sense of agency.

Similarly to Wolin, Giorgio Agamben traces the emergence of totalitarianism from the deep transformation of liberalism. In particular, once the human is stripped of sanctity and is reduced to bare life, the line between individual liberty and total care of the state is blurred:

---

16. Wolin, *Democracy Incorporated*, 1–8.

And only because biological life and its needs had become the *politically* decisive fact is it possible to understand the otherwise incomprehensible rapidity with which twentieth-century parliamentary democracies were able to turn into totalitarian states and with which this century's totalitarian states were able to be converted, almost without interruption, into parliamentary democracies. In both cases, these transformations were produced in a context in which for quite some time politics had already turned into biopolitics, and in which the only real question to be decided was which form of organization would be best suited to the task of assuring the care, control, and use of bare life. Once their fundamental referent becomes bare life, traditional political distinctions (such as those between Right and Left, liberalism and totalitarianism, private and public) lose their clarity and intelligibility and enter into a zone of indistinction.[17]

Both Wolin and Agamben presuppose a deep mythological transformation prior to the emergence of a totalitarian order. This occurs through the willing submission of people and the externalizing of their own knowledge to academic experts, their agency to politicians, and their judgment of the external world to the media. Technology, which once served to fulfill their consumer wishes, slowly turns into a tool to both create and easily manipulate desires in order to harvest docile minds and bodies.[18]

The Leviathan appears just like the Grand Inquisitor in Dostoevsky's prophetic vision. He does not need to coerce his subjects, as they willingly kneel before him and beg him to provide them comfort and security, thereby sacrificing their agency and their individual rights. The supposedly benevolent leader Lenin, whom I grew up with in the Soviet Union, reappears again in a different disguise. Some Germans still lovingly call him "Father State." Yet this time there is no portrait hanging in every state office. Instead, the image of the benevolent state is diffused into the individual conscience directly via technology through the constant promise of the fused powers to care and maintain the bare life. Aldous Huxley already envisioned this soft form of totalitarianism in the 30s in which people would be conditioned from birth and sedated through pleasure and drugs. As long as Western societies remain wealthy, compliance of

---

17. Agamben, *Homo Sacer*, 135; emphasis in original.
18. Shoshana Zuboff paints technological innovations through a dystopian lens. Ultimately, the exploitation of workers and consumers becomes ubiquitous as minds and bodies are harvested by the few who control AI (*Age of Surveillance Capitalism*).

citizens is more likely to occur. The necessity for disruptive change and force arises when resistance begins to grow as people begin to notice the loss of liberties, security, and wealth. However, a disruptive imposition of totalitarian order is also possible by employing technology to create a mass formation. The psychological dynamics and sophisticated technologies of manipulation make it impossible to assess independently a constructed, all-encompassing reality. The proclaimed "state of exception," which has been used as a blank check to bypass checks and balances in order to counter an imminent danger, and has been employed by all twentieth-century totalitarian ideologies, could be much more ubiquitous in the twenty-first century due to the available digital technology.

Once liberalism is transformed from within, any resistance weakens and the door is opened for a more direct, revolutionary upheaval. Once decay progresses far enough, a light push suffices to topple the entire structure. This push manifests itself as proclamation of "state of exception":[19] "One of the essential characteristics of the state of exception—the provisional abolition of the distinction among legislative, executive, and judicial powers—here shows its tendency to become a lasting practice of government."[20]

However, the exception can become the rule only because the subjects participate in this transition of sovereignty away from the individual to the all-powerful entity. Within the twentieth century, the largest Leviathan conceived was the nation-state. Therefore the threat that provided the state with the legitimacy to exercise total control was framed as a matter of national survival:

> No sooner did Hitler take power (or, as we should perhaps more accurately say, no sooner was power given to him) than, on February 28, he proclaimed the Decree for the Protection of the People and the State, which suspended the articles of the Weimar Constitution concerning personal liberties. The decree was never repealed, so that from a juridical standpoint the entire Third Reich can be considered a state of exception that lasted twelve years. In this sense, modern totalitarianism can be defined as the establishment, by means of the state of exception, of a legal civil war that allows for the physical elimination not only

---

19. Recently Agamben reformulated this Schmittian concept both in relation to the history of ideas and in applying this concept to the transformation of democracies (*State of Exception*).

20. Agamben, *State of Exception*, 7.

of political adversaries but of entire categories of citizens who for some reason cannot be integrated into the political system.[21]

Agamben goes on to notice similar patterns in political rhetoric and policies post the September 11 attack. In light of national security, the Patriot Act as issued by the US Senate on October 26, 2001, allowed the suspension of prior-given rights of non–US citizens: "What is new about President Bush's order is that it radically erases any legal status of the individual, thus producing a legally unnamable and unclassifiable being."[22]

After the Second World War, the state of exception has developed into the consciousness of global threat. For the first time in human history, the possibility of global annihilation by nuclear extinction poses a real threat, which requires communication and agreement between world powers. I grew up in the Soviet Union with the constant threat in the back of my head, just as my US-American wife did, that the enemy could push the button and unleash a cataclysmic hell. Soviet and American schools trained their children for nuclear war and thus implanted in them the expectation of imminent doom. With the end of the Cold War, this expectation of collapse was further stoked through the growing discourse surrounding environmental pollution, which was then scaled up to climate change. With raised consciousness of imminent apocalypse, blockbusters stoked the fires of fear with dystopian films portraying differing scenarios of how humanity could end. From natural catastrophes, wars, pandemics—the entire doomsday genre provides a brief avenue of chaos to escape bureaucratic modern life. The most recent perceived global threat is the emergence of AI, which many fear will take control of the earth and, in the end, replace human beings.[23] Universal threats, whether real or imagined, require universal institutions. However, once established, all institutions tend toward perversion of their original purpose. The slope from care to protection to control is a slippery one. As Shoshana Zuboff demonstrates, the progression from predicting the consumers' desires to actively generating their motivations and actions will most likely occur due to the incentive of generating large revenue.[24]

---

21. Agamben, *State of Exception*, 2.

22. Agamben, *State of Exception*, 3.

23. Yuval Harari paints this dystopian future as a possible scenario in his book *Homo Deus*.

24. Zuboff, *Age of Surveillance Capitalism*, 8.

Before one can begin to reflect upon these threats, one has already internalized the sense of dread that hangs over the head of the global population. Since these various crises threaten to wipe out humanity, democratic procedures and structures can be seen as not sufficient to counter them. Since what is at stake is nothing less than the survival of humanity, anything goes. Stoking fear and nudging via various psychological techniques in order to create mass compliance are justified if the danger can be averted.[25] The ignorant masses must be moved at any cost for their own benefit. Institutions that were created to prevent global dangers could slowly take on a preemptive approach in seeking to localize these dangers and then use these projections for intrusive control. The desire for security is insatiable. Thus computational models could be increasingly employed as the primary source to simulate reality and possible risks. Based on these projections, the Leviathan acquires authority as the only power to prevent humanity from Damocles's sword hanging over its head. This sword is a projected hologram, a simulacrum, which replaced the real dangers. However, as reality can't be distinguished from its simulation, there is no reference beyond what appears as real.

Suspension of checks and balances, the elimination of individual rights, seems like an inevitable small sacrifice in order to guarantee the future of all humanity. Instead of long debates, urgency and collective, univocal agency are required. The vague deity does not reveal how it all ends. Anything is possible, and therefore pure power is desired by the people in order to preserve the biological survival of the group. Due to the collective amnesia and the lack of conversation about what makes life worth living, people descend into a stupor, a simple, vegetative, trancelike existence. Like in Plato's allegory of the cave, they turn against anyone who threatens their narrow and shallow but familiar world. Once the Trinitarian Judeo-Christian myth is forgotten and the hope of redemption loses its imaginative force, the entire attention turns toward mere survival in the moment and the frame of perception is funneled into the phlegmatic now. Masses who have lost the larger arc of meaning can be induced with mass hysteria. The totalitarian state is then welcomed as the savior from the imminent universal dangers, and anyone who does not share in this mass paranoia is attacked as an enemy of humanity.

---

25. Alison McQueen argues for "rational fear" as an apocalyptic strategy in order to move lazy masses toward action in light of what she perceives as a global threat (*Political Realism in Apocalyptic*, 203).

The Megalomaniac Leviathan

Hobbes's Leviathan formed itself by mimicking and transforming the church. The legitimacy and authority of the secular state has deep roots in the medieval theological imaginary and succession of the church as the guarantor of peace, care, and security (see ch. 3). The nation-state acquired its legitimacy when the church failed to embody the common good for all. Hobbes's vision appeared as the only option in light of the threat to the commonwealth by religious zealots. As Voegelin noted: "The symbol of the Leviathan was developed by an English thinker in response to the Puritan danger."[26] Once the church mires the highest ideal through its own corruption, another highest principle must be imposed on society. However, as Voegelin described, social reality rarely fits into a simplistic individual imagination. Referring to Schelling, Voegelin diagnosed gnostic thinkers with what he terms *pneumapathology*, which refers to the "condition of a thinker who, in his revolt against the world as it has been created by God, arbitrarily omits an element of reality in order to create the fantasy of a new world." According to Voegelin, Hobbes omits the highest good as the highest principle for orienting society and substitutes it with *summum malum*: "If men are not moved to live with one another in peace through common love of the divine, highest good, then the fear of the *summum malum* of death must force them to live in an orderly society."[27]

Paraphrasing the biblical idea that love drives out fear (1 John 4:18), in the absence of love for the highest good, fear prevails as the only motivation. Consequently, the tragedy of the secular state, which set out to be a better church, consists in the lack of any corrective vision beyond its own boundaries. The megalomaniac thirst for power of the medieval popes could be countered by reference to divine authority. The corrective alternative of medieval sects and the Protestant Reformation originated in their reference to God, whose authority was placed above ecclesial power. However, once there is nothing beyond the immanent frame, every revolution must be fought within the constant fear of chaos and the vague projection of human flourishing. Ultimately, the only point of reference to uphold the structure is the gnostic thinker who envisioned the entire society in the first place: "The society that is governed neither by God's will nor its own, shall be placed under that of the gnostic thinker.

---

26. Voegelin, *Modernity Without Restraint*, 240.
27. Voegelin, *Modernity Without Restraint*, 306.

The *libido dominandi* that Hobbes diagnosed in the Puritans celebrates its highest triumph in the construction of a system that denies man the freedom and ability to order his life in society. Through the construction of the system the thinker becomes the only free person—a god, who will deliver man from the evils of the 'state of nature.'"[28]

Various political religions of the twentieth century fought about the immanent vision of a flourishing society. Three competing ideologies of socialism, National Socialism, and liberalism ultimately fought about the immanent vision of what it means to be human and build flourishing societies. These immanent ideologies employed Judeo-Christian methods of critique to establish their own legitimacy. By reenvisioning history, they first uncovered the original sin by laying bare what went wrong. Then like good prophets they stirred the hunger for the future paradise. Yet contrary to the biblical prophets, they kept their own gods hidden in the background, in not spelling out their normative assumptions and unconsciously borrowing from the Judeo-Christian past.

Hanna Arendt's brilliant analysis of totalitarianism is a striking example of her unwillingness to acknowledge her own indebtedness to the Judeo-Christian background. Arendt presupposes that totalitarianism can be perceived and that it is evil. As I have shown in more detailed analysis elsewhere, both of these assumptions are firmly rooted in biblical apocalyptic literature.[29] Perhaps due to her aversion to the biblical roots, Arendt falls into a naïve solution to totalitarianism by suggesting that totalitarianism can be overcome through the reconstruction of a new humanity. Through a letter exchange with Arendt, Voegelin reminded her that the idea of a new humanity stands at the very core of the totalitarian grip with its pride to engineer the new human being. To the contrary, Voegelin suggests that the rediscovery of Greek philosophy and biblical prophets suffices to resist totalitarian rule.[30] Voegelin traces totalitarianism to the collapse of Christendom and the perversion of religion, while Arendt views totalitarianism as caused by the systemic transformation of society in the age of industrialization. I view both explanations as complementary while emphasizing the deeper historical explanation as proposed by Voegelin.

The phenomenon of the megalomaniac Leviathan stands in continuity with Hobbes and twentieth-century totalitarianism. However, due

28. Voegelin, *Modernity Without Restraint*, 307.
29. Dik, "Discovering Entanglements."
30. Arendt and Voegelin, *Disput über den Totalitarismus*, 33.

to further uprooting from the Judeo-Christian past and further systemic changes, the degree of both the reach and power through technology of the emerging Leviathan has by far surpassed the predecessors. The nature of the encroaching totalitarianism will be so thorough and all-encompassing that it will usurp any space from which its nature could be perceived, extinguishing any suspicion of its very own existence. The megalomaniac Leviathan comes close to the perfect map in the short story of Borges, "On Exactitude in Science." The state will not be defined functionally as enabling human flourishing but ontologically: the state, like a perfect map, will cover the territory so thoroughly that it will equate being human with living in the state. As it was for the tribal humans of ancient times, to be exiled outside the territory of their local bonds and gods will mean to cease to exist. A communal life outside the power of the totalitarian state will become unimaginable and repulsive, similar to the brute, disgusting existence of a primitive remnant outside the World State city of London in Huxley's *Brave New World*.

The powers of the advancing Leviathan exceed the nation-states and ubiquitously pervade all societies. There will be no iron curtain between two competing secular ideologies like we have had in the twentieth century. Instead, the megalomaniac Leviathan will appear like a caring mother, covering everyone with a warm blanket. Once the child is asleep, she transforms into an evil witch and turns the soft blanket into an iron casket. The children begin to panic and gasp for air. Her response is to calmly reassure them that this transformation was necessary in order to protect them from the evil world out there. This metaphor is not exactly accurate, as the encroaching soft totalitarianism does not have personal agency and can't be adequately explained through conspiracy theories wherein a few powerful elites pull the strings. Instead, this order arises organically when certain ideas become manifest in sociopolitical structures. Mattias Desmet employs the Sierpinski triangle to demonstrate that totalitarian social order arises from the bottom up when a mechanistic ideology captures the imagination of people:

> As with drawing the Sierpinski triangle, if everyone follows the same rules, it results in strictly regular patterns emerging in society. Like iron filings scattered in the force field of a magnet, individuals arrange themselves in a perfect pattern under the influence of these forces. Man has always fallen prey to the aforementioned "temptations"—the illusion of rational understanding and control, the resistance to questioning oneself

critically as a human, the pursuit of short-term convenience, and so on. Within the religious discourse, these temptations were considered dangerous, but that changed with the rise of mechanistic thinking.... Leaders and followers were captivated by the limitless possibilities the human mind seemed to offer. The whole evolution towards a hyper-controlled technological society—the surveillance society—is simply unavoidable as long as the human mind remains trapped in that logic and is (to a large extent unconsciously) controlled by those attractors. It is this ideology that redesigned society, created new institutions, and selected new authority.[31]

In accord with Desmet's analysis, I view the megalomaniac Leviathan as the product of possessed humans. The beast is birthed from a collective body. The obliteration of Judeo-Christian myth and rituals allows for a stronger manifestation of the gnostic myth and an all-pervasive presence of the Leviathan in the twenty-first century. The emerging Leviathan will encounter less resistance from a sedated populus. There will be no space, either imaginary or real, from which to resist. Instead, the encroaching order extends its tentacles into the most private realms, down into the brain synapses, thus feeding and building up the Leviathan from the neurons of its subjects. The grip of the new Leviathan will reach deeper than anything that appeared before it. Therefore, previous modes will prove ineffective to counter its ubiquitous nature.

Seductions

The seduction of soft totalitarianism is effective due to its appeal toward four ideal types of intellectuals. To simplify, I classify these modes of perceiving reality as progressive, conservative, fundamentalist, and idealist.[32] The seducer appeals to the best in a particular mode, while the one who is seduced also feels the allure of the dark. There is something in every individual and mode of perception that is drawn by evil.

The strength of the progressive mode lies in its openness toward the new and the courage to explore wider horizons by breaking with the old paths. The weakness of this mode lies in the often-naïve view of history as a linear progression toward a utopian goal. This makes progressive

---

31. Desmet, *Psychology of Totalitarianism*, 132.

32. These ideal types do not refer to specific, historic sociopolitical movements, even though these modes are crucial in understanding historic events.

intellectuals susceptible to every zeitgeist and opens them up to be possessed by spirits that once appeared as progressive but now are unmasked as evil. Eugenics in conjunction with scientific racism is merely one example. Soft totalitarianism could appeal to progressive intellectuals' desire to improve human nature and the world. They might genuinely be convinced that soft totalitarianism is the only way to avoid the otherwise-inevitable global collapse and introduce a new level of global human flourishing. The darker appeal lies in the promise of becoming a part of the enlightened elite, similar to Dostoevsky's Grand Inquisitor, who justified his ubiquitous power over the people with the weakness of the masses.[33] He masked his tyranny as benevolence, his lies as necessary sacrifice of truth due to the inability of the masses to endure harsh reality. Within this progressive logic, a sacrifice of truth and, when necessary, human dignity as well are justified with the necessity of progress toward a utopia. Accordingly, the price of soft totalitarianism pales in comparison to the bright future, which requires that the enlightened elites sacrifice a few people in order to elevate the masses. These few turned out to be millions of corpses in the German concentration camps and Soviet gulags.

At its best, conservative intellectuals are wise to discern the constancy of both human nature and certain historic patterns. As Chesterton's vivid example goes, the conservative does not simply break the old fences without first evaluating their use and benefit. The new is not necessarily better, and it is often worth preserving what one's ancestors fought for. A side effect of this continuity with the past and appreciation of local roots is a deep satisfaction with the way the world is, without a constant need to disrupt.[34] The weakness of conservatives lies in their high desire for security and orderliness and therefore a high maintenance of boundaries. This at times makes them turn inward, sinking into a naïve, nostalgic glorification of the past. This orientation to the past and focus on sustaining the present makes it difficult to paint a captivating vision for the future, thus often defining themselves over and against the progressives. This could dissolve into a worse kind of conservatism as resentment—a bitter, boiling feeling of jealousy, without any valve of constructive release. Instead, the resentful intellectual descends into hatred

---

33. Dostoevsky, *Bratja Karamasowj*, 254–73.

34. Sheldon Wolin advocates for a return toward democratic, grassroots virtues as a bulwark against soft totalitarianism. Similarly, Steven Pinker seeks to conserve Enlightenment virtues. One can see these intellectuals as classical liberals who turn more conservative in light of changes that they perceive as impacting our societies negatively.

and ultimately lashes out against his brother like Cain against Abel. Additionally, secular conservatives find themselves increasingly in a strange dissonance. As progressives acquiesce to the post-individual order, secular freedom-loving intellectuals increasingly begin to see the value of religion to underpin the liberal social order. It begins to dawn on some that if religion is inevitable, perhaps the Judeo-Christian tradition constitutes the lesser evil.[35] Secular conservatives are increasingly split between those who repeat ad nauseam the return to Enlightenment values as the founding myth of Western liberal democracies, and those who are historically more sophisticated and are aware that the Enlightenment is an outgrowth of a particular religious tradition.[36] Yet the tragedy of these sophisticated conservatives consists in the fact that they are doomed to live as parasites: well aware of the fact that they are drawing from the life of an organism they are unable to actively sustain.

The best of fundamentalism consists in the courage to face the attack and the fortitude of character to build a wall in order to protect the weakest. In the irenic-charitable version, the fundamentalists, either religious or secular, preserve their life-giving core and maintain an attitude of pragmatic interaction with the surrounding world.[37] Fundamentalists of this brand will continue to cultivate their guarded shires, hoping that the orcs will not destroy their paradise. One may of course debate the effectiveness of such efforts. At times fundamentalists battle ghosts, without understanding the true nature of the battle. They do not understand that ideas penetrate walls and implant themselves in the minds of people. Often, fundamentalists cling to nostalgia while they are being shaped through the waters of change flowing through them. Without understanding that the current social order emerged from decaying Christianity, they are tempted to fight against "secular individualism" while embodying it fully in their everyday life. Similarly, secular fundamentalists might not recognize the religious nature of the post-individual order, and instead of the spiritual battle, they will fight flesh and blood on the

---

35. Even Richard Dawkins, the staunchest warrior of the New Atheism, recently declared himself to be culturally Christian, in light of Islamic incursions into British culture and politics.

36. E.g., Habermas's admission of religious surplus of meaning in his conversation with Ratzinger (Habermas, *Zeit der Übergänge*).

37. The Amish are an example of the religious brand of charitable fundamentalism. Shoshana Zuboff, who envisions a retreat into nature as an escape from the digital slavery, is an example of secular fundamentalism (*Age of Surveillance Capitalism*).

periphery. There is no escape from the invisible powers; no paradise lost can be recreated in the pure enclave.

With the crumbling of the previous order, some might be tempted to feel Schadenfreude—glee about the collapse of secular liberalism. Without understanding the deeper sources of the social order centered around the sacred individual, they will interpret this demise as their victory. Without learning from history, they will seek to fuse the divine and ethnic within one political order once again.[38] Theirs will be an unintended resurrection of an old idea of Christendom as a bulwark against the decomposing gravitational force of the aged secular liberalism. However, they will resurrect a monster who will compete with the emerging gnostic society. This grand fundamentalism is not motivated by irenic retreat but rather by expansion and the will to power. It will employ the same means as the advancing totalitarian order because it views itself on the right side of history, interpreting the defeat of secular liberalism as confirmation of its own ideas. The resurrected Christendom might turn into a digital "handmaid's tale."[39]

The final, most sophisticated mode in facing the emergence of the post-individual order is idealism. This mode could turn out to be the worst if corrupted because it is fueled often by the best of imaginations. Idealists are able to perceive the larger picture and think in symbols. At their best, idealists are able to illuminate hidden metaphors and point to unexpected connections within a system. Yet at the root of their capacity to illuminate lies the cardinal sin of hubris due to their elevated perception. This vice could pervert their idealism into a totalitarian hell.

Idealists could be split between those who choose to be at the service of the emerging enchanted society and those who seek to recover a larger picture in order to preserve a society centered around human dignity. This can be seen in secular and religious idealists who seek to employ various disciplines to overcome the modern bifurcations between science and religion, aiming at unifying, larger horizons. Increasingly, secular intellectuals are reaching out and borrowing from the Judeo-Christian reservoir of meaning. Yet, they borrow in a gnostic,

---

38. Aleksandr Dugin on the Russian Orthodox side and Stephen Wolfe on the US-American Reformed-Calvinist side are two examples of this type of reactionary-nostalgic brand of fundamentalism.

39. *The Handmaid's Tale* is a novel by Margaret Atwood that was made into a television series. Atwood paints a dystopian future, where the US has been transformed into a theocracy.

selective manner. They break off the symbolic pattern from the socio-material body of Christ, the church.

The strength of the idealist perception is also its weakness. The flight toward overarching meaning detaches them from concrete reality. Moreover, idealists tend to perceive general ideal types, while losing sight of the particularities. Yet life and history are specific. Sometimes, their ability to envision the whole leads them toward overtly cliché, caricatured representations of reality. Christian idealists tend to portray the emergence of the secular as a counterforce against the church. This may lead to defending the church and portraying it as an ideal against the corrupt secular state. Yet the church has been deeply enmeshed in both the dark and bright moments of Western secularization. The danger of Christian idealism lies in the illusion that once a better myth has been reimagined, the re-narration alone suffices to counter the seduction of the enchanted society. Their vivid imagination blinds them to the fact of corporeality.[40]

Theologians and secular intellectuals alike are prone to respond within these ideal-type paradigms. The advancing soft totalitarianism seduces intellectuals to define themselves in relation to its presence. Yet the one who looks into the eyes of the Medusa will turn to stone. My strategy so far—to sketch the emergence of the social order based on the idea of sacred human dignity and its demise—does leave out the question of how this myth and these rituals could be manifested. I don't believe that the solution to the problem lies in any of these intellectual strategies, even though I see some value in all of them at some point in time. In an ideal strategy, all of the best features of these ideal types would be held in perfect balance. However, this can't be achieved through individual modes in particular discursive traditions. What are needed are a higher complexity and energy that could radiate a life, breaking the spell of the encroaching totalitarianism.

So far I have been looking retrospectively. To propose a constructive theological solution now would make theology functional and thus reduce it in the eyes of a believer. My intention has been to humble both the agnostic and the religious believer. Hopefully, the believer will have realized that his perverted worship radiates decay into the rest of society. Hopefully the agnostic will have recognized that she lives off borrowed capital and develops an appreciation for that which previously seemed to her an irrational myth. However, at this point some pragmatically

---

40. This is my temptation as well, which I seek to counter by leading an urban intercultural church, by being rooted in the messy reality of the everyday.

oriented believers and agnostics might ask: So what? What are we to do concerning this encroaching soft totalitarianism? If all social order comes from theology, how do we return to the life-giving myth and ritual? Once the fire has burned everything down, is there even a possibility to build up something on the smoldering ruins? I hesitate to give a simple answer. The deepest myths do provide answers to concrete problems. But even more so, they help to formulate foundational questions, which reach beyond the immediate problems and through their scope sketch wider horizons.

My hope is that both seeking agnostics and believers alike will relativize their previous questions and discover deeper ones. Perhaps the nature of the problem will be reframed in such a way that the urgency to find an answer will disappear. In this newfound place of rest and stillness, larger horizons will emerge. People mostly become worshippers of the triune God because they are touched by his glory and not because they want to fix social problems, although the latter one could be a door opener, a glimpse into the wider horizons. In order to resist the seduction, one must envision a different framework altogether. Voegelin rightly discerned the very problem of any academic attempt to climb out from the gnostic graveyard: "The struggle against the consequences of Gnosticism is being conducted in the very language of Gnosticism."[41] In order to speak a different language, one must step into a different life form; and in order to break out, one must perceive new horizons.

So far, I have been pursuing this route from below, hinting at the necessity of gods and rituals in general and for the necessity of the triune God, who secures sacred human dignity at the center for the particular social order. Yet we can't climb all the way up to him. Instead, he descended to us. His glory interrupts the temporal and spatial. It is at this point that I switch my mode of reflection. Instead of hinting from below, I will now attempt to describe this mode of interruption first and then spell out the consequences for the church and society at large. God's table is set. His invitation precedes our being and our action. From his table, some crumbs fall off and feed the entire civilization.

---

41. Voegelin, *Modernity Without Restraint*, 248.

Critical Interlude

MY ARGUMENT SO FAR could be dismissed as too narrowly focused on the role of Judeo-Christian tradition in the rise and fall of secular liberalism. Moreover, the decline toward a totalitarian state may seem overly pessimistic and deterministic. Various objections could be leveled against my analysis.

First, Christianity is perhaps necessary but not sufficient for the emergence of secular liberal democratic regimes. Throughout history, and even on a global level, Christianity has led toward other sociopolitical orders. Currently, the Russian Orthodox Church stabilizes Putin just like it did the czar. European churches, both Roman Catholic and Protestant, viewed monarchy as a divine ordinance just a few centuries ago. Perhaps one might argue that it is anachronistic now to smuggle Christianity in as the chief reason for equality and liberty. Together with this objection, a second could follow suit. It would appear according to my analysis that other, non-European influences are excluded from the genesis of liberalism.

I believe both objections are valid. My focus on the role of the Judeo-Christian tradition was not meant to claim exclusivity. The second step would consist in opening up my story to wider comparative perspectives. As I have hinted throughout this book, the Judeo-Christian tradition has allied itself with various political regimes, both hierarchical and more egalitarian. This tension permeates the Christian tradition itself, as at its core stands the tension between hierarchy and its permanent subversion. The paradox of God's unfathomable greatness and his concrete servitude in Jesus and presence through the Holy Spirit permeates the very idea of the Trinitarian God. This tension serves as a continuous creative source to imagine various ways of organizing society.

While the church has succumbed many times to the seduction of power, its core remains relational. European Christendom has had its center in the Middle East. This is the irony and the heart of European secular modernity. This story could be elaborated further and in so doing point to the suppressed roots of this modernity, as David Graeber and David Wengrow have shown in their revisionist account. Accordingly, the interaction with the native population of the Americas stimulated new questions and fresh avenues of thought for Enlightenment philosophers.[1] Graeber and Wengrow suggest an existence of heterogeneous political orders existing beside each other, both egalitarian and highly authoritarian, throughout human history. The desire to learn from and write an alternative history by resurrecting the perspective of the conquered people is in itself a Judeo-Christian legacy, which seeks to lift up the oppressed and views all humans as created in the image of God. Therefore, power can't be conflated with truth.

My view of history confirms the anthropological/archeological account of Graeber and Wengrow. History is not ascending linearly toward the secular utopia. Instead, there are various breaks and unexpected turns. Humans are experimenting with various ways of organizing themselves. I only maintain that myths and rituals remain constant amid the highly pluralistic conceptions of organizing society. The hopeful message, which both Graeber and Wengrow paint by looking into the distant past and which I seek to communicate in my last part, is that nothing is inevitable. A deterministic framework is in itself already a conceptual tool of totalitarianism.

All I have sought to establish from a historical view is that myth and ritual are the primary causes to understand social change. Hereby, the role of Christianity is ambiguous. It served as the source of both flourishing and decay. Christians must learn from history. In particular, they must understand how their worship was corrupted in order not to repeat it. However, the attempt to draw conclusions from history as to how to use their religion instrumentally in order to achieve a flourishing society would ultimately fail. This would contradict both their theological creed about God as the highest ideal and the fact of social complexity, as our intentions rarely match the outcomes. The paradoxical effect of worship is the enlarging of the perception beyond the immediate sociopolitical order. A religion that dwarfs itself into a

---

1. Graeber and Wengrow, *Dawn of Everything*.

functionalist mold will cease to exist and fail to shape the sociopolitical order. Even worse, this type of religion will fall prey to immanent political powers, which would subvert it from within.

Twilight is an ambiguous phenomenon, which refers to the in-between, as the light either fades or increases. Thus, twilight can be experienced just before a new day breaks in and before the night envelops everything. Perhaps this is the reason Wagner chose the title *Twilight of the Gods* for the fourth opera of his cycle *Der Ring des Nibelungen*. One interpretation of the final act suggests that as the gods die in the burning Valhalla, hope for the emergence of a new man breaks in.[2] On the ruins of the old world, a godlike man appears. Both socialist and National Socialist ideologues favored this interpretation. However, this interpretation is naïve as humans can't live without gods due to their social nature. Therefore, the rebirth of the new imaginary of man coincides with the rebirth of the gods. The self-image of man is possible only within the larger myth.

Nietzsche interprets Wagner in his *Twilight of the Idols* in such a manner that the gods of old in their Platonic and Christian disguise are mere idols, which must be smashed with the hammer. Here Nietzsche treads the paths of the biblical prophets. I sought to show that all idols ultimately sink into exhaustion after parasitically devouring human societies. Idols must be fed. After exhausting societies and nature, idols begin to drink human blood and chew human flesh. Once civilization is devoured, the idols die of starvation. Nietzsche's pathological suspicion of both Platonic philosophy and Christian morality as weakness breeding resentment could also be turned upon his own philosophy. Therefore, his attempt to envision new gods remains the projection of a sick mind creating a world of his own grandeur. In retrospect, Nietzsche's passionate divinities, who promised to reinvigorate humanity, only accelerated the decay. I seek to point to the one who has been proclaimed dead so many times and yet is alive and whose life still indwells churches and societies.

The last part does not offer an exhaustive theopolitical vision. This is not possible anyway due to the depth of the biblical narrative and the myriad of possible interpretations and enactments within history. All we can do every generation anew is to point to the crucified and risen. I merely seek to be like the long finger of John the Baptist in the painting of Matthias Grünewald. My modest contribution is not to paint all the

2. On various possible interpretation within the historical context of Wagner's opera, see Fridrich, "Richard Wagners Götterdämmerung."

subtleties of Christian worship. Instead, I hope to sketch the paradoxical features that permeate the Judeo-Christian myth and thrive in the communal rituals. Within this paradox as its soil, a society can take root and begin to flourish. To describe this flourishing goes beyond an academic work and lies within the realm of a prophet. I merely point to the crumbs that fall from the liturgical table and demonstrate how they feed the starving world.

Part IV

How Idiotic Worship
Unintentionally Births
a Flourishing Society

CHAPTER 10

Soli Deo Gloria: Envisioning Paradoxical Patterns

Religions devised for a social purpose, like Roman emperor-worship or modern attempts to "sell" Christianity as a means of "saving civilization," do not come to much.

—C. S. Lewis, The Four Loves

Gloria Dei est vivens homo. Vita hominis visio Dei.

—St. Irenaeus, *Adversus haereses*

The Evasive Nature of Pleasure

In Germany, car sharing is quite common. A few years ago, I rented a car and picked up a student who was also going to Frankfurt. The trip took several hours, and he happened to be very talkative. He shared with me that he studied business administration and sports, which he viewed as very practical, due to his love of philandering. He explained to me that in order to manage his simultaneous relationships, his administrative skills come in handy. Simultaneously, he needed to maintain his physique through sports in order to remain appealing so as to keep the supply going.

I asked him about his highest goal in life. He replied that his ultimate goal was to maximize pleasure. The means toward this goal was sex with as many appealing women as possible. He did recognize that this was only a temporary solution, as age will ultimately turn him into an old sugar daddy. At one point, in a more pensive mood, he wondered whether there is something else beyond immediate sexual gratification.

In his sermon "The Weight of Glory," C. S. Lewis surprisingly described modern humans as not pleasure seeking enough.[1] Lewis concluded that the human hunger for fullness and the absence of anything in this world to fill the human heart point to the need for fulfillment from beyond the immanent. We do not find complete satisfaction in ourselves, as we are social creatures. René Girard rightly emphasized the mimetic desire as the core motivating force for human behavior.[2] We desire that which others attribute value toward. The tragedy and conflicts stem from our insatiable hunger for the highest good without fully discerning what it is. Humans sense that the highest good is not contained within themselves but lies outside. Therefore, an attempt to make lesser goods into the highest will inevitably spoil them. Viktor Frankl put it succinctly in relation to sexual pleasure: "The more a man tries to demonstrate his sexual potency or a woman her ability to experience orgasm, the less they are able to succeed. Pleasure is, and must remain, a side-effect or by-product, and is destroyed and spoiled to the degree to which it is made a goal in itself."[3]

The biblical story posits the highest goal for all of creation and humanity in God himself. Ultimately, human desire can be stilled only in God. Therefore, while human desire for pleasure is real, the attempt to find it within oneself or by seeking it through others will fail. Pleasure is a side effect of a larger endeavor.

Paradoxical Glory

The biblical story portrays God as the central character. The main motive for God to create the world and to continuously pursue people in love is to glorify himself. God's own glory is the main axis around which everything else revolves. Theologians sought to pin down the meaning

---

1. Lewis, "Weight of Glory."
2. Girard, *Ende der Gewalt*.
3. Frankl, *Man's Search for Meaning*, 125.

of glory. Jonathan Edwards wrote a treatise on the meaning of God's glory. He describes glory as the following: "The thing signified by that name, the glory of God, when spoken of as the supreme and ultimate end of all God's works, is the emanation and true external expression of God's internal glory and fullness."[4]

Edwards can't avoid circularity in his attempt to grasp the nature of God's glory. Toward the end of his treatise, Edwards concedes "a degree of obscurity in these definitions."[5] Perhaps as the most general understanding, *glory* could be conceived as that which emanates from God's inner being. For example, in the vision of Isaiah, the angels cry out: "Holy, holy, holy is the Lord of Hosts; all the earth is full of His glory" (Isa 6:3). Glory encompasses God's holiness, it is the radiant sum of God's character.

Etymologically, glory can be traced to the Hebrew *kavod*, referring to heaviness. Glory, as that which is the ultimate reason for all of being, is being conveyed to humans via the metaphor of physical experience. In the Letter to the Corinthians, Paul employs this meaning in order to contrast the heaviness of future glory with the lightness of momentary troubles: "For our light and momentary troubles are achieving for us an eternal glory that far outweighs them all" (2 Cor 4:17). Bauckham notices the difference in semantic field between Hebrew and Greek. The semantic field of glory is wider in Hebrew than in Greek. *Doxa* in Greek is commonly used to mean "opinion." However, when Hebrew *kavod* is translated into Greek, it takes on a new meaning of "visible splendor."[6]

In conclusion, glory could be understood as the core motivation of God, emanating from him into his creation. Since glory is of ultimate concern to God, it must be to humans as well. The purpose for human existence is to glorify God through worship. Humans become truly who they are meant to be as they contemplate in adoration upon God's glory. A better mode to comprehend glory is not to provide a water tight definition, but to look at how glory is described throughout the biblical narratives. Its paradoxical nature fits more easily into a story than a systematic treaty.

God's glory is both present in God's creation and at the same time transcends everything immanent. The psalmists reflect on God's glory in creation. In his Letter to the Romans, Paul follows the First Testament in summarizing "God's invisible qualities" which are plain to people

---

4. Edwards, "End for Which God Created the World," 242.
5. Edwards, "End for Which God Created the World," 242.
6. Bauckham, *Gospel of Glory*, 44.

(Rom 1:20). In verse 23, Paul refers to all these qualities as "the glory of the immortal God." Accordingly, the tragedy lies in human failure to glorify the creator and instead installing the lesser glory of creation over God. The hierarchy of being, both within human nature and social order, crumbled and led toward chaos (Rom 1:28–32). Yet the apocalyptic writers glimpsed a future glory, which surpasses any immanent categories. John seemed to be overwhelmed by the sheer grandeur of God as the center of the universe, in which it would appear he struggled to come up with comparisons to describe the radiance of God's glory and the scene of worship in heaven (Rev 7:9–17).

The tension between the revelation of God's glory and its hiddenness is maintained throughout the Bible. Jesus points to himself as the one whose mission it is to glorify the Father, and at the same time it is the Father who glorifies the Son. In the Gospel of John 1:14, glory is mentioned twice and is introduced as the mission of Jesus. The glory of Jesus fulfills the glimpses of God's glory revealed in the Sinai covenant and the visions of messianic glory in the book of Isaiah. Richard Bauckham summarizes Moses's experience of glory: "The story seems to suggest that God's glory is the radiance of his character, of his goodness, of who he truly is. (In fact, the Hebrew uses the phrase 'all my goodness' [Exod. 33:19] as equivalent to 'my glory.') This is what the face of God would reveal, if Moses could see it. A person's identity is made visible in the person's face. Moses cannot see, but he does hear."[7]

Jesus qualitatively surpasses the revelation at Sinai as he points to himself as the face of the Father. Ben Sira, the Jewish sage, asked: "'Who has seen him and can describe him?' (Sir. 43:31). Jesus is the literal answer to this question."[8] Yet while God's display of his glory is at its fullest in the body of Jesus, it nevertheless remains veiled through the human nature of Jesus.

The same paradox also applies to history. God's glory manifests itself within a particular salvation history, yet God's glory radiates from an eternal throne beyond time. God's glory is revealed to a particular people, yet Jewish prophets envision God's universal glory and people from all nations worshipping Yahweh. The ultimate vision portrays God's glory filling all the earth.

---

7. Bauckham, *Gospel of Glory*, 50.
8. Bauckham, *Gospel of Glory*, 53.

God's glory is in both his being and his action. It manifests itself as pure gift, as something that is available to everyone who is willing to perceive and receive. All of creation points to God's glory. However, it also breaks into the immanent through revelatory events and illuminates the given. The emphasis on both the stable, perceivable structure of all reality and the free agency of God is equally present in the biblical stories. The disagreement between the Dominicans and the Franciscans is a false dichotomy and can be explained through the political bifurcation of the church. Simultaneity is held together in the biblical narrative and the liturgy. There is no need to split apart being and action. Nominalism acquired its normativity against the backdrop of an institutional status quo. The Thomist emphasis upon the rational structure of the world and the Augustinian focus upon desire and will are two sides of the same reality, which is paradoxical at its core and can't be grasped within one theological system without losing its complexity.

God's glory appears as nature and grace, which are embodied in Jesus Christ. In him, God's glory as fully manifest and yet also hidden becomes real. In Jesus, both God's hiddenness and revelatory nature become accentuated. God's glory evokes a response in humans and can't be fully grasped. Divine glory disrupts human perception of themselves and the world.

Both Moses and Isaiah experienced the manifestation of God's glory as preparation for their leadership. They were simultaneously crushed and empowered, lowered and lifted up. Moses and Isaiah are instantly struck down and shaken at their core by the presence of God's glory. Moses bows his head down to the ground and worships (Exod 34:8). In light of God's glory, Isaiah instantly perceives his inner state as dirty, not worthy to appear before a holy God (Isa 6:5). Block describes the bodily posture of worship as prostration before a king.[9] In light of the divine overwhelming otherness, the human sinks to his knees.

Like a beam of light penetrating the darkness, God's glory provides instant orientation as it illuminates both the spatial and temporal dimensions of human existence. The psalmist's declaration that God sets his feet in a spacious place (Ps 31:8) becomes real through the illuminating glory. He perceives God as sovereign above creation and his immediate hardships. The life-threatening circumstances fade in light of the proclamation that God created his people for his own glory (Isa 43:7). Consequently,

---

9. Block, *For the Glory of God*, 13.

since God is envisioned as all-powerful and sovereign over both natural and historic events, his people are able to rest and not panic, realizing that God himself desires to and is able to uphold his own glory. All of history aims toward one goal. The seemingly random and meaningless events are structured through this prism. The final goal, wherein God will be glorified, with every knee bowing before him, stands firm. For believers, their immediate historic point is a mere transitional moment toward this inevitable pinnacle.

Moreover, God's glory establishes a moral hierarchy that does not leave humans crushed permanently but elevates them through love. The sheer terror of Isaiah facing his own corrupt state gives way to God's loving action. God's angel cleanses Isaiah's mouth with a burning coal. God's glory brings forth both the depth and the height of the moral landscape. In the light of God's glory, the prophet suddenly becomes aware of the abysmal distance between God and himself and the dark abyss within himself.

God's glory does not remain static but progresses with the increasing revelation. In the Second Letter to the Corinthians, Paul seeks to demonstrate to Christians that the glory that comes through Jesus and is mediated through the Holy Spirit is greater than the glory that Moses received. Focused attention upon this glory in Christ leads toward transformation of the individual Christian and the Christian community toward the true image of God, thus restoring the original creation (2 Cor 3:18). Glory radiates from God through his particular revelations and is encountered in mystical events. Yet glory is also present like steady rays, which can be experienced through turning oneself toward Christ, through reading the Scriptures and meditation upon his creation.

Glory is not a means to something higher. The one who is touched by glory in the first place moves beyond any calculating logic, as he has glimpsed the highest level of reality, toward which everything else pales in comparison. God's glory frees the individual from personal will for power and strategic calculations to achieve a higher status. While glory stands above and beyond any social concerns, when people begin to seek God's glory, the effects of this search produce social patterns, which structure society in a particular way. While the light of God's glory is desirable in itself, it will also expose darkness and imperfection and ultimately illuminate reality.

Illuminating the Given in a New Light

Perhaps the most important contribution of Christianity to Western civilization has been that which cannot be measured or quantified. As Rémi Brague remarked, quoting Irenaeus, the Christian revolution consists in illuminating the entirety of the world, to throw light upon what is already there and through such an act to make the unseen visible.[10] Contrary to the Platonic cave, one must not be dragged to the surface in order to see. Instead, the divine light broke into the dark: "The light shines in the darkness, but the darkness has not understood it" (John 1:5). This is a true tragedy, which everyone could see, but many refuse to open their eyes. The decaying world does not need to be rescued by men. The biblical story describes how the world has already been saved. The only thing humans need to do is to open their eyes and see anew how God's glory permeates every inch of our being and the world around us. Despite the groaning of creation for the final liberation, God has left symbols of hope for the final victory over all of evil. Let me briefly hint at how God's glory illuminates patterns that provide a life-giving structure for our society. Like the instant transformation of darkness when hit by sunrays, so our perception of all relations is suddenly transformed when we glimpse God's glory. Let me briefly describe the patterns produced by God's glory within the self, in relation to others, and in relation to the wider sociopolitical and natural world.

God's glory shatters into pieces all false perceptions about self, others, and the world. The initial reaction is awe mixed with terror, as the falsely constructed reality crumbles and one becomes instantly aware of the vast difference between God and man. The prior sense of unity and integration of self breaks apart. Despair follows as one becomes aware of how pathetic one's attempts are to construct one's own sense of reality. Yet contrary to the relativistic philosophies of constructivism, humans enveloped by God's glory are not left in despair and phlegmatic resignation, handing over their perception of reality to the philosophers, who act as magicians in constructing a simulation. Instead, the pursuit of glory fulfills the double function of both relativizing the immanent and reassuring the worshipper of a reality more solid than any human perception. This seemingly paradoxical function of glory is the best safeguard against suffocating totalitarianism in politics and science. Only through a deeply held belief in ultimate reality can one let go of the temptation to make

---

10. Brague, "Was hat Europa," 29.

an idol of a temporary scientific level of knowledge or political system. Only through the reassurance of God's glory manifest in love can one hold loosely to knowledge in the service of love and not use knowledge to create a steely cage as a bulwark against external threats. God's glory makes it possible for a human to be simultaneously in a state of a radical certainty and radical doubt. From within this paradox a tension arises, which energizes the best possible modes of creating institutions.

In light of the divine overwhelming presence, a human person shrinks and is decentered. This complete humiliation is a great beginning point. In the stories of both Moses and Isaiah, and later in the narrative of Jesus, humbling oneself is a precondition for elevation. The cross will be transformed to glory, yet Jesus must first empty himself and pass through unimaginable pain and abandonment before entering full glory (Phil 2). In this process, hubris as the source of all chaos and decay is eradicated. Christian baptism embodies this reality, wherein the old self is buried with Christ and the new person is raised up with him (Rom 6).

All totalitarian ideological hells of the twentieth century began with the prideful belief that there is nothing sacred about humans and that humans are able to perfect human nature through the utopian dream to create a perfect society. Humility, paired with the deep conviction that every human being is created in the image of God and that every individual's dignity must be safeguarded by all means possible, is the best protection against the growing threat of the next totalitarian ideology. Transhumanism has the potential to recreate the totalitarian hells of the twentieth century on a much larger scale in the name of progress and human well-being. Evil almost always disguises itself as good.

Since God's glory is a gift given from the outside, human hubris is subverted. Balthasar locates the origin of the disciples' faith in the external attraction of radiating glory.[11] A person is torn away from inward obsession with self and redirected toward the radiating beauty. Paradoxically, by losing oneself through the outward-turned gaze, the person is truly found. By bracketing one's own concerns and being lost in God's presence, the person begins to truly care for others and the world. From the soil of humility and realization of the interdependence between humans and also between human and nature, wisdom emerges. From this wisdom, social structures can be built that are aimed at the largest benefit. People who view themselves as being recipients of

---

11. "Hingerissenwerden aber ist der Ursprung des Christentums" (Balthasar, *Schau der Gestalt*, 30).

the greatest gift will be courageous enough to innovate and yet humble enough to correct their course. Diverse personalities, emphasizing both the wisdom of the past and the benefits of improvement, will work together in a fruitful tension, producing development without the utopian notion of transhumanism. This understanding of glory produces an ability to innovate that surpasses the false alternatives of mindless progressivism or fearful conservatism. God's glory enables us to see new, life-giving patterns, which while new to the human perception were, in fact, there all along. Similarly, God's glory makes us realize that perhaps some ideas and technologies that we clung to in the past are mere idols and must be let go. As Karl Löwith lucidly puts it:

> Christianity, far from having opened the horizon of an indefinite future like the religion of progress, has made the future paramount by making it definite, and it has thereby immensely accentuated and deepened the earnestness of the present instant. In this faithful expectation of a definite future glory and judgement is implied the assumption, not that history is indefinitely progressing, either by natural law or by man's continuous efforts, but that history has virtually reached its end. Christian progress from the old Adam to a new creature is certainly a momentous progress, yet it is entirely independent of historical changes in man's social and political, cultural and economic, conditions. . . . Christianity has made no progress for the very reason that a Christian's progress consists in a progressive imitation of Christ, who did not care for worldly improvements.[12]

Paradoxically, by not caring about the world directly, Christians are producing the best possible world as they are not tempted to use the promise of the better world in the future in order to unleash hell to get there. Humility as a healthy realization of one's own limits is a precondition for social cooperation. The immeasurable progress in the imitation of Christ results in the measurable progress of socio-material innovations.

Glory gathers. People who are stunned by something or someone who emanates a captivating energy, which is perceived as love, beauty, or truth, gather around. Glory permeates the group and creates an atmosphere that radiates beyond the particular community. In Durkheimian fashion, the modern, anonymous, highly individualized bureaucratic societies grew out from these smaller communities imbued by the envisioned and experienced glory. Simone Weil sensed the limited nature

12. Löwith, *Meaning in History*, 112–13.

of sociopolitical institutions: "Above those institutions, which are concerned with protecting rights and persons and democratic freedoms, others must be invented for the purpose of exposing and abolishing everything in contemporary life which buries the soul under injustice, lies, and ugliness. They must be invented, for they are unknown, and it is impossible to doubt that they are indispensable."[13]

Weil hints at an important distinction. While the current institutions' function is negative, the new ones must be positive by exposing evil through embodying the good. Just like Jesus embodied the glory of God, the church as his body, despite its brokenness, is gathered as a community of glory. By discerning the real in communal worship, one becomes aware of anything that is a perversion of the real. The institution that Weil envisions was invented by Jesus, who called it his body. Life-giving patterns extend beyond the boundaries of a community that is pervaded by the paradoxical glory. In order for a larger group to cooperate together, the individual must risk to trust; and at the same time, those in authority must not disappoint. Balthasar points to the relation between authority of the church and glory: "The formal authority of the Church, and that of Christ, is ultimately credible only as the manifestation of the glory of God's love—this is real credibility."[14]

In other words, the authority of the church is credible to the degree to which it embodies the received glory as manifested in love, as experienced in the incarnation via sacraments. Glory as manifested in love is a strong antidote to the glory of the power-drunk Leviathan as manifested in totalitarian control and coercion. The progression of evil, however, lends an opportunity for the good to shine ever brighter.

God's glory does not merely shatter and humble, but it also provides an instant, overwhelming glimpse of the entirety of reality. Suddenly, all relations, which previously seemed obscure, appear in their clarity. God's glory reinstates the meaningfulness of the world in a nihilistic society, by enabling nature, society, and every individual within the historic process to be conceived again as both relationally stable and dynamic. People who glimpse larger patterns are energized to shape their lives by building durable institutions, seeking to cultivate the environment in such a way as to secure clean air, fresh water, and a thriving ecology. The will to act emerges when one is able to envision desirable goals. The world infused

13. Weil, "Human Personality," 98.
14. Balthasar, *Love Alone*, 120.

with divinity creates a living pattern. When each person and every tree radiate God's glory, every relation becomes not merely an instrumental means toward an egoistic goal to advance particular power but an intrinsically valuable relation. Illuminated through God's glory, the entire world is lifted from fatal isolation into a communal dance of life. The colors of worship run from the canvas into the wider world and transform the grey into a brilliant, invigorating picture.

God's glory manifests reality beyond any doubt. The modern preoccupation with the loss of the real fades in light of God's glory. The external world appears as solid once again. Once each person perceives their relation to God, to nature, to others, and to self, crippling, nagging doubt is dispelled in a second. Like in a dark room, one is not able to perceive the relation to all that surrounds oneself. However, once light fills the room, everything appears solid in an instant.

To glimpse God's character is to begin to understand the nature of reality. Empirical observations contribute to clearer insights on the nature of the world only within the unifying vision. Empiricism could develop into full-blown methodology in a world where people viewed the natural world as a means toward the worship of God. Christian contemplation and scientific exploration are not merely related through their meticulous discipline but also in the overall ontological and epistemic assumptions on the nature of reality. The former gave rise to the latter. The simultaneous awareness of the overflowing meaning within universe and of human limits serves as a strong motivation for both the Christian and the scientist alike to explore the larger horizons in humble recognition that one can err. The one who has glimpsed God's glory will be committed, whatever he does, to pursue goodness, truth, and beauty over his personal will to mere power. The external motivation will be complemented with the internal awareness that one is related to this stunning outward beauty by being created in the image of God. The relationality emerges and deepens through God's glory. Through this relationality, decay retreats as the personal body, the social body, and all of nature experience healing. Energized through this larger vision, humans once again take responsibility for their divine calling to be stewards of the earth entrusted to them as representatives of God.

However, the return to glory does not come easily, as ecclesial innocence has been lost. Memories of abuse linger in our collective consciousness. In some regards it seems easier to stumble into new utopias than to correct the abused idea of glory. The cost of twentieth-century utopias, which reduced God's glory to human glory on earth, became evident as over a hundred million corpses piled up.

The return toward God's glory as the highest ideal in order to counter social exhaustion and decay might demand a high price. The demolition of Christendom succeeded by portraying the Judeo-Christian ideal as destroying human nature in the process, or at least hindering it in its flourishing. This was the original whisper of the snake in the garden of Eden, arousing doubt about the goodness of God. How would we return to God's glory without resurrecting the perceived potentially suffocating by-products of this overarching ideal? Charles Taylor closes his insightful book *Sources of the Self* with this dilemma. On the one side, recovery of the highest good is necessary. On the other side, we can't overlook the potential perversion of the highest good:

> If the highest ideals are the most potentially destructive, then maybe the prudent path is the safest, and we shouldn't unconditionally rejoice at the indiscriminate retrieval of empowering goods. A little judicious stifling may be the part of wisdom. The prudent strategy makes sense on the assumption that the dilemma is inescapable, that the highest spiritual aspirations must lead to mutilation or destruction. But if I may make one last unsupported assertion, I want to say that I don't accept this as our inevitable lot. The dilemma of mutilation is in a sense our greatest spiritual challenge, not an iron fate. . . . There is a large element of hope. It is a hope that I see implicit in Judeo-Christian theism (however terrible the record of its adherents in history), and in its central promise of a divine affirmation of the human, more total than humans can ever attain unaided.[15]

Taylor rightly hints at the destructive nature of the highest ideal, which judges human imperfection. Humans stand condemned: "From the very beginning of the human story religion, our link with the highest, has been recurrently associated with sacrifice, even mutilation, as though something of us has to be torn away or immolated if we are to please the gods."[16] Moreover, the highest ideal does not only exercise a moral terror but has also been conceived of as a suffocating cage, in its religious or secular-ideological disguise, destroying human individuality. God's glory could also be conceived of as power, which erases the subject. Yet, throughout the biblical story, we glimpse a God who hides

---

15. Taylor, *Sources of the Self*, 520–21.
16. Taylor, *Sources of the Self*, 519.

his glory in order to ensure a realm of freedom for those he has created. Moreover, as the story progresses, God's glory moves closer toward humanity. Glory transforms itself into love. Both the moral and the totalizing terror of the ideal are countered through the ideal becoming human, or as C. S. Lewis coined it: the true myth.[17] The unfathomable glory of God becomes approachable through Jesus. God desires for his glory to indwell every person through the Eucharist.

---

17. Lewis, "Myth Became Fact."

CHAPTER 11

The Eucharist: Embodying the Living Center

Very truly I tell you, unless you eat the flesh of the Son of Man and drink his blood, you have no life in you.

—Jesus, John 6:53

Lose yourself

—Eminem, "Lose Yourself"

THROUGH JESUS, GOD OFFERS the restoration of all relations; healing between humans and God, between humans, between humans and nature, and of humans' inner chaos. This myth is made real through the incarnation, which manifests itself anew every time the communal experience of the Eucharist is celebrated. Those who partake in the body and blood of Christ form the church. The abundance of life radiates beyond the gathered community and lays down the often-invisible and unacknowledged fruitful humus where the seeds of a flourishing society germinate.

You Are What You Eat: At Whose Table Do You Sit?

Humans depend on food and water in order to live. Thus eating is the most basic activity. Yet there is great variability in how we eat. While humans are able to eat and drink alone, throughout history and across cultures, they prefer to eat in community. The communal aspect of eating shapes relations between people. In many myths, gods are believed to shape the climate, which directly impacts the harvest of food, thus eating also symbolically represents the larger sacred cosmos and the human relation to nature. Therefore, eating does not constitute a mere biological process but establishes larger symbolic patterns. In this regard, one can conclude that you are what you eat and drink, as the act of eating secures physical survival and establishes a society within sacred patterns.[1]

While eating can bring people together, it can also evoke disgust and exclusion. My grandfather liked to share the story of how he was invited by Siberian nomads to eat with them. In the middle of the yurt was a huge kettle with chunks of lamb. As the honored guest, my grandfather was allowed to join the eldest of the tribe in the first round to serve oneself from the kettle. They were privileged to fish out the juiciest pieces of meat, taste them, and pass them to the second circle, which was formed of middle-aged men. The last circle was made up of women and children. In Berlin, where I live now, this way of conducting a meal would be condemned as outrageously unjust.

When we organized a community meal in the courtyard of the building where our church meets, we were also confronted with the fact that various people cared not only about what we eat but also how we eat. Some neighbors refused to come because we did not have exclusively organic vegetables. Our Muslim neighbors were concerned as to whether we would serve only halal meat, and on one occasion, when I thought that we had taken into account everyone's expectations, one student asked what kind of meat we had on the grill. I nodded and assured him that it was halal beef. He stared at me in discomfort and declined due to being a Hindu. One refugee asked me who had paid for all this food and whether this was a social program funded by tax money. He wanted to know if the table had been set by the state or if it was being offered by those who had invested freely from their own resources.

---

1. Schmemann points out the irony of Feuerbach's intent to put an end to religion through his statement that "Man is what he eats." "In fact, however, he was expressing, without knowing it, the most religious idea of man" (Schmemann, *For Life of World*, 11).

I explained to him that we as a church community had contributed to this meal. Yet I clarified that ultimately it was Jesus' table. He could not fully understand my assertion. As the church, we are the host, and yet we are at the same time guests at the table of the one who invites us all to eat him so that we can eat with him.

Paradoxical Life

The Eucharist is embedded in a far-reaching narrative arc that must be taken into account in order to understand the particular significance of the sacrament. Judeo-Christian myth portrays God as generous in creating a world for people to enjoy. Eating various fruits and vegetables and delighting in the created order, the human being's destiny was to commune with the giver and thank him in adoration. Eating in gratitude is an act that expresses harmony between God and the world. Consequently, eating in rebellion, mistrusting the loving character of God and seeking to become like him, marks the beginning of a broken relationship. While abundance of food flowed from God's generosity, scarcity and struggle to wrestle food from the soil became the consequence of human estrangement from God. Yet throughout the Bible, God is portrayed as generously prescribing how individuals and the community can experience reconciliation through the offering back of food. Already in the earliest accounts in Genesis, one can glimpse the paradox that humans offer sacrifices to a God who owns everything. Giving back to God what humans need the most expresses a fundamental trust as humans offer their lives back to God, which they once chose to lead in separation from him. The earliest account of this offering is the sacrifice of Abel and Cain. Later in the Exodus story, the sacrificial lamb protects the Israelites from God's punishment. In the story of Abraham's sacrifice of Isaac, God himself provides the sacrificial lamb, thereby foreshadowing the most radical revelation of love in not merely creating the world for humans to consume but in giving himself to be incorporated by his creation.

Throughout Israel's journey in the desert, Yahweh provides the people with fresh water and manna from heaven, in consistency with his character in the creation narratives. The psalmists build on this collective memory and paint a picture of a God who takes care of his people in light of natural disasters and political turmoil (e.g., Ps 43). In Psalm 23, the author employs vivid imagery to underscore how even in the most dangerous situations, the believer can rest and enjoy God's abundance. The prophets weave this particular thread into a universal tapestry. Isaiah envisions Yahweh as a host for all nations, who stream to his table, which is loaded with the most exquisite foods (Isa 25).

In the Second Testament, Jesus embodies what was already foreshadowed in the First Testament. He begins his public ministry by transforming water into wine.

> The first miracle Jesus performs at the wedding of Cana when, for the purpose of revealing his glory, Jesus turns water to wine (John 2). The account of John states that the response of his disciples was belief in him. With the Old Testament prophetic visions as a background, Jesus' action in changing the water to wine serves for them as confirmation of his messianic identity. Moreover, they see the amount of wine and taste its quality. Jesus demonstrates in a very down to earth bodily way, here through the sense of taste that he is able to provide life in its fullest measure (John 10:10). Jesus defies any religious asceticism, which forbids wine on earth and promises rivers of wine in heaven. It is assumed that each jar contained between 20 and 30 gallons of water, which means on a moderate account that Jesus produced 120 gallons of wine for the party. Such abundance and generosity would have been expected in a Middle Eastern context, in which lavish hospitality was the rule rather than the exception and where running out of food or drink would be an occasion of great shame for the host.[2]

Jesus further embodies Yahweh's provision for his people in the desert by feeding multitudes of people. Yet he also refers to himself as the sacrificial lamb, as the ultimate thanksgiving sacrifice. In Jesus, God's character becomes tangible to people: God is the one who gives everything for humans to enjoy, and he ultimately gives himself, out of burning desire for communion with his people. Jesus' command of the Eucharist is therefore the central act not merely for Christians but for the entire world, as this signifies the reality of how the world once was and where it is returning: the world comes into being from the abundant love of God, from sheer generosity.[3] By tasting the bread and drinking the wine, every

---

2. Dik, *Church, Immigration & Pluralism*, 185.

3. According to Schmemann, "It is God and God alone that has made this world His symbol, has then fulfilled this symbol in Christ and will consummate it in His eternal Kingdom. When deprived of this symbol the world becomes chaos and destruction" (*For Life of World*, 149). Subsequently, the Christ event in the form of the Eucharist must be the primary lens through which to interpret all of reality.

individual who comes to the table has the opportunity to experience this reality in a paradoxical manner. Through the Eucharist, humans participate in the divine, grand love story of God becoming man. The Eucharist mirrors incarnation as the grand paradox. Just like God partakes in our humanity, we are invited to partake in his divinity.

During the Eucharist, God, who is the creator of the universe and exists outside of time and space, desires to be joined to humans, who are a mere speck of dust in the universe. In the Eucharist, God offers himself through Jesus and desires to restore the broken relationship. The Eucharist allows each person in a moment to glimpse something of our original state in the garden when both God and man dwelt together. Jesus sought to heighten the unthinkable by stating it as confrontationally as possible: "Unless you eat my flesh and drink my blood, you have no life in you" (John 6:53). These words, which express the burning desire of God to enter again into the most intimate relationship with humans, were too confrontational for many of Jesus' disciples, who upon hearing them turned away from following Jesus.

The Eucharist expresses God's unconditional invitation to his own table, which in our material experience of it must nevertheless be set up by humans. Here the continuous biblical tension is not resolved. God acts and invites humans to coact with him. God is fully sufficient in himself, and yet he invites humans to participate in his own eternal dance of love. Even more so, God makes himself vulnerable by giving people the responsibility to perform the ordained ritual. This simultaneity can't be resolved in a discursive manner. As each person takes in the bread and wine, the simultaneity of God's grace as underpinning all of existence and the moment of human response merge together. In the ritual act, the analytical categories of being and action are experienced as one.

In the fragile human performance of the Eucharist, God's unfailing promise of sovereign care becomes manifest. In the final book of the Bible, the slaughtered lamb appears as the triumphant king at the end-time, who conquers all evil and wipes away every tear. The eucharistic time is condensed time, wherein the entire history, from God's creation to his ultimate renewal of all creation through Jesus and the final union with his people, is proclaimed. The moment of the Eucharist encapsulates the entire human history as all of history is consummated in the final triumphant delight of all saints in God (Rev 7).

In the Eucharist, God's glory is simultaneously revealed and hidden, expressing the paradox of incarnation:

> Though Augustine puts the emphasis on human sin, part of the reason that we fail to see God in things is that God's presence is veiled in things. God is not immediately available in creation; there is no beatific vision of God face to face in the temporal world. A tree can reveal something of God, but perhaps we can be forgiven if sometimes a tree just seems like a tree. The Incarnation is necessary because Christ, as begotten, not made, is able to reveal the nature of divine Form; Christ is the very image of the invisible God (Col. 1:15), but in a manner that humans can fathom. Christ is the Incarnation of supreme Form or Beauty. What we love in loving Christ, even in his human form, is no created thing but divine Beauty itself, "beauty so old and so new." And yet even in Christ we encounter God sacramentally; we are not given a direct vision of God. No one has ever seen God, but Christ has made God known (John 1:18). We can only respond with faith, hope, and love, and thus witness to the restoration of the image of God in ourselves.[4]

This paradox allows us "simultaneously to see God in things and not to make a god of things."[5] This avoids two false alternatives of either making the creation divine or viewing it as merely dead matter. Instead, the tension of the paradox invites an active response. As the realization sinks in concerning the mystery of a God who stands beyond categories of comprehension and yet who chooses to make himself known in a very particular, tangible manner, the pride of Eve and Adam can be transformed into humility. Through the Eucharist, the broken relationships between human beings are restored. The passive act of receptivity breaks down any sense of pride, which is at the root of envy and the desire to dominate the other. Furthermore, this passivity arises from the active commitment to love as one is loved.

The gift from above invites into horizontal community. The Eucharist is received individually yet communally. The antagonism between the individual and society, which has been ravishing the West since the Renaissance, comes to an end. Each person tastes God individually, while being surrounded by brothers and sisters. The simultaneous relation of the individual before God while being in connection with others undermines the intellectualists' construction of eternal enmity between the individual and group, which is kept alive by pitting communitarian and individualist-libertarian ideologies against each other.

---

4. Cavanaugh, *Uses of Idolatry*, 353.
5. Cavanaugh, *Uses of Idolatry*, 334.

The Eucharist decenters the hubris and re-centers the individual as a divine being. Yet this divinity is dependent on the God who infills each one who comes to the table. Human existential hunger is satisfied. As God's love permeates one's body in the form of bread and wine, the inner tears are being healed through the Holy Spirit. The presence of Jesus through bread and wine is made permanent through his abiding indwelling of every person through the Holy Spirit.

Through the Eucharist, man acknowledges his deep dependence upon nature. She humbly receives bread and wine as a gift to be treasured and recommits herself to being a faithful steward. God chooses the human body in Christ and then nature in the form of bread and wine to be experienced by humans. These everyday foods are imbued with divine significance. Matter is not dead. Instead, nature acquires deep significance as a mediatory reality toward God.

The Eucharist signifies the beginning of abundant life, as pride commits suicide. Herein lies the true paradox of the eucharistic experience. By receiving the bread and wine, one confirms that God in all his infinite wisdom and power chooses this humiliating act as a means to mediate his grace to people. In an Anglican church in Beirut, this experience was accentuated when I knelt in front of the priest like a helpless bird. All I could do was merely open my mouth and stretch out my tongue. The priest, representing Christ, placed the piece of bread on my tongue. In the Eucharist, one's intelligence, religious genius, and desire for power must be crucified. There is nothing we can do to reach upward as God himself descends in a most humbling manner and offers himself in the most mundane elements of bread and wine.

In the Eucharist, humans follow Christ into his death in order to resurrect to new life. Without the Eucharist, humanity will shatter upon the rocks of its own hubris. By embracing one's helplessness in the humble reception of the Eucharist, by accepting the invitation to the divine feast, the church unintentionally drops some crumbs and spills some drops, which rescue the surrounding society from either dying of starvation and thirst or turning into a zombie, which is neither dead nor alive.

Crumbs and Drops for a Starving and Thirsting World

The Eucharist forms the nucleus of life around which a flourishing civilization emerges. Without the strategic intention to use religion for social means but rather out of pure desire and love for Jesus, gathered Christians unintentionally till the humus where the seeds for social flourishing can germinate.

Of course one could object to this view that in a stratified, secular society, religion makes up only one slice of the flat cake. The center has dissolved, and if it exists at all, then only as a vague, dissipated civil religion. Normativity is viewed as a mere product of discourse. Thus communication must proceed according to democratic rules in order for each segment within the stratified society to function. This view could hold weight and persist only in a religiously homogenous society in which the Judeo-Christian religion still provided a strong base. With that religion's further dissolution and increasing religious pluralism, Ernst-Wolfgang Böckenförde's dictum begins to exert its weight not merely in relation to the secular state but to the secular society as well. Paraphrasing Böckenförde, secularity nourishes itself from the soil, which it did not create nor till.[6] When a secular system is challenged from outside its framework, it is not enough to merely recur to a functioning discourse. Normative, higher-order reasons must be given. The Eucharist as a practice that is anchored in the divine order exerts a normative force from beyond the immanent frame.

How exactly religious rituals affect the wider society is a matter of thick ethnographic description, which I can't provide here. However, I agree with the Durkheimian description. Rituals create a stratified reality. People are literally elevated in their perception and charged with divine energy. Through ritual, the myth is inscribed into the body of the believer, who begins to perceive the everyday through its plot. As I will show in the following chapter, this does not happen automatically but can also fail and be perverted. Yet even with a holey bucket one can draw water. Holy people are people with holes but who are in the process of being made whole. Something always spills out as the gathered eucharistic community disperses into their daily lives. The following is an ideal-type image of how the Eucharist serves as soil for the germinating seeds of a flourishing society. Even faith like a mustard seed can move mountains (Matt 17:20). Bertrand Russell's mockery of faith and replacement of it with power (see ch. 4) is sobering. Overcoming faith with hubris and certainty cannot dispel, however, a perpetual fear of the possibility of self-destruction through technology. Russell's praise of human power, once

---

6. Böckenförde, *Staat, Gesellschaft, Freiheit*, 60.

it runs its course, must relearn humility or risk accelerating suicide. The crumbs from the Lord's Table and drops from the chalice of the Eucharist can feed and quench the thirst of entire civilizations.

The Eucharist is often preceded by individual and/or communal confession. Confession arises from humans' realization of God's holiness. The Bible uses the imagery of fire to describe the purifying nature of God's holiness (Heb 12:29). Humans realizes their true nature when confronted with God's purity. In the Letter to the Corinthians, Christians are instructed to examine themselves before partaking in the Eucharist. This "examination" occurs through a dialogue with God and humans and is not a pathological navel-gazing. Ultimately, it is impossible to assess oneself apart from an outsider's perspective. The psalmist asks God to search his inner motives, which are unconscious even to himself (Ps 139). Christians are exhorted to confess their sins to each other. Bonhoeffer goes so far as to state that it is through confession that new life can break in.[7] Yet the searching of self and the horror involved in glimpsing one's inner darkness and abyss do not continue indefinitely. The release comes through the words of God reassuring the burdened believer of complete pardon. This is a fact that is grounded in God's character and his redeeming action in Jesus (1 John 1:9). The confessor grants this relief to the one confessing by speaking in the authority of Christ: "Your sins are forgiven."

The practice of confession produces a particular type of character and society. People who are truly free from shame and guilt are not easily manipulated through hyper-moralistic extortions. They can't be coerced easily by political messaging attempting to give them a bad conscience that needs absolution from some inherent guilt. The one who confessed has already gone through the simultaneous sense of guilt and pardon. Therefore, the Christian is able to resist being cemented in a state of guilt by any idol masquerading as virtuous but unable to pardon. Bonhoeffer discerned in Jesus a strange freedom to transcend the binary alternatives posed by the Pharisees.[8] In the same way, liberated Christians receive this strange freedom to glimpse paths of action beyond the seemingly fixed alternatives. In confession, true freedom from human codes of conduct manifests itself as freedom toward love. By glimpsing the highest ideal, one becomes instantly aware of both negative and positive freedom. Liberation from sin is only the first step toward becoming

---

7. Bonhoeffer, *Gemeinsames Leben*, 96.
8. Bonhoeffer, *Ethics*, 33.

more like God, who is perfect love. Thus, the Eucharist redeems the self-mutilating, destructive notion of critique and agonizing negative freedom. In confession, one can experience the scalpel-sharp critique as life giving due to its prior embedding in unconditional grace and its progress toward divine love. The one who confesses is not stripped of identity in a state of non-relationality. Instead, what is cut away is replenished with more abundant identity in Christ.

Herein lies the humus of a life-giving critique, which though painful does not destroy but rather is in service of a better life. Political, scientific, and economic institutions depend on people who have experienced this kind of temporary destruction and the subsequent growth out of it. They will have both the confidence and courage to employ the practice of critique not for personal gain but for the sake of communal flourishing, employing the scalpel of honest examination not to deconstruct the other but to restore the social body back to health. One can more easily risk outsourcing one's responsibility to a person who is accountable to an objective standard outside of himself. Before the virtue of authenticity became completely internalized and self-referential, it was viewed as remaining true to the divine ideal. Relentless self-critique served to move oneself toward this goal. Such a culture of authenticity rooted in the divine ideal engenders trust in intersubjective moral order. Confession evokes a larger reality whereby, in confessing, the person receives both grace and truth from outside of himself, thus unintentionally confirming an objective moral space, under which roof many people can gather. The risk of partially outsourcing one's responsibility, as occurs in all highly developed modern societies, is easier when one is assured of this larger normative space. Trust is the invisible foundation of any society, as I outlined in ch. 4. Trust is like an invisible glue that holds our societies together, or like a bank deposit that allows for investment in order to build strong institutions.

In the Eucharist, grace and truth are experienced simultaneously. One is willing to feel the hurt in facing the truth about oneself due to the fact of being held. The Christian is assured that the exposure of sin will not bring destruction but rather life. A society that is made up of people who embody grace and truth will be both stable and dynamic. A good scientist needs to have an ontological sense of trust that he will not be crushed when pursuing truth relentlessly. Similar to the one who confesses, scientists need to always question and examine their own presuppositions while being willing to discover truth in the objective world. A good politician needs, as Max Weber rightly outlined, moral courage to make unpopular decisions for the common good and humility to admit a mistake when necessary to correct the course.[9] People who work in the economic sector need a sense of solidarity with others in order to not rig the system toward their own benefit. The degree of flourishing in a society is proportional to the degree that the people of that society are filled with grace and truth.

Each person is invited to participate in the Eucharist, but everyone is free to observe. The invitation was very costly for God as he extended himself through Jesus' pain in order to win the love of people. God searches every dark alley for those willing to join his party (Luke 14:16–24). He even patiently waits for those who insulted him and runs toward them when they return broke after wasting all his gifts (Luke 15:11–32). This voluntary participation in the larger communal meal is the fruitful soil where civil society can germinate. Liberal democracies depend on voluntary associations of self-organized, responsible citizens who, without pressure from the state, form successful associations. People who experience their God as a generous host standing with his arms wide open and waiting for their response will have an allergic reaction against a tyrannical state who slips its tentacles into every inch of a person's life and coerces citizens into compliance. A voluntary response becomes sacred through divine invitation. In every tyrannical state the citizen feels like a beggar. In societies where eucharistic practice is strong, the citizens will have the liberating dignity to serve others, as those in power will view themselves in service of all. A society where everyone is willing to serve will elevate everyone. The title "minister" reminds of the function of those in power to minister to the needs of the people who have entrusted them with power. Moreover, a society, just like a game, is permeated by more enjoyment, joy, and durability if those who participate are doing so out of a free decision. Those who freely decide to join the game are willing to sacrifice more, since they are not impinged upon in their dignity. Conversely, force extinguishes the spark of divine freedom granted to humans and hurts them in their dignity. The necessity of force grows proportionally to the degree that voluntary participation is weakened. The imposition of force requires increasing cost in the form of energy, time, and personnel, draining a society of its resources and institutional effectiveness.

---

9. Weber, *Politik als Beruf.*

The Eucharist: Embodying the Living Center 241

In the Eucharist, the human action of walking toward the Lord's Table in order to receive is framed by God's action. Both the invitation and the giving of the Eucharist are performed by the priest. The laity remain passive. The receptive posture expresses complete vulnerability and surrender. In the Eucharist, being and action are interwoven. Human action is embraced by divine being. Man realizes that he is a complete dependent being and everything that sustains him is given. Through creation and the continuous upholding of all order, God enables life. To receive something tips the scale of power. The one who receives is put in a position to return the favor. This is how a mutual sense of obligation arises between humans. This seems to be a universal principle:

> Spelt out it means that each gift is part of a system of reciprocity in which the honour of giver and recipient are engaged. It is a total system in that every item of status or of spiritual or material possession is implicated for everyone in the whole community. The system is quite simple; just the rule that every gift has to be returned in some specified way sets up a perpetual cycle of exchanges within and between generations. In some cases, the specified return is of equal value, producing a stable system of statuses; in others it must exceed the value of the earlier gift, producing an escalating contest for honour. The whole society can be described by the catalogue of transfers that map all the obligations between its members. The cycling gift system is the society.[10]

This cycle of mutual obligation in archaic societies was elevated through the Eucharist toward a much larger group, transcending blood and kinship. The invisible obligation people felt toward a larger group eventually culminated in the notion of a state. The modern welfare state is rooted in a highly abstracted system of gift redistribution, which arose from the sense of obligation toward God to care for all. Once this divine obligation evaporates, humans fall back upon their natural prioritization of tribal gift negotiation. European welfare systems are crumbling not only due to economic recessions but also due to the unwillingness of the homogenous ethnic Europeans to share with the newcomers.[11] Marcel Mauss concludes his masterpiece with a mythological vision of King Arthur's roundtable:

---

10. Douglas, "Foreword," xi.
11. Alesina et al., "Why Doesn't United States."

Societies have progressed in so far as they themselves, their subgroups, and lastly, the individuals in them, have succeeded in stabilizing relationships, giving, receiving, and finally, giving in return. To trade, the first condition was to be able to lay aside the spear. From then onwards they succeeded in exchanging goods and persons, no longer only between clans, but between tribes and nations, and, above all, between individuals. Only then did people learn how to create mutual interests, giving mutual satisfaction, and, in the end, to defend them without having to resort to arms. Thus the clan, the tribe, and peoples have learnt how to oppose and to give to one another without sacrificing themselves to one another. This is what tomorrow, in our so-called civilized world, classes and nations and individuals also, must learn. This is one of the enduring secrets of their wisdom and solidarity. There is no other morality, nor any other form of economy, nor any other social practices save these. The Bretons, and the Chronicles of Arthur tell how King Arthur, with the help of a Cornish carpenter, invented that wonder of his court, the miraculous Round Table, seated round which, the knights no longer fought. Formerly, "out of sordid envy," in stupid struggles, duels and murders stained with blood the finest banquets. The carpenter said to Arthur: "I will make you a very beautiful table, around which sixteen hundred and more can sit, and move around, and from which no-one will be excluded. No knight will be able to engage in fighting, for there the highest placed will be on the same level as the lowliest." There was no longer a "high table," and consequently no more quarrelling. Everywhere that Arthur took his table his noble company remained happy and unconquerable. In this way nations today can make themselves strong and rich, happy and good. Peoples, social classes, families, and individuals will be able to grow rich, and will only be happy when they have learnt to sit down, like the knights, around the common store of wealth.[12]

Mauss seeks to undermine the human desire for honor by imagining a leveling table of plenty. Yet in this myth, Arthur has the highest authority, as he owns the table, and it would be just a matter of time until someone challenged him on ownership of his table. Moreover, globally the "common store of wealth" is neither common nor is it distributed evenly. Isaiah's vision solves this dilemma (Isa 25). Here the host is not human but God himself, who invites all nations to his rich table, where

---

12. Mauss, *Gift*, 105–6.

warfare and pain end. Yet this is possible only if the guests are captivated by God's radiant glory and submit willingly to his authority.

There are some core differences that remain between human and divine giving. While God is complete in himself and the Trinitarian relation is perfect love, humans are dependent beings. The divine gift stems from the overflow of God's abundance within himself. Human beings are able to give only what they have received. Therefore, the sense of obligation also differs. There is a degree to how much one can give back as one gives vis à vis. With God, the idea of giving back seems absurd, as everything is his already. Yet if God's grace can't be repaid, there remains a continuous desire to give back without limits. The Christian story creates an avenue to return the gift, as Jesus is viewed in the person of the fellow Christian, the stranger, and the poor. As Illich fittingly put it:

> The Incarnation invites me to seek the face of God in the face of everybody whom I encounter. And it makes me believe that, even though you and I will be ashes pretty soon, there is something in our bodily encounter, which is outside of this world in which we now are. Our bodyline takes on a metaphysical quality, which it makes more than just an accident of the moment.[13]

Since God's grace has no limits, the receiving believers also can't draw personal boundaries upon their own generosity toward others. Yahweh's universal invitation transcends particular tribal and ethnic boundaries. In principle, every human in the world is a potential brother and sister for the Christian, as there are no restrictions on participation in the Eucharist, with the only prerequisite being faith in Jesus as Lord and the confession of known sins. As Archer lucidly recognized, the ritual can be seen as inexhaustible resource for social capital, which extends beyond the empirical realm into concrete sociopolitical reality.[14] This resource can't run dry, as it is activated simply through the faith of the participants. Whether a believer feels filled by God's divine mercy and love and thus is enabled to give depends solely on an openness to receive the invisible riches.

However, in the Eucharist, the invisible becomes concrete via the experience. In this way the Eucharist follows the logic of incarnation, as Cavanaugh writes:

---

13. Cayley, *Rivers North*, 110.
14. Archer, "On Understanding Religious Experience."

God's "sacramental" presence is found in the Tabernacle and its furnishings, including the Ark of the Covenant and the table of the Bread of the Presence (Ex. 25–31, 35–40). The detailed prescriptions of the Law governing the mundane minutiae of life—from personal hygiene to animal husbandry, from clothing to pots and pans—indicate that God is to be found in everyday interactions with the material world, which, as Genesis 1 repeatedly reminds us, is good in God's eyes. Though Judaism and Christianity differ on the reality of the Incarnation of Jesus Christ, the movement of God in both is in the same downward direction: the life of the faith is not essentially the challenge of climbing a ladder to transcend the material world; rather it is responding to God's descent into concrete human life.[15]

By choosing to move downward and to dwell among men and women, Jesus lends nature sacred significance and elevates the mundane. Any gnostic notion to denigrate the body and the empirical world, to escape into a world of Hegelian idealism, is cut at the root when Jesus speaks: "This is my body, which is given for you" (Luke 22:19). Just as Jesus becomes the living mediator through the bread and wine, so the church is incorporated into his union with the Father and becomes the living sacrament to the world in a very concrete gathering at a particular moment in time. The bodies of believers are gathered and, in their brokenness, transformed into an icon of God's love. Love manifests itself through bodily encounters of people, and through this performance the Eucharist functions as a counter-reality to the growing excarnation that began in the archaic rebellion: "Excarnation is best understood as an attempt to escape human finitude, to transcend the limits of creatureliness. In that respect, it is a version of the primordial sin identified in Genesis 3:5, the sin that is at the heart of idolatry: the attempt to reach out, grasp, and be like gods."[16]

The embodied encounter is the antidote to increasing, excarnating non-relations, which are cemented through digital technology. Reality is first of all that which occurs in concrete encounter with God, with others, and with nature in the Eucharist. From this vantage point, Christians have a normative judgment point from which to view rapid technological innovation. The main question could be framed and discerned communally: Do these forms and tools enhance our relation with God, with each other,

---

15. Cavanaugh, *Uses of Idolatry*, 346.
16. Cavanaugh, *Uses of Idolatry*, 345.

and with nature? As foreboding unease arises concerning rapid innovations, which seem to enslave humanity, Christians have a very concrete, communal practice that could be employed as a normative lens to judge development not as some inevitable force of history but as subsumed under the decision of a sovereign, free people.

This sobriety of judgment is further reinforced through an existential sense of fullness. In the Eucharist, God himself infills each person. Each person is overcome with awe about Jesus choosing to first suffer to restore the relationship between humans and God as well as to dwell in the body of every believer through the Holy Spirit. The elements enable the concrete experience of this fact. The person who is frozen in a relation of non-relation and feels empty from inside can easily be manipulated by totalitarian forces, which promise an easy fulfillment through obedience. However, a person who feels at peace with God, with people, and with self will not be easily swayed through anger or fear. Satisfaction of physical and existential hunger is the best way to prevent the hungry person from devouring garbage. In our age of ever-subtler development of propaganda and psychological nudging techniques through AI, the best way of resistance is to anchor every person in the immediate relational reality. Moreover, in order to overcome the punctual self, who is not able to make any judgment about events due to communal historic amnesia, the Eucharist offers a ritual of remembering the larger narrative arc.

In the Eucharist, time is condensed as one simultaneously looks both backward and forward. One remembers what Jesus has done and celebrates it in the moment while looking forward to the future reality in which what Jesus accomplished in his death will be made fully manifest. Jesus accompanies the command of the Eucharist with the assurance of his coming. The eucharistic celebration foreshadows the destiny for all of creation, which is eternal captivation in the inexhaustible divine glory. By focusing on this goal, one allows the future to radiate into the present. The invitation to the lavish banquet allows the guests to relax. The atmosphere of hysteria due to the constant proclamation of an imminent doomsday recedes as the early mist through the rays of sun. Fear can subside as one experiences the sovereignty of the host. "Fear not"—this often-repeated biblical message becomes a reality at the generous feast. Reflexivity is possible only in a climate of rest, when one dares to stop acting, trusting that the world will not immediately collapse. Memory allows for a stable world within which people are allowed to think and to develop their environment. This stability is further strengthened through the covenantal nature of the Eucharist. Throughout the First Testament, God's unshakable loyalty to his people is repeated, as his promises about the better covenant culminate in the new covenant of Jesus. The new covenant reverberates the notion of the unshakable character of God, who commits to his people and reassures them that his promises stand firm.

In the Eucharist, all of reality appears as a precious gift not to be willfully destroyed. In the Eucharist, stewardship of the world is renewed. A thankful reception shapes the core attitude toward the elements one receives. Gratitude awakens in the heart of people who realize that all of life is a gift. Gratitude destroys entitlement and greed, which contribute to social exploitation and poverty. Abundance as social imaginary creates a soil within which cooperation can grow. The German theologian Martin Dibelius could not appreciate the generosity of Jesus. He remarked that the overabundance of wine in the wedding at Cana "was not necessary" and seemed "not to fit the Protestant ethic."[17] God's wasteful generosity dwarfs our cultural molds and challenges us to break out from narrowly constructed frameworks of mutual obligations.

If people internalize the core view of the world that there is enough for everyone, the zero-sum game disappears and the struggle for the best piece of the cake gives way toward a synergetic cooperation. Mauss rightly concludes that a basic image on the nature of reality may lead toward strife or cooperation. The myth of King Arthur is embedded in the English culture. Isaiah's vision transcends cultural boundaries due to Yahweh's universality. A myth does not simply become normative but must be embodied ritually. Jesus' incarnation makes the myth true. The grand story and empirical reality meet in a mutual embrace, which extends itself through believers participating in the Eucharist. A society permeated by a mutual atmosphere of gratitude and synergy due to communal belief in God's abundance will have greater resources in finding solutions to complex problems.

Gratitude is a core motivation for sacrifice. Sacrifice is crucial in forming foundational communities upon which every larger social unit relies. Through baptism, the believer identifies with Jesus' death and resurrection (Rom 6:8). By entering his death, the believer is promised to be raised to life through the resurrection of Christ. However, even the cross is embraced by the promise of glory. Jesus enters the agony in light of the

---

17. Hirsch-Luipold, *Gott wahrnehmen*, 123.

glory set before him.[18] This sacrificial logic is transmitted from the one-time event of Jesus' death to a regular habitual action of Christians. In the Eucharist, the believer receives with deep gratitude the costliest sacrifice and simultaneously commits himself to lay down his life as well. Just like Christ lowered and emptied himself, so believers must follow him by sacrificing themselves for others (Phil 2). In fact, the Christian ideal calls for the Christian life becoming a single sacrifice out of gratitude. A society made up of people who sacrifice themselves for their family, their brothers and sisters, their colleagues, their friends, and ultimately even the stranger will radiate life. To the contrary, when more and more people demand rights and fewer and fewer people are willing to sacrifice their privileges in order to take up responsibility, when the state must pay its citizens for every act of kindness, this is a sign of imminent collapse, as every system is able to thrive only when more energy is added than taken.

The realization that Jesus made the first step toward humans creates an obligation for humans to make the first step of reconciliation toward the other. Vertical reconciliation is real only insofar as it produces horizontal reconciliation.[19] As the antagonism of humanity toward God recedes, this newfound harmony radiates outward, impacting society by bringing about restoration of broken relationships, opening new avenues of connection, even dismantling ideological strife.

The Eucharist is commanded by Jesus and expresses a primordial reality. Although performed by humans, it refers to the eternal God, who is outside of time and space. Since humans have limited attention, Jesus institutes a regular practice of the Eucharist. As humans we need repetitive acts in order to glimpse the solid nature of an otherwise vague reality.[20] The givenness of the ritual as divine continuous invitation frees the exhausted individual from the pagan compulsion to feed the idol (see ch. 2). The curse of self-creation and a world on the verge of chaos gives way to approaching God, whose throne never crumbles and who desires to lavish good gifts upon his children.

The Eucharist is in itself a signpost of this advancing new reality permeated with the spirit of freedom and love, driving out the spirits of coercion and power. As embodied practice, the Eucharist represents a

---

18. Richard Bauckham shows convincingly how the suffering of Jesus in the Gospel of John is transformed through the overall vision of God's glory (*Gospel of Glory*).

19. This is particularly emphasized through the Lord's Prayer and in the Epistles of John.

20. Catherine Pickstock elucidated this idea in *Repetition and Identity*.

stronger ontology than any discourse could ever establish. It entails much more than is visible on first glance and has far deeper significance for our society than I could possibly unpack in this brief chapter.

Yet even the Eucharist's efficacy is not somehow automatically manifested. It can also be perverted. In fact, the perversion of the best leads toward the worst. Since eating together is so powerful and the Eucharist has been central in European civilization, its perversion constitutes a destruction of the core. The outcry about the mockery of the Last Supper during the Paris Olympics 2024 was surprising, due to the fact that Europe was considered to be secular. Perhaps even the seemingly agnostic Europeans sense deep down in their collective memories that desecration of the Eucharist represents the final blow to Western civilization. By delegitimizing the core myth and ritual, other gods are invited in. However, the strongest perversion of the Eucharist does not come through external ridicule but through internal destruction. External ridicule can, in fact, bring Christians together. Internal perversion leads toward an inner split. True worship involves the why (myth), the how (ritual), and the what (everyday life). As Cavanaugh put it:

> In other words, there is an ethical dimension to the Eucharist that demands attention in any attempt to remedy idolatry. To put a sharper point on it, there are not only different celebrations of the Eucharist, but there are idolatrous ones. The line between genuine and perversely sacramental ways of being in the world does not run between Christian and non-Christian practices; that line runs through the church as well.[21]

Coherence between meaning, ritual performance, and everyday behavior leads toward a powerful demonstration of God's glory and a flourishing life. Conversely, the perversion of the Eucharist destroys the social core and produces a monstrous social body.

There might come a time again, and perhaps the hour is here, when just like at the juncture between antiquity and medieval times, within the interregnum of chaos, the church once again will be challenged at its core to embody its worship in a culture of life. The debris outside its walls would make it impossible to build anything on ruins, which are reduced to ashes. When universities are nothing else than halls of cynicism and propaganda, politics nothing else than temples of self-aggrandizement, which use science and economics for personal power,

---

21. Cavanaugh, *Uses of Idolatry*, 372.

when the cost to reform these institutions from within is incomparably high—this might be the hour when Christians who gather around the living bread begin once again, like in the ancient monasteries, to embody the vision they have glanced in the Eucharist. This will be a powerful witness once again and a source of hope to the decaying society around them. I hope that this time the church will resist the temptation of hubris and power. This has been and still remains the main struggle of the church: to worship God holistically in spirit and in truth.[22]

---

22. Jesus' reply to the Samaritan woman on the nature of worship transcended particular ethnic and cultic boundaries (John 4:1–26).

CHAPTER 12

Peace Through *Ecclesia Militans*

> *Let us honor the Catholic Church, our true Mother, the true Bride of her Husband, because she is the wife of so great a Lord. And what shall I say? How great is that Husband and of singular rank, that he discovered a prostitute and made her a virgin. Because she should not deny that she was a prostitute, lest she forget the mercy of her liberator. How can it be said that she was not a prostitute when she fornicated with demons and idols? Fornication was in the heart of everyone; a few have fornicated in the flesh, but everyone has fornicated in his heart. And He came and made her a virgin; he made the church a virgin.*
>
> —St. Augustine, "Sermon 213: on the Creed"

> *Wenn es keinen Kampf gibt, gibt es kein Christentum.*
>
> —Benedict XVI

THE HEBREW CREATION STORY locates pain and ultimately death in the severance from God as the source of all life. Evil emerges as the perverted hierarchy of relationality, seeking to dethrone God. God overcomes this separation through Jesus and offers people reunion with him through communion with the Holy Spirit. Though the offer stands, the realization of this offer can be perverted. The main struggle of the church lies in worshipping the triune God truthfully, as he wants to be praised. A holistic worship unites myth, ritual, and everyday behavior. From within this praise, the church must suffer and wage war against the sinful nature that is antagonistic to God and others. The result will be peace, which is the unique contribution of the church to the flourishing of society until God himself establishes his will on earth as it is in heaven.

Severance, Pain, and Struggle

Human life begins with struggle. Through pain and travail, a mother must push the baby out from her body. The comfortable, warm cocoon bursts, and the baby is thrust out into the sharp light, the cold, and the sudden vast space. Through the cut by the surgeon the baby is separated from the safe union with the mother and must from now on move ever further from her and through struggle and pain navigate this dangerous world. Life begins with painful separation and continues full of struggle to restore the lost harmony and overcome the alienation from the world, the self, and others. The end of life resembles the beginning with painful separation. Upon breathing the last breath, the body stiffens and is transformed from a living body to a cold corpse. Once life has left the body, the person no longer has a sense of self nor the ability to interact with others. The corpse remains passive, and any notion of relationality collapses as it merges into dust. This short summary exemplifies how severance, both physical and psychological, causes pain and how humans struggle to establish a coherence that can restore the original unity.

Even if for a moment we could forget the reality of physical pain—some are more fortunate in this than others—continuous relational pain remains a fact. Every second of one's life is a reminder of inevitable loss. Pain is both directly and indirectly felt and can't be rationalized away. If I have a toothache, my mental acrobatics can take me only so far. It is therefore rational to center a myth around this solid certainty of suffering, as for example a young Siddhartha Gautama, who later became known as Buddha, did. He sought to explain and escape the reality of pain. Thus, the appeal of Buddhism rests on the reality of human suffering. It is also tempting to declare the reality of struggle and pain as the sole determining factor of human life, as Karl Marx did. Both myths derive their appeal through engagement with the real human problem of separation, struggle, and pain. Although pain presents itself directly to all humans, as beings who seek meaning, humans interpret this experience within the larger myth and mediate it via rituals. How we respond to pain depends on the story we inhabit.

How Not to Beat the Air: Recovering the Story

The Judeo-Christian story explains pain, both physical and existential, as a consequence of severance from God. Suffering was not part of God's original plan. Since God is good, pain and suffering are symptoms of evil. In the first and the last books of the Christian Bible, God is portrayed as the sovereign actor. He is the beginning and the end, the all-powerful ruler over all of reality. While evil exemplifies a degree of reality, it nevertheless has a negative identity as lack of the good. After separation from God, the biblical story tells how all aspects of Adam and Eve's lives and their descendants were permeated by perversion of the original divine intention, resulting in pain and death as the ultimate separation from physical life. Yet already in the First Testament, culminating in the person of Jesus in the Second, the story offers a way for how pain can be transformed into redemption and restoration of the original unity. God takes what is broken and recycles it within his redemptive plan. This double view of pain, in which one embraces it and seeks to transform it, has been influential in the development of Western institutions.

Within medieval Christianity, pain was embraced as the reality of the fallen world, but also the transcendence of pain was sought as a sign of a new reality, which broke through with Jesus' crucifixion and resurrection.[1] In fact, the cross is the symbol of both ultimate pain and its overcoming. With secularization, this complex dual view of pain increasingly shifted toward mere alleviation of pain, ushering in our modern medical preoccupation with eradicating human suffering through technological innovation. In order to recover the reality of *ecclesia militans* as a robust, suffering church amid struggle and pain, one must be aware of this unarticulated background that shapes our perception and value judgment. In a numbed and drugged world, it sounds cruel

---

1. Asad, *Formations of the Secular*, 67–100.

to advocate for a suffering, struggling church. In order to recover a true *ecclesia militans*, I must mention its caricature, as this caricature is often responsible for a visceral, knee jerk reaction in the West against this term. Yet instead of getting rid of a perverted ideal, it is better to recover it and cleanse it from historic misuse.

From the fourth century onward, the church at times externalized evil and projected it as a fixed target. Yet how evil presents itself shifts. When the church assumes evil in front, it is already behind; when evil is seen as without, it has already corrupted the body from within; when finally evil is found out due to its ugliness, it already triumphs over the church in the guise of a beautiful and charming suitor. The Bible portrays evil as a complex, intelligent agent who does not rest.[2] Evil can't be easily perceived, let alone hit with precision. For the past centuries, the church sought to combat the growing godlessness of the world without realizing that the outward godlessness was just a reflection of its own inner perversion. The church sought to combat social ills only to find that by making the betterment of the world its sole focus, it had cut itself off from the deeper reasons of its own existence. While mistaking social progress for the advance of the kingdom, the church allowed a sinister, triumphal relaxation to penetrate it from within and blind its apocalyptic vision.

By framing the struggle in terms of "us," the good, versus "them," the evil, whether heretics in the fourth century, or Muslim infidels during the times of the Crusades, or the fierce battles of the nineteenth-century Roman Catholic Church against secular modernity, or the Protestant fundamentalism of the twentieth century, the church replayed a Manichaean logic, abandoning the complex biblical view of evil, failing to perceive it due to the perversion of its worship through the corrosive effects of power. The suffering church was transformed into a political institution, which inflicted suffering upon those perceived as heretics. For the first three centuries, Christians were willing to endure pain in order to prove their allegiance to Christ as ultimate authority. As Tertullian rightly remarked, the blood of martyrs became the seed of the church. Yet once the church gained social credibility through its martyrs, it was willing to employ pain as a redemptive tool. Pain was justified as a means to bring pagans into the peaceful realm of Christendom.

Most theologians and Christians today would agree that these were pathological expressions of the struggling church. Yet we are in

---

2. Matthew Croasmun demonstrates the complex nature of evil within Pauline writing (*Emergence of Sin*).

the middle of another perversion, which disguises itself as virtue. By solely focusing on the caricature of the *ecclesia militans* and forgetting its healthy expressions, the church today tends to negate the reality of struggle and pain altogether. By forgetting the larger horizon, the church is blind to the real struggles. Instead, the church kicks the air and mobilizes its troops for the battles dictated by the zeitgeist, seeking to receive medals from political and cultural elites.

False prophets proclaimed peace where there was none. They sought to please the king and be praised by the crowd (e.g., Jer 14:13–14). It is therefore not by accident that the church, upon realizing that it had lost its battle against secular modernity, shifted into a mode of dialogue to preserve its power. At the Second Vatican Council, the language of *ecclesia militans* was absent altogether. The call for dialogue became prominent. Although dialogue might appear conciliatory in some regards, yet it remains a gesture of the powerful, who are in a position of control and can dictate the rules of engagement. To be clear, dialogue in the sense of engaging the other through the power of the word is unanimously accepted by all Christians. However, similar to the previous perversions, this time the rich modes of engagement are reduced to a more passive mode of seeking to understand the other. A dialogue can also be viewed through the mode of polemical argument or witness, provoking a response from the other. The established European churches within the mainline Protestant and Roman Catholic denominations shifted to an irenic mode and abandoned the addressing of struggle and pain to its ideological bastard children—mostly Marxist and neo-Marxist political movements. Now if the church dares to address struggle at all, it does so only by parroting the narrative of the cultural elites. The sheltered life of the average European theologian creates blind spots to the pervasive nature of struggle and consequently to the complex character of God. Miroslav Volf, coming from the volatile region of former Yugoslavia, does not seek to explain away God's vengeance and violence as portrayed in the book of Revelation. Instead, he views these characteristics as crucial, if human nonviolence is to be maintained:

> My thesis that the practice of nonviolence requires a belief in divine vengeance will be unpopular with many Christians, especially theologians in the West. To the person who is inclined to dismiss it, I suggest imagining that you are delivering a lecture in a war zone.... Among your listeners are people whose cities and villages have been first plundered, then burned and

leveled to the ground, whose daughters and sisters have been raped, whose fathers and brothers have had their throats slit. The topic of the lecture: a Christian attitude toward violence. The thesis: we should not retaliate since God is perfect noncoercive love. Soon you will discover that it takes the quiet of a suburban home for the birth of the thesis that human nonviolence corresponds to God's refusal to judge. In a scorched land, soaked in the blood of the innocent, it will invariably die. And as one watches it die, one will do well to reflect about many other pleasant captivities of the liberal mind.[3]

Currently, the recovery of *ecclesia militans* arises from the global South, where churches face a sociopolitical environment similar to that of the seven churches which received the apocalyptic vision of John depicting the struggle through a vivid imaginary. Our theologies are not solely determined by the concrete sociopolitical context. Yet, as our minds are embedded in the concrete sociopolitical environment, the context also paints the horizons of the possible. Jenkins rightly hinted at the fact that the instability and the lower sociopolitical status of the church in the South makes the church acutely aware of the conflictual nature of reality and thus more open to the recovery of apocalyptic imaginary:

> Read against the background of martyrdom and exile, it is not surprising that so many Christians look for promises that their sufferings are only temporary, and that God will intervene directly to save the situation. In this context, the book of Revelation looks like true prophecy on an epic scale, however unpopular or discredited it may be for most Americans or Europeans. In the South, Revelation simply makes sense, in its description of a world ruled by monstrous demonic powers. These forces might be literal servants of Satan, or symbols for evil social forces, but in either case, they are indisputably real. . . . To a Christian living in a Third World dictatorship, the image of the government as Antichrist is not a bizarre religious fantasy, but a convincing piece of political analysis.[4]

I can confirm this observation from my field research in Beirut among the underground African and Lebanese Pentecostal churches.[5] While I attended interreligious dialogues at the Jesuit university, where irenic

3. Volf, *Exclusion and Embrace*, 304.
4. Jenkins, *Next Christendom*, 219–20.
5. Dik, *Realness Through Mediating Body*, 196–220.

dialogues in sanitary rooms prevailed, the Pentecostals were venturing into former enemy quarters of the city to engage Muslims in "conversion dialogue."[6] Conversations protected by academic walls and conventions are completely different from encountering someone vulnerably on the street who in the past could have slit your father's throat.[7]

The appeal and the rise of charismatic and Pentecostal movements in the twentieth century among the urban poor stems from those movements' ability to provide a plausible metastory of a struggling church amid the powers of evil. The idea of a spiritual warfare offers a wider view of reality and richer imagery than that of a Marxist duality of oppressor and oppressed, restoring agency to the powerless, who enter into spiritual practices, which also transforms socioeconomic conditions in the long run. The question remains as to how *ecclesia militans* can be conceived of today, beyond the pathologies of the church "beating the air" (1 Cor 9:26).

The idea of a struggling, suffering, and battling church originated in the biblical corpus and was developed through church history.[8] The primary struggle of the Israelites in the First Testament was to worship God rightly. This continues in the Second Testament with the nascent Christian movement developing Jewish worship further into Trinitarian worship: to worship God, through Jesus, guided by the Holy Spirit. Hereby, God is viewed as sovereign over all other powers. Contrary to the Babylonian myths and their secularized version in the form of Marxism, struggle is not viewed as the primeval creative force within human history. God's word is. Creation is not antagonistic at its core. God created a harmonious order, which he proclaimed as very good. When evil seduces the first man and woman, it creates a rupture between humans and God and ultimately alienation on all levels. Yet in the same breath, God already promises the victory through the conqueror born of the woman (Gen 3:15). Evil is conquered through the resurrection, and the final victory is promised when Jesus returns. Thus struggle and pain are framed by harmony. Evil is conquered by good. At

---

6. Dik, "Conversion Dialogue."

7. On the sociological analysis of differences between academic dialogue and street conversion dialogue, see Dik, "Conversion Dialogue."

8. I build the following chapter on the work of Michael Fiedrowicz, "Ecclesia Militans." He presents a biblical-theological case for *ecclesia militans* and collects reflections on this topic by major theologians throughout church history. See Fiedrowicz, *Ecclesia Militans*.

the center of the biblical story is a God who is the primary agent against the powers of evil. Yet evil is portrayed as a cunning, complex power that surpasses the abilities of humans to resist its lure. Again and again, the biblical stories describe how people succumb to its seductions, creating the longing for divine intervention from the outside. The reality and profundity of evil require God himself to fight. Jewish perseverance and Christian hope in the final victory rest on the fact that it is God himself who will restore peace in order to safeguard his glory. The fact of resurrection prefigures the final victory over death. In both the First Testament and the last book of the Second Testament, the reoccurring theme is God's assurance to his people: "The battle is mine."

The primary struggle for the church is to worship God rightly by giving itself fully as a response of thankfulness. Both the First and Second Testaments, although through different means, nevertheless proclaim a similar message of how God reconciles men and women with himself and seeks their response out of gratitude and love. The main message of the Hebrew prophets was to call Israelites to the right worship of God by establishing a ritual practice that reflects God's glory and is in sync with their inner attitude and daily life. All of life must be a reflection of who God is. Consequently, the primary calling for Christians is to abide in Jesus as the incarnate God and to live in deep union with him. All evil, whether internal, structural, or historical, emerges through separation from the source of all life, goodness, and beauty. Therefore, to remain in God is the essential precondition for resisting evil, which requires discernment of its shifting shape.

To say that the battle is primarily God's is to reiterate a core biblical distinction between God and humanity. In the First Testament, there is a moment when God asks his people to stand by and watch as he battles for them (e.g., Ps 46:10). This theme is then extended in the Second Testament, wherein Paul emphasizes that the battle is won by God through Jesus' death and resurrection. This initial victory is finalized in the apocalyptic vision that John received and recorded in Revelation, in which Christ returns as victor. Yet humans are not totally passive in this struggle but rather invited to join it.

Since God is the source of all reality and he will ultimately prevail against anything that seeks to destroy the good, true, and beautiful, the primary struggle of humans is to stay loyal to God and remain in continuous union with him. The primary attack of evil lies in destroying this union and creating a break between God and human beings. Worship extended from cultic rituals to everyday aspects of life. However, being surrounded by various nations, Israel was always being tempted to dance around the golden calf, to compromise their allegiance to Yahweh. Throughout the Psalms, the goodness, power, and faithfulness of Yahweh through turbulent historic events were proclaimed among the worshipping community. Yet the evil powers that sought to seduce or coerce the faithful into idol worship remained a continuous threat. These evil powers worked from within the people of God but also manifested themselves through concrete historic empires. For example, the Egyptian pharaoh is portrayed as anti-Yahweh, seeking to thwart the redemptive purpose of God for the people of Israel. Similarly, Isaiah and Daniel portrayed the manifestation of anti-godly forces, which attempted through various empires to destroy God's redemptive history with his people.

This theme finds its fulfillment in the proclamation of Jesus and Pauline theology. Jesus did not confront the Roman Empire directly head on. Instead, he dwarfed the empire by introducing the larger conceptual reality of the kingdom of God. The tension between the heavenly and earthly kingdoms gave rise to all subsequent Christian political theology. While Jesus left untouched the nitty-gritty questions on the concreteness of power between the Jewish way of life and Roman rule, he nevertheless established a much larger framework of authority, over all creation and history. John rightly spelled out this intuition in the book of Revelation by lifting Jesus up over Caesar and bringing the implicit lordship of Jesus into open confrontation with the imperial cult. Thus, for the early Christians, the proclamation "Jesus is Lord" implied the subjugation of Roman authority and therefore emancipation from the ubiquitous demands of Greco-Roman polytheism. While both the First and Second Testaments admonish the believers to respect earthly authority, the ranking of authority is made clear. Daniel respected Babylonian rule, yet he did not hesitate to protest when the king sought to usurp the realm of Yahweh's law. In this way, God is portrayed as standing above and even working through Nebuchadnezzar. Therefore, the believer is called to maintain highest allegiance to God.

This steadfastness to and confession of Yahweh as the highest authority confronts political authority. The Bible tells numerous accounts of believers who were willing to lay down their lives in order to not compromise their allegiance to Yahweh, when earthly authority demanded it of them. Extending further this tradition, Jesus prepared his disciples, telling them in advance that they would be attacked, driven out, and killed for proclaiming him as Lord and risen Messiah (John 16:2). The author of the Epistle to the Hebrews lists many biblical characters who suffered willingly for the sake of their allegiance to Yahweh.

The formation of the church as a distinct entity within the first century was largely due to the refusal to accommodate Greco-Roman polytheism. The church fathers vehemently defended the highest allegiance to Jesus amid Greco-Roman polytheism. Through the centuries, it remained a liberating act of rebellion when the church proclaimed Jesus as Lord over the political powers of their day. Karl Barth's proclamation of Jesus' lordship for the Confessing Church during a time when the totalitarian National Socialist state sought to usurp the church stands in this long tradition. The most important struggle of the church is to stay faithful to the lordship of Jesus and live in the realization of the battle won, in order not to descend into false activism and fear.

Therefore, while the primary mode of struggle consists in abiding in God, by keeping attention and focus upon him, the Bible also tells a story of active ways to enter into the outward struggle. I see it as a three-tiered battle: first, the inner-life struggle to remain rooted in faith; second, the battle to resist the false teachings that creep into the church; and third, staying firm in light of outer pressures and not compromising, whether through beliefs or behaviors.

Although Hebrew Scripture portrays Yahweh as the only ultimate ruler, lesser evil powers are also mentioned, who wage war against God himself. In the book of Job, evil is personified and equipped with powerful agency. Satan means "adversary" in Hebrew. He opposes God and seeks to seduce people to separate themselves from the love of God. In the book of Ezekiel, the origin of evil is located in the pride of an angel who wants to be equal to God and the subsequent rebellion that emerges from it (Isa 14:12–14; Ezek 28:14–19). The battles of the Israelites against the various Canaanite tribes can't be viewed as mere political conquest. Instead, they exemplified God's concrete punishment upon nations, after a very long period of patience. The driving out of evil groups and establishing of the monarchy of Israel served as a beacon of light to the surrounding nations, a universal invitation to all nations to come to the generous table of Yahweh (Isa 25).

These brief sketches about angels and demons are then further developed in the Second Testament. Both the Gospels and the various Epistles paint a very vivid and dynamic view of the powers and principalities of evil. Satan, as God's opponent, rules over the lower realms.

He is the "prince of this world" (John 12:31), who seeks to thwart God's redemptive plan for this world. Military language permeates the Second Testament, and world history is staged as a battle between God and the devil. The devil knows that he can't topple God. Therefore he turns toward humans, who are loved by God, in order to destroy them. The important difference from the First Testament with the advance of Jesus is the call to his followers from all nations to fight this battle not through military-political means and the establishment of a Christian nation but through spiritual means against invisible powers and principalities (Eph 6), in order to embody the advancing universal kingdom of Jesus, which transcends earthly delineations of countries and nations. Jesus is portrayed as an advancing conqueror who will bring an end to the rule of the devil, who, fully aware of this, intensifies his attacks on the faithful. The resistance and persecution that Jesus himself, his apostles, and the early church had to endure was interpreted in this larger historic drama with a fixed outcome in Jesus' final victory and the subsequent restoration of original harmony (Rev 21–22).

The book of Revelation opens up a deeper view of both sociopolitical reality and history. Behind and underneath the concrete experience, John's visions reveal a larger stage, upon which invisible powers pull the strings. This view of reality enabled the Jewish sect worshipping Jesus to perceive his identity and mission within the larger framework and persevere despite harsh resistance from the Jewish religious elites and, later, Roman authorities as well.

The Judeo-Christian stories blur the clear-cut distinction of evil as coming from an external source. Throughout the entire biblical narrative, evil is portrayed as active within Israel and, later, the church as well. Thus, the battle must be forged against the evil desires of the flesh and the evil that corrupts the church from within. Both the Hebrew and Christian Scriptures do not create a clear-cut separation between an idealized image of believers on one side and depraved sinners on the other. To the contrary, the main preoccupation of the Hebrew prophets is the corruption of Israel. God seems to be foremost concerned about the corruption of his people, as they are the carrier of his mission toward all nations. Therefore, the harshest critique is directed inward. The higher the privilege of being the elected people and the loftier the task of being the light to the nations, the stronger is the responsibility and the deeper the fall. This inner battle within the believer and the church permeates the Epistles of Paul.

After the ceasing of external pressures upon the church in the fourth century, the focus of battle shifted toward battling the demons within and addressing the growing heresies within the church rather than the evil from without. The popularity of the monastic movement since the third century was due to the fact that many Christians recognized that the ceasing of external attacks introduced a more subtle and therefore more dangerous seduction from within. The monastic movement sought to address and to tangibly embody the struggle against the evil within the flesh. The various church councils in the third and fourth centuries sought through clarifying doctrine to battle false teachers and prophets within the church.

This story of struggle against evil, which originated in the beginning story of the Bible, continues in the Hebrew experience through to the life of Jesus, then his disciples, and spills over into church history. Thus *ecclesia militans* is primarily formed through Trinitarian worship. If the church does not struggle as the worshipping church, it will be perverted into the same evil it sought to battle in the first place. The battle of the church, when truly rooted in worship, will appear as paradoxical and in this way provide a life-giving pattern for the surrounding society.

The Peaceable War of the Worshipping Church: Modeling Social Patterns

The primary mode of formation of *ecclesia militans* is holistic worship as expressed in its ritual, narrative, and ethical dimensions. Robust churches gather to worship regularly, they know why they worship, and their worship extends into their everyday lives. It is only from within Trinitarian worship, involving all the senses of every believer, that the church can resist and struggle against evil. Various societies pose different challenges to a holistic, biblical worship.

Traditional cultures insist upon ritual form while often discarding the larger meaning and obfuscating authenticity in everyday behavior. This was the main critique of Hebrew prophets against the Israelites, who kept the ritual as a shell but forgot its significance and therefore contradicted it through daily injustices. On the other side, there is a modern Protestant-Kantian inversion of biblical worship: everyday ethics are distilled from ritual and myth, which are then discarded, assuming that the ethics will somehow be self-evident to every rational individual. This assumption is further reinforced through Western individualism in its gnostic-intellectualist or hedonistic disguise. It follows then that one would ask what point there is to going to church on Sunday if one knows it all. Why bother investing time in something of seemingly little material value if I can do something more pleasurable instead or simply optimize myself? The peculiar evangelical temptation has been to discard the form by insisting on the meaning of the rituals, thus sliding into a gnostic, disembodied mode of worship. Moreover, by failing to connect the ritual to the everyday, Evangelicals have often wasted energy solving problems that they have in fact created through false worship. Endless debates and ink have been spilled trying to reconcile word with action, mission with justice, and many other artificial binaries.

The church must never cease to wrestle with the meaning of the biblical narrative. Comprehending the larger story of God's revelation is a struggle that is not reserved for a few theologians. Jacob wrestled with God. Similarly, Job hurled his anger and doubt at God. In Ps 88 the author expressed his cynicism amid perceived darkness around him. These stories and songs were included in the Bible perhaps primarily to serve the church as an example of honest worship, as people remained in relationship with God. Similarly, the church gathers as an interpretative community and allows Scripture to read them as much as believers are reading the Scriptures through their struggles. People with various gifts and cultural backgrounds are more able to glimpse a larger picture than a lone theologian can. The search for and communal discernment of the true God is of crucial importance in matters of life or death. As Cavanaugh rightly remarked:

> If, on the other hand, our predicament is better described as misenchantment, if we are *homo liturgicus*, worshiping beings who encounter divine presence in all sorts of created realities for good and for ill, then the question "Which divinity?" is necessary to address not necessarily at the start, but sooner rather than later. Idolatry is a different thing from disenchantment. We are not talking only about a beautiful world in which people have forgotten to thank the invisible God for the visible gifts they receive. We are also living in a broken world in which people are oppressed and slaughtered by gods of human creation. If sacramentality is not to become sentimentality—Look at all

the pretty flowers!—then the hard questions of which gods are being encountered in things must be addressed.[9]

The modern man looks back in disdain upon the seemingly naïve religious believers, who fought about whose God is supreme. Yet the twentieth century has been equally ravished by wars in the name of ideologies, which are gods in a secular disguise, as they fulfill the same function as the ancient divinities. From a historical distance the ideological wars of the twentieth century are indistinguishable from religious wars. People in the twenty-first century are faced with a dilemma: how to struggle for the question of ultimate concern without killing the other. Currently, the death is "merely" social, as many have no problem with destroying the reputation and employment of the ideological other. Yet the line between social and physical destruction is porous. Religious wars never disappeared, they were only renamed. Historically, deities outlined the radius of liberties and taboos.[10] Cultural wars are the symptom of a deeper history of religious struggles over whose God is better for society. Paradoxically, the church can establish the widest radius of liberty only if Jesus' authority is elevated in the believer's life above all other allegiances.

By proclaiming the lordship of Jesus, the Christian church proclaims its social vision as well. By praying "thy will be done on earth as it is in heaven," Christians commit themselves to struggle to be loyal to Jesus above all other loyalties. Christians who have glimpsed a higher reality of divine glory and who have incorporated this reality deeply through the sacraments can't but find themselves in everyday life facing a world that often opposes God's will. While Roman Catholics provided deep theological accounts for the reasons for worship, the Orthodox preserved a rich tradition of how to worship. Evangelicals and in particular the Anabaptists showed us how the discipleship culture fleshes out worship in daily life. Furthermore, Pentecostals/charismatics highlighted how a life in fullness with the Holy Spirit ushers in a powerful coherence between who God is and how we celebrate him and live out liturgical commitments throughout our daily lives.

The continuous struggle to glimpse and understand who God is within the biblical story is crucial in order to arrive at a right orientation in life and the unmasking of false gods as idols. Without the highest ideal,

---

9. Cavanaugh, *Uses of Idolatry*, 340.

10. On the genesis of current culture wars through the lens of religious history, see Dik, "Freiheit durch Kreuzigung."

people turn blind as reality blurs and fragments. Entire civilizations can be penetrated by evil without conscious awareness.

The second struggle for right worship lies in maintaining a regular gathering. Already the author of the Letter to the Hebrews reminded the believers not to neglect regular fellowship (Heb 10:24–25). Today many forces seek to disintegrate the gathering of the church: from gnostic dismissal of the body to social fragmentation and obsession with self—the church must recover the why of its corporeal worship and commit to it.

The third struggle for worship is the integration of awe and love of God in story and ritual with everyday life. The church must learn to interpret society through worship. The sacraments are the highest reality, which both manifest the ideal and explain the aberration. While the secular West creates the illusion of absence of anything divine on the surface, it is pregnant with idolatrous myths and rituals at a deeper level. The worshipping church must expose these evil idols in the light of God's goodness. Under the weight of God's truth, they will crumble.

I do not believe that a single theologian like myself is able to prescribe a battle against some particular evil. This must be discerned only from within the worship of the local church. Society exemplifies a high degree of complexity. Evil enmeshes itself into the very individual and social fabric. Therefore, it is impossible to discern the contours from a distance and to lay down a concrete path forward. I have written on particular social ethics for the street church in Berlin that I lead with others.[11] In this book my primary intention is to clarify why the primary struggle of the church is to worship rightly and how this understanding affects the way the church will approach its struggle in sowing the seeds of peace. Evil can't be discerned or addressed directly. It is like Medusa, who will turn us to stone if we stare into her gaze without first glimpsing the glory of Jesus.

By gathering around Jesus, believers affirm the fact that they are in need of repetitive glimpses of a larger and deeper reality. By confessing their sins and receiving the Eucharist, they proclaim their own inability. Humility as the realization of one's own susceptibility to blindness and bias opens one up to the other, even if the other comes with a completely different perception of reality. In our small street church, people with various socioeconomic and cultural backgrounds gather. As our societies fragment along educational, socioeconomic, and political lines, which

---

11. Dik, *Church, Immigration & Pluralism*.

are reinforced by algorithms forming invisible prisons, the church offers a place where oppressive hierarchies are dismantled, through communal kneeling at the cross, where the ground is level. This moment becomes the performance of a counter-reality that relativizes the dominant social categories. Social peace occurs when the boundaries between powerful and powerless become porous, and they dissolve completely for a moment when rich and poor drink from the same cup. This is why in the Epistle of James the author speaks strongly against favoring the rich, as it contradicts the logic of equality before Jesus as Lord (Jas 2:1–13).

Social strife intensifies when hierarchies become cemented along hereditary lines. In the past, these lines were drawn along blood relations, later extending to larger ethnic tribes. In the nineteenth and twentieth centuries, the wars were fought along the boundary markers of nations. Now these lines are erected along new ideological markers like gender, religion, and political affiliation. The logic of antagonism and eternal strife is cemented. Through the Eucharist, the powerful are lowered and the poor lifted up. Yet this occurs in a voluntary, peaceful manner, recognizing the ultimate authority of the host. Within the rapidly splintering social fabric, the church must offer an inviting space in which God's kingdom transcends particular individual and communal identities. Even though, sadly, churches often reinforce the prevalent divisive lines, I have also witnessed churches where the most unlikely people, who due to their difference would not otherwise touch or rub shoulders, found a larger allegiance together. From this particular ritual experience, the tent is widened and perhaps may even become a larger sacred canopy for society, shielding against divisive forces. Without the concrete social body of the church, civil religion will vanish or be transformed into a state-imposed ideology.

One may counter with the objection that Christianity is particular and divisive and can't serve as a unifying bond of solidarity. Despite the obvious historical shortcomings of the church (see ch. 4), there is nothing better on the horizon to counter the maddening swings between suffocating totalitarianism and the atomized individualism of the past century. Either Christians struggle to worship holistically, or the social order will be shaped by other gods. While Christianity was perverted when it turned to violence and exclusion, the true story and practice of it require humility and critique of the self, enveloped in hope. Christians are not exempt from the temptations of hubris and evil. However, they have built-in autocorrecting mechanisms in their myth and rituals.

By focusing exclusively on the uniqueness of Christ, Christians will be the most inclusive and charitable toward outsiders, who always remain potential brothers and sisters. By confessing the lordship of Jesus, Christians drain political powers of their hubris and relativize all other immanent entities who could be tempted to claim absolute allegiance. Of course, one could object that one could also fight in the name of Jesus. Yet Jesus is badly suited for this, as he willingly gave his life for all of humanity and prayed for his murderers. Therefore, if anyone claims to fight in his name, they are sorely mistaken. Christians must not only fiercely critique themselves first but they must also not be afraid to be canceled or killed as they point to the perverted good in others. While speaking truth, Christians will not descend into bitter resentment, as they are continuously enveloped by the eucharistic hope that truth will prevail. The first thing that dies in a war is truth. Conversely, people who love truth will cultivate the humus of peace and keep war at bay.

Even if the church struggles against a particular evil, it will not succumb to its magic spells. The worshipping church will be able to keep evil at bay through God's glory and will not turn bitter and exhausted as it glimpses regularly the original harmony and is filled with hope through the promise of final victory of Christ. Moreover, Christians can't descend into ad hominem, othering dynamics. Christians know all too well that the line between good and evil does not merely run through every heart but must be reinstated regularly through sacraments, in order that hearts be not blinded by the father of lies. Therefore, they will seek to battle evil within themselves first, while helping the ones who are possessed by it as well. The fuel of war consists in perpetuating the view of society divided by good and evil people, while of course every side claims to be good. The maturation of peace occurs when every person begins to recognize and battle the evil within their own heart first.

The church as complementary community composed of diverse people with various gifts will not be fooled by mobilization against an abstract cause or concrete people. Instead, the social body of the church employs all of its senses to wrestle with the concrete reality in a particular place. Prophets envision a deeper reality. Teachers and evangelists proclaim and witness to the peaceful advance of an alternative kingdom. Deacons extend their hands through healing touch and practical help. The entire church tastes the goodness of God and releases a life-giving aroma to the surroundings.

Those who have glimpsed God's glory and become one with Christ, who are filled with his love and power through the Holy Spirit—these people become aware of the glaring abyss between God's will and the reality of evil in this world. These people struggle the most as they desire to see God's will on earth as it is in heaven, and they are willing to bear the cross and suffer without resorting to violence, as they are filled with the pleasure of God's glory. They are called saints, and by being saints, they unintentionally save the world, as Peter Kreeft put it:

> What can save our miserable world? What can save Western civilization? . . . Saints save civilization. It's not their fundamental purpose. But they do. How many saints? Well we don't know. There is a Jewish legend that says: At each time of human history god looks down and asks how many saints are there? And the answer is 12. And he says, okay, I won't destroy the world. But if the number goes to 11, he will destroy the world. Now the 12th saint has just died. Somebody must take his place. Is it going to be you? Maybe if it is not you, it is not going to be anybody. So maybe the survival of the world depends on you. And that's addressed to everybody. It's a universal call. There is no excuse.[12]

Those who encounter God become fools as they glimpse the nature of reality and are catapulted outside of this world while staying in it. They embody an alternative reality and are viewed as fools. Whether Isaiah, who walked naked and barefoot for three years, symbolizing the coming captivity of Israel (Isa 20:2); Ezekiel, who ate bread baked on cow's dung (Ezek 4:9–15); or Hosea, who married a prostitute to make visible God's relentless love (Hos 3)—these performative artists sought to embody a deeper reality. The apostle Paul referred to himself as a fool of Christ (1 Cor 4:10). Jesus also embodied these elements of turning reality on its heads and doing things that appeared to be out of touch with reality. Yet by hyperbolic actions the true nature of reality was breaking through the fog. Both Western and Eastern traditions are full of these holy fools, in art, literature, and philosophy. Perhaps Nietzsche's madman, as a modern embodiment of Isaiah, was a nod to Dostoevsky's Christ figure, Prince Myshkin.[13] The character of Prince Myshkin is an idiot in its proper sense as Webster's dictionary defines the word: "The Greek adjective *idios* means 'one's own' or 'private.' The derivative noun *idiōtēs* means 'private person.' A Greek *idiōtēs* was a person who was not

---

12. Kreeft, "Becoming a Saint," 51:52–52:37.
13. Dostoevsky, *Idiot*.

in the public eye, who held no public office. From this came the sense 'common man,' and later 'ignorant person'—a natural extension, for the common people of ancient Greece were not, in general, particularly learned. The English *idiot* originally meant 'ignorant person,' but the more usual reference now is to a person who lacks basic intelligence or common sense rather than education."[14]

A person who is gripped by God's glory and changed is set apart. Only a misplaced church is able to gift the world with a vision and actions in order to elevate this world toward the intended ideal. In German, the word for crazy is *verrückt*, which literally means "removed." Those who follow Christ are removed from their everyday perception; they are transported into a paradoxical state of being simultaneously in God's ideal and in the now. This tension will not always be resolved harmoniously. Most fools were ultimately torn by the extremes that they could not reconcile in the now. Yet the inner energy drove them to speak and act in a way that interrupted the grip of the immanent and opened a window into eternal play. Idiots embody the real and through their lives present a radical critique of the majority consensus.

The struggle of Christian leaders in the advancing idolatrous totalitarianism will be to abandon recognition in favor of becoming fools for Christ. If churches become truly fools for Christ, they will fight in an unconventional way. They will not fit a cultural, political, and social mold. They will be an odd association, who say no where the ordinary moral citizen says yes, and yes where the majority say no. The paradox will permeate these communities to such a degree that they will become the largest possible imaginary for our society without trying to be so. They will be fierce in their devotion to Jesus and, because of it, the most open to all. They will be hopelessly idealistic and brutally realistic at the same time. They will accidently create the largest space, not through intellectual coercion or some secret initiation but through an invitation to glimpse the true, the good, and the beautiful and experience the fullness of the divine through their worship and daily discipleship.

The struggle of the church lies in continuous worship and the enduring of tensions. Yet this struggle will be light, as it will usher in a culture of joy. By kneeling before God and surrendering everything to him, Christians experience inner serenity and lightness. People laugh because they are hit with the unexpected paradox. Judeo-Christian myth invites

---

14. See https://www.merriam-webster.com/dictionary/idiot.

us to laugh as we encounter the comical effects of the simultaneous presence of the divine in the typically human.[15] Christians laugh with Sara at the thought that an old woman can become pregnant (Gen 18:12–15), they laugh at the foolish idea that the king of the universe is born in a barn. Laughter is the involuntary reaction to the surprise of something revealed that we suspected all along, deep down in our hearts. Laughter is liberating and at the same time disarming. It is no coincidence that one of the first points of attack from totalitarians is comedians, then prophets, followed by philosophers. I grew up with many political jokes, as humor helped Russians to survive the nightmarish hell of Soviet totalitarianism. In the deepest layer of hell, there will be a frozen lake,[16] a totalitarian calm without laughter. Perhaps the first sign of true worship is the holy laughter of fools, at themselves and at evil. At the self, as the sudden realization that all of reality is a gift dislocates the inward gravity. And at evil, realizing that its posturing is comical in light of the inevitable victory of the advancing Christ. Deep joy radiating from within a worshipping community will permeate all of reality.

The main gift of the church to the world and society, which is not aware of its idols, is to uphold divine reality through worship. The worshipping church lays down the best possible core and foundation for the society around it. Despite the prevalent ignorance on the crucial civilizational task of Christian worship, the church will keep society alive, as its core motivation is not social in nature but mere captivation with God's glory. Salt keeps decay at bay even in small quantities. Similarly, a small church that struggles to worship God in spirit and in truth will have a disproportional impact, radiating life from its liturgical center. The key struggle, and the gift of the church to the world, is the realization of all reality being a gift. Without this embodiment of grace a society spirals down into a maddening self-creation.

The ultimate struggle of the Christian church today is to embody God's truth, goodness, and beauty on earth as it is in heaven and endure the fact that there will never be a complete overlap until God himself establishes his full authority at the end of time. The church must endure this tension, filled with hope, without succumbing to the gnostic temptation of control through knowledge. The battle of the church is guided

---

15. Helmut Thielicke views this paradox as the source of Christian humor (*Lachen der Heiligen*, 110).

16. This is a fitting metaphor for the deepest level of hell in Dante Alighieri's poem *The Divine Comedy*.

by much larger horizons than particular sociopolitical constellations. Yet through its spiritual warfare the church gently bends concrete sociopolitical powers to the will of God. Just like the worshipping tiny Christian communities resisted Roman subjugation in Central Asia two thousand years ago, many churches will resist the advancing soft totalitarianism and embody a flourishing alternative. Saint Augustine was right when he observed that earthly peace can be only temporal, as the earthly kingdom operates through coercion, which breeds new ground for violence. The church exemplifies a form of struggle that breaks this cycle. The church wages war peacefully. The church possesses the means to provide an alternative to the cycle of coercion and violence. From within Trinitarian worship, the church is formed as *ecclesia militans*. By waging war against evil peacefully, the church accidently provides a pattern for social struggle, which establishes the precondition of growing peace.

Critical Interlude

THE MOST EFFECTIVE ARGUMENT against my strong theological vision in part 4 is the one closest to my historic analysis while making the Christian story and worship obsolete. Those who agree with my interpretation of social decay as breakdown of myth and ritual, while simultaneously disagreeing with the assertion that creative power flows from the church's center of worship, are the ones who are most effective in undermining the reality of Christ and his body. The more sophisticated critics are not those who categorically disagree but those who mostly agree in theory and disagree in practice. Yet since practice is prior to theory, in this way they pull the carpet out from where Christians stand.

The best way to drain my theological assertion of its efficacy is to suggest that my analysis (chs. 1–9) stands on its own. Theological reality can be subsumed under psychological-symbolic, sociological, or any other disciplinary perspective. Theological perspective is useful in analyzing the human condition, but ultimately it is less effective when it comes to facing the world "as it is." This trick does the job of satisfying theologians hungry for recognition but leaves in starvation all other Christians who look to the Christian story and the church to grapple with their real, everyday-life challenges. Here I would like to reference the work of Hartmut Rosa, who offers not only a brilliant diagnosis of what went wrong in modernity but also a positive sketch of how the malaise can be cured.

As a theologian reading Rosa's sociology, I sensed underlying theological resonance that opened me up to the plot he offers. Rosa elevates the idea of resonance as the highest ideal, which promises to restore the broken relations of humans to nature, society, and self. Since sociologists are still deeply embedded within Judeo-Christian myth, their constructed deities resemble the biblical God. Thus Rosa's highest ideal is similar to Yahweh.

It is sovereign and unavailable (German: *unverfügbar*), yet it reveals itself at moments, thus satisfying the human longing for the harmonious state. Similar to the Christian story, paradise was lost when this resonance was broken. Rosa translates theological myth into sociological analysis. The theological plot is retained, while the dynamic and personal God disappears as the primary agent shaping history and society.

Rosa's admission of religion as one of the means to recover resonance paints a myth where Yahweh is degraded to one of the subservient spirits, underneath a vague deity of resonance. Rosa even makes the case that religion is useful for democracy, reassuring liberal Protestants of their cultural concerns.[1] A sociological apologia is welcomed by theologians, since sociology has surpassed theology in the academic hierarchy through its wider explanatory scope. Yet theologians who swallow the entire sociological cake too quickly are often not aware of the hidden ingredients. Within the relation between sociology and theology the age-old question reappears: Who is the highest God, who is the all-ordering ideal? Sociologists tend to elevate some social category to the status of the highest divinity and to lower religion to a mere function. Idolatry occurs when the good is made into the best.

True to the biblical story, Rosa cautions against the perversion of the highest ideal of resonance. Yet ironically, through all these qualifications of the highest good, resonance evaporates and turns into a whimsical deity. Rosa attempts to avoid all the modern pitfalls. Similar to his teacher, Charles Taylor, Rosa seeks to establish a normative category that somehow enables thought and analysis, thus avoiding a solipsistic dead end. At the same time this fundamental category must avoid an essentialist understanding of human nature. Thus resonance as a category vacillates between fleeting moments of concreteness and general vagueness. Contrary to the biblical narrative, this tension is not upheld through the narrative structure itself but must be maintained by the human dialectician. Resonance is the newest projected deity that must stand in the vacuum left by the "murdered" God.

Ultimately, Rosa's masterful secularization of the Judeo-Christian myth runs into brutal contradictions, which he glimpses and attempts to address. Contrary to Rosa, I trace the origins of the world going mute not merely to the acceleration of the industrial age but in the slow breakdown of the Judeo-Christian myth and rituals. Rosa advocates

---

1. Rosa, *Demokratie braucht Religion*.

for a fundamental break from the matrix of modernity, which destroys resonance. Yet within his outlined system there is no exit, and he offers no rituals beyond the fragmented attempts prevalent in our culture, thus reinforcing the same conditions he critiques. Lucidly, Rosa suggests that individual desires to break out from the logic of acceleration and exploitation of the world are futile due to systemic forces. He salutes small attempts of alternative communities. Yet ultimately resonance remains a human attempt to climb out from the mess moderns have created. Rosa's attempt is akin to Baron Munchausen, who lives in the illusion that he can pull himself and his horse from the swamp by his own hair. No larger myth or ritual is offered that could offer wider horizons beyond the force field Rosa bemoans. He appeals to Taylor for strong evaluative judgments. Yet ultimately the resonance project will become that which Rosa feared: another self-optimizing project of the privileged elites. Those who are able to afford it will create their enclaves of resonance through esoteric religion, nature rituals, and sealed-off communities through suburban houses and private schools. By projecting primary agency upon humans, to fix the mess they have created, Rosa attempts to extinguish the fire of modernity with gasoline. I do appreciate Rosa's translation of the larger myth into a specific German cultural-theoretical construct. However, contrary to the biblical story, this reduction can't speak to a diverse socioeconomic and culturally heterogeneous society.

Moreover, even those who are able to decipher sociological theory and gather crumbs for the reconstruction of resonance are left in desperation: while their desire is awakened, resonance remains unavailable. Rosa hints at this frustration on the last page, quoting Antoine de Saint-Exupéry, confirming that this has been his main intention: to awaken a longing for the endless sea in order to spur humans to construct a ship and gather a team.[2] Herein lies his fundamental error. Resonance as immanent category makes sense only in relation to a higher ideal, which all myths project outside the empirical, without which we would be overwhelmed by the brute material world. Since resonance is a relational category, its perception and negotiation are achievable only from a hierarchical, mythological point. Rosa does exactly that, employing a Judeo-Christian myth while pretending to do so on a purely immanent sociological level. Yet his entire construct makes sense only as long as his thick theological background remains unarticulated. At least his teacher

2. Rosa, *Resonanz*, 737.

Charles Taylor was more transparent about his Catholic background, from which he reasoned. And the Persian and Babylonian kings were at least openly praising Yahweh when witnessing his miracles.

Rosa's narrative certainly made me hungrier to imagine the sea, but the construction he offered was a leaky boat. Sociology as a discipline fails at sketching a good life, because the idea of a flourishing life is the result of a mythological ideal, which transcends the sociological grasp. As Taylor lucidly puts it:

> The paradox of Christianity, in relation to early religion, is that on one hand, it seems to assert the unconditional benevolence of God towards humans; there is none of the ambivalence of early Divinity in this respect; and yet it redefines our ends so as to take us beyond flourishing.[3]

This paradox marks a fundamental difference between theological and sociological conceptions of a flourishing life. As I have shown in this last part, human flourishing is a by-product of God's glory. Contrary to resonance, the triune God does not leave us in despair. His glory disrupts the immanent system from beyond and lets us despair in our human ability to construct a relation of resonance. Yet this complete annihilation of human hubris is the true beginning toward a reconciled relation to nature, others, and self, which begins from the primary restoration with God as the highest ideal. Following Taylor's intuition my story reveals a paradoxical relation between church and society.

Secularity emerged as a by-product of the all-powerful God. Secular society is able to remain secular to the degree its religious core remains alive. Thus the optionality of religion in liberalism is an illusion. Here I depart from Taylor's narrative. From a historical distance, religion can't remain optional. Taylor's turn away from the publicly accessible cosmic order to the exploration of individual resonance is a self-limiting pair of glasses, cutting out the wider horizons of meaning.[4] The fragmentation of wider horizons only awakens the desire for a new collective solidarity. We have seen through political religions of the twentieth century that entire civilizations can suddenly fall into a collectivist frenzy. And I believe

---

3. Taylor, *Secular Age*, 151.

4. "We are now in an age in which a publicly accessible cosmic order of meaning is an impossibility. The only way we can explore the order in which we are set with an aim to defining moral sources is through this part of personal resonance" (Taylor, *Sources of the Self*, 512).

that the further erosion of the Judeo-Christian core will enable an even grander re-enchantment on a collective level.

Some practical theologians might object that my account is not concrete enough to solve any real social problems. This has been my point exactly. Theologians and Christian leaders must focus first on the primary task, which is worship. Worship constitutes the mode that brings us closer to the ultimate reality of God and through which we perceive the world in its core structure. Only from within worship do we learn to struggle against evil without succumbing to its lure. By glimpsing ultimate reality and becoming aware of the power of evil, Christians are humbled. By being filled with divine love, Christians struggle in the everyday, with a messy and ad hoc strategy, which can't be "solved" by a theologian a priori. I sought to show how the church is manifested from and toward God's glory, which the gathering community embodies in the Eucharist. From this eucharistic table, some crumbs will fall off and feed the starving world. As Bonhoeffer recognized, the direction must be from God to the world:

> It is necessary to free oneself from the way of thinking which sets out from human problems and which asks for solutions on this basis. Such thinking is unbiblical. The way of Jesus Christ, and therefore the way of all Christian thinking, leads not from the world to God, but from God to the world. This means that the essence of the gospel does not lie in the solution of human problems, and that the solution of human problems cannot be the essential task of the Church.[5]

Siedentop's caution to Americans to not succumb to a dangerously simplistic version of their faith, I believe, must first apply to all the intellectuals who view themselves as sophisticated enough to solve real problems at their desks. In reverse, those ordinary Christian fools who simply worship Jesus on Sunday morning and struggle to live out the divine reality in their everyday lives will very likely in retrospect be viewed by historians as agents of change for the better. The first shall be last, and the last shall be first (Matt 20:16).

From a global perspective one might wonder whether the relation between Christianity and secular liberalism is sufficient. In other words, will the worldwide explosion of Pentecostal-charismatic Christianity in the twentieth century unintentionally provide fertile ground for the

---

5. Bonhoeffer, *Ethics*, 351.

growth of secular liberalism via religious tilling? I believe that the Western story is unique and depends on many specific variables. For example, Western Christianity developed in the Augustinian tradition, which emphasized a stronger separation between the earthly and heavenly realms, leading toward a continuing fruitful tension. Eastern Orthodoxy lacked this tension and produced a different social order. Christianity does not entail a particular immanent ideal but is able to generate different social imaginaries due to its polyphonic and paradoxical mode. The majority of Christianity in the South must learn from European church history in order to avoid their hubris and downfall. The rapid growth of Pentecostalism could result in seduction toward triumphalism and sociopolitical power. It may well be that secularization as immanent cage does not remain an exception to Europe but could reoccur in any region of the world where the church provides a negative foil through its abuse of power.

However, I do believe that as Christians struggle to worship the triune God, they will unintentionally produce the best society possible in the long run. While the church as an empiric, social entity does give birth to a social order, it can't draw its raison d'être from any immanent reference point. This is the ultimate paradox between church and society: the church is both inside and outside the immanent sphere. It must be fully present in the socio-material world and yet always drawing its reason for being from beyond. The church is fully in the world and yet fully outside it. My sketch of paradoxical worship borrows from various Christian traditions. In order to move forward and embody the living center for the decaying world, we must drink from the ecumenical well. Moreover, my sketch suggests Trinitarian contours of worship: we are enraptured by the glory of the Father, which becomes real in the incarnation of his Son and experienced in the Eucharist. As the church, we struggle to embody this reality in our everyday actions through the empowerment of the Holy Spirit. An ecumenical theology of Trinitarian worship is the trajectory forward, an adventurous path to travel.

Conclusion: Paradoxical Worship and a Flourishing Life

> *There is no such thing as not worshipping. Everybody worships. The only choice we get is what to worship.*
>
> —David Foster Wallace, "This Is Water"

THE CONCLUSION CAN BE summed up in one sentence: a flourishing society exemplifies paradoxical roots, which thrive in the soil of worship of the triune God. Conversely, the destruction of the soil leads to the roots dying and the tree withering. I sought to demonstrate this thesis through a particular Western civilization. The plot of the story I told in this book is paradoxical: The idea of secular individual dignity emerged from collective religious myth and ritual (part 1). The decay of secular liberalism is already present in its success (part 2). The secular realm, both as imagination and sociopolitical construct, is contingent on the Judeo-Christian religious background. Thus permanent dis-enchantment is an illusion. At the height of this illusion an entire civilization is gripped by false gods. At the moment of rejection of the Judeo-Christian spirit, a gnostic spirit returns with full force and establishes soft totalitarianism (part 3). The conclusion for the church from these lessons of history is also paradoxical: the church is at its strongest when it is weak, and most impactful when it is simple in its focus upon the triune God, and most socially effective when it forgets to care about being useful (part 4). However, when the church ceases to worship rightly, the church commits an extended suicide. The church kills itself first and then pushes the rest of society into a long agony of decay by removing its centering core.

A paradox arises from the complexity of reality and the limits of the human mind to grasp it. By presenting human cognition with seeming contradictions, the paradox points beyond the human grasp and thus entails liberating potentiality. Cyril Orji, in his brilliant description of paradox both in everyday life and in various academic disciplines, demonstrates the life-giving function of the paradox. Quoting Henri de Lubac, he describes the function of a paradox as helping "our grasp . . . of 'the provisional expression of a view which remains incomplete, but whose orientation is ever toward fullness.'"[1] In this way, a paradox safeguards the human intellect from sliding into hubris and a self-referential prison. To bring to light seeming contradictions is both to acknowledge a greater reality and to awake wonder, which is a precondition for faith and cognition. The Judeo-Christian myth is permeated with paradoxical elements that are not reconciled on the systemic level but are left in order to awaken hunger and thirst, which can be quenched only through communal worship.

This paradoxical feature marks Western civilization, which is shaped by the Judeo-Christian myth. The collective is centered around sacred individual dignity, just like the God-man Jesus Christ becomes the sole center around which all of history orbits. While dignity is presupposed as something self-evident, its normativity emerges through a particular myth and the ritual of the Eucharist. Unresolved paradox creates fruitful tension, which must constantly be lived out. Thus plurality, cooperation, and constant movement are required. A society that is marked by these dynamics is not in danger of becoming a frozen lake in a totalitarian hell. Yet it also must be permeated by humility, rest, and hope, as people without rest lack an Archimedean point from which to evaluate and exercise their freedoms. Humility acknowledges that paradox requires cooperation of differences. Hope allows for this eternal pursuit to continue without the prospect of ever resolving the inherent tensions and sliding into gnosis. The tension can be endured through the continuous hope for harmonious resolution in the final manifestation of God's glory.

All life-enhancing institutions, be they political, economic, or scientific, exemplify this paradox and are permeated by this tension. Political institutions are able to breathe as long as a pluralistic, peaceful discourse continues. Economics that benefit all of society also require the paradoxical notion of individual freedom and collective bond of solidarity, which

---

1. Orji, *Exploring Theological Paradoxes*, 3.

is rooted in the idea of covenant. Scientific discourse requires a paradoxical notion of complete assurance of objective reality and yet constant subjective doubt. The thick fruitful soil for these social institutions is tilled through the Judeo-Christian myth and ritual performance.

While a flourishing society is marked by paradoxical dynamics, paradox itself thrives primarily in deeper ritual soil. Ritual is the training ground for people to experience tension before enduring it in their everyday lives as they form institutions. Paradox can't be embodied in individual academic cognition, which reasons in a linear fashion and is at home within the left hemisphere of the brain. It is more at home within the right hemisphere, which captures the holistic imagination and is not driven to resolve the perceived tensions. Paradox points beyond the discursive mode toward a larger reality of embodied experience. The whole is more than its parts. I could write that an individual becomes aware of their true nature at the moment of receiving the blood and body of Jesus in union with others. Yet words always fall short to convey this thick, fully embodied experience. All I can do through this medium of encoding a living experience into a reduced form of writing is to point to the significance of the ritual. In worship of God the individual approaches reality. She ascends toward God as she participates in the sacramental reality that God himself brought down to humanity. The communal act hints at the loving dynamic relation within the Trinity.

Consequently, those who embody this reality, even if they lack the ability to articulate its significance, are the true heroes who shape the heart of Western civilization. The illiterate refugee who worships and sacrifices his life daily for the good of his neighbors in Berlin is more virtuous than the German intellectual who is able to speak eloquently but lives a self-absorbed life. Countless Christians all over the world and unknown pastors leading local churches to gather in the name of the Father, the Son, and the Holy Spirit are the true pillars of society, without knowing it. They embody divine reality through true sacrifice, instead of virtue signaling from comfortable professorial chairs. Herein lies the irony of it all. It took an illiterate Syrian construction worker to make me reconsider my simplistic view.[2]

Since worship is the primary response to God as the highest ideal and ultimate reality, the church is formed through worship. As the church struggles to worship God fully, giving all of life, crossing all modern

2. See ch. 1.

segmentations, it will unintentionally hold together a paradoxical tension, which will radiate into all other social segments. Thus the worshipful dynamics will permeate the wider society like an aroma, counteracting the decay that sets in where hubris seeks to solve the reality of paradox. The seduction of hubris has been a danger to the church from its inception. Both Gnosticism and the temptation to create a Christian dominion through coercion and force have perverted Christian worship by splitting myth from ritual and reducing its paradoxical tension toward one side or the other—leading toward schisms, agony, and ultimately a secular illusion and a desire to imagine a society without the church at its symbolic center. While the notion of a secular person and space is born from within the ecclesial womb, secularity can't exist without her mother, the church. The paradoxical tension can't thrive without the ritual soil. Destruction of the Judeo-Christian myth and ritual creates social monsters. The subsequent exhaustion invites ancient gods into a ritual vacuum. Thus re-enchantment is inevitable. The emerging gods resemble ancient Gnosticism, around which a totalitarian society assembles.

The question could be posed as to what significance my thesis might have for today. I have contended that religion is inescapable and forms the core of every society. This insight will humble believers and many agnostics as well. The believer becomes aware of the gravity of his task to worship God truthfully due to the consequences for both the church and society. In light of the repetitive idolatry of the church, the believer must sink to his knees, tremble, and confess. The agnostic's smirk about religion will hopefully vanish as the realization sinks in that the society they enjoy so much, which grants freedoms and well-being unknown in history, is the product of a specific religion. Hopefully, the result will be gratitude toward others, who uphold this social order through their worship. The divisive blame game for social decay must stop. The believer must stop blaming secularism for all the social evils and embrace the estranged child. The unbeliever must stop looking down on believers as backward and stuck in the past. Hopefully my story has demonstrated that religion and secularity are intrinsically intertwined and can't be cut asunder. We must appreciate the other and build this society together. Secular critics were often the prophets to expose the idolatry of the church. Without the church, secular liberal democracies will collapse, emptied of their core and penetrated by bloodthirsty deities.

My plot does not allow for exclusion through othering. It stops the blame game between religious and secular citizens. We are at a point in history where the myth of the Enlightenment as a miraculous break from its religious past can't be maintained in intellectual honesty. Even honest former despisers of religion can't overlook the parasitical nature of their secular convictions. Interesting alliances between thoughtful monotheists and humble agnostics emerge.

I also believe that this new situation will drive thoughtful and humble Christians toward a pragmatic grassroots alliance. There is a Soviet anecdote that the Soviet ecumenical movement began when Orthodox, Roman Catholic priests, and Baptist preachers met for the first time in the Soviet gulags. I believe that my explicitly theological part can be viewed as "mere Christianity."[3] The themes of glory, the Eucharist, and *ecclesia militans* are central to Orthodox, Roman Catholic, Protestant, and Pentecostal-charismatic theology, despite differences in nuance. In times like these, we must harness the best of every confessional, historic theology in order to recover a robust, holistic worship, resisting global, totalizing forces, and embody God's kingdom in light of the decay of the current secular liberal order, which is both tragic and fortuitous. Yet the decay of the old presents challenges to rediscover the sources of life and renewal, which have been taken for granted and forgotten.

It is tragic to observe secular intellectuals mourning the draining of life from the current social order while unable to locate the source of its flourishing in the Judeo-Christian tradition. Instead, they keep repeating ad nauseam the illusory return to "Enlightenment values," lacking a deeper story of how these values came into existence in the first place. Moreover, their insistence on the will to return to this golden age begins to sound like nostalgia, which is ultimately the fate of all revolutionaries who are not rooted in tradition. Those who once rallied masses by painting the past in dark colors and promising a bright future are caught in the trap they set up for themselves. People get exhausted by the utopian promise that never materializes, and once their narrative becomes the status quo, they automatically become conservatives, attempting to preserve the revolt. The once-blazing life cools. Hippies transition into retirement communities. Tattoos on sexy bodies shrivel. Ferocious tigers turn sad on wrinkly skin. When secular utopias fail to materialize, their worshippers become unfaithful. We live now through

---

3. C. S. Lewis's book *Mere Christianity* was an attempt to address core beliefs shared by all Christians.

this unrest, which is an opportunity for the church to reassert itself not in gleeful triumph[4] but in humility and courage.

The hope that secular elites will somehow provide a path beyond the decay of the current order will be disappointed. This is not due to their bad intentions or insufficient intellect. In fact, many begin to perceive the contours of the coming age, and there is no lack of imperatives as to what we ought to do. However, if my plot in this book sounds plausible, a mere ethical imperative will not suffice. Advice to a person who is starved and dehydrated to get up and party would sound cruel. Help must come from the outside. Secular inward exhaustion can be overcome only by revelatory light and energy from the outside.

The renewal of the social order can happen only paradoxically: by turning away from the periphery and by focusing on the center, the peripheral will be renewed as well. The primary agency and privilege to form the social core lie with the church. However, the church can achieve it only paradoxically, by abandoning its desire to be relevant and instead being completely raptured by the glory of God. The church must respond to God through full-bodied worship. This worship is constantly threatened of being shred to pieces. However, the church does not stand alone in its struggle to worship God rightly. The Holy Spirit as the counselor and comforter is actively renewing the body of Christ. Even if the church errs and falls into idolatry, the invitation stands as a hopeful promise to the one who returns and chooses life: "See, I set before you today life and prosperity, death and destruction" (Deut 30:15). This book has been my attempt to reiterate this divine invitation. At the core of history, despite the changes and ups and downs, the same pattern remains. Let our worship flow from thanksgiving, as the author of the Epistle to the Hebrews states: "Therefore, since we are receiving a kingdom that cannot be shaken, let us be thankful, and so worship God acceptably with reverence and awe, for our God is a consuming fire" (Heb 12:28–29). Every false idol will burn when in proximity to the true God. Evil will melt when the church worships God truthfully. As humans we do not have the choice to worship or not; the only choice we have is whom to worship. The choice is to either worship the triune God, flourish, and let life radiate beyond our gathering or be ripped apart by idols. Suicide retreats in light of true worship. Worship is alignment with God, who is the ultimate reality and the source of all life. Let us worship and flourish.

---

4. Germans granted to English a special word for this, which carries a unique meaning: Schadenfreude.

Acknowledgments

THE DILEMMA OF ACKNOWLEDGING one person lies in excluding another. Well, this is life, one might say. Although I agree, the question remains as to what criteria determine the elevation of one person over another. It seems obvious that those who directly influenced my work would be acknowledged as the most important and thus must be mentioned. Another criterion, which is usually not acknowledged openly due to embarrassment of one's own insecurity, is the preference for whose praise one seeks to maintain and whose connection is considered to be more valuable. Academic culture thrives upon acts of reciprocal recognition. The thought is—if I mention you today, you will mention me tomorrow. And if you mention me and you happen to be higher up in the academic hierarchy, your praise might pull me up one rung higher.

There is nothing wrong with this convention. To a certain degree all cultures function in this way, as Marcel Mauss rightly discerned. My problem with it is a simple one: those who influenced my work directly are already acknowledged in the footnotes. Yet there are others who influenced my work indirectly, by cultivating the questions I asked, which led me to write this book. So let me try to be fair and acknowledge some of those who are not mentioned in my footnotes and bibliography.

I will begin by mentioning academic colleagues whose charitable gestures helped me at the inception stage of the project and later as I was reaching the finish line. I happened to teach a course at Humboldt University with a Canadian professor, Christopher Brittain, who was on his sabbatical leave in Germany. A few times we hung out at a coffee shop near the university, and he generously read through my introduction and gave very constructive remarks on how to improve my line of argument, which led me to rewrite my introduction. He helped me avoid derailing the train at the very beginning. I also enjoyed talking with Michael McClymond, whose interdisciplinary horizons energized my research. William T. Cavanaugh gave me very needed encouragement to persevere toward the end of my project. Henning Wrogemann kindly accepted my work as *Habilitationsschrift* at the Kirchliche Hochschule Wuppertal. Finally, I am grateful that Rebecca Abbott improved the manuscript greatly due to her expertise in both German and English.

I thank my grandparents. I spent my childhood summers in their Siberian village. Their earthbound life taught me that if you don't prepare food and supplies for yourself and the cattle during the summer, you will starve and freeze to death during the brutal winter months. This sobering realism seeped into my way of thinking. My thoughts must be tested against the chilling cold.

I thank Ivan, my father. Although himself a high-ranking bureaucrat within the Communist Party, he dared to interpret Marxism/Leninism differently from the majority and refused to be bent and therefore had to pay the price of leaving everything behind and immigrating to a foreign country. His example encouraged me to pursue a story that does not easily fit into the current academic discourse and be willing to stand alone if need be. I thank Olga, my mother. She possesses the rare chutzpa to say things as clearly and briefly as possible, straight to your face. With her, you don't need to play a guessing game, and the conversation flows like a clear mountain spring.

I thank my parents for exposing me early on to volumes of fairy tales from around the world. This shaped my curiosity of and appreciation of myths. Perhaps reading fairy tales from around the world awakened a desire to envision larger narrative plots. I also thank them for exposing me to great Russian literature. I thank my father for exposing me to Vladimir Vysotsky, the Soviet singer-songwriter rebel whose creativity subverted the totalitarian monster.

I thank Lisa, my wife, who over the last twenty years helped to form me into the man I am today. She is a living paradox. Her sharp mind makes her a rare combination of grace and truth, which was powerful motivation for me to pursue truth as I felt held. Lisa helped me to think through nuance. By offering her constructive critique, Lisa served as dialogical partner and assisted me in chiseling my thoughts. She challenged me to think more deeply and to wrestle for words.

I am grateful to my four children for continuously reminding me of what really matters. They ground me in the everyday, pushing my prose to touch the ground and abstain from words that sound grandiose but hide more than they reveal. Children expose pretense quickly and, in this way, contributed to me hopefully writing with greater clarity.

Last, I thank my spiritual father Josef, with whom I spent days riding motorcycles through Pennsylvania hills and letting my thoughts dangle around the campfire. Josef once told me that he does not write books but lets others write books about him after his death. This sentence made me laugh. Jesus and Socrates also did not write books. They spoke more powerfully through their lives. They are my inspiration to lay down my pen and live what I have attempted to put into words.

Bibliography

Adorno, Theodor W., and Max Horkheimer. *Dialektik der Aufklärung: Philosophische Fragmente*. Frankfurt am Main: Fischer, 1969.

Agamben, Giorgio. *Homo Sacer: Sovereign Power and Bare Life*. Stanford, CA: Stanford University Press, 1995.

———. *State of Exception*. Translated by Kevin Attell. Chicago: University of Chicago Press, 2005.

Alesina, Alberto, et al. "Why Doesn't the United States Have a European-Style Welfare State?" *Brookings Papers on Economic Activity* 2 (2001) 187–278.

Ali, Ayaan Hirsi. *Prey: Immigration, Islam, and the Erosion of Women's Rights*. New York: Harper Collins, 2021.

Anthony, Oliver. "Rich Men North of Richmond." YouTube, Aug. 8, 2023. http://www.youtube.com/watch?v=sqSA-SY5Hro.

Archer, Margaret S. "On Understanding Religious Experience: St. Theresa as a Challenge to Social Theory." In *Transcendence: Critical Realism and God*, edited by Margaret S. Archer et al., 138–54. Critical Realism: Interventions. London: Routledge, 2004.

Arendt, Hannah. *Elemente und Ursprünge totaler Herrschaft*. Frankfurt am Main: Europäisch, 1955.

Arendt, Hannah, and Eric Voegelin. *Disput über den Totalitarismus: Texte und Briefe*. Göttingen: Vandenhoeck & Ruprecht, 2015.

Asad, Talal. *Formations of the Secular: Christianity, Islam, Modernity*. Stanford, CA: Stanford University Press, 2003.

———. *Genealogies of Religion: Discipline and Reasons of Power in Christianity and Islam*. Baltimore: Johns Hopkins University Press, 1993.

Atwood, Margaret. *The Handmaid's Tale*. Philadelphia: Chelsea, 2001.

Augustine, Saint. *The City of God*. Gutenberg, 2024. From *The City of God*, edited by Marcus Dodds, vol. 1 of *The Works of Aurelius Augustine, Bishop of Hippo: A New Translation* (Edinburgh: T&T Clark, 1971). https://www.gutenberg.org/ebooks/45304.

———. *Confessions*. Translated by R. S. Pine-Coffin. Penguin Classics. London: Penguin, 1961.

Balthasar, Hans Urs von. *Love Alone*. New York: Herder and Herder, 1969.

———. *Schau der Gestalt*. Vol. 1 of *Herrlichkeit: Eine theologische Ästhetik*. Einsiedeln, Switz.: Johannes, 1961.

Barth, Karl. *Kirchliche Dogmatik*. Vols. 1.1, 1.2. Zurich: Theologisch, 1932, 1938.
———. *Die Theologie Schleiermachers 1923/1924*. Zurich: Theologisch, 1978.
Bauckham, Richard. *Gospel of Glory: Major Themes in the Johannine Theology*. Grand Rapids: Baker Academics, 2015.
Baudrillard, Jean. *Simulacra and Simulation*. Translated by Sheila Faria Glaser. The Body, in Theory: Histories of Cultural Materialism. Ann Arbor: University of Michigan Press, 1995.
Baudy, Dorothea. "Ethology." In *Issues, Topics, Approaches, Concepts*, edited by Jens Kreinath et al., 345–61. Vol. 1 of *Theorizing Rituals*. Numen 114.1. Boston: Brill, 2006.
Bauman, Zygmunt. *Liquid Times: Living in an Age of Uncertainty*. Cambridge: Polity, 2007.
Baumann, Gerlinde. "Das Opfer nach der Sintflut für die Gotheit(en) des Alten Testaments und des Alten Orients: Eine neue Deutung." *Verbum et Ecclesia* 34 (2013) art. 888. http://dx.doi.org/10.4102/ve.v34i2.888.
Baur, Ferdinand Christian. *Die christliche Gnosis oder die christliche Religionsphilosophie in ihrer geschichtlichen Entwicklung*. Tübingen: Osiander, 1835.
Bell, Catherine. "Embodiment." In *Issues, Topics, Approaches, Concepts*, edited by Jens Kreinath et al., 533–45. Vol. 1 of *Theorizing Rituals*. Numen 114.1. Boston: Brill, 2006.
Bell, Daniel M., Jr. *Divinations: Theopolitics in an Age of Terror*. Theopolitical Visions 22. Eugene, OR: Cascade, 2017.
Berger, Peter L., and Thomas Luckmann. *The Social Construction of Reality: A Treatise in the Sociology of Knowledge*. New York: Doubleday, 1966.
Biggar, Nigel. *Colonialism: A Moral Reckoning*. [Glasgow]: Williams Collins, 2023.
Bloch, Maurice. "Deference." In *Issues, Topics, Approaches, Concepts*, edited by Jens Kreinath et al., 495–507. Vol. 1 of *Theorizing Rituals*. Numen 114.1. Boston: Brill, 2006.
Block, Daniel I. *For the Glory of God: Recovering a Biblical Theology of Worship*. Grand Rapids: Baker, 2014.
Blumenberg, Hans. *Arbeit am Mythos*. Frankfurt am Main: Suhrkamp, 1979.
Böckenförde, Ernst-Wolfgang. *Staat, Gesellschaft, Freiheit: Studien zur Staatstheorie und zum Verfassungsrecht*. Frankfurt am Main: Suhrkamp, 1976.
Bonhoeffer, Dietrich. *Ethics*. Translated by Neville Horton Smith. New York: Simon & Schuster, 1970.
———. *Gemeinsames Leben*. Gütersloh: Kaiser, 1993.
———. *Nachfolge*. 9th ed. Munich: Kaiser, 1967.
———. *Widerstand und Ergebung: Briefe und Aufzeichnungen aus der Haft*. Edited by Eberhard Bethge. Gütersloh: Mohn, 1983.
Borges, Jorge Luis. "On Exactitude in Science." *Genius*, Mar. 1946. Translated by Andrew Hurley. https://genius.com/Jorge-luis-borges-on-exactitude-in-science-annotated.
Brague, Rémi. "Are Non-Theocratic Regimes Possible?" *Intercollegiate Review* 41 (2006) 3–12.
———. *La voie romaine*. Paris: Gallimard, 1992.
———. "Was hat Europa mit dem Christentum zu tun?" In *Europa: Ein christliches Projekt? Beiträge zum Verhaeltnis von Religion und europäischer Identität*, edited by Urs Altermatt et al., 25–35. Religionsforum 2. Stuttgart: Kohlhammer, 2007.

Bruckner, Pascal. *The Tyranny of Guilt: An Essay on Western Masochism.* Translated by Steven Rendall. Princeton, NJ: Princeton University Press, 2010.

Camus, Albert. *The Myth of Sisyphus.* Translated by Justin O'Brien. Penguin Modern Classics. UK: Penguin, 2000.

Carr, David. *Time, Narrative, and History.* Bloomington: Indiana University Press, 1986.

Casanova, José. *Public Religions in the Modern World.* Chicago: University of Chicago Press, 1994.

Cavanaugh, William T. *Migrations of the Holy: God, State, and the Political Meaning of the Church.* Grand Rapids: Eerdmans, 2011.

———. *The Uses of Idolatry.* New York: Oxford University Press, 2024.

Cayley, David. *The Rivers North of the Future: The Testament of Ivan Illich.* Toronto: Anansi, 2005.

Chesterton, Gilbert K. *Orthodoxy.* UK: SnowBall Classics, 2015.

Cohn, Norman. *The Pursuit of the Millennium: Revolutionary Millenarians and Mystical Anarchists of the Middle Ages.* London: Pimlico, 2004.

Colino, Stacey, and Shanna H. Swan. *Count Down: How Our Modern World Is Threatening Sperm Counts, Altering Male and Female Reproductive Development, and Imperiling the Future of the Human Race.* New York: Simon & Schuster, 2020.

Croasmun, Matthew. *The Emergence of Sin: The Cosmic Tyrant in Romans.* New York: Oxford University Press, 2017.

Cunningham, Conor. *Darwin's Pious Idea: Why the Ultra-Darwinists and Creationists Both Get It Wrong.* Grand Rapids: Eerdmans, 2010.

D'Angour, Armand. *The Greeks and the New: Novelty in Ancient Greek Imagination and Experience.* New York: Cambridge University Press, 2011.

Dante Alighieri. *The Divine Comedy.* Translated by John Ciardi. New York: Norton, 1977.

Demandt, Alexander. *Der Fall Roms: Die Auflösung des römischen Reiches im Urteil der Nachwelt.* Munich: Beck, 1984.

Desmet, Mattias. *The Psychology of Totalitarianism.* Translated by Els Vanbrabant. White River Junction, VT: Chelsea Green, 2022.

Dik, Oleg. *Church, Immigration & Pluralism: Paradoxical Reformation After German Christendom.* Münster: LIT, 2022.

———. "Conversion Dialogue and Resilient Pluralism." In *Interreligious Dialogue: From Religion to Geopolitics,* edited by Giuseppe Giordan and Andrew P. Lynch, 219–35. Annual Review of the Sociology of Religion 10. Leiden: Brill, 2019.

———. "Die Dilemmata und die Zukunftsfähigkeit des Liberalismus." In *Die Wir-gegen-die-Gesellschaft: Warum der von Arthur M. Schlesinger vor 30 Jahren diagnostizierte Samen der identitätspolitischen Spaltung aufgegangen ist,* edited by Sandra Kostner, 159–79. Stuttgart: Ibidem, 2024.

———. "Discovering Entanglements Between Apocalypse & Totalitarianism." In *Apocalypse & Totalitarianism: Entanglements Between Religious & Secular Patterns,* edited by John Dik and Oleg Dik, 19–31. Theologische Anstöße 14. Göttingen: Vandenhoeck & Ruprecht, 2025.

———. "Freiheit durch Kreuzigung." *Novo Argumente für den Fortschritt,* Dec. 21, 2022. https://www.novo-argumente.com/artikel/freiheit_durch_kreuzigung.

———. *Realness Through Mediating Body: The Emergence of Charismatic/Pentecostal Communities in Beirut*. Kirche-Konfession-Religion 71. Göttingen: Vandenhoeck und Ruprecht, 2017.
Dörnyei, Zoltán. *Vision, Mental Imagery and the Christian Life: Insights from Science and Scripture*. London: Routledge, 2020.
Dostoevsky, Fyodor. *Besi*. Moscow: Act, 2001.
———. *Bratja Karamosowj*. Moscow: Eksmo, 2005.
———. *The Idiot*. London: Dent & Sons, 1934.
Douglas, Mary. "Foreword: No Free Gifts." In *The Gift: The Form and Reason for Exchange in Archaic Societies*, by Marcel Mauss, translated by W. D. Halls, ix–xxiii. London: Routledge, 2005.
Durkheim, Emile. *The Elementary Forms of Religious Life*. Translated by Karen E. Fields. New York: Free Press, 1995.
Edwards, Jonathan. "The End for Which God Created the World." In *God's Passion for His Glory: Living the Vision of Jonathan Edwards*, by John Piper, 117–253. Wheaton, IL: Crossway, 1998.
Ehrenberg, Alain. *Weariness of the Self: Diagnosing the History of Depression in the Contemporary Age*. Montreal: McGill-Queen's University Press, 2010.
Ellison, Harlan. *I Have No Mouth, and I Must Scream*. USA: Worlds of Science Fiction, 1967.
Fichte, Johann Gottlieb. *Grundlage der gesamten Wissenschaftslehre als Handschrift für seine Zuhörer*. Hamburg: Mein, 1997.
Fiedrowicz, Michael. *Ecclesia Militans: Die streitende Kirche-Zeugnisse aus der Frühzeit des Christentums*. Fohren-Linden, Germ.: Carthusianus, 2017.
Foroutan, Naika. *Die postmigrantische Gesellschaft*. Bielefeld: Transcript, 2019.
Foucault, Michel. "The Subject and Power." *Critical Inquiry* 8 (1982) 777–95.
Frankl, Viktor E. *Man's Search for Meaning*. London: Penguin Random House, 2004.
Frenkel, Edward. "Reality Is a Paradox—Mathematics, Physics, Truth & Love." YouTube, Apr. 10, 2023. From *Lex Fridman Podcast* 370. http://www.youtube.com/watch?v=Osho-J3T2nY.
Fridrich, Michaela. "Richard Wagners Götterdämmerung als Untergangsvision." Deutschlandfunk, May 6, 2012. https://www.deutschlandfunk.de/richard-wagners-goetterdaemmerung-als-untergangsvision-100.html.
Fukuyama, Francis. *The End of History and the Last Man*. New York: Free Press, 1992.
Furedi, Frank. *Culture of Fear: Risk-Taking and the Morality of Low Expectation*. London: Continuum, 2002.
Gadamer, Hans-Georg. *Hermeneutik im Rückblick*. Gesammelte Werke 10. Tübingen: Mohr, 1995.
Gauchet, Marcel. *Le désenchantement du monde: Une histoire politique de la religion*. Paris: Gallimard, 1985.
Gehlen, Arnold. *Der Mensch, seine Natur und seine Stellung in der Welt*. Berlin: Junker und Dünnhaupt, 1940.
Giddens, Anthony. *The Consequences of Modernity*. Cambridge: Polity, 1991.
Gillespie, Michael Allen. *The Theological Origins of Modernity*. Chicago: University of Chicago Press, 2008.
Girard, René. *Das Ende der Gewalt: Analyse des Menschheitsverhängnisses*. Translated by August Berz. Freiburg: Herder, 1978.

Godin, Benoît. *Innovation Contested: The Idea of Innovation over the Centuries.* London: Routledge, 2015.
Graeber, David, and David Wengrow. *The Dawn of Everything: A New History of Humanity.* London: Penguin, 2021.
Gray, John. *Black Mass: Apocalyptic Religion and the Death of Utopia.* [London]: Penguin, 2007.
———. *Heresies: Against Progress and Other Illusions.* London: Granta, 2005.
Grimes, Ronald L. "Performance." In *Issues, Topics, Approaches, Concepts,* edited by Jens Kreinath et al., 379–94. Vol. 1 of *Theorizing Rituals.* Numen 114.1. Boston: Brill, 2006.
Grossbölting, Thomas. *Der verlorene Himmel: Glaube in Deutschland seit 1945.* Göttingen: Vandenhoeck & Ruprecht, 2013.
Habermas, Jürgen. *Zeit der Übergänge.* Kleine Politische Schriften 9. Frankfurt am Main: Suhrkamp, 2001.
Han, Byung-Chul. *Müdigkeitsgesellschaft.* Berlin: Matthes & Seitz, 2015.
Harari, Yuval. *Homo Deus: A Brief History of Tomorrow.* London: Vintage, 2017.
Harnack, Adolf von. "Die Versuche der Gnostiker, eine apostolische Glaubenslehre und eine christliche Theologie zu schaffen, oder: Die akute Verweltlichung des Christentums." In *Gnosis und Gnostizismus,* edited by Kurt Rudolph, 142–74. Darmstadt: Wissenschaftlich, 1975.
Harth, Dietrich. "Rituals and Other Forms of Social Action." In *Issues, Topics, Approaches, Concepts,* edited by Jens Kreinath et al., 15–36. Vol. 1 of *Theorizing Rituals.* Numen 114.1. Boston: Brill, 2006.
Havel, Václav. "The Power of the Powerless." Amor Mundi, Dec. 23, 2011. Translated by Paul Wilson. http://hac.bard.edu/amor-mundi/the-power-of-the-powerless-vaclav-havel-2011-12-23.
Heartfield, James. *The "Death of the Subject" Explained.* Sheffield: Sheffield Hallam University Press, 2006.
Hegel, Georg W. F. *Phänomenologie des Geistes.* Berlin: Akademie, 1967.
Hildegard von Bingen. *Der Weg der Welt: Visionen der Hildegard von Bingen.* Translated by Maria-Louise Lascar. Hamburg: Severus, 2015.
Hirsch-Luipold, Rainer. *Gott wahrnehmen: Die Sinne im Johannesevangelium.* Ratio Religionis Studien 4. WUNT 374. Tübingen: Mohr Siebeck, 2017.
Holland, Tom. *Dominion: The Making of the Western Mind.* London: Little, Brown, 2019.
Honneth, Axel. *Kampf um Anerkennung: Zur moralischen Grammatik sozialer Konflikte.* Frankfurt am Main: Suhrkamp, 2003.
———, ed. *Kommunitarismus: Eine Debatte über moralische Grundlagen moderner Gesellschaften.* Frankfurt: Campus, 1993.
Howell, Kenneth. J. *God's Two Books: Copernican and Biblical Interpretation in Early Modern Science.* Notre Dame, IN: University of Notre Dame Press, 2002.
Huntington, Samuel P. *The Clash of Civilizations and the Remaking of World Order.* London: Simon & Schuster, 1996.
Huxley, Aldous. *Brave New World.* New York: Perennial Classics, 1998.
Jaeggi, Rahel. *Entfremdung: Zur Aktualität eines sozialphilosophischen Problems.* Frieden und Krieg: Beiträge zur Historischen Friedens- und Konfliktforschung. Frankfurt am Main: Suhrkamp, 2016.

Jenkins, Philip. *The Next Christendom: The Coming of Global Christianity*. New York: Oxford University Press, 2002.

Jonas, Hans. *Gnosis: Die Botschaft des fremden Gottes*. Edited and translated by Christian Wiese. Weltreligionen Taschenbuch. Frankfurt am Main: Suhrkamp, 2008.

———. *Das Prinzip Verantwortung: Versuch einer Ethik für die technologische Zivilisation*. Frankfurt am Main: Suhrkamp, 2020.

Josephson-Storm, Jason A. *The Myth of Disenchantment: Magic, Modernity, and the Birth of the Human Sciences*. Chicago: University of Chicago Press, 2017.

Kant, Immanuel. *Die Religion innerhalb der Grenzen der blossen Vernunft*. Edited by Bettina Stangneth. Hamburg: Mein, 2017.

———. *Der Streit der Fakultäten*. Edited by Horst D. Brandt and Piero Giordanetti. Hamburg: Mein, 2005.

Kantorowicz, Ernst H. *The King's Two Bodies: A Study in Medieval Political Theology*. Princeton, NJ: Princeton University Press, 1957.

Krastev, Ivan, and Stephen Holmes. *The Light That Failed: A Reckoning*. London: Penguin, 2019.

Kreeft, Peter. "Becoming a Saint: The Practical Psychology of Sanctity." YouTube, July 7, 2014. https://www.youtube.com/watch?v=zJszejDxxVU.

Kusters, Wouter. *A Philosophy of Madness: The Experience of Psychotic Thinking*. Translated by Nancy Forest-Flier. Cambridge, MA: MIT Press, 2020.

Lakoff, George, and Mark Johnson. *Metaphors We Live By*. Chicago: University of Chicago Press, 2003.

———. *Philosophy in the Flesh: The Embodied Mind and Its Challenge to Western Thought*. New York: Basic Books, 1999.

Lambek, Michael. "Body and Mind in Mind, Body and Mind in Body: Some Anthropological Interventions in a Long Conversation." In *Bodies and Persons: Comparative Perspectives from Africa and Melanesia*, edited by Michael Lambek and Andrew Strathern, 103–27. Cambridge: Cambridge University Press, 1998.

Lambert, Wilfred G. *Babylonian Creation Myths*. Mesopotamian Civilizations. Winona Lake, IN: Eisenbrauns, 2013.

Latour, Bruno. "Why Has Critique Run Out of Steam? From Matters of Fact to Matters of Concern." *Critical Inquiry* 30 (2004) 225–48. https://doi.org/10.1086/421123.

Leidhold, Wolfgang. "Das kreative Projekt: Genealogie und Begriff." In *Konzepte politischen Handelns: Kreativität-Innovation-Praxen*, edited by Harald Bluhm und Jürgen Gebhardt, 51–72. Schriftenreihe der Sektion Politische Theorien und Ideengeschichte in der Deutschen Vereinigung für Politische Wissenschaft 1. Baden-Baden, Germ.: Nomos, 2001.

Lévi-Strauss, Claude. *Structural Anthropology*. Translated by Claire Jacobson and Brooke Grundfest Schoepf. New York: Basic Books, 1963.

Lewis, C. S. *Mere Christianity*. New York: Harper One, 2001.

———. "Myth Became Fact." In *God in the Dock: Essays on Theology and Ethics*, edited by Walter Hooper, 54–61. Grand Rapids: Eerdmans, 1970.

———. "On Living in an Atomic Age." In *Exploring the Meaning of Life: An Anthology and Guide*, edited by Joshua W. Seachris, 133–37. Malden, MA: Wiley–Blackwell, 2012.

———. "The Weight of Glory." Doxaweb, Nov. 1941. https://www.doxaweb.com/assets/weight_of_glory.pdf.

Löwith, Karl. *Meaning in History*. Chicago: University of Chicago Press, 1949.

Luhmann, Niklas. "Formen des Helfens im Wandel Gesellschaftlicher Bedingungen." In *Gesellschaftliche Perspektiven der Sozialarbeit*, edited by Hans-Uwe Otto and Siegfried Schneider, 1:21–45. Kritische Texte zur Sozialarbeit und Sozialpädagogik. Darmstadt: Luchterhand, 1972.

———. *Soziale Systeme: Grundriß einer allgemeinen Theorie*. Frankfurt am Main: Suhrkamp, 1984.

———. *Vertrauen: Ein Mechanismus der Reduktion sozialer Komplexität*. 4th ed. Stuttgart: Lucius & Lucius, 2000.

Lukianoff, Greg, and Jonathan Haidt. *The Coddling of the American Mind: How Good Intentions and Bad Ideas Are Setting Up a Generation for Failure*. London: Penguin, 2018.

Lurquin, Paul F., and Linda Stone. *Evolution and Religious Creation Myths: How Scientists Respond*. Oxford: Oxford University Press, 2007.

Luther, Martin. *Von der babylonischen Gefangenschaft der Kirche*. Maarten Luther: Gesammelte Werke—Deutsch, 1520. https://infowerke.martinluther.us/Von_Der_Babylonischen_Gefangenschaft_Der_Kirche.pdf.

———. *Von der Freiheit eines Christenmenschen: Studienausgabe*. Erläuterungen: Geisteswissenschaftliche Textsammlung 18837. Reclams Universal-Bibliothek. Stuttgart: Reclam, 1968.

Lyotard, Jean-Francois. *La condition postmoderne: Rapport sur le savoir*. Paris: Minuit, 1979.

MacIntyre, Alasdair. "Epistemological Crises, Dramatic Narrative, and the Philosophy of Science." In *The Tasks of Philosophy*, 3–24. Vol. 1 of *Selected Essays*. Cambridge: Cambridge University Press, 2006.

Magee, Glenn Alexander. *Hegel and the Hermetic Tradition*. Ithaca, NY: Cornell University Press, 2001.

Mangalwadi, Vishal. *Wahrheit und Wandlung: Was Europa heute braucht*. Basel: Fontis, 2016.

Mauss, Marcel. *The Gift: The Form and Reason for Exchange in Archaic Societies*. Translated by W. D. Halls. London: Routledge, 2005.

McCarraher, Eugene. *The Enchantments of Mammon: How Capitalism Became the Religion of Modernity*. Cambridge, MA: Harvard University Press, 2019.

McGilchrist, Iain. *The Master and His Emissary*. New Haven, CT: Yale University Press, 2009.

———. *The Matter with Things: Our Brains, Our Delusions, and the Unmaking of the World*. Bristol: Perspectiva, 2021.

McQueen, Alison. *Political Realism in Apocalyptic Times*. Cambridge: Cambridge University Press, 2018.

McWhorter, John. *Woke Racism: How a New Religion Has Betrayed Black America*. New York: Portfolio, 2021.

Meadows, Donella, et al., eds. *The Limits to Growth: A Report for the Club of Rome's Project on the Predicament of Mankind*. Washington, DC: Potomac, 1972.

Mellor, Philip A., and Chris Shilling. *Sociology of the Sacred: Religion, Embodiment and Social Change*. Theory, Culture & Society. London: Sage, 2014.

Milbank, John. *Theology and Social Theory: Beyond Secular Reason*. Oxford: Blackwell, 1993.

Milbank, John, et al., eds. *Paul's New Moment: Continental Philosophy and the Future of Christian Theology*. Grand Rapids: Brazos, 2010.

Mill, John. S. *On Liberty*. Kitchener, Can.: Batoche, 2001.
Mulgan, Geoff. *Social Innovation: What It Is, Why It Matters and How It Can Be Accelerated*. With Simon Tucker et al. Skoll Centre for Social Entrepreneurship: Working Paper. London: Basingstoke, 2007. https://youngfoundation.org/wp-content/uploads/2012/10/Social-Innovation-what-it-is-why-it-matters-how-it-can-be-accelerated-March-2007.pdf.
Nagel, Thomas. *Secular Philosophy and the Religious Temperament: Essays 2002–2008*. Oxford: Oxford University Press, 2010.
———. *The View from Nowhere*. Oxford: Oxford University Press, 1986.
Nietzsche, Friedrich. *Also sprach Zarathustra*. Hamburg: Nikol, 2018.
———. *Twilight of the Idols*. Translated by Anthony M. Ludovici. New York: Barnes & Noble, 2008.
———. *Zur Genealogie der Moral*. Gutenberg, 1887. Gutenberg-DE ed. 16.2. https://www.projekt-gutenberg.org/nietzsch/genealog/genealog.html.
Nisbet, Robert A. *The Quest for Community: A Study in the Ethics of Order and Freedom*. Oxford: Oxford University Press, 1953.
Nixey, Catherine. *The Darkening Age: The Christian Destruction of the Classical World*. New York: Houghton Mifflin Harcourt, 2018.
Ophuls, William. *Immoderate Greatness: Why Civilizations Fail*. Scotts Valley, AZ: Create Space, 2012.
Orji, Cyril. *Exploring Theological Paradoxes*. Routledge New Critical Thinking in Religion, Theology and Biblical Studies. London: Routledge, 2024.
Orwell, George. *1984*. San Diego: Harcourt Brace Jovanovich, 1977.
Osborne, Catherine. *Presocratic Philosophy: A Very Short Introduction*. Very Short Introductions. Oxford: Oxford University Press, 2004.
Padberg, Lutz E. von. *Die Christianisierung Europas im Mittelalter*. Universal-Bibliothek 17015. Stuttgart: Reclam, 1998.
Perkins, Mary Anne. *Christendom and European Identity: The Legacy of a Grand Narrative Since 1789*. Religion and Society 40. Berlin: de Gruyter, 2004.
Pickstock, Catherine. *Repetition and Identity*. Literary Agenda. Oxford: Oxford University Press, 2013.
Pinker, Steven. *The Better Angels of Our Nature: A History of Violence and Humanity*. London: Penguin, 2011.
Platon. *Der Staat*. Edited and translated by Karl Vretska. Stuttgart: Reclam, 1982.
Polanyi, Karl. *The Great Transformation: Politische und ökonomische Ursprünge von Gesellschaften und Wirtschaftssystemen*. Translated by Heinrich Jelinek. Frankfurt am Main: Suhrkamp, 2024.
Polanyi, Michael. *The Tacit Dimension*. Chicago: University of Chicago Press, 2009.
Pooley, Gale L., and Marian L. Tupy. *Superabundance: The Story of Population Growth, Innovation, and Human Flourishing on an Infinitely Bountiful Planet*. Washington, DC: Cato Institute, 2022.
Putnam, Robert D. *Bowling Alone: The Collapse and Revival of American Community*. New York: Simon & Schuster, 2000.
———. "*E Pluribus Unum*: Diversity and Community in the Twenty-First Century." *Scandinavian Political Studies* 30 (2007) 137–74.
Rappaport, Roy A. *Ritual and Religion in the Making of Humanity*. Cambridge Studies in Social and Cultural Anthropology 110. Cambridge: Cambridge University Press, 1999.

Reckwitz, Andreas. *Die Erfindung der Kreativität: Zum Prozess gesellschaftlicher Aesthetisierung.* Berlin: Suhrkamp, 2012.
Robbins, Joel. "The Globalization of Pentecostal and Charismatic Christianity." *Annual Review of Anthropology* 33 (2004) 117–43.
Rookmaaker, Hans R. *Modern Art and the Death of a Culture.* London: SPCK, 1994.
Rosa, Hartmut. *Demokratie braucht Religion.* Munich: Kösel, 2022.
———. *Resonanz: Eine Soziologie der Weltbeziehung.* Frankfurt am Main: Suhrkamp, 2019.
———. *Weltbeziehungen im Zeitalter der Beschleunigung: Umrisse einer neuen Gesellschaftskritik.* Frankfurt am Main: Suhrkamp, 2012.
Rudolph, Kurt. *Die Gnosis: Wesen und Geschichte einer spätantiken Religion.* Göttingen: Vandenhoeck & Ruprecht, 2005.
Sandel, Michael. *What Money Can't Buy: The Moral Limits of Markets.* London: Penguin, 2012.
Sanneh, Lamin. *Translating the Message: The Missionary Impact on Culture.* American Society of Missiology. Maryknoll, NY: Orbis, 1990.
Sass, Louis A. *Madness and Modernism: Insanity in the Light of Modern Art, Literature, and Thought.* Oxford: Oxford University Press, 2017.
Sayer, Andrew. *Realism and Social Science.* London: Sage, 2000.
Schafarewitsch, Igor R. *Der Todestrieb in der Geschichte: Erscheinungsformen des Sozialismus.* Translated by Anton Manzella. Meerbusch, Germ.: Lichtschlag, 2016.
Schelsky, Helmut. *Die Arbeit tun die Anderen: Klassenkampf und Priesterherrschaft der Intellektuellen.* Opladen, Germ.: Westdeutsch, 1975.
Schleiermacher, Friedrich Daniel. *Über die Religion: Reden an die Gebildeten unter ihren Verächtern.* Ditzingen, Germ.: Reclam, 1997.
Schlesinger, Arthur M., Jr. *The Disuniting of America: Reflections on a Multicultural Society.* New York: Norton, 1998.
Schmemann, Alexander. *For the Life of the World: Sacraments and Orthodoxy.* New York: St. Vladimir's Seminary Press, 1998.
Schmithals, Walter. *Neues Testament und Gnosis: Erträge der Forschung.* Darmstadt: Wissenschaft, 1984.
Schumpeter, Joseph. *Theorie der wirtschaftlichen Entwicklung.* Leipzig: Duncker & Humblot, 1911.
Schwab, Klaus, and Thierry Malleret. *COVID-19: The Great Reset.* Geneva: World Economic Forum, 2020.
Scruton, Roger. "The Beauty of Belonging." *Plough,* Oct. 22, 2018. https://www.plough.com/en/topics/culture/art/the-beauty-of-belonging.
Segal, Robert A. "Myth and Ritual." In *Issues, Topics, Approaches, Concepts,* edited by Jens Kreinath et al., 99–123. Vol. 1 of *Theorizing Rituals.* Numen 114.1. Boston: Brill, 2006.
Sennett, Richard. *The Culture of the New Capitalism.* New Haven, CT: Yale University Press, 2006.
Siedentop, Larry. *Inventing the Individual: The Origins of Western Liberalism.* London: Penguin, 2015.
Smith, James K. A. "Secular Liturgies and the Prospects for a 'Post-Secular' Sociology of Religion." In *The Post-Secular in Question: Religion in Contemporary Society,* edited by Philip S. Gorski et al., 159–85. Social Science Research Council 7. New York: New York University Press, 2012.

---. *You Are What You Love: The Spiritual Power of Habit*. Grand Rapids: Brazos, 2016.

Snoek, Jan A. M. "Defining 'Rituals.'" In *Issues, Topics, Approaches, Concepts*, edited by Jens Kreinath et al., 3–14. Vol. 1 of *Theorizing Rituals*. Numen 114.1. Boston: Brill, 2006.

Sohn-Kronthaler, Michaela, and Ruth Albrecht, eds. *Faith and Feminism in Nineteenth-Century Religious Communities*. Vol. 8.2 of *The Bible and Women: An Encyclopaedia of Exegesis and Cultural History*. Atlanta: SBL, 2019.

Solzhenitsyn, Aleksandr. *Archipel Gulag*. Moscow: Alfa, 2019.

---. "Harvard Address." YouTube, Apr. 12, 2013. https://www.youtube.com/watch?v=WuVG8SnxxCM.

Sowell, Thomas. *Intellectuals and Society*. New York: Basic Books, 2009.

---. *The Vision of the Anointed*. New York: Basic Books, 1995.

Stark, Rodney. *How the West Won: The Neglected Story of the Triumph of Modernity*. Wilmington, DE: ISI, 2014.

Stausberg, Michael. "Reflexivity." In *Issues, Topics, Approaches, Concepts*, edited by Jens Kreinath et al., 627–46. Vol. 1 of *Theorizing Rituals*. Numen 114.1. Boston: Brill, 2006.

Stausberg, Michael, et al. "'Ritual': A Lexicographic Survey of Some Related Terms from an Emic Perspective." In *Issues, Topics, Approaches, Concepts*, edited by Jens Kreinath et al., 51–101. Vol. 1 of *Theorizing Rituals*. Numen 114.1. Boston: Brill, 2006.

Stenger, Victor J. *God and the Multiverse: Humanity's Expanding View of the Cosmos*. New York: Prometheus, 2014.

Strenger, Carlo. *Diese verdammten liberalen Eliten: Wer sie sind und warum wir sie brauchen*. Frankfurt am Main: Suhrkamp, 2019.

Taleb, Nassim Nicholas. *Skin in the Game: Hidden Asymmetries in Daily Life*. Incerto. London: Penguin, 2017.

Taylor, Charles. "Buffered and Porous Selves." *Immanent Frame*, Sept. 2, 2008. https://tif.ssrc.org/2008/09/02/buffered-and-porous-selves/.

---. "Leading a Life." In *Incommensurability, Incomparability, and Practical Reason*, edited by Ruth Chang, 170–84. Cambridge, MA: Harvard University Press, 1997.

---. "The Politics of Recognition." In *Multiculturalism: Examining the Politics of Recognition*, edited by Amy Gutmann, 25–75. Princeton, NJ: Princeton University Press, 1994.

---. *A Secular Age*. Cambridge, MA: Harvard University Press, 2007.

---. *Sources of the Self: The Making of the Modern Identity*. Cambridge, MA: Harvard University Press, 1989.

Thielicke, Helmut. *Das Lachen der Heiligen und Narren*. Freiburg: Herder, 1974.

Tibi, Bassam. *Europa ohne Identität? Die Krise der multikulturellen Gesellschaft*. Munich: Bertelsmann, 1998.

Tolkien, J. R. R. *The Lord of the Rings*. 3 vols. New York: Ballantine, 2003.

Tröger, Karl-Wolfgang. *Die Gnosis: Heilslehre und Ketzerglaube*. Freiburg: Herder, 2001.

Van Gennep, Arnold. *The Rites of Passage*. Translated by Monika B. Vizedom and Gabrielle L. Caffee. Chicago: University of Chicago Press, 1960.

Vervaeke, John, et al. *Zombies in Western Culture: A Twenty-First Century Crisis*. Cambridge: Open Book, 2017.

Voegelin, Eric. *From Enlightenment to Revolution*. Edited by John H. Hallowell. Durham, NC: Duke University Press, 1975.

———. "Der Liberalismus und seine Geschichte." In *Christentum und Liberalismus*, edited by Karl Forster, 11–43. Studien und Berichte der Katholischen Akademie in Bayern 13. Munich: Zink, 1960.

———. *Modernity Without Restraint: "The Political Religions"; "The New Science of Politics"; and "Science, Politics, and Gnosticism."* Edited by Manfred Henningsen. Vol. 5 of *The Collected Works of Eric Voegelin*. Columbia: University of Missouri Press, 2000.

Volf, Miroslav. *Exclusion and Embrace: A Theological Exploration of Identity, Otherness, and Reconciliation*. Nashville: Abingdon, 1996.

Walton, John H. *Ancient Near Eastern Thought and the Old Testament: Introducing the Conceptual World of the Hebrew Bible*. Grand Rapids: Baker Academic, 2006.

Webb, Eugene. "Voegelin's 'Gnosticism' Reconsidered." *Political Science Reviewer* 34 (2005) 48–76.

Weber, Max. *Briefe 1909–1910*. Vol. 2.6 of *Gesamtausgabe*. Tübingen: Mohr Siebeck, 1994.

———. *Politik als Beruf*. Munich: Duncker & Humblot, 1926.

Weil, Simone. "Human Personality." In *Simone Weil: An Anthology*, edited by Siân Miles, 69–99. Penguin Modern Classics. London: Penguin, 2005.

———. *The Need for Roots: Prelude to a Declaration of Duties Towards Mankind*. Routledge Classics. London: Routledge, 2001.

———. "The Needs of the Soul." In *Simone Weil: An Anthology*, edited by Siân Miles, 105–41. Penguin Modern Classics. London: Penguin, 2005.

Westermann, Claus. *Kapitel 1–11*. Vol. 1 of *Genesis*. BKAT. Neukirchen-Vluyn, Germ.: Neukirchen, 1974.

White, Lynn, Jr. "The Historical Roots of Our Ecological Crisis." *Science*, n.s., 155 (1967) 1203–7. https://www.jstor.org/stable/1720120.

Wolin, Sheldon S. *Democracy Incorporated: Managed Democracy and the Specter of Inverted Totalitarianism*, Princeton, NJ: Princeton University Press, 2008.

Wooldridge, Adrian. *The Aristocracy of Talent: How Meritocracy Made the Modern World*. New York: Simon & Schuster, 2021.

Yoder, John Howard. *The Politics of Jesus*. 2nd ed. Grand Rapids: Eerdmans, 1972.

Zuboff, Shoshana. *The Age of Surveillance Capitalism: The Fight for a Human Future at the New Frontier of Power*. New York: Public Affairs, 2018.

Index

absurd, 49, 119, 122–25, 130, 143, 147, 243
Adorno, Theodor W., 77, 122
Agamben, Giorgio, 196–99
alienation, 101–134, 186, 251, 256
Ambrose of Milan, Saint, xiv
anthropology, 14–43, 47, 58, 64, 88, 104, 131, 174
apocalypse, apocalyptic, xvii, 44, 54, 85, 91, 94, 155, 178, 199–202, 253, 255, 257
Aquinas, Thomas, 82, 104, 141, 162
Arendt, Hannah 97, 100, 202
Aristotle, 4, 29, 83, 153, 161
Asad, Talal, 94, 95, 114, 185, 252
Augustine, Saint, xivn9, 17, 28, 42–54, 92, 104, 234, 235, 250, 270

Balthasar, von, Hans Urs, 44–45, 56, 111, 120, 175, 224, 226
Barth, Karl, 11, 20, 56, 73, 82, 136, 156, 175, 225, 252, 259
Baudrillard, Jean, 182
Baur, Ferdinand Christian, 180
Bell, Catherine, 12, 129
Bonhoeffer, Dietrich, 56, 146, 178, 179, 180, 238, 275
Blumenberg, Hans, 10, 50, 91, 119, 133, 146, 169, 176, 192, 193
Brague, Rémi, 64, 78, 223

Camus, Albert, 122, 123, 124, 125, 143, 147, 148

capitalism, 81, 90, 113–14, 126, 136, 162, 187, 197, 199, 206
Casanova, Jose, 144
Cavanaugh, William T., 191, 235, 243–44, 248, 262, 263, 284
Celsus, Greek philosopher, 4
change, social, 13–23, 35–43, 75, 88–89, 105, 127, 146–47, 160–67, 196–99, 206, 211, 275
chaos, 3–7, 16, 20, 28, 31, 36, 38, 42, 49, 52, 67, 151–68, 182–201, 220, 224, 230, 233, 247, 248
Charlemagne, 93, 191
Chesterton, Gilbert Keith, 130, 133, 161
Christendom, 5, 6, 24, 41, 61, 92–94, 152, 158, 161, 168–69, 174, 177–78, 188–93, 202, 207, 211, 228, 253, 255
church, xiv, 4, 5, 6, 29, 40, 41–74, 90–96, 103–115, 132, 138, 146–61, 167–82, 201, 208–282
Cicero, Marcus Tullius, 4, 28, 130, 189
civilization, civilizations, 3–13, 22–29, 41, 45, 60, 75–80, 89, 99, 115, 134, 144, 147, 148, 168, 172, 174, 178, 187, 190, 196, 209, 212, 217, 223, 236, 238, 248, 264, 267, 274, 277, 278, 279
Cohn, Norman, 94, 178
confession, 43–45, 76, 163, 166, 238, 239, 243, 258, 281

conscious, 5, 8, 15, 18, 24, 46, 51, 64, 67, 90, 107, 113, 123, 130, 131, 135, 148, 158, 196, 199, 227, 264
conservative, 122, 204, 205, 206, 281
covenant, 30–35, 37, 38, 82, 87, 103, 170, 177, 193, 195, 196, 220, 244–46, 279
creativity, 60, 99, 100, 284
crisis, 13, 38, 147, 172, 181, 184, 186, 191
critique, 15, 45, 50–63, 75, 89–99, 107, 111–17, 122, 137, 138, 139, 145, 146, 166, 178, 183, 202, 239, 260–84

decay, 4, 42, 57, 71–148, 153, 157, 168, 184, 193, 198, 206, 208, 211, 212, 223, 224, 227, 228, 249, 269, 271, 276, 277, 280, 281, 282
democracy, 4, 22, 28, 29, 139, 196, 272
Descartes, Rene, 33, 39, 41, 43, 47, 62, 98, 106, 111, 112, 131, 132, 184, 234, 246, 281, 282
dichotomy, 6, 20, 75, 90, 145, 176, 184, 221
dignity, human, 22–25, 46–47, 53, 70, 77, 80, 91, 121–24, 135–40, 168, 180, 195, 205–9, 224, 240, 277–78
divine, 7, 15, 19, 27–30, 36–76, 86, 89, 98, 100, 107, 110–15, 118–19, 123, 128, 132–35, 141–42, 146, 148, 153–54, 158, 161–84, 195, 201, 207, 210–28, 234, 235, 236, 237, 239, 240, 241, 243, 245, 247, 252, 254, 257, 262, 263, 264, 268, 269, 275, 279, 282
Dostoevsky, Fyodor, 3, 55, 157, 197, 205, 267
Durkheim, Emile, xvi, 18, 19, 69, 105, 106, 114, 225, 237, 250

ecclesia militans, 250–56, 261, 270, 281
Edwards, Jonathan, 219
embodiment, disembodiment, xvi, 12, 28, 100, 110, 141, 154, 155, 160, 161, 181, 250, 267, 269
emotion, 18, 85, 108, 113, 170

empiricism, 63, 83, 89, 185, 227
enchantment, also re-enchantment and mis-enchantment, 20, 58, 108, 110, 113, 114, 184, 190–92, 275, 277
Enlightenment, 4, 41, 57, 64, 70, 74, 95, 96, 122, 156, 158, 163, 176, 183, 206, 211, 281
equality, 35, 40 - 47, 57–58, 61, 78–82, 85, 184, 195, 210, 265
eucharist, 38, 41, 45, 52, 103–4, 108, 110–14, 118, 136, 165, 194, 229–49, 264–66, 275–78, 281
evolution, 7, 11, 23, 50, 66–69, 135, 144, 146, 194–96, 204
exhaustion, 100, 120–43, 147, 167, 190, 212, 228, 280, 282

fear, 123, 128, 129, 130, 141, 159, 164, 166, 187, 199, 200, 201, 225, 237, 245, 259, 273
flourish, 3, 6, 8, 11, 17, 21, 36, 85, 90, 92, 111, 138, 188, 190, 201, 202–5, 211–15, 218–82
Foucault, Michel, 194
fragmentation, 95, 102–9, 116, 168, 182, 192, 264, 274
Frankfurt School, 122, 137, 140
Frankl, Victor, 218
fundamentalist, 204–6
Furedi, Frank, 128–30

Gauchet, Marcel, 48–51
Gehlen, Arnold, 8
genealogy, 67, 117
Goethe, Johann Wolfgang von, 120
Giddens, Anthony, 118, 126, 127, 128, 139
gift, 32, 39–41, 45, 51, 78, 96, 99, 100, 146, 154, 158, 221, 224–25, 235–36, 240–43, 246, 247, 262, 266–69
Gillespie, Michael, 11, 112, 117–18, 131
Girard, René, 19, 218
glory, 19, 35–37, 42, 51, 58, 104–5, 142, 162, 187, 191, 209, 218–29, 233–34, 243–48, 257, 263–69, 274–78, 281–82

gnosis/gnostic, 169–89
grace, 39, 42, 45, 56, 78, 104–5, 152–53, 164–66, 173, 176–77, 180, 221, 234, 236, 239–40, 243, 269, 284
Gray, John, xviii, xix
Greek, 4, 13, 21, 27–28, 40–42, 50, 63, 78–84, 92, 104, 172, 175–76, 202, 219, 267
guilt, 75–79, 159, 163–64, 167, 177, 238

Habermas, Jürgen, 98, 187, 206
Han, Byung-Chul, 119, 124, 126, 133–34, 169, 176
Harari, Yuval Noah, 186, 199
Harnack, Adolf von, 175
Hegel, Georg W. F., 96–97, 106–7, 108, 131–32, 161–62, 182, 183, 184, 187, 192, 244
hermeneutic, 16, 62, 93, 179
hierarchy, 17, 27, 28, 30, 34, 39, 42, 44, 49, 81, 119, 124, 141, 165, 194, 210, 220, 222, 251, 272, 283
history, xvii 3, 6, 8, 10, 11, 12, 21, 23, 26, 29, 30, 31, 35, 39, 41, 43, 44, 47, 50–52, 59, 66, 69, 73, 80, 84–89, 92, 94, 97–98, 100, 103, 105–6, 111, 132, 146, 147, 152, 158, 163, 172–73, 181–82, 195, 198, 202, 204, 207, 208, 210, 211, 212, 220, 222, 225, 228, 231, 234, 245, 256, 258, 260, 261, 263, 267, 272, 276, 277, 278, 280–82
Hobbes, Thomas, 62, 82, 97, 129, 131, 141, 162, 168, 195, 201, 202
Holy Spirit, 36, 39, 44, 52, 94, 153, 154, 158, 161–62, 181, 194, 210, 222, 236, 245, 251, 256, 263, 267, 276, 279, 282
hubris, 67, 70, 73, 74, 90–100, 112, 133, 145, 155, 179, 186, 187, 196, 207, 224, 236, 237, 249, 265, 266, 274, 276, 278, 280
humility, 41, 78, 79, 88, 94, 97–99, 153, 179, 224–25, 235, 238, 264, 265, 278, 282

ideal, idealist, 5–9, 13, 15, 17–22, 27–30, 34, 36, 42, 50, 51, 57, 59, 67, 70, 74, 75, 77, 81, 83, 87–91, 96, 98, 102, 106, 108, 111, 116–17, 124, 128, 132–36, 140–41, 151–67, 180, 184, 193, 196, 201–211, 228, 229, 237–39, 244, 247, 253, 260, 263–64, 268, 271–74, 276, 279
idolatry, 51, 170, 191, 235, 244, 248, 262–63, 272, 280, 282
Illich, Ivan, 55, 121, 151, 159, 243, 284
Illusion, 6, 17, 20, 21–22, 51, 54, 82, 86, 90, 97–99, 102, 113–16, 123, 132, 135, 147, 164, 179, 191, 203, 208, 264, 273–74, 277, 291
individual, 8–21, 23, 38–70, 79–89, 93, 96, 100, 102, 104, 107–120, 123, 125, 126, 128, 131–41, 147, 148, 154, 159, 164, 165, 167, 173, 179, 190, 193–97, 200–203, 204–8, 222–28, 232, 234, 235, 236, 238, 242, 247, 261–65, 273–79
innovation, 15, 47, 53, 57, 79–85, 89, 98–100, 104, 147, 181, 197, 225, 252
institution, 3, 5, 21–23, 41–42, 47, 52–53, 54, 60, 77, 80, 85, 88, 90–92, 96, 109, 110, 118, 138, 144, 147, 155–59, 162, 167, 172, 177–81, 196, 199–200, 204, 221, 224, 226, 239–40, 249, 252, 253, 278, 279
interiority, 35, 36

Judeo-Christian, xiv-xvi, 4, 22, 25, 27, 29, 31, 33, 35, 37, 39, 41, 43, 44, 45, 47, 48, 49, 52, 53, 56, 58, 62, 64, 76, 78–90, 102–4, 109–110, 116–17, 123, 125, 126, 132, 134, 142, 144, 152, 153, 163, 165–68, 171, 184–86, 192, 200, 202, 203, 204, 206, 207, 210, 211, 213, 228, 232, 237, 252, 260, 268, 271–81

Index

Kant, Immanuel, 25, 26, 62, 63, 96, 99, 106, 112, 114, 131, 156, 160, 180, 261
Kantorowicz, Ernst, 28, 237
Kreeft, Peter, 267

Latour, Bruno, 166
Leviathan, 157, 188–95, 197–209, 226
Lévi-Strauss, Claude, 292
Lewis, Clive Staples, 70, 193, 217, 218, 229, 281, 292
liberal, 4, 22, 24, 29, 47, 56, 74, 84, 89, 94–95, 112–14, 129, 146, 176, 182, 185, 191, 195–96, 206, 210, 240, 255, 272, 280–81
Löwith, Karl, 11, 20, 73, 82, 136, 156, 175, 225, 252, 259
Luhmann, Niklas, 86, 159, 160, 191
Luther, Martin, 47, 56–57, 80, 94, 104–5, 111, 131, 178

madness, 120, 125, 128, 130–33, 146
Manichaeism, 47, 169–70
Marcel, Mauss, 48, 241, 242, 246, 283
Marcion, of Sinope, 173, 176–81
Marxism, 5, 23, 113–14, 117, 167, 183, 256, 284
McCarraher, Eugene, 110, 113–14, 183
McGilchrist, Ian, 55, 57, 144, 200, 256
mediating, 9, 13, 19, 27, 38, 58, 126, 185, 255
medieval, 25, 28, 29, 41–48, 54, 55, 57, 60, 61, 70, 78–83, 87, 88, 93, 94, 97, 102, 111–13, 131, 138, 156, 168, 177, 178, 181, 191, 201, 248, 252
meritocracy, 81, 82, 138
Milbank, John, 58, 145
modern, modernity, 7, 15, 16, 23, 30, 41, 47–50, 56–57, 61–64, 69, 70, 80, 82, 89, 90, 96–99, 102, 104–7, 109, 111, 112, 115, 117–25, 127, 128–36, 146, 156, 161, 169, 172, 178–95, 198, 199, 201, 202, 207, 209, 211, 217, 218, 225, 227, 239, 241, 253, 254, 261, 263, 267, 271, 272, 273, 279

monastery, monastic, 44, 46, 54, 56, 61, 87, 90, 178, 261
Muhammad, the founder of Islam, xvi 5, 18, 28
myth/myths, 3–25, 101–120

Nagel, Thomas, 67, 141–42
narrative, 7, 11, 25, 52, 66, 69, 104, 105, 108, 111, 115, 116, 145, 165, 167, 175, 179, 192, 212, 219, 221, 224, 232, 245, 254, 261, 262, 272, 274, 284
Nietzsche, Friedrich, xvii, 18, 29, 96, 98–99, 101, 107, 119, 123, 125, 128, 135, 146, 193, 212, 267

Ockham, William of 57, 58, 63, 64
ontology, ontological, 17, 29, 38, 41, 42, 63, 69, 79, 81, 82, 88, 90, 91, 113, 126, 127, 128, 130, 133, 138, 157, 165, 177, 185, 194–95, 203, 227, 239, 248

Padberg, von Lutz E., 93
Paul, apostle, also Saul of Tarsus, 34, 37–45, 53, 59, 67, 77, 82, 103, 108, 134, 154, 157, 158, 163, 171, 174–76, 219, 220, 222, 253, 257–58, 260, 267
peace, 16, 17, 19, 28, 31, 35, 61, 62, 78, 88, 141, 148, 191, 201, 245, 250, 251, 253, 254, 255, 257, 259, 261, 263, 264, 265, 266, 267, 269, 270, 278
perversion, 47, 56, 76–77, 142, 148, 159–61, 165–68, 185, 199, 226, 228, 248, 252, 253, 254, 272
paradox, 9, 48, 104, 108, 131, 143, 161, 178, 210, 213, 220, 224, 232, 234–36, 268, 274, 278, 279–84
Plato, 4, 20–22, 27–29, 42–43, 50, 58, 63, 83, 134, 139, 156, 200, 212, 223
pluralism, pluralistic, 22, 28, 88, 137, 139–40, 162, 164, 172, 191, 196, 211, 233, 264, 278
Polanyi, Karl and Michael, 106, 136

political, 6, 20, 28, 36, 40, 44, 47, 55, 60–62, 69, 74, 78, 80, 84, 87, 88, 90, 92–97, 104, 106, 113, 129, 135, 138–40, 152, 154, 156, 157, 159, 162, 171–72, 179, 191, 197, 199, 202, 207, 210, 211, 221, 224, 225, 232, 238, 239, 253, 254, 255, 258, 259, 260, 264–69, 274, 278

power, 6, 15–20, 23, 26–33, 35, 38, 39, 40, 43, 44, 45, 46, 49, 50, 51, 54, 55, 56, 57, 58, 60, 61, 62, 63, 68, 73, 76, 78, 80, 83, 84, 86, 87, 88, 89, 90, 91, 92, 93, 94, 100, 103, 104, 105, 106, 109, 110, 111, 113, 114, 115, 116, 117, 118, 122, 123, 129, 133, 135, 136, 138, 139, 141, 147, 148, 155–60, 163, 165–67, 170, 173–75, 177, 178, 181, 184, 185–87, 190, 191, 192, 193, 194, 195, 197, 198, 199, 200, 201, 203, 205, 207, 211, 212, 222, 226, 227, 228, 236, 237, 240, 241, 247, 248, 249, 252–60, 263, 265–67, 270–71, 274–76, 284–85

progress, 4, 6, 74–75, 82–83, 85–86, 98, 153, 185, 187, 205, 224–25, 239, 253

prophet, 16–19, 23, 28, 29, 31, 34, 36, 37, 50, 51, 59, 63, 89, 94, 96, 102, 103, 107, 111, 115, 119, 132, 133, 155, 156, 157, 158, 164, 165, 168, 182, 183, 193, 197, 202, 212, 213, 220, 222, 233, 254, 257, 260, 261, 266, 269, 280

Putnam, Robert D. 136, 139

Quran, 26

realism, critical, 89, 284
Reckwitz, Andreas, 100
relational, 3, 6, 7, 9, 12, 13, 15, 19, 30, 31, 32, 34, 36, 43, 53, 58, 96, 97, 102, 110, 116, 123, 135, 143, 144, 146, 155, 167, 173, 186, 187, 188, 211, 226, 227, 239, 245, 251

Judaism, also Hebrew, 16, 23, 38, 60, 147, 244
Christianity 19, 23, 28, 29, 35, 42, 46, 52, 54, 59, 60, 73, 78, 79, 92, 93, 103, 110, 142, 146–47, 152, 155, 160, 161, 169, 171–78, 181, 210, 211, 217, 223, 225, 244, 252, 265, 274, 275, 276, 281
Islam 4, 5, 18, 19, 23, 28, 44, 76, 78, 84, 114, 115, 171, 206
Renaissance, 4, 25, 29, 48, 60, 61, 70, 83, 84, 86, 90, 94, 155, 170, 178, 180, 181, 182, 235
renewal, 39, 47, 98, 112, 184, 234, 281, 282
resonance, 109, 114, 117, 168, 271, 272, 273, 274
revelation, 34–39, 44, 52, 59, 63 - 64, 83, 89, 92, 155–58, 173, 177, 179, 182, 183, 185, 220, 222, 254, 255, 257, 258, 260, 262
Rousseau, Jean-Jacque 96, 98, 113, 115, 116, 122
romantic, 64, 98, 100, 106, 107, 108, 115, 116, 122, 131, 180
Rosa, Hartmut, 99, 109, 117, 126, 271–73, 274

sacrament, 104, 107, 111–14, 118, 127, 131, 145, 152, 179, 226, 232, 244, 248, 262–64, 266, 279
sacred, 6, 13, 18, 19–43, 45–52, 62, 70, 88, 96, 98, 100, 102, 109, 112, 113, 114, 121, 133, 134, 135, 137, 142, 146, 147, 170, 186, 193, 207, 208, 209, 224, 231, 240, 244, 265, 278
sacrifice, 18–19, 22, 32, 33, 37, 56, 76, 87, 95, 97, 162–66, 184, 185, 186, 191, 193, 194, 196, 200, 205, 228, 232, 233, 240, 246, 247, 279
Sanneh, Lamin, 59, 60
Schelsky, Helmut, 118, 153, 192, 269
Schleiermacher, Friedrich D. E., 56, 155, 180
Schmemann, Alexander, 231, 233
Schmitt, Carl, 11, 163, 198

Index

Schumpeter, Joseph, 99, 190, 292
science, 21, 46, 63, 64, 67, 68, 69, 73, 79, 82, 83, 85, 101, 106, 110, 118, 138, 140–41, 163, 182, 185, 203, 207, 223, 238, 248
Scruton, Roger, 142
secular/secularity, 3–144
Siedentop, Larry, xiii-xiv, 38, 40, 45, 46, 47, 53, 54, 55, 57, 58, 61, 62, 275
Sisyphus, myth of, 100, 123–25, 143
Solzhenitsyn, Aleksandr, xiiin3, 77, 164
Stark, Rodney, 5, 6, 42, 75, 79, 81, 82, 88, 118, 194
Stausberg, Michael, 12, 16
stoic, xviii, 39, 43, 128
success, 21, 31, 52–53, 59, 60, 70, 73–75, 77–83, 85–102, 136, 139, 140, 154, 155, 178, 181, 183, 184, 187, 201, 240, 277
suicide, 123–25, 134, 236, 238, 277, 282
symbol, symbolic, 14–16, 27, 32, 41, 55, 58, 63, 110, 111, 121, 142, 186, 187, 189, 195, 201, 207, 208, 223, 231, 233, 252, 255, 267, 271, 280

Taylor, Charles, 11, 23, 42, 43, 52, 55, 65, 102, 106, 108, 109, 145, 164, 187, 228, 272, 273, 274
Theodosius I, 5, 46
Tibi, Bassam, 76–77
totalitarian, 94, 97, 100, 106, 115, 131, 133, 137, 154, 161, 166, 187, 189–91, 196–98, 200, 202, 203, 204, 205, 207–211, 223, 224, 226, 245, 259, 265, 269, 270, 277, 278, 280, 284
transcendent, 6, 49, 50, 63, 99, 105, 110, 114, 117, 158, 177, 183, 193
translation, 48, 51, 58–60, 64–65, 146, 175, 187, 273
triune, Trinity, 5, 40, 52, 53, 170, 191, 193, 195, 209, 251, 274, 276, 277, 279, 282
trust, 12, 17, 39, 62, 67, 77, 82, 85–88, 90, 103, 105, 118, 127, 128, 129, 130, 133, 136, 138–39, 162, 165, 167, 173, 226, 232, 239, 245
truth, 4, 34, 63, 76, 82, 94, 95, 115, 123, 139, 141, 142, 164–65, 183, 187, 205, 211, 225, 227, 239, 240, 249, 251, 264, 266, 269, 280, 282, 284

unity, 9, 44, 50, 59, 63, 83, 88, 92, 102, 103, 104, 105, 115, 116, 137, 143, 154, 158, 161, 162, 167, 170, 178, 184, 191, 223, 251–52

Van Gennep, Arnold, 8, 14
Vervaeke, John, 142
virtue, 41, 46, 57, 76–78, 88, 151–68, 205, 239, 254, 279
Voegelin, Eric, 11, 169, 172, 177, 178, 180, 183, 185, 186, 187, 189, 195, 201, 202, 209
Volf, Miroslav, 254–55

Wagner, Richard, 212
Walton, John, 27–33, 50n2
Weber, Max, 81, 240
Weil, Simone, 97, 124, 165, 225, 226
West, xiii, 5–6, 23–30, 41, 47, 53, 74–85, 88, 89, 90, 92, 93, 94, 99, 110, 114, 115, 126, 128, 129, 135, 138, 140, 142, 144, 163, 168, 185, 186, 191, 197, 206, 208, 223, 235, 248, 252, 253, 254, 262, 264, 267, 276, 277, 278, 279
Westermann, Claus, 27
White, Lynn Jr., 19, 82, 84, 184
Wolin, Sheldon, 196, 197, 205
worship, xvi 17, 19, 25, 29, 31–33, 36–37, 51–52, 58, 87, 110, 114–15, 128, 133, 142, 154–61, 167–68, 179, 196, 208–282

Yahweh, 17, 30–38, 50, 59, 184, 220, 232–33, 258–59, 271–74
Yoder, John Howard, 6n2

zombie, 121–22, 142–43, 147–48, 158–59, 188, 236
Zuboff, Shoshana, 126, 187, 197, 199, 206

"Oleg Dik clearly shows that Christians, churches, and citizens in general need a differentiated understanding of secularization as a 'child' of the Christian-Jewish tradition in order to better understand the foundations of Western liberal societies. The author demonstrates that the contribution of congregations and churches to liberal and democratic society lies precisely in bodily living out the meaning of human existence in worship and committed community of faith: praising God as the Triune One."

—**Henning Wrogemann**, Chair for Science of Religion and Intercultural Theology, Protestant University Wuppertal, Germany

"In this fascinating book, Oleg Dik examines the myths and rituals around which all societies, even 'secular' ones, are organized. Dik weaves a panoramic view of the scholarship together with his own experiences and encounters living in the West as a refugee from the Soviet Union. The result is full of deep and surprising insight, bridging the gap between 'believers' and 'unbelievers,' which argues that Christianity is a source of both decay and renewal."

—**William T. Cavanaugh**, Professor of Catholic Studies, DePaul University

"This is a remarkable book. It has an extraordinary range of cultural reference, from philosophy to theology, ritual to secularity, academics to zombies. It offers a bold and penetrating analysis of potential ways forward for western culture and the place of its churches. Full of piercing insights, its thesis is one that deserves wide discussion and serious reflection."

—**Graham Tomlin**, Director of the Centre for Cultural Witness, Lambeth Palace Library, London

"Others have written on the crisis of the West, but Dik's book is unique in making worship—not whether but what people worship—its focal point. Eschewing any simplistic call to Sunday services, Dik lambasts a modern church that failed through its own successful alignment with worldly powers, thus disembodying the virtues God intended it to exhibit. Take heed: Dik's analysis shows why the recovery of God-centered worship is a life-or-death issue for the church."

—**Michael McClymond**, Professor of Modern Christianity, Saint Louis University

"With its provocative assertion that 'worship is inevitable,' this book offers a timely reflection on the critical importance of choosing the object of one's worship with care. Enriched by personal examples, the analysis is a rich resource for thinking about the significance of the rituals and symbols that shape our lives and communities."

—**Christopher C. Brittain**, Dean of Divinity, Trinity College, University of Toronto